Building Cross-Cultural Competence

Building Cross-Cultural Competence

HOW TO CREATE WEALTH FROM CONFLICTING VALUES

Charles M. Hampden-Turner
and Fons Trompenaars

Illustrations by
David Lewis

YALE UNIVERSITY PRESS

NEW HAVEN & LONDON

Printed in the United States of America.

Library of Congress Cataloging-in-Publication Data

Hampden-Turner, Charles.
Building cross-cultural competence : how to create wealth from conflicting values / Charles M. Hampden-Turner and Fons Trompenaars.
p.   cm.
Includes bibliographical references and index.
ISBN 0-300-08497-8
1. International business enterprises—Management.
2. Intercultural communication.   3. Communication in management—Social aspects. I. Trompenaars, Alfons. II. Title.
HD62.4 .H35   2000
658'.049—dc21   00-028107

A catalogue record for this book is available from the British Library.

The paper in this book meets the guidelines for permanence and durability of the Committee on Production Guidelines for Book Longevity of the Council on Library Resources.

10 9 8 7 6 5 4 3 2 1

*To our wives, Shelley and Cens, whose view of us is more comprehensive
And to Abraham Maslow, one of our earliest mentors*

Contents

Acknowledgments

The following passage from Abraham Maslow's *Motivation and Personality* (1954) was the beginning of our quest:

> The age-old opposition between heart and head, reason and instinct, or cognition and conation was seen to disappear in healthy people where they became synergic rather than antagonists, and where conflict between them disappears because they say the same thing and point to the same conclusion. . . .
>
> The dichotomy between selfishness and unselfishness disappears . . . because in principle every act is both selfish *and* unselfish. Our subjects are simultaneously very spiritual and very pagan and sensual. Duty cannot be contrasted with pleasure or work with play where duty *is* pleasure, when work *is* play. . . .
>
> Similar findings have been reached for kindness-ruthlessness, concreteness-abstractness, acceptance-rebellion, self-society, adjustment-maladjustment . . . serious-humorous, Dionysian-Apollonian, introverted-extroverted, intense-casual, serious-frivolous . . . mystic-realistic, active-passive, masculine-feminine, lust-love, Eros-Agape . . . and a thousand philosophical dilemmas are discovered to have more than two horns, or paradoxically, no horns at all.

The British author passed his sixty-fifth year as this book was being finished, as the twentieth century was drawing to an end. This has put us in a retrospective mood. We were both educated as graduate students in the United States—Charles Hampden-Turner at Harvard and Fons Trompenaars at Wharton. Without our American friends, this book could never have been written.

Foremost among these friends are Fritz Roethlisberger, Russ Ackoff, By Barnes, Robert Freed Bales, Paul Lawrence, Hasan Ozbekhan, George Lodge, Gar Alperowitz, Peter Senge, Rosabeth Kanter, Adam Curle, Warren Bennis, Christopher Jencks, Donald Schön, Chris Argyris, Bob Lifton, Maurice Stein—all on the east coast.

In the Bay Area, we were crucially influenced by Gregory Bateson, Nevitt Sanford, James McGregor Burns, Rollo May, and Mimi Silbert of the Delancey Street Foundation, where "dilemma theory" was born. Other important influences were Frank Barron, Carl Rogers, James Hillman, John Kao, Royal Foote, Ed Lawler, and Jim O'Toole.

An invaluable bridge across the world was created by the Global Business Network, especially Peter Schwartz, Jay Ogilvy, Napier Collyns, Nancy Murphy, Arie de Geus, Kevin Kelly, Eamonn Kelly, Stewart Brand, Eric Best, Lawrence Wilkinson, and Kees van der Heijden. It was largely thanks to Napier that we found our editors Henning Gutmann of Yale University Press and Diane Taylor of John Wiley in the United Kingdom, for whose judgment and skill we are most grateful. We are also indebted to Joe Spieler, our agent.

Crossing cultures is by now a business, and we owe much to Milton and Janet Bennett of the Intercultural Communication Institute and their extensive network, including Nancy Adler, R. S. Moorthy, Bob Textor, and André Laurent. And then there are the many kind and inspiring people we meet on our journeys, especially on shared platforms. These include Tommy Koh, Edward De Bono, Richard Sennett, Elliott Jaques, Danah Zohar, Tim Galwey, Tom Peters, Howard Gardner, David K. Hurst, Charles Handy, Gifford Pinchot, Henry Mintzberg, Gareth Morgan, Anthony Giddens, James Moore, Charles M. Savage, and Jeffrey Pfeffer.

All these individuals might have regarded themselves as too busy at the time to pay us much attention, but from our perspective, these meetings, however brief, were memorable. Our intellectual debt to Geert Hofstede, the "father" of cross-cultural data bases, is also deep.

We owe an immeasurable debt to all those who have supported us, especially in our Amsterdam office, and at the Judge Institute of Management Studies at Cambridge University.

At the Trompenaars–Hampden-Turner Group in Amsterdam we owe much to Maarten Asser, Naomi Stubbé de Groot, Katherine Flook, Annemieke Lof-de Kok, Peter Prud'homme van Reine, Vincent Merke, Tineke

Boucher, and Oscar van Weedenburg, not forgetting our "man in Malaysia," Philip Merry, and in Australia, Cheenu Srinivasan.

At the Judge Institute our thanks go to John Child, Mary Beveridge, Andrew Brown, Nick Oliver, Jane Collier, Michael Dempster, Sven Haake, Ginger Chi, John Hendry, Sakai Sugai, Tim Minshall, Laura Luckyn-Malone, Nick O'Shaughnessy, Elizabeth Briggs, Malcolm Warner, George Yip, Dawn Perry, and especially my voluntary assistant Rob Koepp along with our leader Sandra Dawson.

Finally, our friends in Europe are too numerous to thank individually. But Jaap Leemhuis stands out, as do Georgio Inzerilli, Martin Gillo, Bob Garratt, Anne Deering, Max Boisot, Marja Maijala, Peter Woolliams, Fritz Haseloff, Rei Torres, Erik Bree, Bo Ekman, Brian Eno, and Gerard Fairtlough.

Last, but perhaps most of all, we are grateful to David Lewis, our inspired young artist, whose sense of humor contributed much to the cartoons in this book, in addition to his outstanding graphic artistry. We are lucky to have encountered him at a forum organized by Anne Deering of A. T. Kearney.

Charles Hampden-Turner
Cambridge University
Judge Institute of Management Studies
24 Trumpington Street
Cambridge CP2 1AG
Tel.: 44 1223 339700
Fax: 44 1223 339701

Fons Trompenaars
Trompenaars–Hampden-Turner Group
AJ Ernstraat 595D
1082 LD Amsterdam
The Netherlands
Tel.: 31 20 301 6666
Fax: 31 20 301 6555
http://www.interculturalcompetence.com

Introduction

We believe we have made a significant discovery after eighteen years of cross-cultural research. Or perhaps, in a spirit of greater humility, we have at last noticed what has for years been staring us in the face. As Alfred North Whitehead put it, "Everything was seen before by someone who did not discover it."

We finally noticed that foreign cultures are not arbitrarily or randomly different from one another. They are instead *mirror images* of one another's values, reversals of the order and sequence of looking and learning.

Such reversals are both frightening to some people and a source of fascination and wonder to others of us. This book hopes to lead you through the fright into the fascination. The fright comes about because many of us mistake the reversal of our own value systems for a negation of what we believe in. It is as if we were celebrating some Black Mass by reciting the scriptures backward before an inverted crucifix. Satan, it is said, is left-handed, as is the reflection of a right-handed person. Stay in a foreign culture long enough, some believe, and you will lose your ethical moorings and sink down into a swamp of relativism. But however frightened we feel, the culture that is a reversal of our own is in fact coherent and comprehensible. It works very much like our own, albeit with changed priorities. Values switched over from left to right and from right to left work effectively and logically.

Once we grasp this "reverse view" everything the foreign culture says and does falls into place. We typically do the same when inhabiting this "looking-glass land." Cultures have always been reflections of the world mirrored in the eyes of members. Who is to say where we should look first, or in which direction our eyes should scan? Neither direction is "normal." Cultures have simply made different initial choices.

We should have worked this out many years ago. After all, some cultures drive on the left-hand side of the road and some on the right-hand side. More important, all cultures with roadways use different sides for vehicles traveling in opposite directions.

In China, Japan, and Southeast Asia books start at what is for westerners "the back" and end at "the front." Instead of reading from left to right laterally as we do, they read from right to left and usually in vertical columns.

Family names come second in most western cultures, with the given name first. This order is reversed in Sino-Japanese cultures, perhaps because the family is considered prior to the person. When giving a taxi driver your address in Tokyo or Beijing, the town or district comes first, then the street, then the building, then the apartment number. That way he can start to drive before you finish your instructions. Mirror image worlds make good sense and may even have their own advantages. The initial reversal is frightening at first, but when we pass through the glass, whole new worlds appear on the other side. Nor do we lose our own values; rather, we see these as our own touchstones within a wider context.

The context of mirror image reversal is illustrated below. Here we focus on the first three value dimensions used in this book. These are:

UN–PA
(or Universalism–Particularism)
IN–CO
(or Individualism–Communitarianism)
SP–DI
(or Specificity–Diffuseness)

Universalism emphasizes rules that apply to a universe of people, while Particularism emphasizes exceptions and particular cases.

Individualism emphasizes the individual, while Communitarianism stresses the family, organization, community, or nation in which that individual has membership.

Specificity emphasizes precision, analysis, and "getting to the point," while Diffuseness looks to wholes and to the larger context.

But look what happens when we hold these three dimensions up to the mirror (Figure 1). Apart from the mirror-writing, which is a little awkward to read, the pairs of binary concepts have switched places and their se-

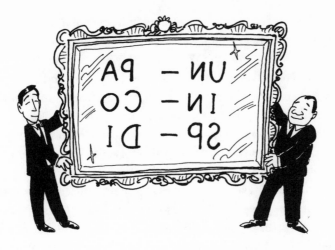

Figure 1 Culture as a Mirror Image

quences are now reversed, so that particularism is prior to universalism, the community comes before the individual, and the diffuse whole precedes the specific parts. Although the culture must still deal with the same dilemmas, the view of what is primary has shifted over to the left.

This book describes our conventional order of things, and then compares this with unconventional reversals of that order, used by some (not all) foreign cultures. In doing this we discover that what we see so clearly, some foreigners miss. What they see so clearly, most of us miss. The ideal we seek in this book is to *perceive and think in both directions*. This is another way of arguing that we must learn to think in circles, or cybernetically.

Let us apply circular thinking to our three dimensions. Not only must universal rules (Universalism) cover more and more exceptions or special cases (Particularism), but those exceptions must be used to improve the universalism of our rules.

Not only must individuals justify themselves by building families, companies, and communities, but communities and the social units within these must justify themselves by nurturing individuality among their members.

Not only must every large context be analyzed into separate elements and specific results, but these specifics must be synthesized and elaborated into whole and diffuse configurations.

As you go around these circles, the first value leads to the second, then the second value leads back to the first. Different cultures value different arcs of the same circle, celebrating the movement from A to Z or, in other cultures, the movement from Z back to A. Although the descending arc may seem to mock and contradict the ascending arc, and vice versa, the truth is that these complement each other, like yin and yang. Thinking in circles, using encompassing reason, is a form of wisdom. The fashionable name for this among the consulting community is *cross-cultural competence,* and it is this learned capacity which this book seeks to illuminate.

In addition to the three dimensions already introduced are three others.

Do cultures regard status as *achieved* by one's record of success or is status *ascribed* to persons for other reasons? Are cultures *inner directed*—that is, motivated or driven from within—or *outer directed*—that is, adjusting themselves to the flow of external events? Finally, do they regard time as *sequential* or seriatim, a passing line of increments, or is time *synchronous,* key conjunctions of events, expertly timed?

The Ubiquity of Dilemma

We all know the old dilemma of the chicken and the egg. Which came first? All six value dimensions investigated in this book represent similar dilemmas. Which came first—the universal rule or the exceptional event? Which is first—the family or the individual, the whole or the constituent element? There is no final answer to these dilemmas. Which is where cultures come in. Cultures tend to assert that to which no final answer can be given. "The resourceful individual comes first," says American culture. "The rice-growing village comes first," says Chinese culture. Wherever people are not sure about basic values, culture makes that assertion for them, and that assertion has often meant survival or destruction.

Consider the famous dictum of Adam Smith, that self-interest leads as if by an "invisible hand" to social and public benefit. Is there truth to this proposition? Certainly. Do individuals competing with one another in serving customers thereby improve service to those customers? Yes. Is this a truth upon which the "science" of economics can be squarely based? Perhaps not.

For have we not ignored the reverse proposition? Do teams, groups, and companies, wherein persons cooperate harmoniously with each other, thereby serve the individual interests of their members, as if by an invisible hand? Certainly. Do cohesive teams encouraging high participa-

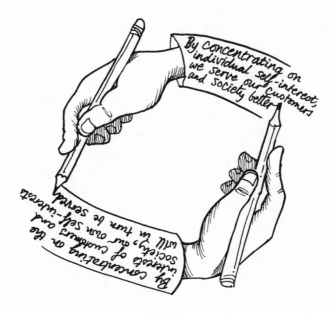

Figure 2

tion thereby improve the morale and power of individual members? Yes. Would it not then be a wiser economic science that encompassed both these sequences, not just one? Perhaps so.

The "circular form" by which values interact is shown in Figure 2. "The descending arc" moves left and top down. This is the traditional western, individualistic view. "The ascending arc" moves right and bottom up. This is the communitarian view, held by at least half the world's people. Note the essential ambiguity of this illustration, based on the work of M. C. Escher. Who is doing the writing, and what is being written? Depending on your culture, the "Individualistic" hand is assuring community benefit or the "Communitarian" hand is assuring individual benefit.

We recommend neither view exclusively but rather the whole circle. F. Scott Fitzgerald put it well: "The test of a first-rate intelligence is the ability to hold two opposed ideas in the mind at the same time, and still retain the ability to function." We paraphrase the remainder of this quotation: "You must, for example, be able to see that just as individuals can contribute much to the life of the community, that community has nurtured and originates the individuality they express."

That is intelligence of an unusual kind, yet essential to a transcultural world.

What Makes Diverse People Generate Wealth?

What does crossing cultures and being diverse have to do with wealth creation? Obviously, traveling to other countries and reaching firm understandings is an advantage, but is there anything beyond that? More than we might expect. Immigrants, refugees, outsiders, and diverse religious and ethnic groups within cultures have so often been spectacularly successful at wealth creation that it cannot be a coincidence.

Among the spectacular successes are the Chinese outside China, Indians outside India, and Jews outside Israel. To be a stranger in a strange land can break you, but surprisingly it often makes you. Refugees and migrants travel light and must rely on what they can carry between their ears. Over 50 percent of the entrepreneurs in Ashton's *The Industrial Revolution* (in Great Britain) turned out to be of Nonconformist religions, many refugees from foreign persecution. At that time Nonconformists constituted 5.0 percent of the population.

While Nonconformist entrepreneurs constituted over ten times more than their numbers indicated, one religious sect, the Society of Friends, or Quakers, contributed forty times in excess of their numbers. The founders of Barclays Bank, Lloyds Bank, Lloyds Insurance, Rowntrees, Cadbury, and Fry were all Quakers. Quakers gave unprecedented authority to women, tithed their community to pay for apprentice training, formed a national network of local groups, and would doff their hats to no one!

One consequence of being diverse, religiously or ethnically, is that many customary avenues to upward mobility are blocked. Nonconformists were barred from major universities and hence medicine, law, church, and government. They did not rely on gentility, charm, conversation, and manners.

What persons of highly diverse identity did and still do is substitute products for their personalities and sell physical things in place of themselves. If most people will not accept you, at least they will use the things you make or supply. Making tangible products is a typical survival strategy of the culturally diverse.

Nor is this strategy purely historical. Much of America's current wealth comes from computer "nerds" and "techno-freaks," consummate outsiders. Silicon Valley is America's great success story, so where do its leaders come from?

A recent study by AnnaLee Saxenian for the Public Policy Institute of

California profiles *Silicon Valley's New Immigrant Entrepreneurs.* The statement "Silicon Valley is built on ICs" refers to "Indian and Chinese immigrants," who account for at least *one-third* of the engineering work force of the region's high-technology firms. Chinese and Indian engineers, who have immigrated to the United States steadily since 1970 to pursue graduate degrees, are now running 25 percent of Silicon Valley's technology businesses. Immigrant-run companies accounted for $16.8 billion in sales in 1998, and created 58,282 jobs in that year alone. This constituted 17 percent of total sales and 14 percent of total jobs.

The proportion of Indian and Chinese immigrants in this region is skewed toward senior positions, with fewer semiskilled workers proportionately than those found in the white population. Because so many of these immigrants run their own companies, or cluster near the top, there are few barriers to upward mobility for Chinese and Indian employees.

In a style similar to the Quakers, Indian and Chinese entrepreneurs are network specialists. They are in touch with most members of their ethnic groups not only in California but also in Bangalore, Delhi, Hsinchu, Taipei, and similar areas. They have created not a "brain drain" but a brain circulation, spending their lives traveling between Silicon Valley and homegrown centers of technology. They are more interested in world than American citizenship. The boom in electronics in Bangalore and around Taipei is directly traceable to the California connection.

All immigrants need ways of engaging the outside world that will make up for their strangeness, for the lack of what the dominant culture defines as "airs and graces" intelligible to that culture. Success in enterprise is a major resort of the otherwise inarticulate, uncomfortable, and ill-fitting. A dense array of dazzling products stands between them and likely prejudice and disparagement. It is not that "prejudice is good for you." It clearly is not. What elevates the enterprising are their ways of overcoming prejudice, from the Asian corner store that stays open twelve hours a day to the transformation of silicon into novel forms.

While those to the manor born are tempted to trickle away their lives in clever conversation and witty repartee, immigrants lack that option. They must build formidable complexes of goods and services, hiring others to do the face-to-face work. By valuing education, especially the "hard" sciences and disciplines—physics, engineering, accounting, mathematics—they concentrate in fields that are relatively stable and impersonal. They avoid most people-intensive, arts-intensive activities where their strangeness could prove a handicap. No wonder that Silicon Valley's Chinese and Indian immigrants are underrepresented in administrative positions.

Value Is not "Added," but Reconciled

One of the half-truths of economics is the idea of "added value." In Adam Smith's pin factory, the pins went through successive stages of manufacture, each stage "adding value" until the total pin was formed and finished.

This is an archaic vision. Modern development and manufacture is far more complex. Since values are differences, it is fallacious to believe that these easily add up. Values, as we have seen, come at opposite ends of continua, analyzing and synthesizing, making rules and discovering exceptions. You cannot simply add a rule to an exception or add a synthesis to an analysis; you must integrate these, reconcile the dilemma. Exceptions must be integrated into a new rule, individuals must be integrated into the community, analyzed pieces must be integrated into a new synthesis.

This also applies to many products. Consider the differences incorporated into an automobile. We wish it to be *high-performing* yet *safe,* to *economize on fuel* yet *accelerate sharply,* to be *sporty* yet *reliable,* to give *freedom* to the driver yet *reassert control* in emergencies, to be *compact* yet *roomy* inside, to *absorb* the impact of a collision so that the occupants *escape* that impact. We want it to be *low-cost* yet *distinctive.*

Clearly this list of values is full of contrasts. A car that performs more sluggishly is safer; acceleration uses up fuel; a compact car, all things being equal, is less roomy; and so on. These values are in tension with each other. The conventional wisdom is that we must choose *between* these values, so that a Volvo, for example, is safe and reliable but not high-performing and sporty.

But if we look deeper, we see that despite some trade-offs, automobiles are considerably safer *and* better-performing, more fuel-saving *and* more responsive to the throttle than they were just a few years ago. The industry consistently improves *both* values-in-tension. The makers of the original Volkswagen "beetle," for example, turned its engine sideways and put it in the back, thus making the vehicle much roomier than comparable small cars.

It is not easy to reconcile economy with luxury—or freedom for the driver with antiskid and crash-protection devices—but it is possible. Moreover, the greater the challenge, the greater the value created for the customer. If reconciling contrasting values is hard, instances are likely to be scarce and hence valuable.

This principle is not confined to a single industry. We need food to be good-tasting *and* fast to prepare. We need computers to be complex and multifunctional yet "user friendly"—a considerable challenge! We need clothes to be elegant yet hard-wearing, the Internet to be open yet secure and encrypted. We need police services to assail criminals but not innocent civilians. None of this is easy. All of this is possible.

What is true of finished products (or services) is true of the processes involved in supplying these. Value conflicts and clashes emerge within research, development, manufacturing, marketing, distribution, and after-sales service departments, and many conflicts erupt *between* them. Yet only those managers and workers who are reconciled with one another can reconcile the supply processes, to distribute reconciled products and services. It is routine for manufacturing departments to wish to churn out quantities of product that sales cannot move. Conflicts are everywhere.

Strategies are full of values-in-tension also. You create a strong strategy that everyone in the company applauds and lose sight of business opportunities it has failed to anticipate. You downsize the work force to save costs and find that the low morale of your staff is being inflicted on customers. You create an elaborate mission statement and find that the changing environment renders it obsolete.

If creating wealth reconciles value differences, this would also explain why some immigrants have proved so adept at free enterprise. Creating wealth solves the problems of being very different from your environment. It is a "training ground for reconciliation."

Are There Universal Dilemmas of Wealth Creation?

Because differences abound between functions, disciplines, genders, industries, ethnic groups, and nations of the world, reconciling such dilemmas should be an important part of creating wealth, and of developing a humane, peaceful, and just system of world governance.

Among the multiplying variations in cultural responses, many of them angry and discordant, we believe a finite number of *universal dilemmas* exist. We cannot think of a nation, tribe, or tiddlywinks team, for example, that does not make rules and is not then shortly faced with exceptions to those rules. We cannot imagine any group anywhere that is not at times in tension with the demands of its individual members. We have created six of these "archetypal dilemmas," and we plan to show that where these differences are reconciled whole organizations grow healthier, wealthier, and wiser as a consequence.

It is true that human creativity and innovation are infinitely variable, but we see this variation as an endless series of responses to the same underlying dilemmas. The answer to business problems may not be to apply "The American Way" to every conceivable one, but to view the six dimensions and their mirror-image reversals as alternative ways of coping with life's exigencies. These dimensions, all reversible, create twelve different logics that in different combinations constitute 24 or 64 variations. If we assume a third integrative position, the number of variations rises to 729.

Serious Humor

There remains the need to justify the style of this book, filled with cartoon depictions. Are we dumbing down an otherwise serious work and appealing to a tabloid audience? The cartoons are playful but serve a serious purpose. They reflect the fact that cultures stereotype and satirize themselves, creating archetypal, one-dimensional images of good and evil. By sharing a culture's laughter, we both acknowledge the surface representation and remind ourselves of the superficiality and excess to which the satirist draws our attention. The United States is "like that" but "*not* like that" or it would not laugh at itself! That this is a joke signifies a deeper reality.

In Ancient Greece the comic cycle of plays preceded the tragedies. It was said that if you could not laugh, you would presently cry. In this book we expose cultural stereotypes because they cannot be ignored, but everyone can and must get beyond them. For the realities lie in the subtle interaction of satire and satirist, in the ground between the convention and the critic. We cannot avoid the use of polarized values, but we can be aware of our exaggeration.

Images and configurations are necessary for another reason. Our third dimension contrasts specific items and units with diffuse wholes. Numbers and words are specific. Patterns, configurations, and images are diffuse. Hence a book on culture which lacks visual-spatial forms of explanation is biased against diffuse cultures and fails to convey their experiences.

The use of Chinese *kanji,* or picture words, primarily conveying composite meanings; the recently published *Japan Inc.,* by Shotaro Ishinomori, consisting largely of strip cartoons translated (by Alan G. Gleason) from Japanese; even the *manga* read by sober Japanese commuters on the subway—are all evidences of diffuse ways of thinking not confined to artists and children.

The Six Dimensions of Cultural Diversity

Some fourteen years of research, largely conducted by Fons Trompenaars and based on his doctoral thesis at University of Pennsylvania's Wharton School of Finance, has resulted in a sample of forty-six thousand managers from more than forty countries on at least six dimensions:

1. Universalism
    (rules, codes, laws,
    and generalizations)

    Particularism
    (exceptions, special circumstances,
    unique relations)

2. Individualism
    (personal freedom, human
    rights, competitiveness)

    Communitarianism
    (social responsibility, harmonious
    relations, cooperation)

3. Specificity
    (atomistic, reductive
    analytic, objective)

    Diffusion
    (holistic, elaborative
    synthetic, relational)

4. Achieved status
    (what you've done,
    your track record)

    Ascribed status
    (who you are, your potential
    and connections)

5. Inner direction
    (conscience and
    convictions are located inside)

    Outer direction
    (examples and influences
    are located outside)

6. Sequential time
    (time is a race along
    a set course)

    Synchronous time
    (time is a dance of fine
    coordinations)

The odd-numbered chapters in this book explore and describe the particular dilemma or values dimension.

The even-numbered chapters describe how these dilemmas have been reconciled, using both storytelling and business case studies to show how organizational dilemmas have been resolved to create wealth.

The odd-numbered chapters detail

- How the dilemma is defined
- How we measure the dimension
- Why American business culture is that way
- At its best, this culture . . .
- But taken too far . . .
- At its best, this (contrasting) culture . . .
- But taken too far . . .
- Culture clashes and derivative conflicts: in business, industry, religion, society, science, ethics, and politics

The even-numbered chapters (with exception of Chapter 2, which has a broader framework) detail:

- Stories told by American culture
- Mirror-image stories told by contrasting cultures
- Domination or reconciliation
- Business cases 1, 2, 3, etc.
- Vicious and virtuous circles

1 Universalism–Particularism

THE DILEMMA

The view taken here is that all values take the form of dilemmas. We would not even know what a universal rule was unless we could contrast it with an exception, a "not-rule." Evaluative terms are differences on a (usually) tacit continuum. When we say this object is "the same" as others, we are insisting that it is "not different."

Why do values such as Universalism–Particularism constitute a dilemma? Because we have a difficult choice. We can search for those many respects in which two or more objects/people are the same. Or we can search for the many respects in which these are different. We can, for example, insist that men and women are both human and should be treated the same, thereby upholding the universal rights of both genders. Alternatively we can insist that men and women are different and should be treated differently. Each approach has advantages, but also serious disadvantages. Some cultures, in the United States especially, stress sameness regarding gender. Others cry "Vive la difference."

How the Dilemma Is Defined

Universalism	*Particularism*
(rules, codes, laws, and generalizations)	(exceptions, circumstances, relations)

Should we apply to this situation the most appropriate rule, even if the fit is inexact, or do special circumstances and unique occurrences raise questions about the rule itself?

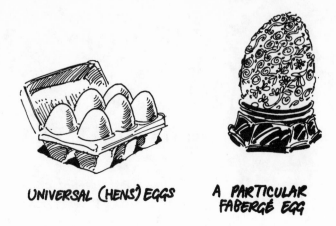

UNIVERSAL (HENS') EGGS   A PARTICULAR
                             FABERGÉ EGG

Figure 1.1

Consider the contrast between two eggs shown in Figure 1.1. On the left are "universal hens' eggs," a popular commodity. On the right is a Fabergé egg, a unique and decorated work of art.

Universalism searches for sameness and similarity and tries to impose on all members of a class or universe the laws of their commonality.	Particularism searches for differences, for unique and exceptional forms of distinction that render phenomena incomparable and of matchless quality.

Since every situation we encounter is in some respects similar to earlier situations and in some respects different, whether we apply "customary rules" or "new circumstances" is a dilemma that keeps recurring.

Take the following corporate rule: "All employees with one year of service may buy X number of company shares at a 5 percent discount." This applies equally to all members of the universe, and no exceptions should be made. If the CEO's nephew is an employee, for example, he should have the same entitlement, with the same limits, as any other employee. To extend special favors to him—say, a 10 percent discount—is nepotism and favoritism.

Universalism is important in both legal and scientific spheres. "Common" law requires that every citizen be treated "in common" and that nothing be done to obstruct the course of justice. However, courts take into

consideration mitigating circumstances, that is, the exceptional characteristics of a case.

Scientific laws must also be tested, so that if there are exceptions to the
scope of any law this will be discovered. Strictly speaking, scientific laws
cannot be proved. They can only be refuted, so we generally extend laws,
principles, and technologies until such time as exceptions multiply, in
which case the law is either wrong or has reached the limits of its "universe." Newtonian physics, for example, cannot be applied to subatomic
phenomena. These are beyond the range of its applicability.

Particularism refers to the claim that a particular event or phenomenon is
outside the scope of any rules and is *sui generis*, "of its own particular kind."
The nephew of the CEO could receive shares at a 10 percent discount if
his uncle made him a present of the difference. But he is doing this as an uncle for a particular relative and not as a CEO handing out a universal employee
entitlement. In practice, it can be difficult to separate the two roles and keep
the benefits of kinship and friendship apart from the fair administration of
rights and entitlements. It is for this reason that we measure Universalism–
Particularism by telling stories in which both values clash.

How We Measure Universalism–Particularism

We measure the extent to which different cultures are universalist or
particularist by presenting a dilemma and forcing a choice upon respondents. One of our questions poses the following dilemma.

You are riding in a car driven by a close friend. He hits a pedestrian. You
know he was going at least thirty-five miles per hour in an area of the city
where the maximum allowed speed is twenty miles per hour. There are no
witnesses other than you. His lawyer says that if you testify under oath that
he was driving only twenty miles per hour, you will save him from serious
consequences.

What right has your friend to expect you to protect him?

1a. My friend has a definite right as a friend to expect me to testify to the
     lower speed.
1b. He has some right as a friend to expect me to testify to the lower speed.
1c. He has no right as a friend to expect me to testify to the lower speed.

What do you think you would do in view of the obligations of a sworn
witness and the obligation to your friend?

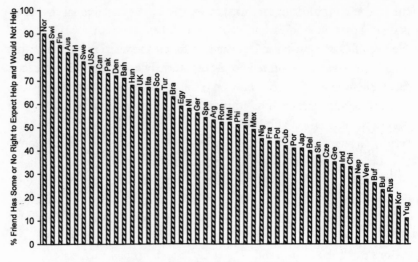

Figure 1.2 The Car and the Pedestrian

1d. Testify that he was going twenty miles per hour.

1e. Not testify that he was going twenty miles per hour.

The results of this research are interesting (Figure 1.2). Seven out of eight of the most universalist countries are Protestant and stable democracies: Switzerland, the United States, Canada, Sweden, Australia, the United Kingdom, and the Netherlands. Ireland is the exception, but this country was under British rule until 1921 and shares a common law tradition. Catholics are, on the whole, less universalist: see the scores for Brazil, Spain, Poland, France, Mexico, Cuba, and Venezuela. Buddhist, Confucian, Hindu, and Shinto countries are more particularist still: see South Korea, China, Indonesia, Nepal, Japan, and Singapore.

Another variable would seem to be "trust in the legal system." This is known to be low in Venezuela, Nepal, South Korea, Russia, and China. Without acceptance of national regulations it is difficult to universalize the duty to uphold the legal system. Because people can usually trust their friends, however bad the legal system, in turbulent times citizens tend to count only on friends and family.

Why Is American Culture Universalist?

We ask this question not because we are exclusively concerned with the United States but because America has contributed disproportionately to the total volume of business studies. It is therefore crucial to ask: What aspects of business studies consist of North American cultural preferences? We need to distinguish between what promotes wealth creation and what wealth creators in the United States espouse. The answers are not necessarily the same.

The business culture of the United States is universalist because:

- Protestants teach that God's word has been codified in the Bible for His faithful to read (Switzerland, where Calvinism originated, scores even higher in Universalism than does the United States).
- The founders created a New World or universe, with a written constitution and a Declaration of Independence.
- Most immigrants to the United States over three centuries have been invited to share American beliefs and pledge their allegiance.
- Immigrants have voluntarily relegated their ethnic origins, places of birth, and so forth to a commitment to a new belief system.
- Protestant cosmology holds that God wound up a celestial clock and bid His saints to discover, through science, how it worked.
- The European Enlightenment doctrine of America's founders commended discovery, science, laws, and methodologies of inquiry.
- Early in the twentieth century, educators codified professional business education, which was systematized and mastered (hence the MBA) in an attempt to create an administrative science.
- As the United States has grown more and more powerful economically and militarily, it has been increasingly able to develop and enforce upon the world its own rules.
- Because many of the foreigners Americans meet are also recent immigrants, there is a tendency to assume that everyone, everywhere would "Americanize" if they could and knew how.
- The process of global westernization and the ubiquity of the English language in world business reinforces the impression that "The American Way" is universally acceptable.
- When someone speaks your language, you tend to assume that they also share your thoughts and assumptions.

At Its Best . . .

The universalist culture accepts and serves all comers equally, whether they want citizenship or hamburgers. The sheer variety of ethnic groups coming to America and living prosperously, for the most part, under the rule of law, is without precedent in the world.

None of this could work unless the citizens themselves could choose their lawmakers. A universalist society counts every vote, even if it cannot make every vote count. Free and fair elections are crucial to a universalist culture.

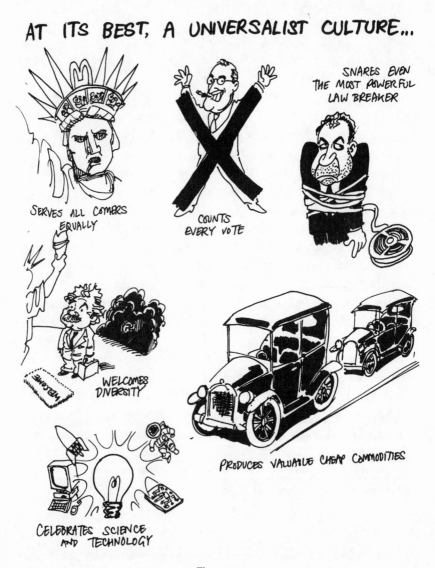

Figure 1.3

An extraordinary feature of a culture high in Universalism is that even people of extraordinary power with many particular relationships can be forced to yield to the supremacy of law. As Archibald Cox, special prosecutor for the Watergate investigations, put it just before President Nixon fired him, "Whether this is to be a government of laws or men, must now be decided." It turned out to be a government of laws, and Nixon was forced to resign to avoid impeachment.

The great strength of American Universalism is its tolerance for diversity. When the United States welcomed Albert Einstein to its shores it not only protested anti-Semitism, it included a scientist who would eventually advise Roosevelt on the potential of atomic weapons. What might have been German science and weaponry became American.

Universalism celebrates science and technology in general. From lightbulbs to telephones to space exploration to the computer revolution to the Internet, the United States leads the world in Nobel Prizes won and in the practical applications of scientific principles. The search for new laws is an all-consuming passion (Figure 1.3).

And, of course, Universalism is crucial to mass manufacturing and mass marketing. America's huge domestic market, created by the millions who choose to live under its laws, has created a larger universal "mass" than exists anywhere else in the world. Universalism pays off when the universe is large. Moreover, prices fall as scale increases. When Henry Ford doubled the wages of his workers, much to his shareholders' anger, he put the Model T within reach of his own workers. America is the home of the valuable, cheap commodity, with so many competitors that the laws of neoclassical economics actually work and real prices fall continually.

But Taken Too Far . . .

No single end of a value's dimension is an unlimited good. Not everything in life can be easily rubricated. There are whole subjects and areas of cultural interest that are particularist—the arts, for example, and the spirituality of people (see Figure 1.4).

American Universalism and general enthusiasm for simplistic moral formulas have led to televangelism and fundamentalist dogmas. From the nineteenth century onward "spiritual technology" has been popular, and we have seen endlessly repeated the career of the Reverend Dimmesdale in The Scarlet Letter, where the ascent of his rhetoric was accompanied by the

BUT IF TAKEN TOO FAR...

TELE FUNDAMENTALISM

I'M SO PROUD AND HAPPY

COLONISES HUMAN RELATIONSHIPS

HOW TO WIN FRIENDS & INFLUENCE PEOPLE

OBJECTIFIES BEAUTY AND CHARACTER

100% AMERICAN

BENCH MARKING

MAKES EVERYTHING LINEAR

Why are they using lawyers instead of rats in animal experiments? *

22 TIMES AS MANY LAWYERS PER CAPITA AS JAPAN

Figure 1.4

descent of his trousers. Scandal follows on scandal, yet instant salvation remains in high demand—fast food for spiritual starvation.

Dale Carnegie's best-seller *How to Win Friends and Influence People* remains a foremost example of the technological approach to friendship. Remembering and repeating people's names during a conversation and lavishing them with praise are typical keys to unlock "friendship." That you might enjoy the unique particularity of your friend and share something incomparable seems to be of no interest!

The stereotyped nature of "universal" criteria is never more obvious than in beauty pageants, where the measurements and sentiments of Miss America are ludicrously limited to a narrowly construed "ideal of beauty" that excludes 90 percent of women. That such contests are under assault from those advocating greater political correctness merely shows how old formulas are attacked by newer ones. The formulas remain. At Antioch College, for example, each level of sexual intimacy between students must be formally negotiated.

Although many scientific laws are nonlinear, cultural "scientism" tends to maximize forces borrowed from nineteenth-century physics and deemed objective. Quantity is seen as good in itself. Hence you must be "100 percent American," more received in your wisdom than anyone else. Not long ago citizens of less than 100 percent purity could be summoned before the House Un-American Activities Committee or put on a Hollywood blacklist. That certain thoughts can be classified in advance as subversive regardless of context is evidence of a vulgar, doctrinal Universalism. Benchmarking, the comparative measurement of industrial processes, tends to assume that the major challenge is doing things right, as opposed to doing the right things. But this assumption is only occasionally true and leads to "doing the right things" being overlooked in the search for perfection.

Finally, an excess of Universalism results in a litigious society and the "lawyer from hell" sitting in Reception with nightmare news. Apparently, America requires twenty-two times as many lawyers per capita as Japan. The phenomenon of the lawyer joke in America is testimony: "Give me three reasons why they are using lawyers instead of rats in animal experiments."

1. Because there are more lawyers than rats
2. Because research assistants feel sorrier for the rats
3. Because there are some things that rats won't do

The number of lawyers has doubled since the sixties. As more law students pass the bar, more litigation is stirred up, and each disagreeable experience is universalized into a federal case.

At Its Best . . .

A particularist culture celebrates what is unique and incomparable about people, situation, and events. If we were afraid of the unprecedented or the original, we could not create. Before the general rule *must* come the events or phenomena concerning which the rule is made. When a customer demands a new level of service, do we curse him for being much more particular than other customers, or do we grasp that a particular request today could well start a universal trend in the future?

Customization, where the product is specially made for the recipient, is an important source of prototype devices. The scarcity that enhances values is not simply a scarcity of the skills needed to be at the leading edge of development, but the scarcity of really close, really complex relationships. There is no time to have more than a few particular friends and associates. The individual who builds unique mutualities is in a very strong position.

Somewhat more particularist cultures like France are famous for certain superlative products—haute cuisine, haute couture, gourmet foods, fine wines, exquisite furniture—all dedicated to the well-developed tastes of the connoisseur. For Particularism is an aesthetic, a fellowship of refined sensibilities (Figure 1.5).

Particularism is also involved in our intimate and passionate relationships. There has never been a love like ours, a passion like ours, an understanding like ours. Moments of life are endowed with eternal significance— a glance, a smile abounds with subtlety and meaning. In ambiguity, irony, and suggestion lie the most elusive yet most enchanting experiences.

Particularist phenomena, like Japanese flower arrangements, Zen rocks in an ever-changing garden, and the elegance of a handmade broom of green birch sticks, are closer to nature. Living systems, although governed by biological laws, have the aspect of growth, flowering wildness, chaos, and vitality. Shinto, a Japanese religion based in nature, takes inspiration from the tumultuous, the blooming, and the flowing. To be alive is to break out of the serried ranks of uniformity and be a person like no other.

AT ITS BEST, THE PARTICULARIST CULTURE...

... IS THE BEGINNING OF SOMETHING NEW

... IS ESPECIALLY MADE FOR YOU

... IS ORIENTED TO EXQUISITE TASTES

... IS INTIMATE, PERSONAL, INCOMPARABLE

... SWEEPS UP THE DETRITUS OF UNIVERSALISM

... AND HAS VITALITY

Figure 1.5

But Taken Too Far . . .

A particularist culture becomes hostile to human rights and universalizing claims of equality. This has happened in East Asia, in Serbia's ethnic cleansing, and in the resistance to universal human rights found in some areas of the United States. Hence the Ku Klux Klan sets fire to crosses, transforming a symbol of worship into an object of terror. This group is racist, anti-Semitic, anti-Catholic, and anti-Communist and claims to be protecting white society against rampaging ethnic diversity. White men wearing bedsheets believe themselves descended from the clans of Old Scotland.

Another strand of Particularism attacks science, with "Eastern" religions, obscurantist mysticism, Hippie "happenings," and mind-expanding drugs, and by deliberate reversals of conventional values, as typified by the counterculture. "We are the people our parents warned us against."

Without the sanction of legality, Particularism often resorts to power and coercion, using intimidation, mystification, complicity, and conspiracy. The Mafia and criminal gangs are particularistic, whether in Sicily, the United States, or Russia. The loyalty is to the extended family, but violence rules beyond its bounds. There is no way of resolving rival particularities, in the absence of law, save through force. The historic quarrel between the Montagues and Capulets in *Romeo and Juliet,* which resulted in the death of two lovers, is a moral fable about Particularism.

Nationalism, tribalism, super-patriotism, and appeals to ethnic identity are all particularistic (Figure 1.6). International law does not apply to the French agents who sank *The Rainbow Warrior* in New Zealand. French interests came before lawful international conduct.

Much Particularism in the world is a protest against rules imposed from the outside by cultures seen as foreign. Such rules are not legislated internally but generalized across the globe and mandated by "alien" influence. What is considered sacred and religious is affronted by the "Great Satan" of American Universalism, intent on turning the world into a fast-food emporium—hence the assaults by French protesters against McDonald's restaurants. Protests are likely to be violent and hatred unremitting because the plea "But we are different" goes unheard.

Especially perilous is "Particularism dressed up as Universalism." This happened in the United States during the Prohibition era (1918–1933) when the Eighteenth Amendment banned alcohol. Ostensibly this was a universal answer to crime, divorce, alcohol addiction, and electoral block

BUT AT ITS WORST, PARTICULARISM IS...

OBSCURANTIST

SECRET, CONSPIRATORIAL, RACIST

UNIQUELY AVARICIOUS

PRONE TO FAVORITISM AND SPECIAL PRIVILEGES

A SOURCE OF FAMILY FEUDS AND MAFIA VIOLENCE

Figure 1.6

votes delivered by intoxicated mobs rounded up by political bosses. But if we note how people actually behaved, we see that this was a struggle between older, rural-based immigrants to America against the urban influx of newer Irish, German, and southern European immigrants. The attack was upon them as new, "less moral" immigrants. The amendment was later repealed.

Culture Clashes and Derivative Conflicts: In Business and Industry

The clash between Universalism and Particularism takes many forms. There are "family resemblances" in different aspects of business.

One example is the historic clash between scientific management, a most universalist approach to business introduced by engineer-inventor Frederick Winslow Taylor, and the human relations movement, championed by Elton Mayo and by Fritz Roethlisberger of Harvard Business School and culminating in the famous Hawthorne Experiment.

Taylor, followed by Henry Ford and "efficiency experts" in general, argued that an engineering-type discipline could be imposed on blue-collar factory workers to make them substantially more productive. They were to perform a carefully specified number of simple hand motions and when these reached the standard set for them, incremental piecework incentives were to be paid.

Taylor believed that his methods would resolve all industrial conflicts, since the "one best way of working" could be mathematically demonstrated in advance. Business hoping to remain competitive and workers seeking continued employment must yield to the verdicts of "science" (Figure 1.7).

Mayo and Roethlisberger investigated the phenomenon of *work restriction*, the deliberate attempt by a work force to restrict output and hold down the level of productivity—sometimes organized by unions, but usually a form of spontaneous revolt against coercion and dehumanization in the workplace. Against the formal system of required tasks and interactions, there arose an informal system that sought to defy management, by means of sabotage, featherbedding, and the social ostracism of "rate busters," high-producing workers.

While scientific management is now discredited, "operations research" and more ominously "reengineering" have taken their toll on human relationships in the workplace.

THE UNIVERSALIST—PARTICULARIST DISTINCTION STRUCTURES BUSINESSES AND INDUSTRIES AND YIELDS THE FOLLOWING DERIVATIVE DICHOTOMIES...

SCIENTIFIC MANAGEMENT ———————— HUMAN RELATIONS

MASS PRODUCTION ———————— CUSTOMIZATION

THE FORMAL SYSTEM ———————— THE INFORMAL SYSTEM

Figure 1.7

What gave scientific management its vast momentum were the triumphs of the Machine Age, especially mass manufacturing and its accompaniment, mass marketing. These swept all before them from the early twenties to the late sixties.

Universalism–Particularism also elucidates the two contrasting strategies of *developing core competence* and *getting close to the customer.* This is because core competence, like "Intel Inside," is a core scientific development, while closeness to customers makes every relationship particular. Such relationships may include jointly developed strategies and shared secrets.

Another contrast is between low-cost strategy, which utilizes the near-universal appeal of cheapness, and premium strategies, which stress the uniqueness, incomparability, and status of owning a product. Like Moët et Chandon champagne, the premium product has a cachet, "a hidden virtue." It is of note that both the champagne and the word are French. Both premium quality and closeness to the customer inspire loyalty. Customers may continue to buy from you and advise you, even when profits and revenues are heading down. They may provide you with a crucial second chance.

Another common polarization that reflects Universalism–Particularism is the distinction between global corporations, typically centralized on their home country, and multinational corporations, with highly decentralized business units particular to their local cultures. The distinction was made by Christopher Bartlett and Sumantra Ghoshal and is taken up in Chapter 2.

The global corporation has the advantage of world scale for products that have much the same function everywhere, for example, microchips, VHS recorders, and fax machines. The multinational corporation has the advantage of fitting into diverse cultural niches. For example, taste in food and styles of washing and cleaning are particular to different cultures. Hence AT&T is typical of a global, universalist corporation, while Unilever is typical of a multinational, particularist corporation (Figure 1.8).

Culture Clashes and Derivative Conflicts:
In Religion, Politics, and Society

The tension between Universalism and Particularism spills over into religion, politics, and society. We have already seen that Protestant cultures score higher on the Universalism scale than most Catholic cultures. The

UNIVERSALIST – PARTICULARIST DISTINCTION CONTINUED DERIVATIVE DICHOTOMIES...

CORE COMPETENCE ———— CLOSE TO CUSTOMER

LOW-COST STRATEGY ———— PREMIUM STRATEGY

GLOBAL CORPORATION ———— MULTINATIONAL CORPORATION

Figure 1.8

image of Jesus is less commonly featured in Protestant liturgy. The cross is usually depicted bare—more an abstract, universal symbol, than the portrait of a real event. Protestants worship God as "the word." For Catholics the crucifixion is depicted in elaborate detail, blood trickling from the crown of thorns. A very particular being is suffering in very particular ways.

Universalist cultures seek moral absolutes, typified by the Ten Commandments; for particularist cultures, "it depends." Indulgence may sometimes be extended, and forgiveness follows confession and repentance. In Japanese culture, multiple points of view coexist. The ideal is to find a harmony among the varied particulars of nature. The relativist view is well expressed in *Ecclesiastes:* "To everything there is a season. . . . A time to break down and a time to build up; A time to weep, and a time to laugh."

Universalism has always sought a "higher law." Its classic expression is the Writing of the Wall at Belshazzar's Feast in ancient Babylon. Despite the king's magnificence and power, the ceremony was interrupted by a hand that wrote, "You have been weighed in the balance and found wanting." His kingdom collapsed on the morrow. Particularist cultures appeal to the mystery, magnificence, and splendor of kings. Louis XIV, the Sun King, is an example of French Particularism and grandeur.

The argument carries into architecture and literary criticism (Figure 1.9). The so-called international school of architecture is an expression of modernism. It is "international" because geometric forms and simple functions were deemed to be the same everywhere. Technology drives construction and is global in its scope and predictable in its application. It is the machine aesthetic—abstract, intellectual, numerate, with flat or curvilinear, undecorated surfaces. Because it was reproducible anywhere it was universal. Its advocates were Mies van der Rohe, Walter Gropius, and Le Corbusier.

In contrast to this trend is postmodernism, which reintroduces the expressive flourishes of particular architects. A famous example is Philip Johnson's AT&T building in Manhattan, which looks like a grandfather clock with a Chippendale pediment and is ironic and ambiguous, with multiple meanings.

Postmodernism also attacks logo-centrism, the idea that great writers have a singular message to impart and that novels have a meaning and logic the critic can grasp and expound. On the contrary, postmodernists and deconstructionists say, great novels have multiple meanings, capable

Figure 1.9

of being interpreted by readers with diverse life experiences according to their particular outlooks. Some have criticized logo-centrism, the belief in some logical unity of all things, for privileging certain interpretations, especially those of dead, white European males and bastions of academic orthodoxy.

It would be absurd to call Universalism "right" and Particularism "wrong," or vice versa. We all need to generalize to some restricted universe of members, and we all need to know when this process has to stop. Rules need exceptions to keep them relevant and just. Exceptions need rules to prove their exceptionality.

Cultures with great enthusiasm for universals sometimes go too far. In 1972, for example, the Pruitt-Igoe high-rise public housing project in St. Louis, Missouri, had to be dynamited down. Yet it had won prizes from the enthusiastic advocates of the international school. It may have been "logical" to store the poor vertically, thus saving on land costs, but the residents hated it. The buildings became nests for crime, which proved impossible to police. The formal system was overwhelmed by informal systems, and the universalists confronted a host of unpredicted events that reproached their "science."

But these examples should not be used to argue against universalizing as a process. They should stand as a warning against doing so rashly and precipitously.

Particularism taken too far may be even more objectionable. Up to 2 million ethnic Albanians, most of the Muslim faith, were recently "cleansed" from Kosovo because the land claims of Orthodox Christian and ex-Communist Serbs were regarded as superior. The expulsion was not for crimes committed but for ethnic identity itself. This kind of ultranationalism represents Particularism gone mad and is reminiscent of the Nazi era. As the NATO bombing showed, this kind of activity is widely condemned by internationalist forces as a defiance of their Universalist creed.

We have a choice then. We can claim that Particularist cultures, who would bear false witness, are not fit to share this earth with us truth-tellers. Alternatively, we can claim that Universalist cultures, who would not even help their best friends in trouble, are too bloodless to belong to the family of humanity. There is fuel for righteous indignation at both poles.

But there is a third option, explored in Chapter 2. We can ask what rules and exceptions have to teach one another and how to create an integrity of the two. To this cross-cultural learning process we now turn.

2 Reconciling Universalism and Particularism

STORIES AND CASES

Our position is that human integrity inheres not in universal codes or particular instances, but in the mutual development of the entire continuum. As William Blake put it, "He who would do good must do it in minute particulars." If "good" is the universal abstraction, then this must be instanced in many particular acts covered by that rule.

We show in this chapter that wealth is created and value "added" when contrasting values are reconciled. What effective business offers customers is the proceeds of its organizational integrity. These high-level integrations are incorporated into products and/or services.

We look first at the stories cultures tell that idealize their favorite values but typically include the contrasting value as well. Hence an American story will put Universalism first, but a French story may put Particularism first. We then show how reconciling both values is superior to imposing our own rules or particular interests on others. We finally turn to business cases in which reconciliation has proved advantageous and has helped create wealth and to moral issues in general. Finally, we warn against the vicious circle, the degenerative spiral.

The sequence of our argument is as follows.

1. A story told by a universalist culture
2. A (mirror-image) story told by a particularist culture
3. The particular exception tests the universal rule
4. Freedom exists within the law
5. Corporate stories reveal the culture
6. How we managed a copyright dispute

7. Beyond globalism and multiculturalism
8. Business strategies of universal and particular appeal
9. New paradigms create scientific revolutions
10. Developing moral judgment
11. Culture as a fractal phenomenon
12. Vicious and virtuous circles
13. The answer lies not in values but in their interactions

All these illustrations show how universals interact with particulars for good or for ill. It is not the existence of universal rules and particular exceptions that elevates or dooms a culture, but the quality of their relationship.

A Story Told by a Universalist Culture

A very powerful way of passing on your culture is through storytelling. The story features a crisis or dilemma, which the American hero or protagonist solves by putting universalism first. Such stories have an almost mythic and archetypal structure within the culture.

One story was told by the American director Fred Zinnemann in *High Noon*. Here, the town's marshal must place his sworn legal duty before his honeymoon and his private happiness. The story begins as the town's marshal, Will Kane, is marrying Amy Fowler, his Quaker bride. They are receiving the congratulations of a small wedding party, including the town's judge and selectmen. Will takes off his gun and his badge and hangs these on a peg. The gesture is symbolic. He has just resigned his job. Tomorrow the new marshal arrives. There are jokes about him becoming a storekeeper. Amy will insist. They prepare to leave on their honeymoon.

Here is a film occurring in "real time." It starts at 10:50 AM and reaches its climax seventy minutes later, so that the audience and the protagonists join in counting the minutes to "high noon." The wedding party is rudely interrupted by the telegraph operator from the railroad station, bearing a message that Frank Miller, arrested by Will and sentenced to death by the judge five years ago, has been unaccountably pardoned by up-state politicians. He is arriving by the noon train in Hadleyville. He has sworn to kill both marshal and judge.

The immediate reaction of the wedding party is that Will and Amy should leave for their honeymoon without delay. He must "think of Amy now." He is no longer marshal. The couple drive quickly out of town, but two miles down the road Will reins in the horses.

He cannot run away, he tells her. If they run now, they will always be running. This is their town, their people. Although he is no longer the marshal, he is the same man who put Frank Miller away last time and whom Frank Miller hates. Amy is furious. She has seen both her brothers shot and is a convert to Quakerism. Will is asking her to wait until noon to discover whether she is a wife or a widow. She won't do it. If he does not come with her now, she will be on that noon train when it leaves.

In the meantime, Ben Miller, Frank's brother, and two other gunslingers are riding ostentatiously through town. They will meet the noon train and then ride back into town wreaking vengeance—the Four Horsemen of the Apocalypse bringing to an end the brief security and quietude the town had recently enjoyed. Frank has his supporters in the town: the gamblers, gunsmiths, drinkers, and coffin-makers.

The first man to flee is the town judge. At Indian Falls last year the townspeople offered up their law enforcement officials to gunmen. He is not exposing himself to that. Will then contacts his deputy marshal, but the young man has a grievance. Why was he not offered Kane's job? Why was another marshal appointed? Kane cannot say. It was not his decision. The deputy tries to sell his services in the present crisis in exchange for the marshal's job. But Will is not buying. The deputy quits.

Now desperate, Will interrupts the Sunday service at the local church to plead for deputies. The minister invokes "Thou shall not kill" and reproaches Will for not getting married in that church. Several worshippers ask if this is not a private quarrel. Is it not true that Frank Miller and Will quarreled over Helen Ramirez, the Mexican owner of the town's hotel? (Will saved Helen from Frank's fists.) Why should the town intervene in a grudge match?

Others complain that the state has never given them sufficient law enforcement funds. Are they now expected to risk their own lives after paying taxes? But it is Will's "friend," the chief selectman, who puts in the knife. Who will invest in this town if they hear of gunfights in the street? It's bad for business. Will is "the best marshal we ever had," but if he is gone when Frank comes, there won't be any fighting. Will should not have come back from his honeymoon. Even Helen Ramirez acts to stop her male business partner from joining Will. She wants to sell him her hotel and get out of town before Frank beats her up.

One by one the pillars of the community desert Will. Even the one who volunteered backs out when told there are only two of them. But now the train is arriving. Amy and Helen get on. Amy gets off again. She cannot leave Will. The Four Horsemen ride into town where Will alone waits to oppose them.

The theme song tells of Will Kane's dilemma: "Oh to be torn twixt love and duty/S'posing I lose my fair-haired beauty?" He faces not simply death but desertion by all he holds dear: "Do not forsake me, oh my darling/On this our wedding day."

Schematically we can depict the story as a struggle between Universalism, or the Rule of Law, and Particularism, or private devotion to another person (Figure 2.1).

On the vertical diagram is the duty Will has as a lawman to the "universe" of townspeople, not to mention the spread of American civilization into the wilderness of lawlessness. On the horizontal dimension is the particular love and intimacy he feels toward his new bride, who abhors violence.

Figure 2.1 High Noon

The resolution is depicted by the direction of the arrow in the diagram. The marshall first upholds his duty, which then allows him to resume his interrupted love life. The second value is realized through the first.

The dilemma is resolved when Will and Amy succeed in killing all four villains and Will returns to Amy's arms. The ordering of these values makes good sense. How would he have felt on his honeymoon if he had run out on the townspeople? How much domestic bliss could there be in a town run by brigands? To what kind of "home" or "job" could he have returned?

Does this mean that universalism must always or necessarily be put ahead of particularism? No, it does not. It means that Americans, who live in a universalist culture, will make films and tell stories about the triumph of universalism and these will be successful at the box office, since the audience already thinks this way.

A (Mirror-Image) Story Told by a Particularist Culture

Consider a story in which conflicting values are resolved in an opposite sequence. It comes from France, a Catholic country much higher in particularism. The hero is Jean Valjean of *Les Miserables,* the novel by Victor Hugo, which has been adapted for the stage as a musical. Valjean has been imprisoned for nineteen years, initially for stealing a loaf of bread and later for attempting to escape. Note that "the Law" is not always fair or commensurate.

Once released, Valjean cannot find work because the conditions of his parole require his yellow parole certificate to be displayed. Hungry and destitute, he is offered dinner and a bed by a kindly bishop to whom he tells his life story. But Valjean wakes up in the night and with an armful of the bishop's silver tries to escape. But he is caught sneaking out of town, dragged back to the bishop's house, and thrown at the bishop's feet. He is invited to repeat his "pretty story" about the silver being a gift, but the bishop interrupts with an astounding confirmation. In the musical version, he sings

That is right!
But my friend you left too early
It has surely slipped your mind
You forgot I gave these also
Would you leave the best behind?

And he gives Valjean two additional candlesticks. He dismisses the constabulary and when they have left, he says to Valjean:

> But remember this my brother
> See in this a higher plan
> You must use this precious silver
> To become an honest man
> By the witness of the martyrs
> By the passion and the blood
> God hath raised you out of darkness
> I have bought your soul for God.

The solution to this dilemma is the obverse, the mirror image, of the previous one and is full of personal and particular passion (Figure 2.2). The order of priority is depicted by the direction of the arrow. The "lying bishop" reasons that Jean Valjean will understand the universal law of God only if he is first shown a particular act of love and kindness. Sending him back to lifetime imprisonment under a law that has already embittered him would crush his spirit. The danger (shown at the bottom right of the diagram) is that the bishop's act of forgiveness will be exploited and confirm Valjean in his thievery. Instead, the criminal is redeemed. His life changes forever. He has discovered the law of God in the love of humanity.

The story is a moving tribute to the human capacity for redemption and renewal. When Javert, the police chief, finds himself at the mercy of his old enemy (Valjean) and is spared, he kills himself rather than live in a world where people can change the meaning of their lives and where judgments are not fixed.

Such a story is better adapted to French history than to American. In the history of France, cruel and unjust regimes have had to be overthrown. Nazi occupation was endured. Rebellious acts had to be forgiven and laws remade from the ideals of brotherly love and human interaction. What persisted over the centuries was not the rule of law but the resilience of the human spirit—the capacity of the French people to reinvent themselves.

If the United States and Switzerland are, respectively, the world's most powerful culture and the country with the world's highest per capita income, and if these two score higher on the scale of universalism than any other culture, then surely it is better to be universalist. That is not our interpretation. Nor does this make sense in light of the recent economic

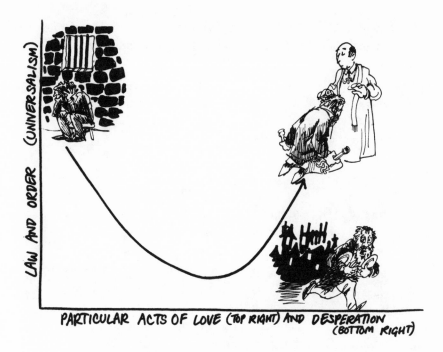

Figure 2.2 Redeeming Jean Valjean

successes of East Asia, which comprises nations quite high in Particularism.

Let us consider the two cultural "folktales" just related. In neither case did the culture reject the value at the other end of the dimension. The moral of *High Noon* was not that the marshal should neglect his bride or cease to love her, but that after he had done his duty of law enforcement, there would be time enough for marital bliss. Similarly, the moral of the "stolen silver" scene from *Les Miserables* was not that the universal law of God, the "higher plan" as the bishop called it, was unimportant, but that, for this man, a particular act of love must precede his commitment to this law. He had to be shown before he could be told.

What we see from both these stories is that cultures *reconcile* universalism and particularism. They seek one through the other and have their preferred sequences. In other words, the solution lies not in universalism or particularism but in the integration of both. Laws by themselves are no guarantee of virtue—what makes for a good society are laws that account for a diversity of particular interests and contingencies. Similarly, exceptions are not good in and of themselves—what makes for a good society is a diversity of novel forms and expressions that transcend known laws and standards.

A corporation, business unit, or whole society learns by making rules and laws, studying the exceptions that arise, and revising those rules to accommodate the exceptions. The process of rule making and exception finding never ends. It is circular.

The Particular Exception Tests the Universal Rule

The most crucial nexus between rules and exceptions is where rules are meant to limit the number of exceptions and exceptions are meant to transcend existing rules and standards—a dialectic that never ends.

We all make rules. We have to. This includes simple business procedures like "Give customers this level of service." But no sooner do we promulgate rules when exceptions arise. The world is changing. Markets shift. Customers want something *else*. Do we simply ignore the mounting number of exceptions or revise our rules to cover these?

Successful businesses do the latter. They constantly reinvent rules to accommodate more customers more effectively.

For example, in the early eighties People Express reinvented the rules of air travel, so that 30 million Americans who could not afford to fly were now included. Huge savings were made by removing kitchens, selling tickets on board, and not checking baggage but hefting it into enlarged overhead lockers. Prices fell to $50 or less.

But a second rule change killed People Express. United Airlines and American Airlines used management yield software to predict how full their flights would be, and then slashed their prices on slow-selling flights. Flexible low costs beat fixed low costs. People Express, whose own management yield software had been delayed in development, could not survive the competition.

Making rules that better cover multiplying exceptions is essentially a way of thinking. We all generalize until our generalizations break down and then we reconceive our categories of thought. It is we who invent rules and we who must accept responsibility for how adequate these are.

Exceptions can be used to "prove" or test the rule we have made (Figure 2.3). Rules and exceptions are not adversaries but potential complementors. To be "exceptional" is to rise above current rules and standards. To in-

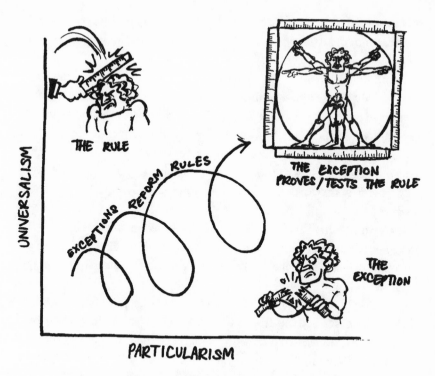

Figure 2.3 Universalism/Particularism

clude more exceptions within your rules is to universalize or generalize better. It is to legislate more skillfully.

There can of course be conflicts. The rule may beat us around the head (top left of Figure 2.3) so that we are provoked into breaking the rule (bottom right). But this tension also helps us learn, hence the helical pattern by which rules get better as more and more particulars are covered by their scope.

But it could be a mistake to believe that rules, codes, and laws will eventually account for every particular. Unprecedented and incomparable works of art and literature will never be completely accounted for by rule-based axioms. There will always remain, as in physics, areas of indeterminacy and uncertainty, a tendency for knowers to influence what is known.

Freedom Exists Within the Law

It is important not to polarize freedom with lawfulness. The lawful growth and development of living organisms shows a freedom within the process of development. No flower, no animal, no human being is quite like another. All are engaged in a growth process, but no two will turn out exactly the same as a result of that process.

You can be determined at one level and free at another level. For example, Gregory Bateson first reinforced dolphins for doing specific tricks by rewarding them with fish. He then switched to rewarding a trick not witnessed before. Initially the dolphins were greatly confused, until one by one they worked it out and performed a series of original antics. Were they determined? Yes. They had to perform tricks to survive in captivity. Were they free? Yes: the particular trick they would perform next could not be predicted.

A way in which human societies recognize freedom within the law is by doctrines of human rights. We are given rights within which we are free to behave as we wish, so that we may lawfully assemble, protest, worship, and so forth.

It was Sir Thomas More, the Roman Catholic martyr, and the author of *Utopia*, who described this freedom at his trial for treason, in Robert Bolt's *A Man for All Seasons*. Told that "by the light of the law" he was guilty of treason against Henry VIII, he replied: "The law is not a light for you or any man to see by. . . . The law is not an instrument of any kind. The law is a broad highway, on which, so long as he keeps to it, a man may walk freely in matters of conscience."

More was arguing for a freedom of personal conscience *within* the law. Just as you can go this way or that while keeping to the highway, so the road that wound to More's Utopia respected each man's freedom of conscience. We see this in Figure 2.4. At top left is the famous Old Testament story of Belshazzar's Feast, during which appeared a ghostly hand "Writing on the Wall." "Thou hast been weighed in the balance and found wanting." This is an early example of the Israelites' insistence on a written Law of God, which in this instance cast down the mightiest of pagan kings.

How such monarchs ruled is illustrated at bottom right by Percy Bysshe Shelley's poem "Ozymandias," which describes a crumbling monument, "Two vast and trunkless legs of stone / Stand in the desert." These were all that remained of a once mighty monarch, ruling by fear and mystery in pure particularism. The inscription read

"My name is Ozymandias, king of kings:
Look on my works, ye Mighty, and despair!"

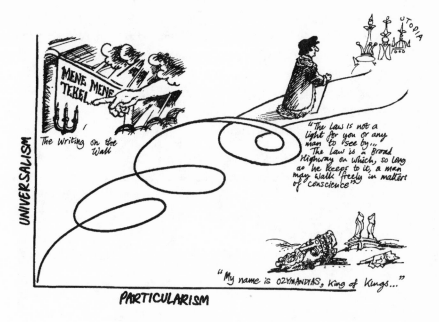

Figure 2.4 Universalism/Particularism

Nothing beside remains. Round the decay
Of that colossal wreck, boundless and bare
The lone and level sands stretch far away.

His was an absolute power without logic or legitimacy, an absolute power that corrupted absolutely. We develop only when laws protect our autonomy and discretion.

It follows from the arguments above that universalism and particularism develop *together* in corporate and societal cultures. The United States and Switzerland may indeed be more universalist than other cultures, but, paradoxical as it seems, this universalism survives by being tested against more particular instances and by legally protecting diverse and particular expressions. It matters less which value is given priority than that both values should be reconciled and integrated.

Corporate Stories Reveal the Culture

Universalism and Particularism are not commonly used words in the discourse of employees and managers. If people do not identify themselves by these labels, how are we to discern their mental models? One way is to look at the stories they tell, much as we looked at *High Noon* and *Les Miserables* to discover what values these cultures were extolling and in what sequence. Stories that make us feel good usually have reconciled values. In stories that make us laugh, cry, or grow angry, reconciliation is not usually a priority. Our intuitive liking or disliking are vital clues. What dilemma is raised by the following stories (Figure 2.5)?

- *Case 1: Refinery Fire*   Tim K. was a personal assistant to the managing director of an oil company. Suddenly Tim heard his boss cry out in alarm. "Look! The refinery is on fire!" Sure enough, they could see from the top floor of the office a plume of black smoke on the horizon. "Get down to the refinery in a car and report back to me." So Tim took the elevator to the parking garage in the basement. "I need a car!" he cried breathlessly.

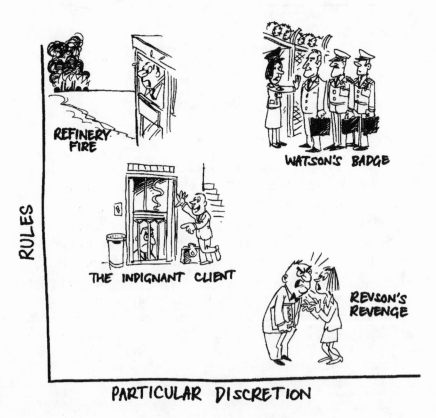

Figure 2.5 Four Corporate Stories

"I'll take that one," and he pointed to an old Mercedes. "Oh no you won't!" said the garage supervisor. "You're job-group 3. Mercedes is for group 2 and above." So Tim had to wait twenty-five minutes for a Ford from Avis.

- *Case 2: Revson's Revenge* Charles Revson, head of Revlon Corporation, insisted that everyone sign the time of his or her arrival in the office in a book kept in Reception. A new receptionist was at her first week on the job when a man she had not seen before walked into Reception and walked off with the book. She chased him. "Excuse me, Sir! But that book is not to be removed. I have strict instructions." Revson turned and stared at her. "When you pick up your last paycheck this evening, ask them to tell you who I am."

- *Case 3: The Indignant Client* There was a rule at one advertising agency that copywriters were not to speak to clients. When an august client was due to be entertained for lunch in the penthouse suite of the agency, the directors all waited, oozing obsequiousness, outside the top floor elevator. But the client had gotten stuck in the elevator, with his head and shoulders visible through the gate on the fourth floor and his legs and briefcase hanging around the third floor. One of the copywriters happened upon his top half. "I say, little man, are you stuck?" he asked cheerfully. "Well, never mind, we'll feed you through the bars. In the meantime, no peeking up the girls' skirts!" The agency lost the account. Ever since that day the account executives and creative people have maintained a segregation and a standoff.

- *Case 4: Watson's Badge* A 19-year-old, ninety-pound female security guard was at the gate of IBM's high-security building, when Tom Watson and a group of senior managers and top brass from the Pentagon approached. "I cannot let that man through," she said in a quavering voice. "He does not have his security clearance badge." Another manager hissed, "Don't you know who that is? It's the chairman himself!" But Watson halted the whole party and sent for his badge. "She's quite right," he said. "We make the rules. We keep 'em."

All these stories describe unique situations and outcomes, yet the themes of conflict are curiously similar. What are these?

All four stories are variations on universal rules versus personal and particular discretion in exceptional circumstances. In Refinery Fire, the rules are so strict that you cannot investigate an accident, in a case of clear emergency, even when you are representing the managing director! Hence, Refinery Fire is a story about strong rules that minimize discretion.

The obverse of this situation is Revson's Revenge. Here the new receptionist is fired at the whim of Charles Revson, precisely because she is following his rules. Her "offense" is that she does not know who he is and does not realize that he overrides any rule that gets in his way. To survive in such an organization, you must know which particular person is "in power" and mollify him. Following rules is no protection.

The Indignant Client is a compromise, because while keeping creative people away from the client bypasses exposure to their irreverent wit, it precludes the opportunity to delight him. Creative people have been locked into a particularist compartment, while the account executives play it strictly by the rules. The rules cannot easily be changed by creative employees with such a division of labor.

Only when we come to Watson's Badge do we recognize that values can be integrated. Watson chooses to obey the rules he himself has made, exercising his personal and particular discretion within these rules. He probably has the power to amend the rules, but until he does this he will comply with them. This is a trivial incident. It is not a "good story" worth telling for its own sake. The Indignant Client is more entertaining. That the story of Watson's Badge was told and retold at IBM for twenty-five years testifies to the importance of the cultural message conveyed. "In this organization the leaders live by the rules they have made, and employees using these rules are vindicated and supported." These kinds of corporate stories are very important to know if you are a new employee entering the corporate culture and wondering how you should behave.

How We Managed a Copyright Dispute

This case actually happened to the Trompenaars–Hampden-Turner Group in its dealings with Samsung, the South Korean *chaebol* (a family of businesses). We received a very friendly letter thanking Dr. Trompenaars for a previously published book of ours and conveying the "good news" that it had been translated and widely used by Samsung executives, who had found it most enlightening. There was only one problem: the copyright was ours. We had given no permission for translation or publication in Korea. The advice of our original British publisher who owned the translation rights was clear. Sue them! What we had here, they explained, was a clear breach of the international copyright convention, to which South Korea was a signatory. There could be no excuse.

Yet we hesitated for obvious reasons. The letter was so nice, they clearly expected us to be delighted. It was flattering that Samsung, a world-league player, found our book so useful. Were we not, as experts in cross-cultural communication, obliged to explore this incident for sources of misunderstanding?

We considered, and quickly dismissed, the idea that Samsung did not understand international copyright law or had signed it for reasons of subterfuge. We knew that South Korea was one of the most particularist cultures we had surveyed. Might it be, therefore, that they thought a particular and warm relationship should *precede* the exercise of legal rights?

Samsung had had our book translated into Korean at their own expense. It was sent to us with their original letter as a gift. Inquiries revealed that the translation was of the highest quality. Had we commissioned our own translation, the cost would have been $18,000, with very real difficulty in guaranteeing quality work.

But we were reluctant to say to Samsung, "Help yourself." It was, after all, *our* work. Should we relinquish our rights for the vague hope of some future consulting projects?

It occurred to us, in addition, that we might compromise. We could tell Samsung that it had broken the copyright convention but that we were prepared to make a deal. We would agree not to sue, for payment of a negotiated fee, representing all or part of the rights to which we were entitled. But we felt that this would "irritate everyone," our publisher included. We would almost certainly lose Samsung's goodwill, and if they were angry with us they would spread the word. Future commercial publication in South Korea might prove elusive.

The solution we arrived at was to first pay our respects to South Korean particularism. We thanked them warmly for the translation and expressed delight that Samsung's executives found the book valuable. We then asked their advice on how to locate a good Korean commercial publisher. Within two weeks we had three offers. Within a month we had a legal contract that protected our copyright. The fact that Samsung commended the book and had commissioned the translation was displayed on the cover. Sales in Korea have been brisk. Royalties have been received. The value of royalties

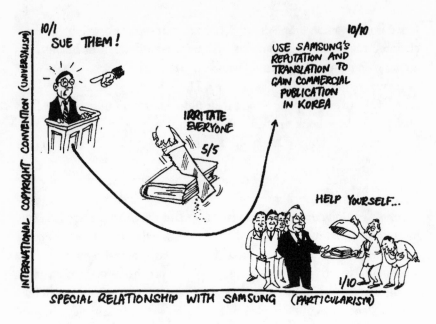

Figure 2.6 The Right to Copy

forgone when Samsung published its own version was less than the translation costs (Figure 2.6).

The line drawn in Figure 2.6 begins with our impulse to sue (top left), moves downward and rightward to affirm our particular relationship with Samsung (at bottom right), and then uses this relationship to win our universal rights (top right). We have integrated Universalism with Particularism, but in reverse sequence, by putting our special relationship with Samsung first. As with the story of Jean Valjean, we have accepted that deep personal relationships of particular respect are the foundations of laws that respect human rights to property.

Beyond Globalism and Multiculturalism

We earlier saw that a derivative dichotomy of Universalism–Particularism is Globalism–Multinationalism. Should corporations create a single global system of universal applicability or should they reflect particular, multinational diversities, in which every national business unit takes on local coloration? This issue has been addressed by Christopher Bartlett and Sumantra Ghoshal. According to these researchers there are three models designed for three different purposes, along with a fourth, which is a reconciliation of the three. The three models are:

1. The *multinational corporation* is designed for local and national responsiveness to varied demands.
2. The *global corporation* is designed to meet the needs for integrated operations and efficiency.
3. The *international corporation* is designed to innovate continuously and to learn from its environment.

However, none of these three types meet the exigencies and challenges of modern world markets. The authors advocate a fourth type: the "transnational corporation," which has the capacities of the three other types, along with virtues of its own.

Each Structure Has Its Historical Era

The three types of structure have evolved in response to key historical events. All carry with them an administrative heritage.

Earliest was the multinational structure, which evolved in periods when the world was more divided, with high tariff barriers in the thirties and during World War II, which split corporations like Philips of Eindhoven and Unilever into corporations controlled by both the Allies and the Axis powers. Without near total autonomy of their parts, multinationals could not have survived these years. The watchwords were "local initiative and decentralized control."

The global corporation, highly centralized upon the originating culture, grew up in the immediate post-war years of American hegemony.

The Heyday of U.S. Trend-Setting

International corporations are typically, if not always, American, originating in the sixties when the United States was the archetypal consumer society, leading the world in living standards and hence the first to want to buy consumer products. During this time, the United States led other economies by so wide a margin that it was emulated worldwide.

Although knowledge originates with the international corporation's headquarters, it may be regenerated en route. Hence Procter & Gamble created its European Technical Centre in 1963 to do research and development (R&D) for its European subsidiaries. Nonetheless, product cycles commenced in the United States and were repeated at staggered intervals in other countries, so that American experience was replicated in culture after culture.

Japan's Technological Globalism

The global organization was given a new lease of life with the rise of the Japanese economy and organizations in the seventies and eighties. Excelling in the fusion of electronics and mechanical engineering, companies like Toshiba and Matsushita produced superlatively manufactured products of very high quality by using flexible manufacturing, which permits a higher degree of variation. Still insular in many ways, because of centuries of isolation, the Japanese used the "universalism" of precision engineering to funnel products made for its large domestic market to all corners of the world—a vigorous strategy of globalism. That this strategy is no longer enough may be one reason for Japan's current difficulties.

Three Models Summarized

We are now in a position to contrast the three models of worldwide organization—before considering a fourth. Summaries of the multinational, global, and international structures follow.

The multinational corporation is decentralized and locally responsive, taking on considerable local coloration and typically managed indigenously.

The global corporation is highly centralized, treating "offshore" business as ROW (rest of world). It is highly integrated and typically stresses efficiency and scale, overseas operations, and delivery pipelines.

The international corporation is halfway between the first two models. The prime export is really knowledge, although typically such knowledge is American, Japanese, and so forth. Some knowledge gathering is done regionally, and the corporation may make concessions to local taste.

All three models discussed so far have difficulty in rising to the variety of world challenges. This is why we propose the transnational corporation. This is less anchored in some administrative heritage than constituted of a novel state of mind and a way of thinking/acting. It is designed to overcome contradictions and resolve dilemmas. No longer are efficiency and responsiveness ends in themselves; rather, both are now means to becoming more competitive and innovative worldwide. Recognizing the part-truths of centralizing and decentralizing, the transnational corporation

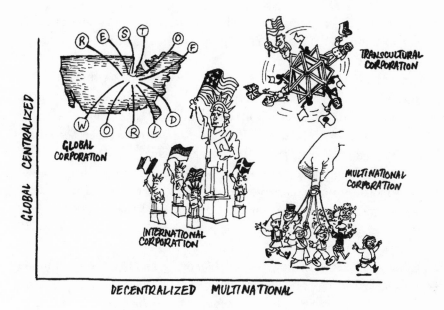

Figure 2.7 Universalism Versus Particularism

generates innovativeness in all parts of the world by cross-fertilizing diversity with common themes.

Centralization may itself be decentralized so that manufacturing is performed in the nations most adept at it. R&D is "headquartered" where ideas are most seminal. Hardware and software are mined from veins of cultural excellence. In short, a function is performed at that place on the worldwide network where experience shows it can best be done. Because cultures are diverse, innovation and excellence may emerge from any locality and this learning can be communicated through the network. It is crucial to grasp that the image of transculturalism *rotates* (Figure 2.7). The United States is at the apex for some purposes and functions but not others.

Knowledge and authority flow from one apex to all the others. New customers, new markets, new satisfactions may originate from any point. It is an integrated network with all ends "up" at a particular moment and is simultaneously local and coordinated. An efficient "local" plant can be converted for international production; a diverse local stratagem can be copied universally. Knowledge is developed jointly, with every difference capable of forming creative combinations.

In this new type of model, multiple perspectives are legitimate, coordination is flexible, and commitment by individual units to a shared vision is essential. But multidimensionality is no easy task, especially when administrative heritage has favored one group over the other. Rather, centralization and decentralization both need to be balanced along with centrifugal forces that threaten to pull the corporation apart and the centripetal forces that threaten to pull it into a destructive vortex, or "black hole."

We see Philips, Matsushita, GE, Ericsson, Procter & Gamble, and others as making tentative steps toward transnationalism.

These four corporate models are all variations on Universalism–Particularism. Globalism is the extreme case of universalism. Multinationalism is the extreme case of Particularism. The international corporation borrows from both and is a compromise, with local variations on the know-how supplied centrally.

Note that the transnational corporation represents a high-level synthesis and reconciliation of global universalism and multinational particularism, having the virtues of both and the vulnerabilities of neither. It is both more particular (any culture can innovate) and more universal (that innovation is potentially available to all). It is also a learning organization superior to the transferred technology of the international corporation, because what has been discovered in any one particular location can be communicated to the whole universe of business units. Enlightenment may come from any or all directions. It is a net with multiple nodes—authority follows upon knowledge and expertise.

Business Strategies of Universal and Particular Appeal

It was Michael Porter who distinguished between two archetypal and generic (one-of-a-kind) business strategies. You could produce a low-cost product, in which case you were engaged in the universal game of cost-cutting, a game inevitably won by the cheapest. Or you could create a premium product, one of particular, rare, and unique distinction and so commanding a premium price.

Porter warns against confusing these two strategies. Those who do so may obscure their competitive advantage, being neither a low-cost bargain for the consumer nor a product of real distinction. Porter reveals the American bias toward specificity, which we take up in Chapters 5 and 6. He likes his strategies clear and separated.

Products typically earn a premium to begin with, when these are new,

Figure 2.8 Low-Cost and Premium Strategies

but as markets mature they tend to commodify with the advantage moving toward the low-cost production.

Porter's famous dichotomy is depicted in Figure 2.8. Despite his warnings, we fail to see why a product should not be distinctive *and* low-cost for the degree of quality on offer. Moreover, we see this combination as unbeatable. The "generic" nature of the premium product derives in our view from the desire to make a quick profit from rarity, before competitors move in. The "generic" nature of the low-cost product is to make a profit from scale economies before rivals also merge.

But the company or the country who delivers growing value at ever-declining cost simply leaves its competitors standing in the learning race. It moves so far ahead, like the Japanese in fax machines or video recorders, that the market is essentially theirs for the long term. But surely it is possible to be lean, fit, and luxurious and still be priced relatively competitively. Ford has turned around the fortunes of Jaguar by using common platforms that lower cost while maintaining a premium product.

New Paradigms Create Scientific Revolutions

Thus far we have largely considered "laws" to be legal and moral, but they are also scientific. Indeed, the only genuinely universal propositions

may be those of the hard sciences. If a law genuinely reveals the nature of
the universe, it is presumed to be immutable.

Yet Thomas Kuhn in *The Structure of Scientific Revolutions* introduces the
notion of a paradigm. This constitutes a set of a priori assumptions about
the nature of what is being investigated and how to go about researching it,
which is so generally accepted by scientists as to be universally binding
upon them. For example, the idea of the cosmos as a celestial clock is a paradigm, not a law or a theory. Paradigms are taken for granted—for example, "We examine the facts" is a statement presupposing an object-like universe of atoms.

Kuhn, a historian of science, argues that a series of paradigms constitut-
ing a "normal science" of universally shared assumptions have been challenged historically by an increasing number of anomalies (or particulars)
leading to a paradigm shift, in which a new paradigm arises that makes
sense not only of the data covered by the old paradigm but of the multiplying anomalies, thereby unifying the rule and the exceptions. Figure 2.9
borrows from Edward de Bono's illustration of lateral thinking.

The "rectangular paradigm" represents normal science, or the conventional wisdom. Note that it makes sense of pieces 1, 2, 3, 4 and 5. But when
it encounters a particular exception, 6, it cannot make sense of this and so

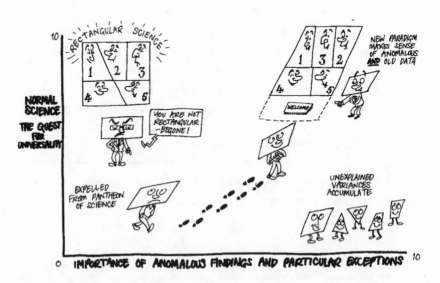

Figure 2.9 Shifting Paradigms

drives 6 out of the citadel of science. This happens when behaviorist psychologists say "Conscious statements are not scientific," knowing that these will prove anomalous.

But a paradigm shift, in which "reality" is regarded as a parallelogram, allows all six pieces of evidence to be incorporated. Even the exceptional piece of evidence has been invited back into the pantheon—nay more, it has been seen as a microcosm of the larger "reality." De Bono sees this paradigm shift as an example of "lateral thinking," while fitting all data into a rectangular mold is "vertical thinking" or extending normal science. Lateral or combinational thinking is what we call reconciliation.

So science, according to Kuhn, progresses both by small deductive steps where normal science reigns, and by discontinuous and revolutionary upheavals, whenever paradigms shift. It is this capacity of new paradigmatic universals, to account for the accumulating numbers of particular exceptions, that is the focus of this chapter.

Developing Moral Judgment

Does the dilemma between universals and particulars also account for the growth of moral judgment in the personalities of people? Yes, according to Harvard psychologist and moral development theorist Lawrence Kohlberg. He identified six levels in the growth of moral judgment, the lowest ones being "pre-moral." Here we concern ourselves with levels 4, 5, and 6, set out in Figure 2.10.

Level 4 is reached when the subject grasps that there is in society a system of law and order essentially independent of his own desires, although it may come to attract his allegiance. The various encouragements and prohibitions of his formative years are made sense of by this wider system of lawful order, applicable to the universe of citizens.

At level 5 dawns the awareness that the subject essentially makes his own laws through interpersonal commitments to chosen people. These include contracts freely entered into and commitments such as marriage and parenthood.

At level 6 a principle of conscience is abstracted from both laws and personal commitments; for example, "I should keep my promise."

It is by use of dilemmas that Kohlberg pitted various levels of moral judgment against one another, arguing that respondents would cite the highest level of which they were capable to justify their decision. He uses

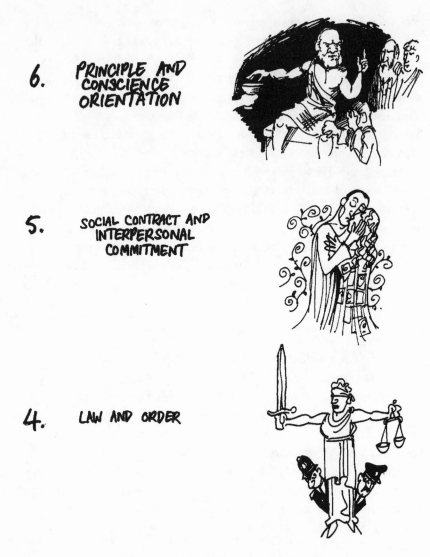

6. PRINCIPLE AND CONSCIENCE ORIENTATION

5. SOCIAL CONTRACT AND INTERPERSONAL COMMITMENT

4. LAW AND ORDER

Figure 2.10 Moral Hierarchy: Stages 4—6

the story of Hans, a young husband who needs medicine to save his wife from dying, although the drug maker is charging more than he can possibly afford. Consequently, he faces the dilemma of whether to steal the drugs or let his wife die. Kohlberg is less concerned with whether the respondent steals or does not steal the drug than with the level of moral judgment used to justify or forbid the chosen action.

A level 4 respondent might answer, "I cannot steal the drug even for my wife because the Law forbids it."

A level 5 respondent might answer, "I will steal the drug because my marriage vows and our relationship mean more to me than the Law."

A level 6 respondent might answer, "I will steal the drug, but as an act of civil disobedience, so that my society will understand what all poor partners face when those they love are sick and drug makers seek to profit from their desperation."

We can also express these three higher levels of moral judgment as one of our dual-axis dilemmas, with level 6 as the reconciliation between levels 4 and 5, illustrated in Figure 2.11. The law and order orientation (or Universalism) is depicted at top left. The interpersonal commitment orientation (or Particularism) is at bottom right, while the Socratic reconciliation is at top right, wherein Hans accepts the penalty of law in order to dissent from that law and sustain his commitment.

This reconciliation is similar to a paradigm shift. Instead of regarding the dilemma as a personal moral quandary and private problem, it is redefined as a question of national health policy. If addressed at this broader level, the whole society has a chance to improve its provision of health to its citizens—an important issue in the United States at this time.

It was Kant who argued that you can protest against a law ("confront universalism with your particular objection") but you must do so in a way that allows a new law to be made out of the manner of your protest. This is what Socrates did. He argued at his trial that the democracy of a state like Athens required his dissent, like an ox needs a gadfly to awaken it and keep it alert. If the court wished to sever him from the city, or sever dissent from the rule of law, then they would have to execute him. He would neither go into exile nor stop dissenting, "not if I have to die many times." He proposed that protest be a civil right.

Similarly, Hans, at level 6, is pleading not only for the right of all poor spouses and parents in general to sustain those they love but also for his own wife in particular, thereby reconciling the two values and standing some chance of amending the law, if people respond to his plight.

In our view it is not the mere utterance of a principle of conscience that is moral, but the capacity of that utterance to renew laws and commitments so that the whole hierarchy is repaired. Mahatma Gandhi and Martin Luther King both turned their peaceful dissents into laws.

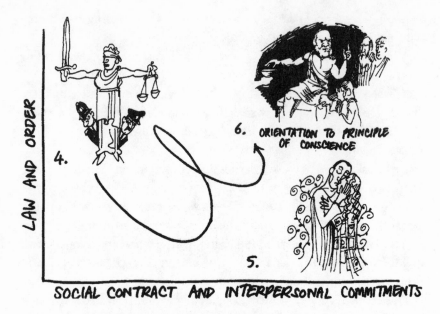

Figure 2.11 Reconciliation of Kohlberg's Stages 4, 5, & 6

Culture as a Fractal Phenomenon

Is there a name we can give to the phenomenon that is part orderly and lawful and part chaotic and free? When predictability and unpredictability merge, what patterns arise from this curious combination?

We must turn to chaos theory and studies of complexity to understand that many natural phenomena are *fractals,* a term coined by mathematician and scientist Benoit Mandelbrot. Fractals constitute a geometry of broken, wrinkled, and uneven shapes, either dynamic or the result of dynamics. They are both chaotic at one level and self-similar and repetitive at another level. Their chaos includes principles of order, like the twisting trajectory of a hurricane.

Mandelbrot produced a mathematical equation into which he inserted a wild card, so that the answer to the equation when calculated and recalculated would give an ever-changing result. This equation is displayed in Figure 2.12.

You start with one of the numbers on the complex plane and put its value in the "fixed number" slot of the equation. In the "changing number" slot put zero. Now calculate the equation, take the result, and slip it into the

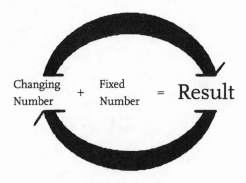

Changing Number + Fixed Number = Result

Figure 2.12

"changing number" slot. Iterate the equation and watch the numbers change.

Mandelbrot gave fast- and slow-changing numbers different-colored pixels on his computer and produced a "fractal image of chaos" which is reproduced in Figure 2.13. Note that the equation is circular with a "spiraling motion" that throws off a pattern that is self-similar in its beetle-like iterations *and* has artistic and chaotic flourishes, so that it is both science and art. Our black and white rendering cannot capture the flaming, multicolored corona around the beetle shapes, nor does it reveal the beauty of the magnifications, which include "a jewel box" and "an orchid pattern."

Some clarifications are in order. These aesthetic examples of the Mandelbrot set are but a few of the images created by thousands of repeated tries. Like evolution, not everything generated from the equation is selected. But the hummingbird who likes brighter flowers, or the pollinating bee or insect, or the gardener's eye for beauty are all capable of selection, so that beauty and brightness abound. What is clear from this example is that mixing order with chaos can create phenomena of great beauty and value. It is an analogy of how value is created—by freedom within laws.

Figure 2.14 shows to what extent we are surrounded by fractals. Perhaps easiest to understand is the formation of a snowflake (top left). Seed crystals drop from the sky in a chaotic pattern, tossed by the streams of colder and warmer, drier and moister air through which they fall. Yet amid all this chaos is a principle of nonlinear order (or multilinearity) produced by feedback. Whichever arm of the snowflake is shorter is also warmer and therefore attracts tiny deposits of ice in its downward journey, so that ice accumulates evenly on all the snowflake's spikes or arms.

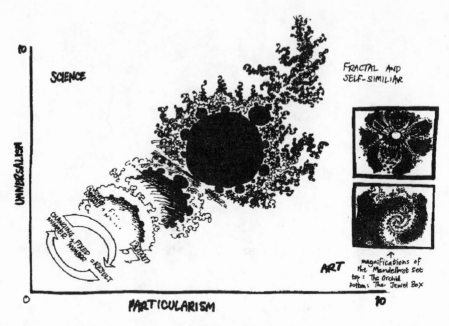

Figure 2.13 The Mandelbrot Set

We can predict the approximate symmetry of a snowflake but we cannot predict the thinness or thickness of the ice deposits since every flake falls in different conditions. The flake's beauty is that of chaotic order.

Among fractals that help to shape human beings are our brain waves, which behave like strange attractors on an electroencephalograph. In Figure 2.14, the image at top right is that of a brain-wave pattern during the process of solving a seven-step arithmetical problem. Other fractals are the pattern of dendrites in the human brain (middle left) and the pattern of a beating heart (middle right). Note that healthy hearts are chaotic, beating unevenly in response to environmental inputs. The human circulatory system is fractal (bottom left), as are the tightly coiled intestines and the gray matter of our brains. Finally, fractal images abound in art, especially Persian, Islamic, Indian, and Japanese art (bottom right). In Hokusai's famous rendering of The Great Wave, the shape of the whole picture is repeated in the foaming crests of each wave. Nature constantly reiterates its themes from the roots of a tree, to the trunk and branches to the twigs and leaves, inside which tiny branching spines, or miniature "trees," can be detected.

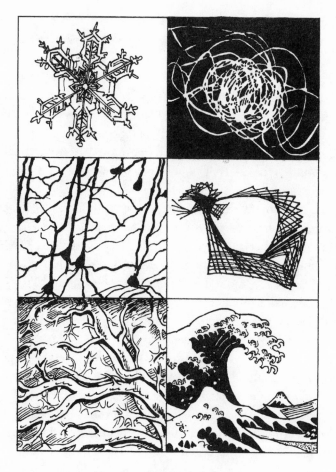

Figure 2.14 Six Fractal Shapes

Among these fractals are human and corporate cultures, where the way the CEO treats her executive employees will likely be repeated all the way down and across the corporation and even show up in the treatment of customers. Like the human heart, the corporate culture must respond to its environment, now faster, now slower, supplying just the amount of blood and level of adrenaline required.

Vicious and Virtuous Circles

Thus far our account of conflict and reconciliation has been tinged with optimism. Two values collide, and with sufficient awareness and intelligence we discover that even more wealth and value can be created from their combination than from their isolation or antagonism. In fact, real life is far more perilous. Many conflicts never heal but fester and grow steadily more destructive.

We write this very near the end of a century that historians may call the "Age of Genocide." More people were massacred in the twentieth century than in any previous one. Our scientific progress is belied by our moral stagnation. In over twenty centuries we have gone from the beauty and pathos of *Antigone* to the booty and bathos of television evangelism—no sign of progress there!

For the truth is that virtuous circles are only half the reality. Shadowing and threatening human existence itself is the vicious circle. Here the polarities lash each other into a frenzy of mutual reproach. Naive idealists excite and enrage crackpot realists as the League of Nations enraged Hitler. Those advocating law and order shoot at dissenters at Kent State University and kill students on their way to class, while a father tells his son that he would gladly pin a medal on the soldier who shot him and Nixon refers to anti-war demonstrators as "bums."

The real danger arises in those cases where the "universal" being advocated is not in fact a viable rule capable of benefiting members of the culture. An interesting example is America's Prohibition Era, in which the prohibition of alcohol was "dressed up" as a universal panacea for social ills, including crime, wife-beating, divorce, and unemployment but was, in fact, an anti-immigrant movement.

Earlier American settlers attacked the symbols of the new immigrants—German brews, Irish whiskey, Italian Chianti, and alcoholic drinks imbibed by recent immigrants from Southern Europe—even then crowding cities like Chicago and New York. The Eighteenth Amendment pitted Main Street against Wall Street, the idyllic small town against the "wicked cities," those left behind in the new era of rapid industrialization against those benefiting therefrom.

What is the effect of forcing what claims to be a legal-moral panacea of universal value that is in fact experienced as an attack on one's ethnic lifestyle? Prohibition failed, for the obvious reason that it was a pseudo-universal to begin with, but it succeeded in stirring up a hornet's nest of particular ethnic hatreds. Crime has always been difficult to control when the communities where criminals operate give them tacit or overt support. Where bootlegging was perceived as protecting the lifestyle of key ethnic groups, then Al Capone, the notorious gangster, could work with the mayor of Chicago to intimidate his political opponents.

It is legitimate to accuse the Prohibitionists of pseudo-universalism, because they consistently refused the money needed to enforce the law, to police the Canadian border, or to make medical and industrial alcohol undrinkable.

They clearly wanted an underclass of sinners beneath them socially and morally, and to have ethnic lifestyles criminalized. This led to a vicious circle of intrusive policing resisted by organized criminality.

Prohibition represented a self-exciting system. The more unjust, discriminatory, and insulting the "universal" law, the more vicious, criminal, and ethnically particularist was the revolt against it. Because immigrants from Southern Europe tended to be more particularist anyway, an attack on their lifestyle fermented more than alcohol! As for those who sought to prohibit alcohol, they felt utterly vindicated. Had they not warned against this? Was not alcohol the poison of the immigrant hordes, now corrupting American society? Were not Al Capone and Bugs Moran just what you would expect from Italian and Irish immigrants? So positions hardened on both sides, as abstract moralizing and organized crime became permanent features of American culture. The vicious circle in which Prohibition excited crime, which excited Prohibition is depicted in Figure 2.15.

The man with the top hat and the umbrella is the caricature of Prohibition enforcement used by the American media at the time. Gangsters lashing back at discriminatory laws are depicted beneath. The writhing snakes are the motif used in this book for vicious circles in general. Wherever people suspect that their lifestyles are the real target of attack, as do many modern drug takers, then laws passed in their name for "their good" are regarded with hatred and suspicion. The problem continues to this day.

But Prohibition was long ago in America's history, and the movement has been thoroughly discredited. Overexcitement about "universal truth" is surely a thing of the past, like phrenology and eugenics. Modern business does not make mistakes on anything like this scale—or does it?

In fact, there is a very recent example of the "science" of money making costing the American economy and taxpayers $3.6 billion. In September 1998, Long-Term Capital Management (LTCM), commanding leveraged funds of $130 billion, went bust. It lost up to 90 percent of its assets and pushed prominent banks and brokerages into multimillion-dollar write-offs. Only a federal bail-out saved the world's financial system from cata-

pseudo-universal

particular ethnic hatreds

Figure 2.15 Ethnic Particularism Biting Back at Prohibition Enforcement

strophic reverberations. Nicholas Dunbar likened LTCM to the Flying Island of Laputa in Swift's *Gulliver's Travels*. It was closer to a conceptual structure than a real island. He commented: "Yet none of this involved real oceans or landmasses. No one died—or was physically injured in the catastrophe. The country—if we may call it that—was a vast human construction and in its own way a true modern 'wonder of the world.'"

The creators of LTCM, Robert C. Merton and Myron Scholes, had won Nobel Prizes for their theory of option pricing. They were so obviously smart—why were they not also rich? LTCM was their attempt to profit from their brilliance, and for four years they did just that.

They had invented nothing less than a money machine operating on mathematical principles. Derivative financial products known as swaps and options allow you to buy, sell, or swap a stock, bond, commodity, or currency at a specified time in the future. By exactly balancing your portfolio so that you gain whether the stock rises or falls, it is possible to hedge most, but not all, risks. Computers on trading floors and offices were programmed with the appropriate formulas, and the work of these scholars shaped derivatives trading worldwide.

Their system is too complex to be explained here, but we can trace some of its "scientific" pedigree to try to understand why it claimed to be a universal system for inventing money.

From statistical theories it borrowed the idea of measuring volatility by its standard deviation from the mean. Assuming that volatility is random—which is not always the case—you can calculate the odds on prices fluctuating beyond two standard deviations from the mean, along with the likelihood of such volatility diminishing over time, as prices come into line.

From classical economics it borrowed the idea of markets moving to a perfect equilibrium point. Newton's celestial clock was self-correcting. You can "rationally" expect fluctuations to diminish because underpriced stock will soon be bought for more and overpriced stock will soon be sold for less, as thousands of players iron out the imperfections among them.

Finally, the hedging proposed by Merton and Scholes was a *martingale,* a process in which stakes increase as certainties mount. A simple martingale at the roulette wheel bets that, say, black numbers will not come up six times in a row, so that you stake on the color red $1, $2, $4, $8, $16, and $32. By doubling your stake after each loss you are guaranteed to gain— save in the unlikely case of six successive blacks. Typically such systems work well for a time, but when the loss comes, it is catastrophic. To bet that black would not come up eight times you would have to bet $64,000 to make $1,000 on the eighth spin of the wheel. Even assuming your money had not run out, your nerves would probably fail.

There is a consistent cultural bias behind all these calculations. The universal is valued over the particular, the rule is valued over the exception, the standard is valued over the deviation, equilibrium is valued over volatility, the "rational" is valued over the "irrational," the abstract is valued over the concrete.

One does not have to be around mathematical economists for very long to grasp that they seek to banish from academic discourse that which cannot be quantified. Hence the slang name for them in the investment community is "quants." Actual business is a mess of uncertainties. You invent a product or service and offer it to strangers. Quants seek to banish real business from the Kingdom of Pure Forms.

Being well-educated, quants are too sophisticated to express openly their

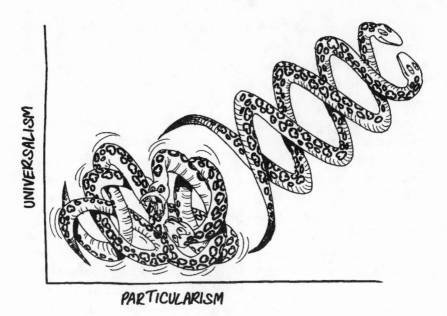

UNIVERSALISM

PARTICULARISM

Figure 2.16 Vicious and Virtuous Circles

hatred of the particular, the exceptional, the unbalanced, and the "irrational" (defined as elements outside their model)—but the animosity is very much present. When Frenchman Benoit Mandelbrot trespassed on Anglo-American turf to explain to investment houses why numbers were inherently chaotic and could blow up a storm, he was shown the door.

So what went wrong? How did this super-sophisticated construction collapse? Because the values at its foundations were half-truths. Yes, of course these were useful generalizations widely used by traders, but particularism never goes away. What happened in the past may not be true in the future. A deviation is no less important than a standard. Yes, markets equilibriate in the longer run, but what *is* the longer run? Can we afford to wait? It is at least possible that more volatility may precede convergence, that disequilibrium is as fundamental as equilibrium.

What was seen as "irrational" was all the chaos of business, lying outside the mathematical model, which is the majority of industry and commerce! The fluctuations were only "random" and "unexplained" because quants had ignored the explanations. In fact, the explanations for runaway volatility in the summer of 1998 were quite obvious. On top of the banking crisis in Southeast Asia came the Russian default in international payments. Perfectly rational people withdrew their funds.

Had LTCM set aside its "universal money machine" until the upheavals subsided, it might well have survived and prospered. Most of us know when to abandon a generalization. But no! LTCM was sucked into the vortex of its own universality, obsessed by its prize-winning mental constructs. It had to be bailed out by the federal government. Dunbar notes "Bewildered Congressmen struggled to make sense of it all. LTCM was invisible. It did not have any votes or factories or armed forces. How could it threaten the global system so badly?" ·

The American media also ignored the event, for the most part. It had Monica Lewinsky on its mind and President Clinton's fall from "universal" conduct to moralize about, a subject altogether simpler and more salacious.

So Prohibition is by no means America's only false universal, threatening to bring the culture to its knees. There are dreams of money-making machinery. There are high-rising concrete buildings of unsurpassing ugliness, celebrated as "the International Style" and modernism. There are "moral majorities" claiming to know God's Will, with divine license to shoot doctors. Genetically modified crops may already have changed our ecology irreversibly. The World Trade Organization touts so-called free trade as a universal panacea even amid riots.

Too easily we turn useful and limited generalizations into unbounded, universal truths, but these are idols not values. It was Aldous Huxley who warned us: "All idols, sooner or later, become Molochs, hungry for human sacrifice."

3 Individualism–Communitarianism

THE DILEMMA

Individualism–Communitarianism is a major dilemma for any business unit or any culture. We cannot even define individuality without specifying a group or social context from which that individual is abstracted and separated. Similarly any group, corporation, or society is constituted by its individual members. The group could not exist but for multiple allegiances.

We constantly need to ask ourselves which is more important: the welfare, development, personal fulfillment, self-expression, affluence, satisfaction, and freedom of each individual person, or the shared resources, endowments, and heritage enjoyed by the group or society, together with blessings naturally shared, clean water, soil, and air, group pride, cultural riches, common memories, and experiences? Is our prime responsibility to ourselves or to others in the commonweal? Why were we born—to set shining examples of personal prowess, or to make permanent contributions to our family, neighborhood, and nation?

How the Dimension Is Defined

Individualism	Communitarianism
competition	cooperation
self-reliance	social concern
self-interest	altruism
personal growth and fulfillment	public service and societal legacy

Should we pay heed to individual convictions and dissenting ideas, even when these appear to undermine hard-won agreements, or should the welfare of the wider group, corporation, and society, consisting as these do of multiple persons, be our principal concern?

Take, for example, the payment of bonuses for work of unusual quantity and quality. Should these be paid to individuals on the basis of hard work, heroic capacity, and personal distinction, or to the whole team or group, who together created the climate of enthusiasm and support that made these successes possible? Is it even possible to separate personal from group contributions?

We must be careful to define individualism and communitarianism correctly. It is not true, for example, that individualistic societies are dismissive of charity, participation, succour, compassion, and social improvement. What makes a society individualist is the belief that such motives originate with individuals and are the result of choice and voluntary commitment.

Similarly, a Communitarian society may take great pride and set much store by how many graduates it has produced, how many engineers, the life expectancy of its population, and the doubling of per capita income. What makes the society communitarian is the belief that such gains originate in shared knowledge, communal values, and mutual supportiveness.

Without societal values a culture may underinvest in public education. For example, Lester Thurow argued in *The Future of Capitalism* (1996) that the individual payoff for college and higher education in the United States barely justifies the expense. If you invest the money spent on education in the stock market and the time spent on education working for a corporation, you will probably do better financially. Our educations, Thurow argued, principally benefit other people—our spouses, children, neighbors, and colleagues at work. Without more community concern Americans may neglect learning for the average citizen. Of course, this argument narrows individualism to calculations of economic gain, when in fact it is much broader. Even so, the communitarian perspectives deserve respect.

The decisive contrast between Individualism and Communitarianism, then, is the extent to which the individual is self-made and the extent to which the wider social system is responsible for personal success (Figure 3.1).

Individualism seeks to locate the origins of value in the creative, feeling, inquiring, and discover-	Communitarianism seeks to locate the origins of value within the social discourse of the living

Individualism   Communitarianism

Figure 3.1 Individualism/Communitarianism

ing person who seeks fulfillment and is solely responsible for choices made and convictions formed.

society, which nurtures, educates, and takes responsibility for the spirit engendered among its members.

Since no one is entirely free of social influence and no one is absolutely bound to act out the dictates of the social milieu, this dilemma keeps recurring.

For example, who is responsible for an error made at work by a new member of a work team? The individual accepted employment, received instruction, but even so made an error, which led to several hundred units of product having to be removed from the assembly line and reworked. We could reasonably take the view that this person alone must carry the responsibility and that if he or she were dismissed, the other members of the team would work with greater diligence.

We could equally argue that the team and immediate colleagues should have looked out for a new member and checked that everything was going smoothly, and that the instructions had been properly understood. Had the new member been adequately trained? Were the instructions clear? Unless such questions are answered satisfactorily the problem may persist.

Individualism may hugely increase the rewards of individuals in the form of salary and dividends, but it logically also increases the penalties and the blame, so that substantially more Americans end up in prison for crimes engendered by vicious social environments. Communitarians may be willing to share both the rewards of success and the blame for failure and criminality.

How We Measure Individualism–Communitarianism

We measure the extent to which a culture is individualist or communitarian by once again presenting a dilemma and forcing a choice upon respondents. One of our questions poses the following dilemma.

Two people were discussing ways in which individuals can improve the quality of life.

A. One said: "It is obvious that if individuals have as much freedom as possible and the maximum opportunity to develop themselves, the quality of their life will improve as a result."
B. The other said: "If individuals are continuously taking care of their fellow human beings the quality of life will improve for everyone, even if it obstructs individual freedom and individual development."

Which of the two ways of reasoning do you think is usually best, A or B?

Figure 3.2 shows how various nations scored. If you know that, say, an opto-electronics industry is possible, educative, and potentially profitable, you can mobilize society to follow fast—Acer has done this in computers. With the exception of Israel and Nigeria, where the respondents represented a tiny sample of the indigenous elite, Canada and the United States are the most individualist nations, with Japan, Singapore, China, and France among the most communitarian. Protestantism is again an influence, but not as strong as in cultures high in Universalism–Particularism. All pioneer capitalist countries are individualist—such as Britain, the United States, Australia—but Communitarianism may be of help in quickly catching up. Consider, for example, France, Singapore, Japan, and Taiwan. Rurally based feudal elites typically resist industrialization, but when they change their minds and make it national policy, development can proceed very quickly.

Consumerism probably boosts Individualism to some extent, but Japan and Singapore appear to have held out against this. Once again, it is the history of countries that decides their preference. You cannot grow rice

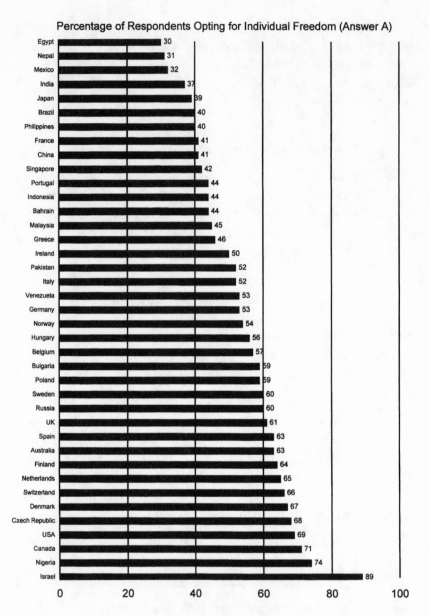

Percentage of Respondents Opting for Individual Freedom (Answer A)

Egypt	30
Nepal	31
Mexico	32
India	37
Japan	39
Brazil	40
Philippines	40
France	41
China	41
Singapore	42
Portugal	44
Indonesia	44
Bahrain	44
Malaysia	45
Greece	46
Ireland	50
Pakistan	52
Italy	52
Venezuela	53
Germany	53
Norway	54
Hungary	56
Belgium	57
Bulgaria	59
Poland	59
Sweden	60
Russia	60
UK	61
Spain	63
Australia	63
Finland	64
Netherlands	65
Switzerland	66
Denmark	67
Czech Republic	68
USA	69
Canada	71
Nigeria	74
Israel	89

Figure 3.2 The Quality of Life

with fewer than twenty people. Cultures with dense population concentrations like Japan and Singapore are obliged to encounter societal pressures. This is in direct contrast to the American experience, to which we now turn.

Why Is American Culture Individualistic?

The business culture of the United States is highly individualist because:

- Most people do not leave the only society they have ever known, hazard their lives on a vast ocean, and create new social systems out of personal convictions. Those who have immigrated to the United States have tended to be self-reliant.
- Early immigration did not end with arrival in America. There was a vast frontier to be explored and expanded westward.
- Because of the relatively small population of Native Americans and the absence of land ownership among these, never in the history of the world has so much real estate been available to migrating persons. Under the Homestead Act, you staked your claim and the property was yours.
- Puritans believed that they had an "errand to explore the wilderness," that they were God's agents, dedicated to building His kingdom on earth.
- In 1776, the year of the Declaration of Independence, by which American colonists severed their links with Britain, Adam Smith, a Scottish schoolmaster, wrote *An Inquiry into the Nature and Causes of Wealth of Nations,* a book extolling the economic sovereignty of self-interest and the Invisible Hand. Since a country's right to create its own indigenous industry was partly what the War of Independence had been about, Adam Smith's book became the bible of economic development and an inspiration to the founding fathers.
- The American Civil War, while of complex origins, was ideologically justified by the freeing of all slaves and the prohibition on slave ownership. The idea that men and women entered freely into contracts and that such contracts originated in free choice was confirmed by the victory of the North and enshrined in American law.
- A very rapid increase in both population and industrialization provided more opportunities for outstanding individuals to seize than at any other period of human history.

Just how strong American Individualism has now become after two world wars were fought and a Cold War endured in its name has been testified to by Robert Bellah and his collaborators in *Habits of the Heart*.

We believe in the dignity, indeed the sacredness of the individual. Anything that would violate our right to think for ourselves, judge for ourselves, make our own decisions, live our lives as we see fit, is not only morally wrong, it is sacrilegious. Our highest and noblest aspirations, not only for ourselves, but for those we care about, for society and for the world, are closely linked to our individualism. Yet . . . some of our deepest problems both as individuals and as a society are also closely linked to our individualism. We do not argue that Americans should abandon individualism—that would mean for us to abandon our deepest identity. But individualism has come to mean so many things and to contain such contradictions and paradoxes that even to defend it requires that we analyze it critically, that we consider especially those tendencies that would destroy it from within.

At Its Best . . .

Individualist culture allows outstanding individuals to mobilize resources so vast as to be without historical precedent. These include people who have given their names to famous institutions: John Davison Rockefeller, Matthew Vassar, Leland Stanford, Cornelius Vanderbilt, Andrew Carnegie, and Andrew William Mellon. Many brand names are directly traceable to their founders: Henry Ford, J. Paul Getty, Richard W. Sears, Alvah Roebuck, Clarence Birdseye, W. K. Kellogg, Philip Danforth Armour, W. R. Grace.

Henry Ford is of special interest because he innovated not just technologically but socially. Upon reading Emerson's essay "Compensation," he doubled the wages of his work force, slashed the price of the Model T, and reduced the turnover of workers in his factory from over 100 percent to single figures by making it a desirable place to work and helping them to buy cars from their wages.

Of course, the shareholders were furious, but Ford stood up to them. He told them: "Business and industry are first and foremost a public service. We are organized to do as much good as we can, everywhere, for everyone concerned. I do not believe we should make such an awful profit on our cars. A reasonable profit is right but not too much. So it has been my policy to force the price of the car down as fast as production would permit and give the benefits to the users and to the laborers with resulting surprisingly enormous profit to ourselves."

But it would not be America if pro-business sentiments were the only ones to get a hearing. Individualism means vigorous dissent. William Jennings Bryan's famous plea still moves the heart: "Do not press down upon the brow of labor this crown of thorns, nor crucify mankind upon a cross of gold."

More recently, and apropos of the automobile industry, we have Ralph Nader following the tradition of the muckrakers with his famous book *Unsafe at Any Speed*. General Motors tried to use prostitutes to entrap him and had to apologize before a Senate investigative committee. The business of America may be business, but individual dissenting opinions can be powerful assailants of that business.

America's worldwide campaign for human rights was unforgettably acclaimed by demonstrators atop the Brandenburg Gate, when the Berlin Wall finally fell, just as it was tested by events in Kosovo and the Balkans. A war that began to free slaves in 1852 has barely let up in one and a half centuries, and millions owe their freedom to American intervention.

Individualism also takes to the air, soaring like a lone eagle, as did Charles A. Lindbergh's *Spirit of Saint Louis* when it crossed the Atlantic in 1927. The unknown has always attracted individualists, and when the frontier was no more, Americans explored space. The "errand into the wilderness" first pledged to by the Puritan settlers continues into the twenty-first century.

But American individualism has also discovered how to perpetuate itself through philanthropic foundations. The principles were spelled out in Andrew Carnegie's *The Gospel of Wealth*. Money should be provided, but never to the pitiful, the defeated, the hopeless. Money should be spent to create opportunities, to educate and inform. It should be given not to the most needy, but to those most determined to change the conditions perpetuating that neediness. You "use a bucket of water to prime a pump." You search out every spark of initiative and fan the flames. Carnegie died in 1919, worth $22 million. He had given $351 million away.

One result of American individualism is that philanthropy is among the most innovative, idea-driven, and stimulating in the world (Figure 3.3). It gives meaning to the phrases "Help people to help themselves" and "A hand up, not a hand-out."

AT ITS BEST, AN INDIVIDUALIST CULTURE...

ALLOWS OUTSTANDING INDIVIDUALS TO MOBILIZE VAST RESOURCES

ALLOWS VIGOROUS DISSENT

SUPPORTS FREEDOM WORLDWIDE

LONE EAGLE

EXPLORES THE UNKNOWN

THE GOSPEL OF WEALTH

HELPS PEOPLE HELP THEMSELVES

Figure 3.3

But Taken Too Far . . .

In Figure 3.4, the man lying shot is illustrative of the theme of blaming the victim. The figure also alludes to America's long history of complicity with Latin American strongmen. The attitude appears to be that the perpetuation of the methods of the conquistadores will prevent incipient re-

BUT TAKEN TOO FAR...

SUPPORTS HISPANIC STRONGMEN

IT BLAMES THE VICTIM

CELEBRATES GREED

GREED IS GOOD

KILLS AND PERSECUTES TRADES UNIONISTS

COMPETES AGAINST CONSUMERS

TOP SECRET

CONSUMES TOO MUCH OF THE WORLD'S RESOURCES

Figure 3.4

volt. America's secret assistance to General Pinochet in Chile (depicted at top left), who overthrew a democratically elected left-wing president, was symptomatic of an individualistic society's fear of cooperative movements. Over three thousand people were murdered and many more tortured and imprisoned. Even as Pinochet, charged with war crimes, fought extradition from England, Henry Kissinger and George Bush continued to support him.

America also has a very checkered history concerning trade unions' rights to organize. The same Andrew Carnegie who wrote *The Gospel of Wealth* left Henry Clay Frick in charge of his plant in Homestead, Pennsylvania, where men from the Pinkerton detective agency killed strikers and broke the Amalgamated Iron and Steel Workers Union. History repeated itself on Memorial Day in 1937 when a thousand men, women, and children at a union gathering outside Republic Steel were fired on by Chicago police. Ten people were shot dead, seven in the back. A woman and three children were wounded. Twenty-eight more sustained serious head injuries. A year later the National Labor Relations Board found in the union's favor.

In the meantime, Henry Ford had slipped back into the paranoia that often afflicts the ultra-individualist. He was now anti-Semitic, pro-Nazi, and anti-Catholic. The Ford Company had fallen behind General Motors and Chrysler as he clung to personal control. Workers spoke in "a Ford whisper" for fear of being overheard and reported to Harry Bennett, his mob-connected director of labor relations. As early as 1932 four strikers were shot at the River Rouge plant. But the climax came in 1937 in the Battle of the Underpass when Bennett's hired thugs attacked Walter Reuther and other leaders of the United Automobile Workers.

When they discovered that their assault had been photographed, they turned their truncheons on the press, especially *The Detroit News*, smashed their cameras, and exposed their film. But some of the evidence survived. In May 1941, many years after unions had been recognized in Western Europe, 70 percent of the Ford workers won representation by the UAW.

A further pathology of individualism is the runaway greed it celebrates. If charity and the compassionate individualism of civil rights workers is defended as a personal choice, so can greed and unlimited acquisition be defended. Ivan Boesky was among the celebrants, along with Michael Milken and Charles Keating.

One result of runaway acquisitive individualism is that the United

States consumes a disproportionately large share of the world's resources. Were it to be emulated by other economies, disaster would result. While individualistic societies produce as well as consume, save as well as spend, the spending-consuming side of individualism threatens to go out of control and become an end in itself.

Finally individualistic companies have a tendency to compete promiscuously, not just with other companies, but with relatively powerless customers and consumers. Capitalism works best when individuals and firms compete with each other to serve customers. It ceases to work well when customers themselves become targets of sharp practice and are shaken down by aggressive individualism. But the kind of individualism that hates all cooperative impulse competes with everyone and everything, "beating" even the customer, who is often the softer target.

At Its Best . . .

Communitarian culture shares burdens equally. For example, Singapore has made across-the-board wage cuts to allow it to ride out the East Asian recession more effectively. Such willingness to share burdens is found in Western individualist countries only in wartime. Singapore and France have also levied taxes on those who do not train their work forces and try to "free-ride" on the employee training of other companies.

A communitarian culture encourages its members to leave a legacy to society, neighborhood, and family, which lasts beyond the individual's life span. We all need to live for a purpose beyond ourselves, to leave some lasting sign that we passed this way, that our contributions were significant. A corporation is a potential means of immortality, as is a society—a place where our influence lives on, where the mark we made is not erased.

Several communitarian cultures offer international corporations very high levels of productivity, quality, and esprit de corps. This is especially true of Singapore, Malaysia, and Hong Kong. Worker education and health is increasingly important in knowledge-intensive manufacturing, and these cultures are adept at instilling high levels of literacy and numeracy in the bulk of the population (Figure 3.5).

Communitarian cultures are especially adept at industrial catch-up and the strategy of fast following. They watch very carefully what technologies are being created in the West and choose to specialize in those that are cleanest to produce and most educative to design, manufacture, distribute,

AT THEIR BEST, COMMUNITARIAN CULTURES...

SHARE BURDENS EQUALLY

LEAVE A LEGACY TO FUTURE GENERATIONS

CREATE ESPRIT DE CORPS

ACHIEVE LOW COST OF CAPITAL THROUGH LONG-TERM BANK LENDING

PROMOTE HEALTH AND EDUCATION FOR WORKING PEOPLE

CHOOSE LEADING EDGE TECHNOLOGIES TO CREATE INTELLIGENT ISLANDS

Figure 3.5

and service. By coordinating educational policies with the arrival of foreign companies, they are often able to assure those companies an abundant and hence inexpensive supply of knowledge, workers, and skilled engineers.

Following rather than innovating is lower-risk, since you know the technology you are making is viable and in demand. By using industrial banks with long-term, low-interest loans, communitarian cultures achieve a lower cost of capital and a source of lending that remains loyal and supportive over extended periods. Chinese and Japanese work ethics, for example, may be communal in their origins and part of a Confucian tradition and what Robert Bellah called *Tokugawa Religion* (1985).

Finally communitarian cultures tend to connect business, education, finance, government, and labor into one overall push toward greater knowledge intensity. These cultures are influenced by Confucian traditions, in which the purpose of working becomes to learn together—and the more you know, the faster you learn. Singapore's aim is to become an "intelligent island," admitting only those technologies, products, and purposes that will further educate its own people. Every square mile of scarce terrain is crowded with complex processes.

Part of the legacy of the Cold War makes us associate communitarianism with statism, communism, and command economies. But this is only one expression of communal values and a notoriously ineffective one. Most fast-growing communitarian economies mobilize their people around economic growth targets and added-value objectives, so that the average employee grows more and more knowledgeable and productive. In such societies, few are excluded and marginalized.

But Taken Too Far . . .

Communitarianism has severe downsides and makes quite predictable errors. One problem is that the mutual assistance provided by cross-shareholding, in which banks, suppliers, and customers own shares in each other's companies, allows ailing industries to prop each other up. The system works well when only one or two companies are in trouble and the intervention of powerful friends restores them to profitability. But it does not work so well when all or most of the collegial companies are sick. In such cases they prop each other up, when, in fact, it is better for the economy as a whole for them to fail.

Going bankrupt serves a purpose in reallocating funds to more vital parts of the economy. Communitarian cultures have problems with renewal because they resist letting redundant enterprises die. In Japan, for example, smaller banks that should have gone out of business years ago constitute a group of "walking dead." Many are permanently affixed to the economic equivalent of life support machines.

Another problem with communitarianism is that it often occurs at the expense of an outsider. Cooperating industries may collude against customers, since managers are often closer to each other psychologically than to consumers. Japanese consumers, for example, have taken quite a beating over the years. Domestic prices in Japan are generally well above world prices, and consumers have been sacrificed to build a strong domestic platform for Japan's export drives.

All too easily a communitarian ethic can become a pyramid of sacrifice, with those lower down sacrificed to those on top. This happens not just in Serbia and Kosovo, where Albanians are exploited by Serbs and Serbs by their own leadership, but it occurs when the interests of consumers are subordinated to the interests of producers. Because production is a group activity but most consuming is done individually, these societies typically expect the individual consumer to subsidize "the common good."

Communitarian societies work very hard to gain consensus, as opposed to calling elections and expecting losers to keep quiet. A consensual workplace ideally mobilizes everyone, but technologies may now be changing faster than it takes to create a consensus. And the old consensus may lie sloth-like in the path of progress.

Anyone who has worked with poor or disadvantaged persons knows how lethal a poor community can be to the initiatives of individual members. Like people in a pit of misery, they actively sabotage any attempt by members to escape their shared fate. Those who try to improve themselves in any way are "selling out to the oppressor." Certain communities have a knack of keeping all their members in wretched circumstances. Because some have escaped poverty by standing on the necks of their neighbors, all attempts to escape are savagely censured.

We cannot bring ourselves to be neutral between Individualism when taken too far and Communitarianism when taken too far. Of the two, the latter is far more dangerous. The ludicrously inflated importance of some rogue individual can usually be contained and controlled before long. But nations on the march and in the grip of crazed communitarian ideologies

BUT TAKEN TOO FAR...

ALLOWS AILING INDUSTRIES
TO PROP EACH OTHER UP

COLLUDES TO FIX PRICES
AND EXCLUDE CUSTOMERS

PRODUCES A SLOTH-LIKE
CONSENSUS

PREVENTS INDIVIDUAL
ESCAPE FROM SHARED MISERY

ENGENDERS PYRAMIDS OF
SACRIFICE

PRECIPITATES REVOLUTIONS
THAT DEVOUR THEIR OWN
CHILDREN

Figure 3.6

are a danger to the whole world. Communitarianism is used to forge such cultures into lethal fighting weapons, and their victims are numbered in the millions—in Nazi Germany, the Soviet Union, and Maoist China (Figure 3.6).

This happens even when the community guides itself by "reason" and proclaims Enlightenment doctrines. The revolutionary concept of a "general will" became an idol. The community as an abstraction "devoured its own children" as the Terror spread in eighteenth-century France.

Culture Clashes and Derivative Conflicts: In Business and Industry

Business and industry are full of derivatives of the Individualism–Communitarianism dichotomy. There is, for example, the argument between shareholder value and stakeholding in the organization. According to shareholder value, those external to an organization, with no necessary knowledge of the organization or participation in it, are nonetheless sovereign over it. It exists to pay them a return on their individual investments. Such owners may be widely scattered and unknown to each other or to the companies in which their funds are invested. These organizations exist for the benefit of individual investors.

For stakeholders the corporation exists for its own sake for those groups with stakes in its success and prosperity. Hence, employees, customers, lenders, shareholders, and the community all hold stakes and co-generate value between them. The ideal is for a community of employees to serve a community of customers and for a community of managers to cooperate with a community of workers. Americans buying shares in Japanese corporations have discovered that this gives them very few rights except to payments. Not being members of the working community, they have scant powers.

Individualist cultures like to maximize profits since this is something individuals can take away from the company and use as they see fit. If your money is still in the corporation, you are attached to its members. Profits allow you to switch your allegiance from one company to another, to divest and reinvest, and the urge to independence may be present in the sheer volume of transactions and resulting market turbulence as buyers pile in and fall out.

Individualism is further encouraged by unit funds and pension funds, in which your money is invested entirely at the discretion of individual fund managers who have no goal beyond profit maximization and certainly no time to discuss other considerations with those for whom they act. Sometimes companies invested in are limited to those deemed "ethical," but the rules remain much the same.

Communitarian cultures, in contrast, are much more interested in market share, what the company has done for customers, or for Japan, Singapore, Hong Kong, as measured against their share of these total domestic markets. Typical Japanese strategies may shave profits wafer-thin, cut costs to the bone, and engage in "predatory pricing" as individualist cultures call it. Profits may be postponed or almost abandoned as the company "buys market share" by undercutting competitors.

In such contests (very common in the eighties), Western companies may withdraw since profits are meager, while East Asian companies persevere, since their market shares are rising. This dynamic cannot go on forever, and part of Japan's recent economic troubles may stem from profit starvation. Market share strategies are very much for the longer term. It is hoped, but less often realized, that when profit-oriented competitors withdraw, the previous margins can be restored. But often this fails to happen. The strategic calculation is more usually as follows: higher market share = higher volume throughput = faster learning on the job = further price reductions = higher market share. Such calculations are as good as what they omit; too often profits are omitted, and the whole community begins to "run on empty."

Profits and individuality are clearly associated with risk-taking and creative innovation. The more you pioneer and the greater the unknown contingencies, the more you should reasonably pay to those underwriting those risks. In contrast, market share is the calculation of the fast followers and catch-up practitioners who want to know to what extent they are overhauling the leaders. As markets mature customer relations grow in relative importance, and those cultures that are more Communitarian may become more effective.

Individualist business culture tends to regard teams, work forces, and even corporations themselves as "social technology," that is, as ways of getting things done and ways of making money for individual shareholders. The very word *organization* derives from *organon* ("instrument"). Teams and teamwork therefore are seen as instruments of private owners, used to reach their personal goals, and dissolved as soon as their usefulness has passed, possibly to be reconstituted in new configurations.

Where deemed necessary, massive downsizings may be forced upon a working community, making thousands of their members redundant. Share prices typically jump on news of layoffs, not because the policy is sound—it rarely is—but because considerable monies have been taken from one kind of stakeholder, the employees, and can now be shared by other stakeholders, including shareholders.

One wonders where the rights of shareholding individuals end. They may be "owners" for only a matter of hours, are nearly always absent from actual working venues, may not know in which companies their money is invested—yet their rights over those who have given their working lives to an organization are absolute. Of course, shareholders are free to become involved in organizations they "own" but rarely choose to do so. Hence protests at annual stockholders' meetings are routinely swamped by proxy votes and institutional shareholders.

As a democratic community, shareholders hardly make the grade. The absent, uncommitted, and unknowing have vast powers over those present, those committed to the company and those most knowledgeable about it. Even Hollywood films have explored this theme. Movies like *Wall Street* compare takeover specialists to geckos (predatory, nocturnal lizards), while *Pretty Woman* portrays a relationship between a prostitute and a man who acquires companies with strong hints that their callings are equivalent. If we are serious about the "learning organization," can we leave it at the mercy of those without time or inclination to discover anything about it? "Here is some money," says the shareholder to the employee, "all I want is your working life." Such bargains are curiously one-sided. The shareholder has extensive rights but very few duties or obligations.

Yet Communitarian business cultures are no less problematic. They tend to regard individuals, and teams of individuals, as their "personal technologies," to be used—and, if necessary, used up—to fulfill corporate purposes. It is hard to know where the corporation ends and the *keiretsu* (family of businesses), cartel, or nation begins. Every larger purpose has an even larger purpose about to envelop it, until all become dwarfed in an ever larger scheme of giant forces.

Even so Communitarian business cultures are less dismissive of their memberships. Mass layoffs, lockouts, and redundancies are less common and hostile takeovers rare or unknown. Threats to social cohesion and group morale are avoided if possible (this is not always possible). There is an expectation that leaders are benign, parental, and caring. If employees have responsibility for several children, the company will take commensurate additional responsibility for that employee. Caring is indivisible. The more you care, the more you should be taken care of. Many of these traditions are currently under serious strain, in Japan especially.

Communitarian cultures are not always broadly inclusive, however. Cohesion can occur at the level of families, tribes, religions, cliques, factions, or ethnic groups. If too narrowly drawn, such groups may feud forever. If too broadly drawn, one group can become suffocated in a grandly inclusive project, like the Greater Japanese Co-prosperity Sphere. Where the community defines itself by what it is not, those left outside may be in peril (Figure 3.7).

Is the supreme value of business enterprise competitiveness or cooperation? Most individualist nations would choose competition as the all-important driver of free enterprise, where we all struggle to outdo those in similar occupations. The best will rise in influence, with resources allocated to them as an outcome of their relative success. The genius of free markets is that winners acquire progressively more funds to win with, while losers hand over the resources they have mismanaged to those who can do better.

Among the many advantages of competition is that individuals soon discover what they do relatively well and not so well and are motivated to move from their weaknesses to their strengths. Nonetheless, capitalism seen exclusively in the light of furious competition soon comes to resemble a "demolition derby," in which the pieces falling from shattered vehicles are seized by other contestants and cannibalized for their own advantage.

We must always ask, "Where does competition stop?" Are we the rivals of everyone selling customers anything, on the grounds that they are after the same disposable income, or should we see at least some businesses as augmenting our own? If we determine "never to give a sucker an even break" then the average consumer is much easier to beat than a rival professional outfit. Might we all start preying on the most vulnerable?

The truth is that we are supposedly competing at serving customers, so cooperation must be a crucial feature of business, too. One reason that some products achieve astounding quality is that skilled professionals have cooperated in creating that integrity. Southeast Asian Communitarian cultures call this *wa*, or harmony, as when many different instruments or voices blend their melodies to create a symphonic whole. In Japan, for example, the chief personal virtue of a businessperson is held to be, not

SHAREHOLDER VALUE ─── STAKEHOLDER VALUE

PROFITABILITY ─── MARKET SHARE

PIONEER CAPITALISM ─ CATCH-UP CAPITALISM

Figure 3.7 Derivative Dichotomies of Individualism and Communitarianism in Business and Industry

competitiveness, but *amae,* or indulgent affection, typically between a superior and subordinate. *Sempai-kohai,* or an elder brother–younger brother relationship, among executives who mentor their juniors is similarly admired.

These are cultures capable of very high levels of competition with the West. Cultures like Singapore, Malaysia, Taiwan, Hong Kong, and the People's Republic of China have all borrowed, at least in part, from the model of Japanese catch-up communitarianism. This has proved a much better path for once-Communist countries like China than has the sudden swing to individualism, which appears to have afflicted Russia and much of eastern Europe, sending their economies into reverse. It is a supreme irony that China's growth rate, the fastest in the history of economics, has occurred in a country not simply communitarian but still communist. Even in troubled Japan, Toyota production methods, for example, still lead automobile manufacturing worldwide. We must accordingly confront the fact that just as competitiveness may solidify us into rival groups, so harmonious groups may seek to test the quality of their harmony by competing with other groups. We should not assume that cooperation is a negation of competition; it can be its secret weapon, much as team spirit motivates sporting contests (Figure 3.8).

A variation on this theme is rivalry versus complementarity, with individualists being rivalrous and communitarians complementary. Is the business environment largely competitive and hostile, so that for us to win, other companies must lose? Or is the business environment largely complementary, so that videos of movies, for example, played in the home increase rather than decrease the revenues of film studios? For some years the movie industry assumed rivalry, but it now assumes complementarity.

One reason businesses cluster together—movies in Hollywood, theaters in London, and agencies and publishers in New York—is that complementaries may be stronger than rivalries. You go to London to see a play, to New York to see a publisher, to Tokyo for consumer electronics, and so on. What these businesses share—people, skills, resources—may be more vital than what they capture through rivalrous activity. The standards they push upward between themselves and the suppliers they retain may propel the entire industry to higher levels.

While companies like Coca-Cola and Pepsico are still locked into zero-sum games (i.e., win-lose conflict with the winner's gains exactly equaling the loser's losses), companies in computing and software have long since acknowledged their complementarity, as have denizens of the Internet. Communitarian cultures like Singapore have made the creation of clusters, within industrial parks, an urgent national policy. Companies that wish to locate in Singapore are co-located with complementary companies in industries like multimedia, precision engineering, and microchip development, together with suppliers and shared training facilities. The

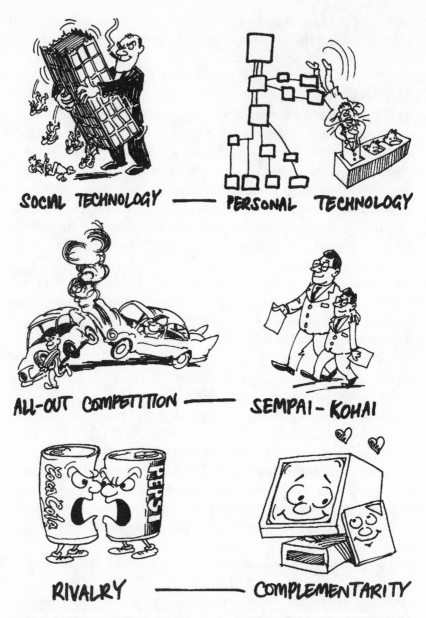

SOCIAL TECHNOLOGY ——— PERSONAL TECHNOLOGY

ALL-OUT COMPETITION ——— SEMPAI - KOHAI

RIVALRY ——— COMPLEMENTARITY

Figure 3.8 More Derivative Dichotomies of Individualism and Communitarianism
in Business and Industry

ideal is for whole industries to develop as interactive clusters of complementary activities, and extremely successful this policy has been.

Culture Clashes and Derivative Conflicts: In Religion, Ethics, and Politics

Individualism–Communitarianism does not simply shape industry but
structures the whole social environment. It would be a serious mistake to
believe that because America is individualist, it dislikes or avoids groups.
On the contrary, American culture may be among the most prolific gener-
ators of group activity in the world.

Individualism is characterized not by the absence of groups, but by the
kinds of groups created. The quintessential American group is the voluntary association: a group formed by the free association and voluntary commitment of like-minded individuals who choose to work or socialize together (Figure 3.9).

This was how America was founded, by individual religious refugees
who formed a covenant with one another to observe commonly held con-
victions. In the years since, this kind of covenant has been called a New
Deal, a Contract with America, and so on. Famous self-help groups include
Alcoholics Anonymous, Mothers Against Drunk Driving, Common
Cause, the Student Non-Violent Coordinating Committee, the Promise-
Keepers, People that Love, the Southern Christian Leadership Conference,
and the Moral Majority—among thousands.

Such groups have certain abiding characteristics. They tend to be
"movements" that pledge to carry out agreed policies to their fruitions.
Their membership is of one mind, for example, to outlaw or to uphold a
woman's right to abortion. They typically go out of existence once their
aims are met, or defeated. They are vehicles of the interests of their members and may bar from membership, for example, those whose children
have not been struck by a drunk driver or those who have never been alcoholics, gamblers, addicts, and so on. They are held together almost entirely
by their socio-political agendas. Any disagreement about ends, or even
means, will lead to a split, with each persuasion going its own way.

In contrast to the group formed deliberately to pursue individual convictions, which happen to be identical, is the group which pre-dates the birth
of the actual individual. This is the family. We are born into a family that
shapes our being, and many of us leave a family that will survive our individual decease. Not unsurprisingly the condition of the American family is

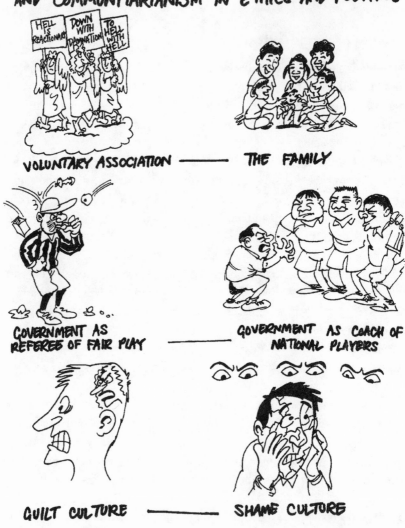

Figure 3.9 Derivative Dichotomies of Individualism and Communitarianism in Ethics and Politics

widely lamented, with latchkey kids returning to empty houses and a high divorce rate as couples seek "individual fulfillment" in place of family development and cohesion.

The family is one of the very few places where different generations meet and negative feedback can be expressed in a context of love and acceptance. Once we are out of the home and into voluntary associations there is no real need to engage with people of differing views, save in a fight or demonstration. Only groups that are ends in themselves—families, neighborhoods, friendship societies—are able to mediate among diverse opinions. Voluntary associations are typically armored in righteousness and ready to push for what their members seek. If you do not agree with the agenda, you do not join.

The family is still the bulwark of Communitarian business cultures, originating over 85 percent of such businesses. Even in publicly owned Japanese corporations, family metaphors are rife, with "brothers," "sisters," "mothers" and "aunts." The Japanese Ministry for Information, Technology, and Industry (MITI) is known as "worried auntie." A male executive will say without blushing, "I am the Mother around here." The family ideal is particularly important in binding seniors to juniors and avoiding the social distance typical of formal bureaucracies. It is the antidote to alienation and the formula for educating the rising generation. Communitarian economies, which idealize the family, are considerably more successful than socialist economies, which idealize the State.

Individualist cultures are characterized by a totally different relationship between government and private enterprise. In these cultures, governments are necessary to act as a kind of referee, whereas in Communitarian cultures the government acts more as a coach of star corporate players. In "referee cultures," all players should be free to compete as they will, provided no rules are broken. Governments are necessary evils that prevent other competitors from committing fouls and order them off the field if they persist.

This view includes a degree of Universalism from Chapters 1 and 2. The individual is free *within* the constraints of the legal process. What prevents runaway individualism is a system of laws before which all individuals are considered equal. Contests will accordingly be won by the best legitimate players, according to the rules of the game, embodied in the referee.

There are some problems with this model. Referees are rarely popular. It is hard to convince fans that the referee is not secretly in cahoots with one side or the other. Many decisions made by referees evoke boos, catcalls, even rotten fruit. Where the referee gets close to any contestant, a whiff of corruption taints the air. Even simple friendship is suspected. Great efforts must be made to "separate the powers" of the contestants and the judiciary.

Where governments stray beyond their refereeing role they are seen as "big government" and as encouraging a Communitarian ethic subversive of individualism. Government should not itself join the game, and to do so is "unfair competition," not to mention a corruption of its role as an impartial umpire or referee. You cannot both join the game and judge its fairness.

The coach government is clearly on the side of its own industries, typically the "national champions" who do the exporting. They are part of the community. This is sometimes called industrial policy, Colbertism (in France), or (by its enemies) "corporatism." Governments "advise" rather than mandate compliance, although the advice may be hard to resist, since the government represents the nation at its most inclusive, while a business represents only a part of that nation.

That said, industry can resist. The most famous case is the Japanese automobile industry's refusal to merge despite MITI's advice that its units were too small and too many. At their best, coach governments are popular (as is a coach in football), are seen as the friend and facilitator of economic development, and are able to encourage the provision of low-cost finance, trained labor, crucial contracts, and help in export drives. Typical coach governments include Singapore, Japan, Korea, and, under socialist governments, France. In most cultures both varieties are included. For example, Scottish Enterprise has a coaching role, as have most development agencies.

The government as coach should not be confused with socialist "command" or "planned" economies. These are also Communitarian but so ineffective that they are typically in retreat. The coach government accepts the free market but believes it can improve the caliber of "players" and their chances of winning.

Coach governments are most effective when economies are catching up, and there is an issue of which industries to specialize in when the choice is very broad. Cultures influenced by Confucianism tend to choose industries and products where skills are most advanced and knowledge most intensive. They prefer to make leading edge products in the field of biotechnology or microelectronics. The more skill that is needed, the more money their national citizens will earn, so the aim is to be the smartest work force available anywhere.

Another key distinction is between guilt cultures and shame cultures, which are Individualistic and Communitarian, respectively. In a guilt culture we are made to feel personally responsible for our sins and hence guilty. "That's no way to speak to your mother!" says a voice within your head. The person feels he has done something unworthy of himself.

In contrast, shame is the sense that many disapproving eyes are staring at your face in reproach and accusation. You have "lost face" because you appear in the eyes of others far less favorably than before. Under their hostile gazes your original "face" has disintegrated and fallen away, replaced by an object of disapproval.

Hence a Japanese executive who was habitually late for meetings did not improve his record when privately criticized for lateness. But he was never late again when his lack of punctuality was publicly commented upon at a meeting.

There are other telling signs as to whether a culture is Individualist or Communitarian (Figure 3.10). Individualist cultures like to depict their leaders as alone—the Lone Ranger, the Lone Eagle, Han Solo in *Star Wars*, Jonathan Livingston Seagull, soaring above the concerns of lesser birds, the sublime architect in Ayn Rand's *The Fountainhead*, and similarly isolated heroes.

Communitarian cultures depict their leaders as flanked by admirers and helpers, leading concourses of closely associated colleagues. "He has no power" is the worst thing you can say about a Japanese executive, but power does not mean unilateral or dictatorial power over subordinates, it means the ability to read the crosscurrents within the community and use group dynamics effectively. It is the harnessing of the community's spontaneous power.

Individualistic cultures like to vote. This gives victory to the majority of individuals present and the minority are expected to yield peacefully, not to remain silent but to offer no more than verbal dissent to the will of the majority. In business settings, they are usually expected to accept the majority decision and work to implement it without foot-dragging. Voting is used as a method for cutting off debate after all views have been aired and the prospects of changing anyone's position have receded.

Communitarian cultures are much more concerned with forging consensus and are upset when people in their midst are not reconciled to

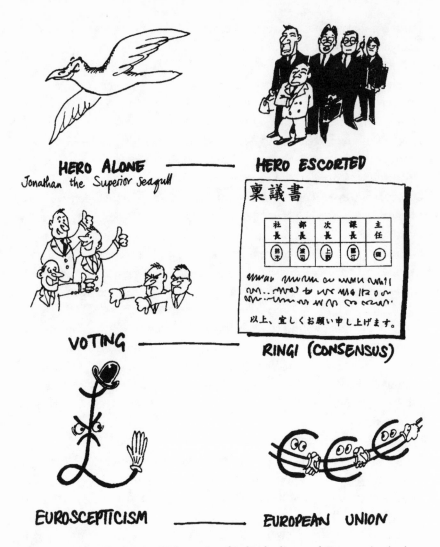

HERO ALONE —————— HERO ESCORTED
Jonathan the Superior Seagull

VOTING —————— RINGI (CONSENSUS)

EUROSCEPTICISM —————— EUROPEAN UNION

Figure 3.10 More Derivative Dichotomies of Individualism and Communitarianism in Ethics and Politics

the policy being pursued. The Japanese *ringi* (going in circles) method, by which draft policies drawn by middle managers are circulated and modified until everyone has put their seal upon them, is typical of Communitarian styles of decision making.

Typically, decision making is fast and incisive in individualistic cultures, but implementation may be slow and difficult because underlying consensus is missing and dozens of dissenters impede the process of operational-izing the decision. Decision making is much slower in Communitarian cultures—so slow that reaction times may suffer, yet the decision once made is implemented smoothly.

Finally, individualism versus communitarianism helps to explain Great Britain's reluctant Europeanism. Great Britain identifies with its former, English-speaking, white colonies—the United States, Canada and Australia are all highly individualist, even more than Great Britain itself. Europe, whose Christian Democrat parties are strongly influenced by Roman Catholicism, has a Communitarian tradition, even within its right-wing parties, while Mrs. Thatcher realigned Britain's Conservative Party behind the hard-nosed American tradition of laissez-faire capitalism, where it remains to this day. Such forces are deeply suspicious of foreign entanglements and extremely skeptical that Europe can ever become more than a giant bureaucracy, qualified by corruption.

Among free-enterprise individualists, there is special antipathy toward France, the most Communitarian member. Mrs. Thatcher inveighed furiously against "Socialism by the back Delors," a reference to Jacques Delors, then president of the European Commission, a Frenchman, former trade unionist, socialist, Catholic, and intellectual—all categories repellant to Thatcherite individualism.

Yet the harnessing of individualism to communitarianism in order to reconcile and combine these powerful human values is a far more fertile and productive process than the sterile joust between them. A third way must be found. To this reconciliation we now turn.

4 Reconciling Individualism and Communitarianism

STORIES AND CASES

Just as Universalism (or rule making, in Chapter 2), is incomplete without Particularism (or exception finding), so Individualism needs the community to complete it, while a community justifies itself by the qualities of Individualism nurtured. We cannot live at either end of a values continuum. We have to move to and fro as the situation demands.

This chapter further demonstrates that it takes both Individualism and Communitarianism to generate wealth. It is when we "fine-tune" these contrasting values that organizations become outstandingly successful.

As in Chapter 2, we recount a famous American movie in which the redoubtable individualist, at the very last moment, chooses to place his selfhood at the service of the larger community. Then we tell a Japanese story wherein the self is negated, almost annihilated, through its manner of public service, only to be reborn in a children's playground to make a lasting social contribution.

While both American and Japanese cultures seek the integrity of the individual and the community, each approaches this reconciliation in opposing sequences. Each has a different order of priority. As before, we analyze these priorities before turning to several business examples.

A Story Told by an Individualist Culture

Casablanca is among the most admired films in the world. Set in the year 1941 and made in 1942, it features a hero who has to make the choice that America had made, months earlier, to break out of isolationism and join the war against fascism. Admittedly, the United States was attacked first, at

Pearl Harbor, while Rick Blaine, the movie's hero, needs no such provocation. Yet his choice is an idealization of America's decision.

Blaine runs Rick's American Bar in Casablanca, the capital of French Morocco, then part of unoccupied France, under the authority of Vichy, France. The United States is still neutral, and so, it seems, is Rick.

That Rick will not compromise his security for anyone in "this nest of vultures" is made clear when Ugarte, a "cut-rate parasite" who sells visas to desperate refugees, gives Rick, for safe keeping, two letters of transit stolen from murdered German couriers. When the police, headed by Captain Louis Renault, the Vichy government's prefect of police, arrest Ugarte in the bar, Rick refuses him a hiding place.

Captain Renault, self-described as "a poor, corrupt official," introduces Rick to Major Strasser, a Nazi villain who has come to Casablanca to negotiate the capture of Victor Laszlow, an escaped Czech resistance hero. Because this is unoccupied France, Strasser cannot act unilaterally. Over drinks Renault vouches for Rick's neutrality "even over women." Rick makes a disinterested wager that Laszlow will escape Casablanca.

Moments later, Laszlow himself enters Rick's bar accompanied by his beautiful wife, Ilsa. Ilsa asks Sam, the piano player, to play and sing "As Time Goes By," whereupon Rick storms into the bar to remind him that he is never to play that song. But upon seeing Ilsa, he stops short. It is clear they have "known" each other.

Romantic love is, of course, one hallmark of individualism. Two strangers meet and spontaneously assuage their loneliness. Now we know the hurt that has embittered Rick. He goes up to his apartment, gets drunk, and memorably exclaims, "Of all the gin joints in all the towns in all the world, she walks into mine."

While Sam plays "As Time Goes By," we watch flashbacks of the Parisian idyll of Rick and Ilsa, enraptured in a doomed city with the Germans closing in. They agree to take the last train from Paris to Marseilles. But moments before the train leaves, Sam delivers Ilsa's message. She cannot come. She cannot tell him why. She loves him. The falling rain makes the ink run down the paper.

So this is what has embittered Rick. By the time Ilsa comes to his room, he is drunk and contemptuously dismisses her attempts to explain.

We get our first hint of Rick's more sympathetic side when he saves Annina, a young Bulgarian bride, from the clutches of Captain Renault. Renault will give Annina and her husband visas . . . if Rick arranges for the boy to win the price of two visas at his roulette wheel. Rick brusquely brushes off all expressions of gratitude, and the captain's jibe at his "sentimentality."

But we have second thoughts about Rick when Laszlow comes to ask him personally for the two letters of transit, now the only means of escape for Ilsa and himself. He pleads his cause. Fascism must be fought. But Rick is implacable. He will not even sell the letters, not at any price, saying, "If you want to know why, ask your wife."

So Ilsa comes to plead with Rick, but he tells her, "I'm not fighting for anything any more. I'm the only cause I'm interested in." This is a personal grudge match. In desperation, Ilsa finally pulls a gun, but when he tells her to shoot him she drops the gun and collapses into his arms, saying, "If you knew how much I loved you."

Now we hear her story. Laszlow is her husband. She married him for his ideals, his nobility of character, his resolute stand against the Nazis. She had thought him dead when she and Rick met in Paris. But two hours before they were to escape by train, she heard her husband was alive, lying wounded in a freight car. She had to go to him.

All she is asking for now is one letter of transit for Victor. She has not the strength to leave Rick a second time. "You'll have to think for both of us," she tells him, anguished by her dilemma.

At this point the audience believes Rick has won the battle of rival suitors. We watch Rick outplot everyone. Luring Captain Renault into arresting Victor and Ilsa with the letters of transit on them, he instead pulls his gun on the captain. All four drive to the airport, where the captain must ensure Victor's safe departure.

But then comes the shock of changed plans. Ilsa is to accompany her husband, not stay behind. To his distraught love, Rick explains: "You said I was to do the thinking for both of us. Well, I've done a lot of it since then, and it all adds up to one thing: you're getting on that plane with Victor where you belong . . . Inside of us, we both know you belong with Victor. You're part of his work, the thing that keeps him going. If that plane leaves the ground and you're not with him, you'll regret it. Maybe not today. Maybe not tomorrow, but soon and for the rest of your life. . . . Ilsa, I'm no good at being noble, but it doesn't take much to see that the problems of three little people don't amount to a hill of beans in this crazy world. Someday you'll understand that. . . . Here's looking at you kid."

At this point Major Strasser arrives to prevent the plane from leaving, a few fateful seconds before his escort. Rick shoots him as he tries to tele-phone the control tower. Then the escort comes running through the fog, looking to Captain Renault for instruction. He utters the immortal words, "Major Strasser has been shot. Round up the usual suspects." He, too, has joined the Allies. It is "the beginning of a beautiful friendship."

Why does this story, although beautifully reconciling Individualism with Communitarianism, remain quintessentially American and individ-ualist? Because individualism *precedes* Communitarianism in time. Be-cause it takes a world community crisis of momentous proportions to bring Rick (and America) into a world war.

Moreover, Rick had won his personal battle with Victor before giving up his prize. He knew Ilsa loved him above everything—her husband, her marriage, even their greater cause. She could not even leave him again by her own volition. When they made love, Rick knew not simply that she was his but that she always had been. She had left him at the train station for the same good reasons that he would soon leave her.

Finally, Rick had to think of Ilsa's individuality too. Her dedication and core beliefs were centered on Victor and the work they shared. In order to bring out the best in her, he would have to give her up.

Figure 4.1 shows the trajectory typical of the stories told in individualist cultures. Rick is a hard-bitten, cynical, forsaken individualist (top left). Liv-ing as he does among "vultures," he does not let any sympathy show, lest it be exploited. During his crushing defeat (bottom left), when he becomes drunk and despairing, his individuality has been annihilated because, as he puts it, his "insides have been kicked out." He has neither sympathy with the sufferings of Europe nor respect for himself. He is near zero on both dimensions of Communitarianism and Individualism.

In contrast, Figure 4.1 positions Captain Renault in the middle, too cyn-ical and temporizing to be severely hurt by anything or anyone. Yet he is so deeply compromised as an official of the Vichy government that values as such are matters of irony. When Rick points a gun at his heart, Renault de-scribes this as "my least vulnerable spot." The sexual attention he has forced on refugee women has blunted all finer feelings. The sole advan-tage of his position is that he can jump either way.

Then there is Laszlow, at the Communitarian end of the continuum (bottom right). He is a man who irritates Rick with his nobility and purity, all the more so when he puts Ilsa's survival before his own and sorely tempts Rick to take her away.

Figure 4.1 Triumphant Individualism—Casablanca

Victor is the least successful character in this drama. His personality is wooden, his heroism clichéd, and his selfless devotion far too good to be true. No wonder Ilsa prefers Rick, who has more than one dimension to his personality. It is clear that American writers find it difficult to make a Communitarian value system either credible or interesting. Laszlow, positioned at bottom right, is the stereotypic foreigner. Even though the writers intended him to be heroic, he remains a foil for Rick.

This brings us finally to Rick's renunciation at the foggy airport, when he persuades Ilsa to return to her husband and Victor says, "Welcome back to the fight. This time I know our side will win." But in case we fear that community spirit might now become a habit with Rick, he assures Ilsa that he soon will be alone again. "But I've got a job to do, too. Where I'm goin' you can't follow. What I've got to do, you can't be any part of." So although Rick's individuality has been dedicated to serve a suffering world, he remains triumphantly alone, as do most popular idealizations of American character. You actually serve your society better by not being part of it, by riding into the story—from God knows where—and riding out again at the end, fondly remembered but far away.

A Story Told by a Communitarian Culture

One of Akira Kurosawa's most celebrated films is *Ikiru* ("to live"). The protagonist, Kanji Watanabe, is a middle-aged, beaten-down bureaucrat in a local government prefecture. He visits the doctor and receives a diagnosis that is his death sentence. He has cancer of the bowel; a shadow passes across his stricken face.

Just as Individualist cultures like the United States tend to suffer from the various pathologies of excessive individualism, so Communitarian cultures like Japan suffer from the pathologies of excessive Communitarianism. Watanabe has worked in a municipal government office for thirty years as a minor official. The film's narrator calls him "our hero," but also "a corpse" who has actually been dead for most of his working life.

Japan's municipal governments have a particularly dismal reputation. Watanabe is a time-server. He has an almost reflexive habit of looking at his watch. One day in the office a female clerk is reprimanded for giggling. She explains that she was reading in a magazine of a man who never missed a day's work in twenty-five years for fear of discovering he was not needed. Watanabe has never missed a day's work.

After visiting the doctor, Watanabe is in shock and is nearly hit by a truck. He tries to approach his son, now married and moved away, but their relationship is tense and awkward. He tries to tell him of the cancer but is brusquely misunderstood. He tries to hug him, but the son freezes. There are flashbacks of this strained relationship. A boy playing baseball who commits some infraction, a lost child at his mother's funeral afraid he will lose sight of the hearse, a young soldier leaving for the war, desperately afraid but unable to share this with his father. Now there is no relationship left.

So Watanabe makes the round of bars and nightclubs in an attempt to lose himself in drunkenness and gaiety. His boozing companion is a writer who jokingly calls himself "Mephistopheles," and they are followed by a black dog. We see Watanabe singing raucously with other revelers, as his tears trickle down. A popular song, about making love while you still can, haunts him.

But Watanabe finds some comfort. He runs into the girl that once giggled in his office. She now works in a toy factory. They gossip about people in the office and she regales him with the nicknames she gave them all. What was his nickname? "The Mummy."

Watanabe explains that he worked so loyally over the years for the sake of his son, to give him a better chance, but now they cannot communicate. The girl takes the side of her generation. "He didn't want you to become a mummy. You can't blame him for that." Watanabe wants to know her secret, what makes her so vivacious. She shrugs. "I just eat and work, that's all," she mimes the making of a toy, "but I feel I am friends with all the children in Japan." That statement proves crucial.

Back in the office we see how the municipality works, or rather does not work. A very polite delegation of mothers is petitioning to have some landfill turned into a municipal park. Because such a decision requires multiple consents and each department passes the buck, they must move from department to department. Despite the ceremonial courtesies, nothing is going to be done. Their petition is finally consigned to the back of Watanabe's drawer.

And it is from there that Watanabe later retrieves it and decides that building the park is what he will do in the time remaining to him.

He takes the petition from office to office, patiently waiting for an audience—gently, insistently, humbly begging for an approval. Several insult him to make him go away. The mayor is annoyed with him.

"Doesn't it make you angry to be insulted like this?" a colleague asks. "No, I can't be angry with anyone. I don't have time to be angry."

Indeed, and what is his ego worth with so little time to live? He might as well sacrifice his self-esteem to get the playground built, to leave some legacy behind him.

The film is somber, but some ironic humor emerges when three gangsters come to see Watanabe. "Build that playground and your life won't be worth much!" A beautiful, slow smile breaks across Watanabe's face. He knows, better than they, what life is worth.

We have to understand Japanese culture to appreciate the methods Watanabe adopted. Because Communitarian culture is supposed to be benignly led, those in authority will yield to pleas that are sufficiently persistent and full of pathos, like the ten-year demonstration of Japanese mothers against mercury poisoning by powerful companies, who were ultimately shamed into conceding liability.

Watanabe has to humiliate himself to succeed, but succeed he does. The last we see of him, he is sitting happily on a child's swing in the fading light of day. Snow is falling and he is singing, now happily, the same tune that earlier made him weep. In the morning he is found frozen to death, his mission completed.

Although the audience knows what happened, the co-workers who discuss his life at the all-night wake in his rooms get much of it wrong and finally descend into maudlin drunkenness and empty platitudes of praise. It is Kurosawa's final swipe at the excesses of Communitarianism in which mediocrity cannot learn. Only one man in the office sensed the truth, and he watches the sun set over the playground in the final moments of the film.

Let us, then, consider a values trajectory largely opposite to the one in *Casablanca,* one that reconciles the preponderant Communitarianism of Japanese culture to the Individualism of "our hero," more alive in his death than in his life.

Figure 4.2 shows (bottom right) Watanabe's mummified existence at the municipal government office, his total despair over his medical diagnosis (bottom left), and his empty pleasure and contrived gaiety in drinking and partying (top left). When he at long last follows his personal incli-

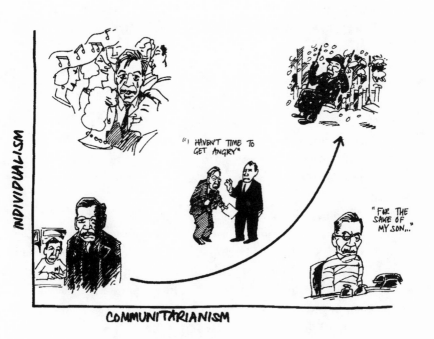

Figure 4.2 Triumphant Communitarianism—Ikiru

nations it is too late, and such indulgent individualism is considered "dev-ilish" in a Communitarian culture. He does not have a personality worth expressing.

So Watanabe seizes an opportunity to accomplish something that will outlast the short time he has left. He will plead and bow before his seniors to complete the project. Children will play at this place of his final labor. He will have made a difference after all. What if his personal dignity is annihi-lated in the process? Has he not left his legacy to the coming generation? And so he sings to himself on a children's swing (top right).

We see, then, that it is possible to reconcile Individualism and Com-munitarianism in two contrasting ways: by fierce self-assertion, Rick's strategy in *Casablanca,* or by humble self-negation, Watanabe's method in *Ikiru.* Rick's self-assertion led to personal sacrifice and identification with a civilization besieged; Watanabe's self-negation led to a lasting monu-ment to his individual efforts.

Which story is to be preferred? Westerners will find Rick far more fun, but Watanabe's quiet, desperate labors are more accessible to the average individual—a more realistic path to heroism that even the least of us can take. In the end, both paths lead to integration and integrity, what values are all about. The more ways we can see to reach virtue, the better we can live and work.

Should One Value Dominate or Should Both Be Reconciled?

It must be clear by now that values at the opposite ends of a continuum are dependent upon one another. What confirms our individualities is the work we have successfully performed for communities. What makes a community dynamic and creative is its ability to nurture and generate in-dividuality.

When the individual stands alone, be it on the wide open prairie or apart from the opinions of colleagues, he or she is only physically alone (see Fig-ure 4.3, top left). Similarly, when the person is closely surrounded by fam-ily or friends, he or she is only physically associated (bottom right). Psy-chologically, matters are far more subtle. The person standing alone may be filled with memories of love or of praise for moral stands taken earlier, while the person physically surrounded by family or friends may disagree fundamentally with their views or with the pressures they exert.

This is why the person depicted at the top right of Figure 4.3 is surrounded by ghosts. Because we each have a mind, we are ultimately alone in our decisions—hence the truth of individualism. But each of us has tested innumerable times the effect of our judgments upon our community, the continuation and success of which will vindicate or fail to vindicate that judgment. Consequently, the person who takes a moral stand is surrounded by the ghosts of everyone who has ever loved him.

The confidence to dissent comes from the success of our past social experience in the family and the community. If our social judgments have been validated in past encounters, we become more convinced of their accuracy and more likely to speak out. In the sixties, psychological experiments conducted by Stanley Milgram established these facts.

In Milgram's experiments subjects were tricked into inflicting electric shocks on a "learner" who was in fact only pretending to suffer. The real purpose of the experiment was to see whether persons paid to inflict electric shocks as punishment for error would continue to do so after the learner started to scream and even pretended to pass out. A large majority of subjects conformed to the role of apprentice torturers, to the very end. Our concern here is with the roughly 30 percent who refused to inflict such pain.

Figure 4.3 Individualism Versus Communitarianism

Since Milgram called these "the Independents," we might expect them to be more individualistic. And so they were—more creative, more outspoken, more verbal. Many of them threw their money back in the face of the experimenter and told him to go to hell. Rick would have been proud of them.

Interestingly enough, those who refused also came from larger and closer families, were closer to their mothers, had more friends and more intimate relationships, and had more varied social experience. Not everyone who refused to continue the experiment first confronted the experimenter; many rushed to the "electric chair" to release its victim.

So what really prevents periodic descents into barbarity is that a minority of people, but just enough, have created an integrity of personal conviction and social attachment that resists cruel acts. Whether one is moved most by compassion for victims or rage against illegitimate authority, both impulses combine to prevent abuse.

Case 1: Collaborative Competition—Tim Galwey and IBM

Author and consultant Tim Galwey recently related to us his success with an IBM sales force. Salespersons competed with each other every quarter for who could sell the most. At the quarterly sales conferences, the winner would be announced and would receive a prize, plus a vacation for the family. There was much excitement and much hoopla. Competition was fierce, which was part of the trouble . . . as it turned out. Salespersons were very careful not to pass on information that they discovered in talking to customers. If new opportunities opened up or if there were new patterns of demand, they kept this to themselves. Each contestant had no intention of helping anyone else to win. Information was the secret weapon.

There was also some grumbling from customers. At the end of each quarter, salespersons tried to unload as much product on customers as they could. This increased inventories and left the customers with carrying costs. There was also a marked increase in sales resistance. The more salespersons tried to push customers into buying, the harder the customers pushed back. The suspicion grew that instead of serving customers, sales staff had their own agendas—which was true enough. There was a marked rise in tension, and absences resulting from mental health problems rose from 3 percent to 7 percent. Yet the spirit of competition was strong, and neither IBM nor Galwey wanted to see it diminished. Individual effort and creative ingenuity in spotting new patterns of demand are crucial to IBM's success.

This is clearly a conflict between competitiveness, a derivative of Individualism, and cooperation, a derivative of Communitarianism. Because IBM is an American corporation, we would expect competition to be furious and opportunities to cooperate to be potentially neglected.

What could Galwey do? What you cannot do as a consultant, unless you want to be sent packing, is to disparage the dominant value of that culture—in this case, competitive individualism. Galwey's challenge was to somehow qualify that competitiveness with more cooperative modes, but he could not, dared not, reduce the intensity of competition. Like Rick in *Casablanca,* each salesperson was out for his- or herself and objections to that reality would get Galwey nowhere.

What Galwey did was change the rules of the competition. Instead of giving the prize to the person with the highest sales, IBM awarded it instead to the salesperson who had learned the most from the customer in the last quarter.

How was such "learning" to be judged? By the simple expedient of having each salesperson ascend the rostrum in turn and tell all his or her comrades not "This is how much I sold," but "This is what I learned from customers." The audience would then vote on the value of this information to each of them. The person with the most votes won the contest.

Was Galwey successful? Very much so. Sales increased by more than 20 percent. For the most part, the person who "learned most" from the customer also sold most. The performance gap between salespersons narrowed as the less informed learned from the best informed. And nearly all the customer complaints vanished. There was no longer an incentive to load customers up with products they did not need, or to achieve sales by a certain date. Instead of trying to "beat" the customer resistance, the salesperson now listened and took notes. It was the information not the sale that would count, and the more the salesperson learned the more genuinely helpful that person became. No wonder the rate of absenteeism from mental disability fell, even as tension eased.

Galwey had left the value of competition in place, but he had made it impossible to compete successfully without first cooperating with, and learning from, the customer. He also made it impossible to win without first re-

Figure 4.4 Tim Galwey's Intervention

laying all important information to the other members of the sales force, so that it was the best cooperator who won the competition, and the person whose information had won most votes.

The dilemma between competition and cooperation is illustrated in Figure 4.4. At top left is the situation as Galwey found it, with overly assertive salespeople browbeating customers, overloading them with inventory and stiffening the customers' sales resistance. On this end of the continuum, the sales force is overly competitive and insufficiently cooperative.

If we follow the direction of the learning circle, we see efforts to move toward sustained listening to customers. We are no longer trying to force products on them. We are listening to their needs and aspirations. This approach actually makes products easier to sell. People who learn more from their customers are better able to help them and hence better able to help themselves competitively. As information flows ever more freely among salespeople, sales soar.

Galwey has argued that within every game is a "hidden game." In this case the game was cooperating with each person to learn what the best competitors knew.

Case 2: Motorola's TCS Competition

For the past ten years or so, Motorola has run a Total Customer Satisfaction (TCS) competition on a worldwide basis. Only teams may enter this competition, and the condition of entry is that your team must have come up with an effective solution that totally satisfied a customer. The benefits received by the customer should consist of demonstrable gains and hard measures of substantial improvements.

In order to stand a chance of winning, these "total solutions" must be innovative, the testimony of the customer must be on record, and team members must be able to explain their contributions and how these combined to solve the customer's problem. It is important that the gains be calculated and be part of the presentation, which should also be written up in handy formats so that Motorola "University" can incorporate this into the experience and learning of the whole community.

Up to eight hundred teams, worldwide, are nominated by customers to enter the competition. To be nominated and entered is itself an honor, so that all contestants have already "won" and are representative of the best national practices. So popular have these competitions proved that the host country may run parallel contests of its own. For example, two nominated teams from Malaysia and Singapore are typically invited to compete also against Malaysian and Singaporean teams from other businesses and industries within those countries. This enables those cultures to learn from Motorola's practices and to compare best practice in a leading transnational corporation with equivalent practices in that country.

National Heroes

The effect is to give industrial problem-solving teams the same kind of respect and recognition as, for example, local football teams, except that the contribution of the problem-solving team is much greater and more lasting. Photographs of TCS teams hang not only on the walls of the company but in local newspapers and government offices. These teams are pathfinders for the economic development of their nation.

There are many opportunities to win. Teams win at plant level to get nominated, at provincial and national levels, in parallel contests within the nation, at the level of the region, the subcontinent or continent, and ultimately, at the finals held in Schaumberg, Illinois, at the Paul Galvin Center. Here the finalists present on stage, often in a costume of their own design—for example, the Singaporean Slickers—sometimes preceded by a national dance or pageant. The idea is to celebrate cultural diversity as well as the diversity of winning solutions.

Putting Winning Ideas to Use

After everyone has presented, the judges give their verdict and reasons for this. One of the criteria is the generalizability of the solution, that is, the extent to which it can be borrowed by other parts of the corporation and applied across the board. All presentations in multiple formats can be used for strategic and training purposes. The value to Motorola of eight hundred customer-delighting solutions could be incalculable if properly used and could be made the bases of new strategies.

The genius of these competitions is that they fine-tune cooperation and competition. You cannot even enter if you are not a successful team player who has already delighted a customer. This comes easily to the Communitarian cultures of Southeast Asia, which have tended to win these contests over the years. But left to itself, Motorola might overlook these successful teams because the style of many, if not all, Communitarian cultures is to be shy and modest about their achievements.

One important purpose of the TCS competitions, therefore, is to persuade communitarians to show off and claim full credit for their achievements by proclaiming these from a lighted stage.

Competing is easy for Americans but cooperating is harder, whereas for Southeast Asian countries like Singapore, Malaysia, and China cooperating is easy but competing with other teams is harder and must be learned.

But, in fact, of course, we need both styles. Competing allows you to discover which ideas and processes are best. Cooperating allows you to apply these ideas to customers in helpful ways and to nurture the talents of your team. What works better than either competition or cooperation is alternate phases of cooperation to better compete and competition to better cooperate. The values join together in virtuous circles of learning, which reconcile them both with one another.

The process of collaborative competition is depicted in Figure 4.5.

Case 3: The Dynamics of Co-opetition

Adam M. Brandenburger and Barry J. Nalebuff coined the word "co-opetition" to denote a strategic synthesis of competing (individually) and

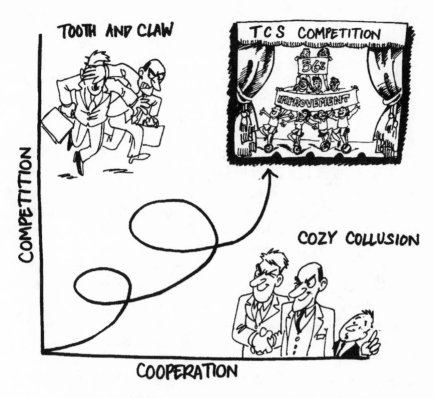

Figure 4.5 Collaborative Competition

cooperating (communally). They argue that the sporting-cum-military metaphors can be dangerously misleading. In order for your company to succeed, it is not necessary for others to fail. The authors claim to have borrowed from game theory various situations where it pays to cooperate rather than simply compete head-on. Games have several players, and you should be able to get out of the game what your playing contributes to the gains of other players.

It is a mistake to view such games egocentrically, that is, only from one's own position. You must be allocentric, putting yourself in the position of all the players and asking what you bring to them and what you contribute to the game in its entirety. Once you grasp that it is the whole game that is creating wealth, then you need to ask yourself, "How can we change that game, so that more can be won by more players?" She who has shaped the game itself and redefines its rules can become the main beneficiary of those changes. For example, Nintendo invited software companies "to play" but limited the number of games it would buy from each supplier, so none could dominate the market. It also kept its retailers in short supply so prices would not be cut.

General Motors faced an industrial "game" where competition was head-to-head and hence mutually destructive. Dealer discounts and year-end rebates were cutting into the profitability of manufacturers. Consumers were even postponing purchases until rebates came into effect.

So GM "moved sideways," into the complementary business of providing credit, some of which could be applied toward the purchase of a GM car. Five percent of charges on a GM credit card, up to $500 per year, with a maximum of $3,500 could be used to obtain a rebate on a new GM car. The credit card has been extremely successful.

This was not simply a successful strategy. It broke GM, Ford, Chrysler, and others out of the "rebate wars," allowing them to raise their prices. Brandenburger and Nalebuff see this as very important. You can gain more by letting your competitors gain too. In an altered game it is no longer price versus price, or rebate versus rebate.

In order to better explain the whole "game" Brandenburger and Nalebuff propose a "value net," shown in Figure 4.6, which enumerates the players and schematizes their relationships. This net distinguishes between competitors and complementors, and customers and suppliers.

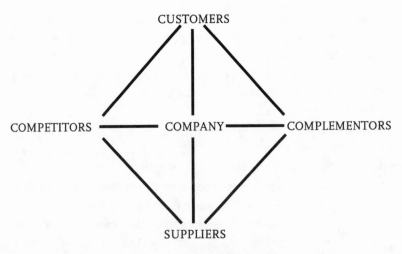

Figure 4.6 Players in the Value Net

Competitors, sometimes called "substitutors," are those players with whom other players could work with instead of you. The danger is being left out of the game. Clearly any company that closely resembles you, like Coca Cola's resemblance to PepsiCo, is a competitor/substitutor as opposed to a complementor.

Complementors are any players who make your own contribution to the game more valuable. GM, for example, is complemented by auto insurance companies and by finance companies who give credit for an automobile purchase. An obvious example of complementors is computers and software. One makes the other more valuable, which in turn sustains the one. Hence Pentium chips complement the Microsoft office, resulting in a virtuous circle. Complementors for GM include anti-theft devices, highway construction, synthetic rubber for tires, and emission controls. It can be a good move to invite complementors to play.

Brandenburger and Nalebuff are convincing on how much more complementarity there is than countries high in the competitive ethic realize. Whatever happened to the "threat" of video cassettes to the movie industry? Remember the "paperless office"? Remember how first television, then computers, were going to put an end to the book trade? The fact is that movie companies get richer from video cassettes than from their core business, that electronics increases the use of paper, and that hundreds of books are published every year on the very media that were supposed to destroy them! Complementarity is everywhere, in every synergy and every industrial cluster.

There are two fundamental symmetries in the game of business, as represented by the value net. The first is between customers and suppliers. The second is between competitors and complementors. You often combine with both customers and suppliers to improve the game or "enlarge the pie." This is complementarity. But there are also times when the pie gets divided and consumed. This remains competitive. If you are too competitive, you will miss opportunities to design a better game. If you are too complementary, you will lose out when the pie is divided among you. The bargaining power of each is in its known contribution to the whole game.

Finally, there is the question of scope. Should the boundaries of the game remain fixed, or has the scope of the whole game shifted, so that two formerly unrelated "games" merge?

Is a GM executive car a way of getting from one office to another, or is it

Figure 4.7 Co-opetition

in itself an office that is in touch with satellites designed to help it steer to its destination and that has the equipment of a modern office? The latter vision represents a transformation in scope. Combining a car and an office is a whole new combination and a whole new game, with a whole set of new complementors, including office systems in addition to vehicle systems. Now the "office" can move to where the customers are. These are new rules for a new game.

It is this combination of competition and complementarity that helps to build more complex systems, with the qualities of both an office and car. This reconciliation is depicted in Figure 4.7.

Complementarity steadily enlarges the system, increasing the number of its interdependent elements, while competition tests its viability against other, rival combinations. It is complementarity and rivalry working together that helps generate wealth, the first elaborating the second, streamlining, economizing, and paring down.

Virtuous and Vicious Circles

A cornerstone of Western economies and of individualism is Adam Smith's concept of the Invisible Hand. According to this view, if economic actors concentrate upon competing with one another, a by-product of this process is that customers, and hence the community at large, will benefit from these efforts. "It is not from the benevolence of the butcher, the brewer or the baker, that we expect our dinner, but from their regard for their own self-interest." The individual, Smith argues, "intends only his own gain, and he is in this, as in many other cases, led by an invisible hand to promote an end which was no part of his intention" (*An Inquiry into the Wealth of Nations*, London, 1776, p. 651).

This has always struck us as a curiously unbalanced view of human motivation. Is Smith saying that businesspeople get no pleasure from doing superlative work for their fellow beings, that pride in skill and craftsmanship is negligible and that the customer's delight and gratitude is of no consequence? No wonder they call economics "the dismal science"! This argument will hardly do.

A more moderate position is defensible. If Smith is saying that self-interest is the prime motivator and pleasure in customer satisfaction a secondary motivator, then this sounds more plausible. But our view is that even this generalization is chiefly true only of individualist cultures.

What, then, of Communitarian cultures? Some would say these do not work as well economically. But this is hardly accurate. The growth rates of the East Asian "tiger" economies, sustained for ten to fifteen years, are the fastest in the history of economics. There is clearly a strong drive toward economic development in at least some Communitarian cultures. What, then, motivates them?

Our view is that Adam Smith's dictum can be turned upside down, as shown in our Introduction, and the so-called invisible hand refers to whichever ends of the values continuum that particular culture has subordinated. In other words, it makes as much sense to say, "If everyone concentrated on serving the community of customers, then self-interests would also be served" as it does to say, "If everyone concentrated on their self-interests, then the larger community would be served."

Business cultures would be wise to put their emphasis on whichever value is the weaker of the two. Hence Individualistic cultures should think more about customers and the public good, while Communitarian cultures should show more concern for individual ambitions and human rights. Both might improve if they fine-tune their value system.

Do serious vicious circles surround the issue of Individualism–Communitarianism as surround Universalism–Particularism (Chapter 2)? There is at least one recurring pathology in American society that historian Richard Hofstadter has called "*the paranoid style in American politics.*" This has to do with recurrent fears of seditious aliens, anarchists like Sacco and Vanzetti, and the more recent Red Scares. Even with the collapse of Communism, these terrors do not cease: witness the state of mind which gave rise to the bombing of a federal building in Oklahoma.

The view we take is that the strong American emphasis on individual freedom and the right to dissent and the relatively weak emphasis on the community and family put unbearable strains upon a sizable minority of Americans, which leads to periodic backlashes and theories of conspiracy and subversion.

The problem of America's radical right is how to justify what they want in the language of political individualism. To some extent they do champion the family and religious communities, and in those respects they add needed balance to the Individual–Community continuum. But if that is all they did, they would lose politically, since the spirit of individualism dominates American political discourse. The strategem they use instead is to claim the existence of a Communitarian conspiracy against "true" American values. This puts them on the side of individualism, while enabling them to behave in a highly Communitarian manner in limiting dissent and attacking unconventional expressions of opinion. After all, if the nation is being besieged by subversives, all "good Americans" must close ranks until the threat is eliminated.

The vicious circle generated by these associations is depicted in Figure 4.8. Note that both sides incite each other to mutual antagonism. As the sheer volume of diversity increases, claiming free expression of right, the readiness to believe that Jews, gays, blacks, peaceniks, and Native Americans are all joined in monstrous conspiracy to subvert God-fearing communities and Christian family life, grows apace. But the real payoff for subscribing to this belief system is that you can spend your entire life in a restricted group of those with similar convictions and lifestyle while ostensibly defending an "endangered country."

So, far from America being in any danger of turning Communist, it cannot even support and elect democratic socialists and for most of the twen-

Those whose individuality and dissent "weaken" America and make her vulnerable to...

VICIOUS CIRCLE

The Communist Conspiracy must be opposed by patriotic citizens closing ranks against...

Figure 4.8

Figure 4.9

tieth century had fewer Communists than any other Western democracy in the world.

The targets of the witch hunts were independent thinkers, liberals, and those whose creativity upset conventional opinion.

The problem with shouting "Conspiracy!" is that the threat when carefully and calmly examined turns out to be imaginary. So the witch-finders must turn their accusations against anyone whose scepticism scuppers their investigation. The anti-Communist scourge conducted by Senator Joe McCarthy of Wisconsin ended when he accused the U.S. Army of being "Communist dupes" and finally auto-destructed in televised Army-McCarthy hearings, where his accusations became ever wilder.

Figure 4.9 shows the Army's counsel, Joseph Welch, a Boston lawyer, reproaching McCarthy's ever more frantic assertions. The Senator finally accused a junior law clerk in Welch's own office, which occasioned the rebuke in the caption. McCarthy was censured by the Senate and soon died along with his accusations.

The crucial contrast between vicious and virtuous circles enables us to distinguish between a company, culture, or nation that is tearing itself apart by internal conflicts over values, and a culture that has managed to integrate and reconcile those values. The battle between Individualism and Communitarianism reached the point of frenzy during the Cold War and during incidents like the Cambodian incursion over the legitimacy of dissent against America's common purpose in Vietnam. American society was not far from the breaking point. The distinction between viciousness and virtue is depicted in Figure 4.10.

The vicious circle is irreconcilable because the truth is not being told and the underlying social reality is not being faced. The truth is that people are being driven to frenzy by an excess of individuality, and by an ever greater range of political, sexual, gender, ethnic, racial, and lifestyle diversity. But those enraged cannot admit that their distress originates in America's foremost value.

Vicious circles have their own mad momentum. People often feel they have reached the pinnacle of "morality" when combating "immorality." If there are Reds under the bed a lot of time can be spent under the bed looking for them, so that you imitate your enemies while combating them. Had we started a nuclear war during the Cold War period, two values which are essentially interdependent would have destroyed each other.

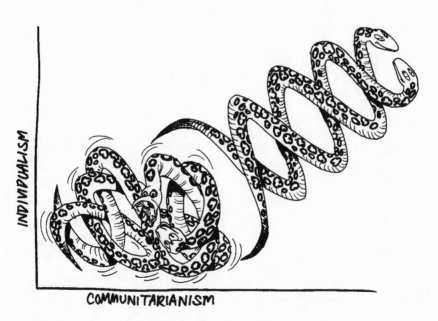

Figure 4.10 Vicious and Virtuous Circles

The conventional explanation is that we "won the Cold War" because Individualism is superior to Communitarianism. We do not agree. The West deservedly won the Cold War because we better reconciled Individualism with Communitarianism, while the Soviets tried to crush Individualism and suffered ever-increasing vicious circles of dissent, apathy, and alienation.

5 Specificity–Diffuseness

THE DILEMMA

Cultures vary considerably in how specific they are, that is, how precisely and minutely they *de-fine* (put an end to) the constructs they use and to what extent they prefer diffuse, patterned wholes, put together in overall configurations and systems.

Nature illustrates this dilemma in many ways, the egg (specific) or the chicken (diffuse), the enzyme breaks down to specifics, while molecules build up into diffuse wholes. Entropy dissipates energy into small, specific pieces, while negative entropy builds up again to constitute and to continue life. Our cells are continually breaking down and continuously building up, until at life's end entropy proves stronger, but not until we have reproduced ourselves, so that our genes survive.

While in nature the specific and diffuse are clearly complementary, in culture there are pronounced preferences for one over the other.

Much of this originates in the Protestant Reformation of the sixteenth and seventeenth centuries. Catholicism was diffuse, picturesque, multisensual, passionate, elaborate, mysterious, and romantic. It was accused, rightly or otherwise, of luxury, self-indulgence, and mystification. Protestantism was specific, verbal, literal, emotionally controlled, spare, plain-speaking, and classic. It was accused, rightly or otherwise, of frugality, abstemiousness, and fundamentalism.

These differences were regarded as matters not of taste but of heresy. Catholic imagery was smashed as being "idolatrous." The mystery, panoply, and ceremonies of the priesthood were dismissed as "bells and smells" that appealed to the viscera, not the brain. While Catholics depict Christ on the cross with blood trickling down His agonized features, Protestants prefer an unoccupied, abstract cross symbol.

The specific versus diffuse distinction, which might today be regarded as a thinking style or a preferred mode of experience, was then charged with fears of hell and damnation. In places like Northern Ireland it continues to divide populations. As we write this, peace is once again upon the brink.

We deal in this chapter with the residues of this dilemma in business, in contemporary social affairs, and in moral sciences. To illustrate the dispute, we refer to William Blake's painting of Sir Isaac Newton as a musclebound giant, bent forward in a grotesque crouching posture, using his dividers to make specific measurements (Figure 5.1). While the left of the picture is specific, the right side, depicting a subject ignored by Newton, is diffuse. Here we see beautiful creatures floating in the water and covering the rocks—patterned, diffuse, and whole—on which Newton has turned his back.

Blake was criticizing "natural religion," the Puritan conception of a mechanical universe—or Newtonian physics, as it later became. He wrote to a friend: "May God us keep from single vision and from Newton's sleep."

Yet Newtonian science was to be the driving force in the British and American industrial revolutions in the eighteenth and nineteenth centuries.

We have to ask ourselves what penalty has been paid for our highly successful yet dangerously narrow conception of the world, what Thomas Carlyle called our "steam engine intellects" running on narrow rails. For our

SPECIFIC ———————————————— DIFFUSE

Figure 5.1 Specific/Diffuse

traditional Newtonian world view is so specific as to ignore relationships, aesthetics, value systems, emotional bonds, waveforms, frequencies, and the very organization that makes life possible. Instead the universe is conceived of atoms or objects in absolute time and space, emulating the operations of a celestial clock.

E. A. Burtt has written movingly of the decisive shift to specificity occasioned by Newtonian science. It totally transformed our image of ourselves and of our habitat. It had reduced the individual "to a puny, irrelevant spectator imprisoned in a dark room. The world that people had thought they were living in—a world rich in colour and sound, redolent with fragrance . . . speaking everywhere of purposive harmony and creative ideals—was crowded now into minute concerns in the brains of scattered organic beings. The really important world outside was a world hard, cold, colourless, silent and dead."

Even today, British and some American analytical philosophy holds values to be meaningless "exclamations of preference." The horrors of World War II convinced Bertrand Russell to logically atomize every proposition, thereby preventing their use by the Hitlers or Stalins of the future. Unfortunately this spiking of fanaticism also kills any insight or proposition that reconciles cultural diversity. We are left with objective agreements on the detritus of lifeless objects. Newton is still turned in on himself, ignoring most of the phenomena that make life worth living. We become very, very certain of things with the least meaning and everything else is consigned to a bog of relativism and of subjective preferences. Economics, for example, regards all human values as subjective, until such time as the market sets a price on particular goods or services. Only then is value objectified and verifiable. "Pushpin is as good as poetry."

How We Measure Specific–Diffuse

In our research we measure Specific–Diffuse preferences using various measures. One seeks to discover how a corporation is conceived. Is it as a system of specifics or as a diffuse whole? We ask: Which way of perceiving a company do you regard as most normal?

A. One way is to see a company as a system designed to perform functions and tasks in an efficient way. People are hired to perform these functions with the help of machines and other equipment. They are paid for the tasks they perform.

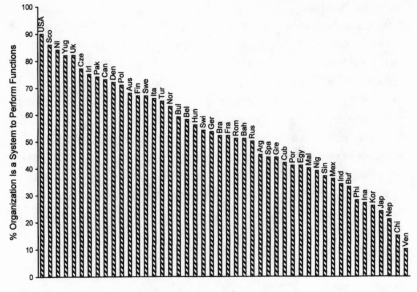

Figure 5.2 Nature of an Organization

B. A second way is to see a company as a group of people working together. They have social relations with other people and with the organization. The functioning is dependent on these relations.

The results are displayed in Figure 5.2.

Eastern European countries—Bulgaria, the Czech Republic, Russia,
Poland, and Hungary—have clearly suffered under communism and do
not respond well when the whole group and its social relations are in-
voked. With the exception of these recent converts to specificity, the United
States, the United Kingdom, the Netherlands, Canada, and Australia are
all relatively specific, while South Korea, Japan, Thailand, Malaysia, Singapore, the Philippines, France, Portugal, Brazil, Venezuela, and Mexico,
and countries in East Asia, Catholic Europe, and South America are more
diffuse.

A second question has to do with "a mistake made at work" by "a member of a team." Is the person making the mistake specifically held responsible—one person, one mistake? Or does responsibility for preventing and
noticing this error spread diffusely through the whole team? After all, the
team could have watched the member more carefully, trained her better,

supported her work. And it may take the whole team to prevent such errors from recurring.

On the other hand, if "everyone" is responsible, no one is taken to task. Accepting responsibility becomes a noble gesture rather than genuine acknowledgment of error. The team may even protect its members from individual sanction, and management will lose its right to hire and fire.

Whether responsibility is specifically assigned or diffusely accepted is a major dilemma in the workplace, and, not surprisingly, different cultures take contrasting views. Figure 5.3 depicts an example of the number of persons choosing to blame a specific individual.

It is interesting to note how discredited "group responsibility" has become in some formerly Communist countries. Some of these are now more punitive toward individuals than are the traditionally individualist countries.

The newly "liberated" countries of East Europe and Russia are now more "Western" than Westerners. American values appear to have been seized upon. The United States, Canada, and Denmark are moderately specific, and East Asia and Latin America are more diffuse. Nevertheless, diffuse thinking has many adherents in the West. It does not dominate on

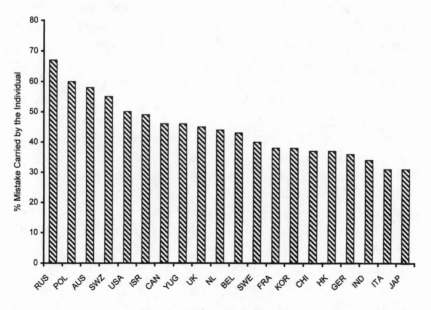

Figure 5.3 Whose Fault Was It?

the same scale as communitarianism (Chapter 3) and particularism (Chapter 1).

Taken together, the two scales reveal only a narrow majority for specificity in the United Kingdom and the United States and strong majorities for diffuseness in France, South Korea, Japan, and so forth. Which style one chooses may depend on the circumstances one faces and the function within the corporation one represents.

Why American Culture Is More Specific than Diffuse

The business culture of the United States is primarily specific because:

- The Protestant Reformation championed "the Word" and objected to images and decorations.
- The Newtonian worldview, with its emphasis on objectivity, detachment, and mechanism, grew out of Protestant cosmology. God had wound up the universe and left it for His saints to discover.
- Universalism, in which phenomena are classified by similarity, leads to quantification and measurement with "more" or "less" or a fixed quality.
- Western capitalism is increasingly responsive to global money and financial markets, which operate with specific profit indexes.
- Financial analysts have risen to positions of immense influence and power. They break down corporate performance into specifics.
- American business, philosophy, and folklore are highly oriented to results, that is, specific outcomes.
- The tradition of debate in Congress and on television polarizes opinion into two exaggerated extremes, thereby activating "the law of the excluded middle." To be seen as decisive, leaders must champion one or another of two specifics.
- Television and media messages are increasingly fragmented and isolated into "sound bites," and the number of impressions made on the number of people is enumerated by politicians and advertisers as more and more specific messages are beamed at already known attitudes. Leadership and originality suffer.
- The digital revolution, in which the *difference* between 1 and 0 makes up the binary code by which computers operate, has greatly increased the bias to specificity.
- In a culture that greatly values literacy and numeracy, there is a tendency

for the specificity of words and numbers to become confused with the diffuseness of the phenomena these describe. As Alfred Korzybski put it, "The word is not the thing."

American specificity is exemplified by such statements as "The buck stops here," "General Motors is not in the business of making cars but making money," "If it ain't broke don't fix it," and the cry of Harold T. Geneen of International Telephone and Telegraph (ITT), "Give me the cold, unshakeable facts!" This exclamation echoes the Puritan belief that everything should be stripped to its "bare bones." (In fact, a "Barebones Parliament" once existed in Cromwellian England.) The belief is that stripping propositions to their bare bones reveals the truth. This is questionable at best. Even high-profit figures exist in a context. If customers or suppliers have been exploited to achieve high profit, if new entrants are even now crowding into the market, then those profits will soon disappear. "The facts" by themselves can enlighten or mislead and are vulnerable to selection. To assume, as Geneen does, that every attempt to qualify facts is varnish, excuse, or obfuscation is both ungenerous and untrue. We survive and prosper by communicated meanings, to which facts contribute, but for which they are no substitutes.

At Its Best . . .

Specific culture operates on feedback. What makes "for-profit" organizations generally superior and more effective than "nonprofit" organizations and government departments is that profits measure not simply gains made from trading but what the company has done for other people. Satisfied customers and satisfied investors supply the monies that keep the company in business.

Most nonprofit organizations soon become ends in themselves—intent on surviving, however meager their contributions, but also unable to measure the value, if any, of those contributions. Profitability is at least a rough estimate of how valuable you are to other people. Although profits can be increased in the short run by antisocial devices—by not, for example, considering damage to the environment—these are failures to measure the right specifics, not failures of specificity per se. It would be nice to know more exactly social and environmental costs.

Specificity seeks truth through analysis, by breaking the whole into pieces and seeing in which specific part a fault or trouble lies. This is not an insignificant procedure. You can pinpoint, for example, exactly the reason a machine malfunctions and replace the defective part. Financial analysis has the same utility. You can discover with great acuity just where money is being made and where it is being lost, or you can isolate "the five main reasons for late delivery" and eliminate these one by one.

In science, specificity substitutes facts for fancies. You may wish or believe the moon is made of cheese, but this will not alter facts. Reality is apart.

Among the most important contributions of specific thinking is the doctrine of human rights. Large parts of the world do not pretend to misunderstand these rights; they are genuinely mystified because the idea that human rights are pieces of property held by each person is by no means self-evident.

Human rights, or "individual dignity entitlement" as these are called at Motorola Corporation, are imaginary pieces of property akin to real estate, which members of Western cultures are held to own. We have property *in ourselves*. This conviction, so obvious to us but so strange to many, derives from the fact that democracy began as a franchise of property owners. When everyone was allowed to vote as a result of political pressures, landless voters were said to have property in their persons, hence civil "rights."

Specificity is also vital to promise-keeping. When you "give your word" you must keep it, if transaction costs are not to rise sharply. Lloyds Bank, Lloyds insurance, Barclays Bank, and others were all started by prominent Quaker families whose motto was, "My word is my bond." In financial transactions, deals may be made in a second and verbal transactions can run several days ahead of written records of those transactions. Clearly a person who would not deny or "forget" an inconvenient promise was a boon to business, and Quakers found they could trust each other and so grow rich.

It has been estimated that the Quaker contribution to Britain's industrial revolution was forty times greater than would be expected from their numbers alone. To make your word your bond is clearly advantageous in business, however inconvenient that may be for those who miscalculate.

In addition, specificity can greatly clarify issues by separating what we know from what we infer or conclude from known facts or results. We can often agree on the facts by observing these, and this permits us to discuss

AT ITS BEST, SPECIFICITY...

ANALYZES THE PROBLEM

HUMAN
RIGHTS —
PROPERTY IN
YOUR PERSON

"Art thou going back on thy word?"

ACTION RESEARCH

FANTASY IS
NOT REALITY

Figure 5.4

the plausibility of different explanations. Which of these best accounts for the facts?

Results are crucial to business operations, since successful action may, and often does, precede detailed knowledge of how that success occurred. Very often we "stumble over the truth" and have to go back and examine exactly how this truth occurred. In action learning, action precedes learning and the specific result may be our first clue to a valuable lesson worth investigating.

Specificity is vital in one additional respect. According to Ashby's Law of Requisite Variety a company needs to make at least those distinctions that are made by the actors in its environment. It must match their combined categories of thought. If the actors make forty distinctions and the company only twenty-five, it will fail them. If they make forty and it makes sixty-five, it may confuse them, blind them with its formidable complexity. Specificity, then, is not an absolute good. You need to specify what those in your environment care about, what they require, and then match each specific request with your own response (Figure 5.4).

But Taken Too Far . . .

Specificity has some very serious downsides. Peters and Waterman describe "paralysis-thru-analysis." If you go on and on reducing, analyzing, and subdividing, the world turns to rubble. A great pile of bricks does not make a house. Analysis not only forestalls action but spreads confusion and bewilderment, because an opportunity cut to pieces is no opportunity at all.

Persons high in analytical skills are typically of formidable intelligence. Indeed, IQ, because it must be measurable and consistent, tests analytical skills, not the capacity to generate new syntheses or to be creative. Analysis is the sword of the critic and the evaluator, not of the originator or the entrepreneur. When Meredith Belbin selected a group of super-intelligent executives to solve a simulated business problem, they performed quite poorly. They tore every suggestion to pieces and "deconstructed" every constructive initiative. Specificity, because of its inability to reexamine thought categories, can be very sterile. When we make a list of "bullet points," each one shorn of ambiguity and qualification, we lose nuance, subtlety, and meaning.

When analysts are in competition with each other, each vies with his or her rivals in the fineness and minuteness of distinctions. Work projects die "a death of thousand cuts," as everyone slices the issue differently from everyone else. This results in total immobility, an interminable comparison of breakdowns as everyone is knee deep in debris.

There may be scores of statistical breakdowns, but when we ask what these mean, no one can say. Asked why the data has been collected, the answer comes back that it always has been collected in the past and so has continued to be collected.

The ideal of the specific thinker is machine efficiency, so highly specific constructs become self-perpetuating, self-validating, and self-sealing—exclusive of all other ways of thinking. Suppose we want to hire someone. It all starts with a job description. Let us suppose that the description is only partially correct. In fact, several additional qualities are required to do this work. But it is too late. The description has gone to the headhunter, another servant of specificity.

If the headhunter does his work efficiently, only those with the misspecified capacities will be candidates for the job. When the "best" is selected, the error will be minutely described in her work contract. When she is evaluated this will be against her (inaccurate) job description. If the company favors pay for performance, she will receive specific increments of pay for conforming to this original error. We are, in effect, paying her to hide our error from us and to vindicate the initial job description. By such specific categorization we may avoid meeting anyone who disagrees with us and so perpetuate our errors indefinitely.

Specificity also turns, all too easily, into "single-principle imperialism." The part or unit specified grows and grows in salience until it usurps the whole. As any biologist, doctor, or systems expert will tell you, a living organism maintains a precarious balance. If you increase the strength of any one part, it will at first disturb the whole and eventually destroy it.

Consider the concept of pay for performance, a great favorite for specific-minded cultures like the United States. The idea is a good one. Let money accrue to success as it does in markets, where the successful attract ever greater resources.

But in practice "p for p" runs into a host of problems, as a result of being part of a tightly knit, coherent organization that markets are *not*. For example, an individual may be reluctant to help others if that help simply leads to those others being paid more than the individual. Employees will choose the easiest among the higher-rewarded tasks, avoiding genuine challenges. P for p assumes that some authority knows exactly how valuable each job is and how difficult it is to complete, but does he? In innovative organizations this is almost impossible to gauge.

Most innovative organizations exert their energies on learning how best to improve and develop their core competencies. What is the effect of superimposing upon this learning calculations about how to get the most money out of the reward system? Might not such logics conflict and confound each other?

All intelligent employees know that their salaries must be earned. To be paid at the end of each month is to be trusted to do good work. But to have a percentage of that salary contingent upon pleasing your boss empowers her and disempowers them. It also injures trust. Your employer can claw back a portion of your salary after the work is done.

The human importance of many jobs dwarfs the pin monies used to incentivize these. How much should a nurse get for holding the hand of a dying teenage crash victim and then breaking the news to her parents? Fifty dollars? A T-shirt with a heart? Specific monies insult the diffuse importance of much of the work we do. Alfie Kohn, in *Punished by Rewards*, reports that kids who were paid to fasten their seat belts stopped fastening them when the money was stopped. They missed the point of the campaign, which was not to win pocket money but to value the extension and the meaning of their own lives.

How does a supervisor convey a subtle message to a subordinate? A very common message, but difficult to communicate, is, "I like and support you, but some of your work needs to improve." That is neither a reward nor a punishment. It is a steer. But you would totally undermine its balance and subtlety if you added, "So I'm giving you/not giving you the $500." You *can* be too specific (Figure 5.5)!

Finally, we must understand that objects and objectives are more specific than living people, who are more diffuse. Human beings have social bonds and attachments. Objects have none. Those who are ultraspecific become materialist and lose all human and spiritual qualities. A famous American presidential candidate, William Jennings Bryan, once reproached the American body politic for its obsession with money and its willingness to break people in order to make profits. In a marvelously oratorical style, he warned: "Do not press down upon the brow of Labor, this crown of thorns, do not crucify mankind upon a Cross of Gold."

Figure 5.5

He rekindled the ancient fable of King Midas, who turned everything to gold and starved physically and emotionally as a consequence.

Drugs, alcohol, gambling are all specific substitutes for diffuse human relationships, with their highs, lows, thrills, spills, and sweet surrender.

At Its Best . . .

Diffuse culture is very aware of quality. Quality is a characteristic of whole products and whole design, development, and manufacturing processes.

Traditionally, Western cultures have tried to assure quality by adding one more specific role, that of the quality inspector. But this rarely produces top quality because the inspector must intervene after the error is made. This delays production, invalidates work already done, creates resentment and counterpressures on the inspection process, and is typically too lax or too severe, since the inspector is not a producer.

Quality, like safety, has to be everyone's job, with everyone looking out for everyone else and for the quality of combined efforts. The problem with quality specialists or safety specialists is that others may leave these responsibilities aside. Quality and safety can be guaranteed not by specific persons but by every pair of eyes and hands searching for any defect in any part of the product or process.

Hence quality and safety are essentially seamless. The problem with divided labors is that no one takes responsibility for the seam or fit between two specific jobs. But where quality or safety is everyone's responsibility, seams are eliminated. Western cultures have learned about "Quality circles" from Japan and Singapore and have tried to imitate these, although without diffuse thinking processes these imitations may fail.

As we have seen in our research question, responsibility for an error by any member of a work team diffuses to all others. They all feel responsible because they should have noticed and prevented the mistake and should have looked after the quality of each team member.

Diffuse styles of thinking create ways of assuring quality that are strange to most Western cultures. Hence, Taichi Ohno's Toyota production system asks "five times why" something has gone wrong. While for specific cultures there is usually a single cause, for example, "The drill bit was defective and broke," for diffuse cultures there may be five or more places to intervene in a diffuse system. These might include:

1. A stronger drill bit
2. Slower drill speed
3. Softer metal being drilled
4. Better lubrication
5. Improved training for the drill operator

The costs of one or more interventions may be lower than the costs of others. Perhaps just two interventions can prevent 75 percent of all breaks, so the others are not necessary.

Diffuse thinking is much more alert to remote consequences and the need for balance. There are many of these remote effects. In complexity theory a butterfly wing can potentially trigger a typhoon. For example, laying off one employee in ten in a thousand-person work force is for the specific thinker a 10 percent payroll saving—an addition of, say, $400,000 to the bottom line and a quick jump in the share price, so that top executives can exercise their options.

For the diffuse thinker, this layoff severs nine hundred relationships, in many of which vital knowledge has been stored and is accessible. It negatively affects the morale of the nine hundred survivors, the best of whom will probably seek a better employer and the worst of whom will keep their heads down. The company will have lost the trust of its employees, and those lofty mission statements will now be objects of derision. How you think of downsizing—specifically or diffusely—will decide how readily you resort to it (Figure 5.6).

While specificity focuses on the product, diffuseness considers the entire process by which the product is conceived, designed, developed, manufactured, distributed, and maintained. While America leads the world in product innovation, Japan, Singapore, Korea, and other East Asian cultures may imitate Western products but originate new processes of making these. By reengineering, by omitting several manufacturing steps, and by parallel processing, the "same" product can be produced in less time and at far lower cost. Fixing the process rather than the product may generate superior results.

Robert Reich has pointed out that companies in the United States typically put manufacturing at one site and research and development hundreds of miles away in a leafy environment. Products move from stage to specific stage, first developed, then manufactured, then marketed. In contrast, East Asian cultures typically develop and design for easier manufac-

AT ITS BEST, DIFFUSENESS...

...IS FRACTAL AND SELF-SIMILIAR

...MAKES QUALITY EVERYONES' JOB

FIVE TIMES WHY

COMPLEX INTERACTION

WORK AS PROCESS

KANJI FOR "TENSION"
BOW + STRING + STRETCH

Figure 5.6

ture and distribution and locate all these functions at single sites, where the researchers make the product easier to distribute and to service. A diffuse view of manufacturability, easier distribution, and cheaper maintenance sees a single process linking all stages of supply, distribution, and use.

Diffuse ways of thinking make it possible to connect ideas that in Western cultures are polarized. Japanese and Chinese pupils learn thousands of *kanji* (composite Chinese characters) while still at school. Many of these have composite meanings like "crisis in which there is opportunity," "competing while cooperating," "optimism aware of pessimistic possibilities." For example, the *kanji* for "tension" is a diffuse composition of characters denoting "bow," "string," and "stretch." In Chapters 2 and 4 of this book we have already seen that wealth is created through reconciliation. We have to grasp that reconciliation is a diffuse not a specific process, although it may combine specific objectives and thereby represent a composite of specifics.

The insight that values thought to be opposed are, in favorable circumstances, complementary (a theme touched upon throughout this book) cannot be realized without thinking diffusely. There is also an increasing realization that we face complexity, as product is connected to product, computers to peripherals, automobiles to satellite navigational systems—all embedded in vast seas of knowledge. The single, stand-alone product is becoming a rarity, and at the economy's leading edge increasing complexity is the rule.

Finally we need to think diffusely to understand networks, especially the Internet. In much of economics there is a law of diminishing returns. Raw materials are exhausted, markets mature, products become commodities, new entrants crowd in, consumers become satiated. This is a variation on entropy, the gradual deterioration of organized natural phenomena. But more recently we have noted a "law of *accelerating* returns," which results from the "net effect" of business units joined into a network.

This effect comes about because every additional member of a network hugely increases the number of relationships. Hence the one-thousandth member to join a network generates nine hundred and ninety-nine additional relationships. The huge share prices for those Internet companies, yet to make any profit at all, testifies to investors' confidence in accelerating returns.

But Taken Too Far . . .

Diffuse culture can become a behemoth. Diffuse or "grand theories" like Maoism regard every crime they commit as occurring "in its historical context." This vast sweep of history dwarfs all specific cruelties, so the death of this or that bourgeois reactionary is as nothing compared with the larger revolutionary struggle.

Diffuse thinkers tend to subscribe to the "ethic of ultimate ends," as Max Weber called it. If the ends are sufficiently glorious and revolutionary, then the trails of blood leading to those ends can be overlooked. Every member of the struggle will be washed clean in the final hour (or shower) of victory. The ends are so ennobling, so edifying, so humane that specific cruelties will be as nothing compared with the vista of human benefits. Of course, this is a delusion. Each cruelty corrupts its perpetrators, and when the New Age dawns it will be as full of hate and recrimination as was the previous age.

Many theories like Freudianism and Marxism are diffuse in a way that prevents them from being invalidated by any conceivable events. If we believe that a child "hates his father" but he denies this, can we then conclude that he "hates his father at an unconscious level"? If our bourgeois enemy has "false consciousness," are we justified in ignoring his protests at being persecuted? Whether the child admits or denies his hate, we persevere in our diagnosis. Whether the bourgeois citizen protests or accepts his persecution, we still believe it justified. The holders of such beliefs need to explain how they would know if they were wrong. The truth is that their diffuse thinking styles have erected barriers against invalidation. Any objections by their victims are explained away.

Diffuse thinking tends to stress the aesthetics, the harmony, the closeness of relationships. Relationships of *amae* ("indulgent care") between seniors and juniors are especially prized. But what if a subordinate disagrees? What if she has an independent (specific) thought that conflicts with prior understandings? The problem with "beautiful relationships" is that any rebellion is seen as ugly, ungrateful, and insensitive. You finish up hugged to the corporate bosom by so many diffuse connections that any genuine dissent is impossible (Figure 5.7).

In a diffuse organization dissenters are pushed out to the peripheries where fewer and fewer people engage them, and they lose influence as they lose their centrality. You arrive in a meeting to discover that the decision has already been made informally, by those who have preserved their relationship. You may be permitted to object, but no one will support you. The harmony of insiders defeats the isolation of outsiders. This has the effect of slowing down needed changes and preventing incremental adjustments to the outside world. A *shokku* (shock), to use the Japanese word, is necessary for diffusely connected insiders to recognize the need to change. When the change comes it may be radical, but it is overdue. Japan's history

BUT TAKEN TOO FAR...

THE CONTEXT OF HISTORY

THE UNFALSIFIABLE THEORY

HUGGED TO THE CORPORATE BOSOM

EVERLASTINGLY GRATEFUL

...ONLY SHOKKU CAN CHANGE IT

Figure 5.7

is punctuated by *shokku,* from the black ships sailing into Tokyo harbor to atomic defeat in World War II to its recent prolonged recession.

Diffuse relationships have a tendency to maintain hierarchy through reciprocal obligations. Because a powerful superior can always do more for a relatively powerless person than the latter can do for his superior, the powerless person is forever obligated. However hard he tries to repay his moral "debt," the powerful superior always remains ahead in this exchange. The junior must therefore reciprocate gratitude and deference, because his boss is so much "kinder" and "more generous" than he can be. Gratitude can keep us all in thrall to superiors whom we are afraid to disappoint. Moral indebtedness can constitute a burden before which we are obliged to bend.

Culture Clashes and Derivative Conflicts: In Business and Industry

One major difference between specific and diffuse cultures has been likened by Akio Morita, a founder of Sony, to the differences between bricklayers and stonemasons. A bricklayer orders bricks of specific kind in advance—whole bricks, half-bricks, glazed bricks, plain bricks—and slots them into prespecified places. The stonemason picks rough, uneven stones and chisels these until they fit together perfectly.

This contrast illumines the personnel policies of American and Japanese corporations. There is a market for specified skills (or bricks). You hire a machine operator, a director of marketing, a public affairs officer, all of whom are specialized in these specific roles. Japanese corporations prefer to mold and keep molding their personnel so that they fit into a variety of corporate roles. By the time an executive climbs to the top, she has represented the union, worked on the plant floor, acted as a salesperson, researcher, manufacturer, distributor, and so on. This diffuse multidimensional experience allows the person to understand all points of view and promote harmony.

"The bottom line" is one of American industry's most specific specifics, and for good reason. It is supposed to be a distillation of everything else of importance that is happening. Are customers pleased? Are costs being controlled? Is quality rising? The answers to these questions will eventually have an impact on the bottom line, which is the summation of all other specifics. You could also argue that the import of various other measures, like late deliveries, work in process inventories, and so on, is equal to their impacts on the bottom line.

Diffuse cultures, however, may be more concerned with more vague criteria, like goodwill and support from customers and the willingness of customers to remain loyal in the face of difficulties. Diffuse cultures would not deny that profits are necessary, but they would argue that the multiple bonds established with customers are the origins of these profits and the reason these profits can continue, even after mistakes have been made. Moreover, you lose or gain customer loyalty before profits start to dip or to rise, so that the relationship produces the bottom line, not vice versa.

Specific indexes are always more definite and unambiguous. They may force you to face facts. Yet diffuse relationships may inform you of what you have to do to restore your credibility and value to the customer. These may give you early warnings of a potential downturn in your business. It is noticeable that in market research, the United States and many Western economies prefer opinion sampling and statistical breakdowns, while the Japanese prefer open-ended conversations with customers. In a market research survey you can learn only what you think you need to know and have so specified in advance. In conversation, customers can change the subject, correct your misapprehensions, and communicate, in its totality, their point of view as opposed to yours.

Another important contrast in ways of conducting business is between *report* and *rapport,* a distinction made by linguist Deborah Tannen. In "report cultures" the emphasis is upon reporting specific facts, which would include your product and its "selling points." The assumption is that if the would-be customer is interested in the proposition you have to report, then there will be time to get to know each other and establish rapport. But if the customer is not interested, creating rapport wastes valuable time.

Rapport cultures approach this problem in the reverse sequence. The emphasis is on establishing rapport with customers, partners, and suppliers. If you come to like and trust one another, then you report on your specific proposition. If the potential partner does not seem amenable and trustworthy, you back off, thereby saving valuable time and not revealing your hand.

Deborah Tannen has argued that report versus rapport describes gender differences within the United States. Boys and girls are raised in different cultures and environments and have different life expectations.

For example, "Cynthia told Greg she was hurt because he fixed himself a snack without offering her any. So he offered her the snack he had just fixed. She turned it down. He asked why. Because he had not prepared it for her. Greg was exasperated. Was she hungry or not?" Greg is concerned with accurate *reports* on Cynthia's hunger. But for Cynthia, this is not the point. Greg has revealed his lack of rapport by not considering whether she would like a snack too.

BRICKLAYERS ———————— STONEMASONS

CUT THE WAFFLE — WHAT'S THE BOTTOM LINE?

THE BOTTOM LINE ———————— CUSTOMER GOODWILL

REPORT ———————— RAPPORT

Figure 5.8 Derivative Dichotomies of Specific–Diffuse in Business

What Tannen's research suggests is that all cultures need specific reports and rapport, and that pressure is put on American women to supply what would otherwise be missing (Figure 5.8).

Traditionally, men assumed the role of "breadwinner" (specific) and women were uniformly cast as "homemakers" (diffuse). Today, women, rightly in our view, regard those roles as evidence of a power play.

The eighties witnessed a fall in per capita income, partly repaired by two-income families in which women went out to work. Although women have as much right as men to the specific end of the continuum, children and families may suffer if no one agrees to play diffuse roles. The culture could shred itself on specifics.

Another variation on the theme of specific and diffuse is the division of labor (specific) versus the integration of labor (diffuse). Ever since Adam Smith's famous pin factory, classical economics has celebrated the division of labor. Smith held that a nation's wealth is a function of the extent to which its labor is divided. Common sense would decree that what has been divided must be reassembled and reintegrated, yet curiously the diffuse integration of labors has never received the equal treatment or attention it deserves.

One reason is that integration is not, in the early stages, problematical. Boss A instructs subordinates B, C, and D to specialize in the production of a pin. The pin emerges as a finished product because all three subordinates work for their boss to make the product.

But when you are making a forklift truck, the process is far too complex to be integrated by the diffuse authority of one person. Ways of integrating labors, departments, functions, and so on have to be devised. Yet the typical condition of U.S. corporations discovered in a series of classical studies by Paul Lawrence and Jay Lorsch is that of overdifferentiation and under-integration, Figure 5.9. The alternative to "chimneys" or "silos" with their overspecificity and isolation would appear to be the Big Boss, which no one wants either, and is typically rejected as a solution. Many corporations are thereby trapped between too great a division of labor, leading to bureaucratic divisions of labor, and too much "bossism" attempting to integrate those labors.

Other sources of specific versus diffuse dilemmas are two rival metaphors of the corporation, first summarized in detail by Gareth Morgan. There is the specific metaphor of the organization as a machine, or mechanism, designed to make money for its owners. Like any machine, it is reducible to its parts and is nothing more than its separate parts assembled. It should run efficiently, in the manner of a machine, so that when a manager steps on the brake or the accelerator, the machine should respond, with minimum waste of energy.

Like a machine, the organization consists of specific, replaceable parts, so if any part, human or mechanical, misfunctions, it should be replaced with a more reliable component.

Since real machines are among the most expensive assets a corporation owns—capable of manufacturing, say, 7 million cigarettes a day—it is often considered necessary for employees to serve machines, which are so much more expensive than they. Where employees operate computers, they may digitalize their thoughts to facilitate the human-machine interface. They may eschew uncodified ideas.

The alternative diffuse approach conceives of the corporation as an organism, a living system with the capacity to grow, unfold, and realize the information within its DNA. Here parts cannot be replaced without trauma, although certain organs may regenerate and grafts are possible. The organism transacts with its environments, absorbing nutrients and shedding fruits and/or leaves. The Japanese Sharp Company uses the image of an audio-digital technology tree, with the roots and trunk feeding knowledge to a branching set of products, depicted as twigs and leaves.

Neither the mechanical nor organic metaphor of the corporation is a perfect analogy. Arguably, a human system transcends both these analogies, but preferences for machine imagery or organic imagery reveal whether the corporate culture is specific or diffuse. An early study by Burns and Stalker suggested that the organic (or diffuse) image is characteristic of successful high-technology companies. Certainly an organism is a more complex image than a machine, and has the qualities of life.

Business planning also takes specific and diffuse forms. The straight-line forecast is a form of specificity. You are given a figure for future sales, or expected growth, that twinkles on its own like the morning star in the empty heavens. You are almost never told what the forecaster assumed or took for granted, or what kind of shift would invalidate the forecast, necessitating its revision. Just about its only virtue is its precision. You have been told exactly what to expect, yet the history of forecasting is pockmarked with fallen stars. The belief that the future will be like the present, only more so, is among humanity's more naive extrapolations.

A diffuse answer to the forecast is the scenario—an imagined, alternative future. From three or four of these model potential futures the company adopts whatever scenario appears to be coming more true. The idea is neither to guess nor to gamble on any one future, but model and hence recognize whatever future may eventuate. The concern is that in an increasingly turbulent world the shape of the future may not be recognized as a coherent system unless modeled in advance of its arrival. Once this future dawns it can be adapted to by those prepared to face it. Current conflicts and disturbances may have several possible outcomes, and scenario planners describe these potential futures with care.

Of course, scenarios may suffer from the limitations of diffuse thinking in general. They can be vague and impressionistic. Alternative outcomes require contingency plans. If one comes substantially true the others are "wasted." None have the precision of forecasts, yet they usually prevent a company from being unprepared and ready it to "see" and recognize what it has modeled. One reason companies like Shell develop scenarios is the volatility of oil prices, green protests, and Middle East politics. You should be ready for very different business environments.

A final distinction is between explicit knowledge, stored in recognized places like manuals, software, accounts, records, libraries, instructions, methodologies, and proprietary processes, and tacit knowledge, which is stored between people in relationships, cultures, understandings, meanings, and interactions. Tacit knowledge is often, although not always, creative and generative. When ideas are being hatched they remain tacit within and between us. Equally tacit is the knowledge of "who knows what." Individuals have made key inquiries, and communicating that learning from private experience to the public realm is no easy task. It requires A to remember that B and C had crucial experiences relevant to D's problem.

Knowledge is stored in cultures, but most of it has not been formally referenced, indexed, and filed. Rather, it is diffusely distributed within the corporation, among people who once worked together and have tacit recollections. Using explicit knowledge creatively may require that the existing meanings of the words and their classifications be suspended in order to make that knowledge tacit once more.

Tacit knowledge is also in our bodies and nervous systems, our judgments and intuitions. Why does a master baker produce delicious bread and cakes? The knowledge is in the kneading and in his hands. How does worker X produce dies accurately to one thousandth of an inch? She probably could not tell you, but if you pointed a video camera at her workstation you might make her tacit knowledge explicit. Her art can be your method. When we learn skilled habits, these seep from conscious awareness into tacit responses, diffused through our bodies and relationships.

The mind stores information in at least two ways: in specific parts of the brain (you would lose key abilities if those parts were damaged or surgi-

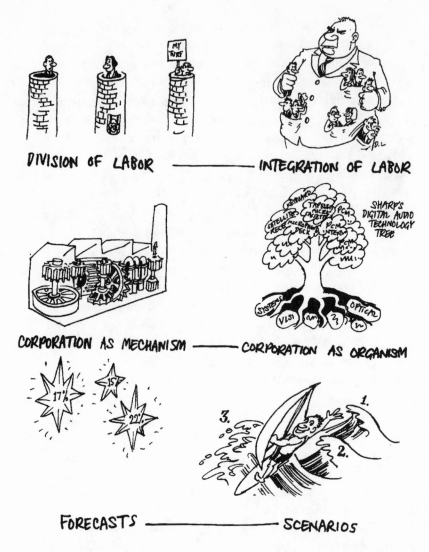

Figure 5.9 More Derivative Dichotomies of Specific–Diffuse in Business

cally removed) and distributed across areas of the brain in diffuse patterns. This is how memories are stored, so that one memory typically triggers a train of associations. If the memory area of the brain (the striate cortex) is damaged, virtually no single memory is lost. Memories do not seem to inhabit different areas. Rather, the entire pattern of memory appears to be distributed across the striate cortex.

What happens in those with severe brain damage is that their memories grow fuzzy and begin to fade. It is as if the whole pattern is mutually rein-forcing in its repetitions in order to clarify. With loss of repetition, clarity is lost. Like our brains, cultures store knowledge as specific structures and distribute knowledge diffusely. Yet cultures value these contrasting attri-butes in unequal ways (Figure 5.9).

Culture Clashes and Derivative Conflicts: In Ethics, Science, and Politics

One of the oldest bifurcations, depicted in classical literature, is that be-tween Scylla (the rock) and Charybdis (the whirlpool). These were suppos-edly located in what is now the Straits of Messina, between Italy and Sicily. Sailors navigating this narrow passage were in danger of being sucked down into the whirlpool if they were overly concerned with avoiding the rock, and of being smashed against the rock if they tried to skirt the whirlpool.

Now this mythical rock is clearly specific—hard, solid, high, visible, public, and static. In contrast, the mythical whirlpool is diffuse—soft, liq-uid, deep, invisible, private, and dynamic. You see the rock looming up be-fore you hit it. You feel the whirlpool pulling down before it absorbs you. In every way these two phenomena contrast with each other. Yet in their wis-dom, the ancient Greeks knew that survival depends on being equally con-scious of both forces.

Another ethical dichotomy is between consequence ethics and deontol-ogy (or duty ethics). Consequentialism, which includes the "happiness cal-culations" of Jeremy Bentham, the utilitarianism of John Stuart Mill, and the pragmatism of John Dewey, is concerned with the results of ideas, methods, and policies. "That which truly guides us is true . . . we take it as our point of departure that ideas have consequences," wrote Dewey. This statement has an obvious appeal to the commercial sector. A good strategy produces the goods. Good intentions may be insufficient if we have not learned to translate them into results.

Deontology, or duty ethics, regards certain acts as good in themselves, emanating as they do from good intention and a sense of duty and obliga-tion. If such acts result in human benefit, so much the better. But their goodness does not spring from the result as much as from duty translated into action, translated into result—a much more diffuse concept.

The Golden Rule is deontological (from *dei*, which means "must"). You must do unto others as you would wish them to do unto you. You can disobey a law, argued philosopher Immanuel Kant, but you must do so by an act from which a new and better law can be made. Arguably, this kind of disobedience was achieved in the United States by nonviolent civil rights demonstrations, which were followed by passage of the Civil Rights Act.

Consequence ethics are strongest in English-speaking cultures and are part of Anglo-American empiricism. French companies, in contrast, employ deontologists to advise on ethics; duty ethics is generally closer to the continental tradition of diffuse constructs mediated by conscience. Confucianism is also deontological, as is Hinduism.

While all political elections are results-oriented, the type of electoral system preferred varies among more specific and more diffuse cultures. Specific cultures like clear and specific outcomes. "First past the post" with a clear winner is popular with the most specifically oriented cultures—Britain, the United States, Canada, Australia. It does more than produce specific results, it exaggerates that specificity. Hence a 10 percent plurality in a British, North American, or Australian election may produce a 40 to 200 percent majority in parliament or electoral colleges. Mrs. Thatcher never had a majority of the British electorate voting for her, although her demeanor and sense of conviction suggested otherwise. Specific cultures give vast powers to the largest organized minority.

In contrast, more diffuse cultures prefer proportional representation, which permits a more diffuse range of political affiliations to share in government and tailors the proportion of votes cast to the proportion of representatives elected. Specific-thinking persons object that this weakens the responsibility of specific representatives to specific constituencies and favors small centrist parties in ad hoc coalitions with shifting allegiances—a diffuse "fudge" or messy compromise in smoke-filled rooms.

Cultures also vary considerably in whether they look at specific acts of criminality, the text, or concern themselves with the wider social environment in which crime occurs, the context.

In specific cultures like the United States, criminality is held to consist of specific acts. There can be no excuse for their commission, and the circumstances surrounding the act are given less weight than the act itself. Specific persons are held responsible for specific acts, for which society may specify the penalty. This may even take the form of a tariff, defined in advance, like "three strikes and you're out." The United States has over 1.1 million citizens in jail.

A diffuse culture is more concerned with the social context that helped

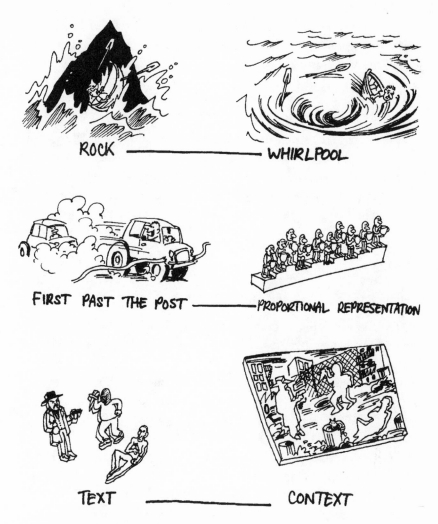

ROCK —————————— WHIRLPOOL

FIRST PAST THE POST ————— PROPORTIONAL REPRESENTATION

TEXT ————————— CONTEXT

Figure 5.10 Derivative Dichotomies of Specific–Diffuse in Ethics and Politics

generate the crime in the first place—unemployment, lack of opportunity, racial prejudice, poor education, drug addiction, and welfare dependency. It is more concerned with the culture of prison (which teaches criminality to first offenders), with the social dynamics of gang culture, with the effect of organized crime and drug cartels.

Specific and diffuse approaches may depend on who commits the crimes. When black criminals in ghettos commit crimes a specific view is taken and greater toughness advocated. When white middle-class high school students shoot other students, as in Littleton, Colorado, there is much soul-searching as to the role of their social environment, parents, teachers, belief systems, and the availability of handguns (Figure 5.10).

What Are the Origins of the Specificity–Diffuse Dimension?

So far we have not speculated on the origins of the Specific–Diffuse continuum. Indeed, it may not matter to cultural studies what these origins are so long as we recognize the pervasiveness of the distinction.

At least four possible sources of the Specific–Diffuse dimension recommend themselves.

- The complementary aspects of energy
- The duality of brain functions
- How we get to know strangers
- Public and private cultural space

The source does not, of course, have to be any one of these. All four may reinforce a single cultural distinction, or we may be studying an important cultural bifurcation with multiple origins. These may be distinctive forces that overlap and superimpose themselves in practice. Cultures are pretty messy and include many successive overlays and accretions.

The Complementary Aspects of Energy

For many centuries since the Greek atomists, we have assumed that energy is atomistic and object-like, consisting of specific particles. Matter was analyzed into smaller and smaller entities until the bottom fell out of the whole corpuscular concept.

Energy was found to have two complementary forms, that of particles and that of diffuse waveforms. Moreover, the discovery of these dual forms depended upon the instruments used by investigators. If a wave detector was used, waves were found. If a particle detector was used, particles were found. So small were the phenomena being investigated that our instruments affected the phenomena being studied. This was known as the Principle of Complementarity.

According to Heisenberg's Uncertainty Principle, we could specifically measure the position of a subatomic phenomenon, but in that case its diffuse momentum would be uncertain. Or, we could measure its momentum only to lose sight of its specific position.

What is clear from such discoveries is that we do not know subatomic phenomena "as they really are" but only as these interact with the mind of the investigator. The mind helps create the reality it perceives.

This happens in theoretical physics because the entities being examined are so small that our instruments are gross invasions. It happens in culture for a different reason, however, because the phenomena being investigated are alive and therefore react to the demeanor of the investigator.

The Duality of Brain Functions

This reactivity to the knower by the known parallels the two hemispheres of the human brain. Could the dual nature of energy, as particles and as waves, represent the imposition of left and right hemisphere brain functioning upon phenomena?

In most persons, the left brain hemisphere controls the more assertive right side of the body. It is analytic, reductive, rational, verbal/numeric, sequential, segmented, and propositional. The right brain hemisphere, controlling the body's left side, is holistic, synthesizing, intuitive, tacit, visual-spatial, continuous, and appositional (Figure 5.11).

In the English language the right brain, wired to the left side of the body, is generally distrusted. Hence the word "sinister" means not only on the left side but also strange and potentially threatening.

There is a vast popular literature on left-hemisphere dominance in the United States, but the specificity bias shows itself most clearly in the polarization between the brain hemispheres. Pop psychology literature classifies people according to left and right: *Men Are from Mars, Women from Venus, Drawing on the Right Side of the Brain*, and so on. But the emphasis on differences and stereotypes is itself specific. You have not overcome specificity by joining the counterculture or identifying yourself as right-brained. You have simply strengthened one more polarity. What remains largely neglected is the communication between, and the integrity of, the right and left hemispheres. Yet this is almost certainly where moral development lies.

How We Get to Know Strangers

All cultures must break down barriers and communicate with strangers, both within the culture and with foreign cultures. How they do this takes two distinct forms: starting specifically or starting diffusely.

This contrast is shown by the two spirals in Figure 5.12. The one on the

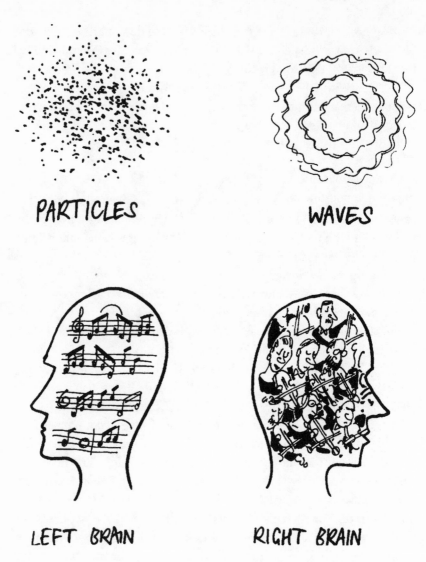

PARTICLES

WAVES

LEFT BRAIN

RIGHT BRAIN

Figure 5.11 Origins of Specific–Diffuse Dimension

left starts at the center with specifics and spins outward to include relationships. The one on the right starts at the periphery, relating diffusely, and then spins inward to encompass specific aims.

For example, do I start with my specific proposition—the product, its selling points, how much profit the foreign distributor is likely to make from handling it—and go on to make friends only if the potential distributor shows a lively interest? Or do I start by diffusely relating to my potential distributor—getting to know her, establishing trust, finding out about her background, gauging her level of courtesy, respect, diligence, and responsiveness—and then talking about products, profits, and specific advantages?

Specific communication styles tend to be forthright, blunt, and confrontational. You "tell it like it is," "call a spade a spade," and hope that you will not cause offense. Diffuse communication styles are indirect—drop hints, and let the other interpret your full meaning. You "tread gently" and hope the implications of what you have indicated have been fully grasped.

At its best, specificity is bold and assumes that the recipient can take it on the chin. At its worst, specificity can be tactless and hurtful. At its best, diffuseness assumes in the other enough sensitivity to decode your message, if and when he is ready to do so. In the meantime you save his face. At its worst, diffuseness is evasive, slippery, and full of euphemisms, designed to let both of you off the hook.

Which approach is superior? It is very hard to say. You can waste considerable time cosying up to a would-be partner only to discover that she lacks the drive and enthusiasm needed to represent you effectively. However, you can waste even more time by appealing to the greed and opportunism of a crook and finding out years later that he is unreliable. Engaging persons on very broad agendas smokes out the unreliable, those whose "friends" turn out to be victims. The dishonest cannot prepare in advance for rambling conversations.

Francis Fukuyama has suggested that diffuse approaches to initial trust building are more typical of low-trust countries in Latin America and Southeast Asia. In these countries, trust may not extend far beyond the family and therefore must be carefully built by extensive interaction. In the United States trust can be taken for granted, so the parties will first discover if either is interested in the specifics of the business. We are not as confident as Fukuyama in this thesis, but it is worth studying. Do Southeast Asian and Latin nations spend more time on diffuse socialization because they lack trust or value trust, or both? Whatever we conclude, the differences are plain. It is "rude," "crude," "aggressive," and "narrowminded" in the eyes of diffuse cultures when Americans try to persuade them to sign contracts. It is "evasive," "time-wasting," "ritualistic," and "ceremonial" in the eyes of Americans and English-speaking businesspeople to "beat around the bush" instead of "getting to the point."

Public and Private Cultural Space

Our fourth and final origin of the Specific–Diffuse distinction has to do with the uses of public and private space within cultures.

Do its members locate themselves in a shared public space or in mutual private spaces? The distinction, carefully drawn in Figure 5.12, derives from the work of the German-American psychologist Kurt Levin, who compared U-type culture (American) with G-type culture (German).

Specific U-type cultures have large public spaces in which even personal issues are discussed as if they were public issues, not private ones. For example, I may hear at a cocktail party in California from the mouth of a complete stranger that his daughter attempted suicide, his wife is leaving him, he has fired his psychiatrist, and he believes the problem lies in his failure to achieve simultaneous orgasm with his wife. I may have done nothing to invite these confidences. Indeed, he may be practicing being "open" and testing this out on me. His sex life is not the only item placed in the public realm. So is his car, to which he tosses me the keys. So is my refrigerator, which he opens and then helps himself. So is every room in my house, which he inspects and admires. When we both leave the area to move to other states, much of our furniture will go into a yard sale and be repurchased in our new homes.

One result of a large public space and a small private one is the objectification of much of our lives. His sex life, his car, his wife, his daughter, my refrigerator, my rooms are all specific items located in public space and are casually picked over and discussed as if they were public events.

Another characteristic of public space is its segmentation. I may be the superior of my friend at work but his equal socially and his inferior at accessing the Internet. He will accordingly call me "Professor Hampden-Turner" during a public lecture, and "Chuck" or even "Chuckles" when helping me get on-line.

Diffuse, G-type cultures are quite different. Here the public space is quite small. I reveal to others only my most formal, polite, and surface attributes. My private space is very large and within it would be my Mercedes, which I lend to no one, and my refrigerator and private rooms, which even dinner guests should not poke around in. My sex life is completely private, and if I were to discuss it with a third party, I would choose a close relation to confide in.

It is not easy to get into my private space, but once in, my friend is dif-

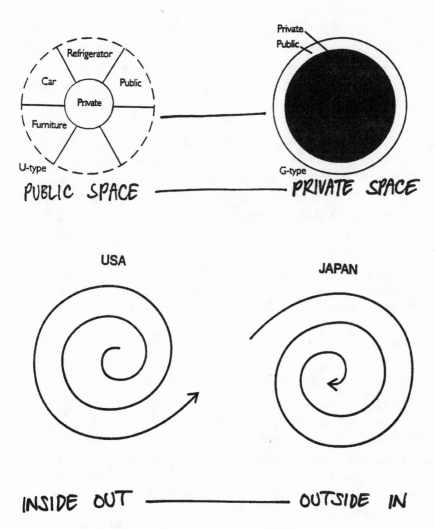

Figure 5.12 Origins of Specific–Diffuse Dimension, Part 2

fusely related to me. I know many private things about him as he does of me, about which both of us are discreet. Such friendships are close and long-lasting, sustained by shared confidences. There may be small rituals to celebrate our intimacy. He will call me *du* and not *sie* or *tu* and not *vous*, and we will drink to it.

Our relationship will not be segmented. If I am senior to him at work, our friendship may be taboo. In any case I will be Herr Doktor Hampden-

Turner at work, in the faculty club, in the supermarket, and even when tinkering with my computer at home. My wife will be Frau Herr Doktor to everyone who knows her formally and "Shelley" to those who know her intimately. There is no segmentation, except between a small public space and a large private one.

You do not have to be in France or Germany for long to notice the relative reserve, emphasis on privacy, shuttered houses, private gardens, and high walls. If you go to dinner you do not follow your host into her study, where she has gone to fetch a book. You do not enter the kitchen uninvited or explore the house. Because close, diffuse relationships are special and rare, you spend time and effort cultivating them.

One result of operating in public or in private space is that existing relationships may be very tenacious in the face of new specific data and promises. We recall a salesperson from an American electronics company in Germany who proved to a customer, using industry figures, that his product was measurably superior. Why did he not win the account immediately?

He discovered why when he tiptoed back into the customer's office to retrieve his umbrella. His customer was on the phone telling his regular supplier that he had two months to equal the new specifics. The diffuse relationship was being used to demand specific improvements.

There is one more bifurcation, which we address in detail in Chapter 6 but should be mentioned here. Money is specific but wealth creation is diffuse, as is the approach we take in this book concerning the creation of value. We ask, "Does the finance and banking sector of an economy help the process of wealth creation or feed upon it?" As we shall see, this is a very significant issue.

6 Reconciling Specificity with Diffuseness

STORIES AND CASES

Unlike the previous two dimensions we have identified, Universalism–Particularism and Individualism–Communitarianism, the dilemma of Specificity–Diffuseness is much more evenly contested in the United States. While specificity is clearly the stronger, especially in business, there has always been a strong dissenting voice within the culture. Moreover, while Newtonian science traditionally champions specificity, the arts and literature tend to champion diffuseness.

The very act of telling a story involves a narrative flow, a continuous stream of conscious experience by the protagonists. What we get from classic American literature, as opposed to contemporary best-sellers, is a theme that highlights cultural excess and champions a remedy. We get a critique of specificity, its cruelty and perils, and we get an account of the human spirit resilient in the face of oppression and showing the way to the reconciliation of the crisis.

A Story Told by American Culture

The Scarlet Letter, by Nathaniel Hawthorne, is a marvelously eloquent critique of Puritanism's excessive specificity, in this case an attempt to stigmatize and disgrace a young woman by making her wear the letter "A," for "adulteress," upon her bosom. The novel is a sustained plea to qualify the culture of Puritanism with the spirit of Renaissance humanism, left behind in Europe when the early settlers sailed to the New World.

Hester Prynne is the first and, arguably, the greatest heroine in American classic literature. She is an eloquent plea, not simply for gender equality but for the spirit of New England Transcendentalism, which included Margaret Fuller and championed women's rights, the abolition of slavery, and respect for the ecology of the natural world. Hawthorne knew Fuller, Ralph Waldo Emerson, Henry David Thoreau, and the denizens of Brook Farm, their utopian community, where he stayed.

Transcendentalism grew out of the Unitarian Church. Emerson, its pastor, led a revolt by a group of members. Unitarianism opposed the specificity of Father, Son, and Holy Ghost, the trinity, with the vision of one diffuse unity, or reconciliation. But Emerson was to go further. Transcendentalism preached the mythical unity of all humanity, and all faiths, with nature itself joined by the Divine Spirit.

It held that acts of individual conscience potentially transcended the individual to resonate with, and dwell among, the wider unity of nature. Act from conscience and a diffuse bond joins you to a developing universe, animated by ideals of justice and compassion. It is one of the greatest spiritual and literary movements to spring from American soil.

Hawthorne saw this philosophy as embodied in the nature of women, who were immensely influential in his life. He wrote *The Scarlet Letter* as self-imposed therapy following the death of his mother. The book was his testimony to her presence within him. He owed his literary circle to Elizabeth Peabody, who formed a modest literary salon around his works. He married her sister Sophie, to whom he read the chapters of *The Scarlet Letter*.

On several occasions in this book, Hawthorne mentions "the sainted Anne Hutchinson," an early dissenter from Puritan orthodoxy. Hutchinson had opposed the "covenant of works" (specific) with a "covenant of grace" (diffuse). You were saved not by an itemized list of your works, a doctrine which favored men, but by the grace of your entire influence and presence before your kindred creatures, a quality women could share. Anne was excommunicated when she tried to institute a dialogue with her persecutors and other religions. She led her followers to exile in Rhode Island, and she died in an Indian raid in a later settlement in New York State.

Desperately short of money, Hawthorne obtained a post at the Salem Custom House, from which he was dismissed shortly before his book was published. He came to associate the routine bureaucracy and the dull specificity of his working life with its Puritan origins. His essay "The Custom House" was used as an introduction to *The Scarlet Letter*. In it, he claims to have found "the letter" embroidered on a piece of cloth in a disused attic (unused imagination) of that dour edifice.

The story opens with a beautiful, dark-haired mother, Hester Prynne, emerging from the door of a prison, a baby in her arms. She is likened to the wild rosebush growing nearby. Sent ahead of her husband to establish their new home, she has succumbed to a seducer whom she will not name. She is condemned to sew and to wear upon her bosom the letter "A" as a public mark of her disgrace.

As she walks to the scaffold in the marketplace, we become aware of the first stirrings of inner defiance. Her head is high, her aspect is graceful yet bold, and on her bosom she has sewn a decorative "A" with such "fantastic flourishes" of gold thread that it has already become an emblem of her passion, her skill, and her fortitude. She will not name her seducer because she loves him still.

The man calling her to confess all is none other than the Reverend Arthur Dimmesdale, the town's new minister and Oxford divine of surpassing eloquence and learning, even now rising to the spiritual leadership of the community. Dimmesdale is the fictional forerunner of a long line of American evangelicals whose religious fervor is at odds with his urge to fornicate. It hardly surprises us anymore that he is her seducer. Of course!

The author makes it clear that Hester symbolizes Roman Catholicism and the diffuse aspects of religion now firmly repressed. "Had there been a Papist among the crowd of Puritans, he might have seen in this beautiful woman, so picturesque in her attire and mien, and with the infant at her bosom, an object to remind him of the image of Divine Maternity."

In the crowd surrounding the scaffold is her husband, Roger Chillingworth, an elderly physician, pale, thin, and musty as his books. She had thought him dead when his ship was attacked by Indians, but he survived capture and was ransomed. He presses a finger to his lips. He, too, will not share her disgrace. He treats her baby in prison and swears her to silence. He also swears to discover the identity of her seducer, and we see in his misshapen shoulders and the rage that transforms his features a diabolic zeal to seize not Dimmesdale's life, but his soul.

Hester makes her living by the skill of her needle. In Puritan society only the dead, the young, and the mighty are permitted adornment, so she lavishes her needlework on her child and on the ruffs and shrouds of prominent citizens. Her wretchedness and her outcast status give her a curious feeling that she can see into the hearts of the lonely, the suffering, and the oppressed.

Her child, Pearl, so called because of the great price paid to bring her into the world, has the grace and beauty of her mother but a wild, impish nature, a brilliant and flighty disorder, an embodiment of the tension in Hester's own soul. Treating the love of her mother as some fantastic sport, she has a nature uncomprehending of sorrow or quietude. Knowing other children will not play with her, she rushes at them with tiny fists flailing.

The first major crisis of Hester's motherhood occurs when the elders decide to remove Pearl from her care. Not waiting for the blow to fall, she seeks out the Governor, who is luckily in conversation with the Reverend Dimmesdale. In his rooms, she sees her scarlet letter hideously magnified by the Puritan breastplate of armor hanging on the wall. It is a relic of the Pequod War, in which an entire Indian tribe was massacred. The war within the breast of Puritanism is not unconnected to the wars without.

When Pearl refuses to recite her catechism before the Governor, matters come to a head and Hester passionately defends her right to motherhood. " 'God gave me this child!' cried she. 'He gave her in requital of all things else, which ye have taken from me. . . . See ye not, she is the scarlet letter, only capable of being loved, and so endowed with a millionfold the power of retribution for my sin? Ye shall not take her! I will die first!'" Then she turns to the agitated Dimmesdale, terrified that she will give him away. "Look thou to it! I will not lose the child! Look to it!"

The minister intercedes and Pearl is restored to her mother. But already we see the transcendental themes being worked out. The scarlet letter stands for ultra-specificity, the condemnatory mark, the Puritan hatred of privacy and personal relations, where rebellion may lurk. Like Hester, everything must be dragged from prison into the public market so that disgrace or piety can be pinned upon each person, just as the sins of two are pinned upon the one.

Pearl is the outraged offspring of this prejudice. Because she is diffuse, not specific, she is capable of being loved and giving love. Her mother is fighting for both their souls, the redemption of which lies in the relationship between them.

Transcendentalism is also at work in the varying fortunes of the protagonists. The Reverend Dimmesdale grows feebler and sicker by the day, even as his sermons and his ministry earn him fame and worship. There is a clear connection between the repression of truth and passion within him, and the moving eloquence of his sermons that denounce this evil. Specific words are not enough to save us, where diffuse integrity is lost. Dimmesdale is divided against himself. In the pulpit, he preaches: "He had told his hearers that he was altogether vile, a viler companion of the vilest. . . . The minister well knew—subtle, but remorseful hypocrite that he was!—the light in which his vague confession would be viewed. . . . He had spoken the very truth, and transformed it into the veriest false-hood. . . . Therefore, above all things else, he loathed his miserable self!" The minister increasingly lays his hand against his heart as if his hurt lay there.

In the meantime, Roger Chillingworth has effected a devilish division between mind and body, which so typifies Newtonian science. He moves into the minister's house the better to take care of his body, yet the better to torment his soul and so keep the division alive. He steals a look at the minister's breast as he sleeps, and what he sees convulses him in venomous delight.

Only Hester remains strong because she lives authentically. The pain in her heart and the defiance in her bosom is declared before the world. She stands for the truth that error is redeemable, suffering is redemptive, and grace joins the individual to a living world.

Increasingly worried about Arthur Dimmesdale's failing health, Hester confronts her physician husband. But he will not yield, so she decides she must warn Arthur. She contrives to meet him on one of his walks in the forest. Hawthorne uses the forest, with its disordered wildness, its fallen trees and murmuring brooks, as a diffuse counterpoint to the specific literalness of the Puritan settlement. Chaos confronts order. Complexity confronts simplicity. Spontaneity confronts calculation. This is Hester's territory, on the borders of conventional wisdom.

She tells Arthur of the devil beneath his roof and when he blames her, cries "Thou shalt forgive me!" While Pearl plays at some distance away, the lovers embrace fiercely. There is a whole, wide world, Hester tells him. Is not America vast, and beyond the forest is the sea. Desperately she urges him, "Exchange this false life for a true one. Be, if thy spirit summon thee to such a mission, the teacher or apostle of the red men. Or,—as is more your nature,—be a scholar and a sage among the wisest and most renowned of the cultivated world. Preach! Write! Act! Do anything save to lie down and die!" When Arthur tells her he cannot be alone without human support, she answers "Thou shalt not go alone!" They arrange to book passage on a ship to England.

After seven years of falsehood the minister has now enjoyed an hour or so in the company of one who knows and loves him for what he is. He strides back to the settlement with new vigor in his step, yet assailed by doubts, temptations, and heresies. He is also pleased that their planned flight will occur after the election sermon he is to preach the next day. He will have the last word!

In the interval of years, the meaning of the scarlet letter, the supposed Word of God, true for all time, has begun to change. Although the townspeople well remember the original occurrence, they now tell children and each other that it stands for "Able," "Admirable," even "Angel." The message of Transcendentalism is that the human spirit can transcend and transform the specific letter of the law.

Yet the escape of the two lovers is blocked when Roger Chillingworth books passage on the same ship, having discovered their plans to flee. Dimmesdale delivers an election sermon of more pathos and power than ever before. When the procession passes the old scaffold, near which stand Hester and Pearl, he suddenly breaks away and, leaning on Hester for support and pushing Chillingworth away, mother, child, and minister ascend the scaffold and stand before the community holding hands, between which a great charge of energy surges.

Before everyone, Dimmesdale confesses his adultery and owns his family, then rips apart his vestment to bare his chest. There, seemingly burned upon his skin and hideously inflamed, is the Scarlet Letter. He begs Pearl to forgive him and to kiss him—an act she had refused in the forest. "Pearl kissed his lips. A spell was broken. The great scene of grief, in which the wild infant bore a part, had developed all her sympathies; and as her tears fell on her father's cheek, they were the pledge that she would grow up amid human joy and sorrow, nor for ever do battle with the world, but be a woman in it."

Minutes later, Arthur Dimmesdale expires on the scaffold as Hester tells him they will spend their immortal lives together. "Surely, surely, we have ransomed one another, with all this woe!" Yet typically, Arthur cannot hope.

Chillingworth dies within the year, lost without the man who had fueled his hatred, but he leaves his estates to Pearl, who returns to Europe with her mother. There Pearl marries into Italian nobility.

Many years later, with her daughter married, Hester returns to the settlement, reoccupies her house at the edge of the forest, and sews back upon her breast the Scarlet Letter, now worn voluntarily and as a source of wonder and esteem. She decides to be a living testament to the power of the human spirit to transcend stigma. Forlorn once herself, she will comfort the afflicted as she once afflicted the comfortable.

"People brought all their sorrows and perplexities and besought her counsel, as one who had herself gone through a mighty trouble. Women, more especially—in the continually recurring trials of wounded, wasted, wronged, misplaced . . . passion—or with the dreary burden of a heart unyielded, because unvalued and unsought—came to Hester's cottage. . . . She assured them, too, of her firm belief, that, at some brighter period, when the world should have grown ripe for it, in Heaven's own time, a new truth would be revealed, in order to establish the whole relation between man and woman on a surer ground of mutual happiness."

As to the mutual happiness of men and women, or specific report being reconciled with diffuse rapport, we are still waiting, 150 years after Hawthorne wrote. But at least it is possible to diagram what Transcendentalism was trying to say.

When, years later, Hester dies, there is inscribed on her tombstone, next to Arthur's, "On a field, sable, the letter A, gules [shines]."

As Figure 6.1 illustrates, *The Scarlet Letter* begins (top left) with a dour, overly specific culture that brands a young woman for what a man has done to her. This leads (bottom right) to the raising of a wild, passionate child, enraged by her social ostracism. This child is reconciled to her father when he owns her publicly. In this process the stigma of adultery is transcended and transformed into Able, Angel, and Admirable, as the diffuse quality of human passion qualifies the rigid letter of the law. But more than this, the letter "A" shines upon its somber, black background, witness to the capacity of the human spirit to transcend the status quo.

We now wish to consider a second story, much more recent and made into a successful film. *The Apartment* does not compare with *The Scarlet Letter* in the demands made of its audience, but it does bring the conflict between Specificity and Diffuseness up to date.

While time has changed our attitudes toward sexuality and illegitimacy, it is not the threat to community survival that once it was; the conflict between the Specific and Diffuse lives on, as does the bias toward the specific. Also similar are the cruel consequences, with women suffering disproportionately.

SPECIFIC
LETTER
OF THE LAW

BLE
NGEL
DMIRABLE

"On a field, sable
the letter A, gules"

DIFFUSE SPIRIT OF PASSION AND TRUTH

Figure 6.1 The Scarlet Letter

The film's hero, C. C. Baxter, called Buddy or Buddy Boy by his male colleagues, is employed in a large insurance company, "Consolidated Life," in New York City. The film opens with a mass of insurance statistics. There are 8,842,783 inhabitants of New York, average height 5′6″. Laid end to end, they would reach to Karachi. The company employs 31,259. Baxter works in Ordinary Policies on the 19th floor, desk 861.

The three specifics in Baxter's life are his apartment on West 67th, the key to his apartment, which he lends to those who might promote him, and the key to the executive suite, which he covets. He works late because his apartment is occupied by colleagues for purposes of sexual adventure. In the opening minutes of the film he is kept waiting for over an hour to re-occupy his rooms and overhears the borrower tell his pick-up that it "belongs to some schnook from our office." Baxter has to work hard for a good "efficiency report."

Baxter's apartment neighbors, Dr. Dreyfuss and his wife, believe that Baxter is a serial seducer because of the "doubleheaders" they witness night after night. Rather pathetically, Baxter clings to this reputation. He is very much "one of the boys," discussing the charms of Fran Kubelik, the el-

evator girl, whom everyone sees each morning and who is a favorite subject for male bonding. Baxter chats up Fran with fascinating statistics on
average head-colds in the city, and he has learned her height, weight, age,
and illnesses from the card group insurance file.

Baxter's scam seems to be paying off as he is summoned to see Jeff Sheldrake, the personnel director, from whom he expects a promotion. But Jeff
has learned about the key and, after scaring Baxter with threats about the
vice squad, agrees that Baxter is "executive material" and should be promoted, provided that he, too, will get the key to the apartment.

We now discover who Sheldrake wants to bed. It is Miss Kubelik. They
meet in their favorite haunt, a Chinese restaurant, where he succeeds in
rekindling an affair that began the previous summer, by claiming to be
ready to divorce his wife. Fran is both in love with him and conscious that
she is being exploited. She calls his overture "music to string her along by,"
but goes with him to Baxter's apartment.

Next day, Baxter returns to Jeff a woman's compact found in his apartment. The mirror is cracked. "She threw it at me," laughs Sheldrake. "You
see a girl a couple of times a week, and sooner or later she thinks you'll divorce your wife. Not fair, is it?" Baxter agrees, "No, especially to your wife."

The Christmas party has started. Miss Olsen, Sheldrake's secretary, gets
drunk and tells Fran that there have been six girls, including Olsen, all
taken to the same booth in the same Chinese restaurant and fed stories of
imminent divorce. Fran is devastated and has to hear from Baxter how he
is now the second youngest executive in the company.

That night at the apartment, which Sheldrake has occcupied, Fran
weeps. She apologizes for not being "a million laughs," tells him of Miss
Olsen's disclosures, and gives him a Christmas present, a record of music
from the Chinese restaurant. At this point Sheldrake reaches the acme of
specificity by giving her a hundred-dollar bill. She can buy what she likes.

Sheldrake leaves Miss Kubelik in the apartment to repair her face. Seeing some sleeping pills (the specific "cure" for cultural specificity), she
overdoses, leaving an envelope for Sheldrake with his money inside. Baxter, with a drunken pick-up in tow, returns to his apartment to find Fran co-
matose. He rushes next door to Dr. Dreyfuss. Together they save Fran's life,
making her sick, slapping her face, dosing her with coffee, and marching
her endlessly back and forth, "One, two, three, four!" She is finally placed
in Baxter's bed to sleep it off. Dr. and Mrs. Dreyfuss are furious with Bax-

ter, especially when he repeats Sheldrake's mantra. "You see a girl a couple of times. . . ." They protest, "Why don't you grow up? Be a *mensch!*" [yiddish for "human being"].

But Baxter still strives to maintain the illusion of ruthless seduction, a man who picks up a second girl while the first is dying. He is partly protecting Sheldrake but partly basking in the glory of "Easy come, easy go," as he puts it.

Baxter calls Sheldrake at home on Christmas Day, informing him of Fran's suicide attempt. Won't Sheldrake at least talk to her? No, says Sheldrake, he is delegating that specific task to Baxter.

So Baxter has company over Christmas while Fran recovers. He falls in love not just with her but with the diffuse process of caring for someone so vulnerable. Back at the office an angry Sheldrake has "let go" of his secretary, Miss Olsen, whom he blames for Fran's suicide attempt. But Miss Olsen, who has overheard her boss talking to Baxter about the overdose, telephones Sheldrake's wife and tells of all his affairs.

Next day Baxter gets his reward for having "managed" the Kubelik problem so well for his boss. He has been promoted again. He is about to offer Sheldrake "to take Miss Kubelik off your hands." But this is precisely the offer Sheldrake makes to him! His wife has fired him. He is on his own. He aims to live "the bachelor life" again.

But back in his office, the same day, the worm finally turns. Sheldrake has persuaded Fran to celebrate the New Year with him. He wants Baxter's key because he threw his duplicate from the window of the commuter train following Fran's overdose.

It is the moment of truth. "You will not take anyone to my apartment," Baxter says, "especially not Miss Kubelik." Sheldrake reminds him that it can take years to reach the executive suite but just thirty seconds to be out on the street. "Do you dig?" Baxter pulls a key from his pocket and drops it on Sheldrake's desk. "Now you are being bright," Sheldrake observes.

It is not the key to Baxter's apartment, however, but the key to the executive suite. "The old payola won't work," he tells his boss. "I'm taking doctor's orders. I've decided to become a *mensch*, a human being." Baxter goes home and starts packing.

Cut to a New Year's party at the Chinese restaurant. Sheldrake has been on the phone. He finally gets rooms for Fran and himself in Atlantic City. He explains, "You can blame Baxter. He point blank refused to let me use his apartment. He walked out. Quit. Threw that big fat job back in my face.

Figure 6.2 The Apartment

He said I couldn't bring anyone back to the apartment, especially Miss Kubelik! What's he got against you anyway?"

It is the stroke of midnight. The whole restaurant sings *Auld Lang Syne* and Sheldrake turns to toast the other diners. When he turns back to their table Fran is gone, running as fast as she can back to the apartment.

The championing of diffuse and romantic perspectives may, of course, be just good business. It was Hortense Powdermaker who observed of Hollywood that on the screen, love always triumphs, but behind the screen money wins. Whether or not we wish to be cynical, *The Apartment* portrays beautifully the struggle between specific and diffuse values in society.

Figure 6.2 illustrates this values clash in terms of the film. At top left are the prized objects and symbols of the macho business culture—keys, booze, pills, and black eyes. Female casualties are simply trophies of the chase, as love is exploited (bottom right). The cure and reconciliation includes harsh specifics (top right)—the slaps to Fran's face that make us wince, as does the coffee poured into her, the relentless marching up and down the apartment for much of the night. Baxter faces long hours of nursing and two nights in a chair. He must work his passage back to humanity to discover the value and fragility of life. Finally, he must sacrifice "the old payola," the corrupt rewards of his previous existence.

Should One Value Dominate or Both Be Reconciled?

Is the United States advantaged by its bias toward specificity, which classic literature and intelligent cinema join together in exposing?

One serious problem with a specificity bias is its tendency to substitute specific things—drugs, alcohol, gambling, one-night stands, and money—for diffuse social relationships. Alcohol and drugs mimic the effects of satisfying intimate relations, replete with thrills, highs, lows, and deeply relaxing comfort and contentment. But there is a crucial difference. Relationships demand social skills of mutuality. You give as good as you get, and you teach each other to please. Benefits to yourself are by indirection and reciprocity. You help calm your partner and through his or her serenity you share in what was co-created. You tease, provoke, excite, play, assuage, caress. There is co-responsibility for success or failure.

Drugs, alcohol, and exploitive sexuality, in contrast, "short-circuit" relationships. They are direct stimuli to your own nervous system, forms of emotional masturbation. You can kick a rival drug dealer to death and, instead of feeling disgust or remorse, use his stash to "mainline" and give yourself a high. Americans call this "substance abuse," as if it were the specific substance that were suffering the abuse! This kind of abuse has now reached epidemic proportions in the United States. Is it one more symptom of excessive specificity?

Gregory Bateson, the social anthropologist, conducted extensive research into alcoholism at the alcoholism ward in the Veterans Administration Hospital in Menlo Park, California, in the early sixties. He subsequently wrote a now famous article called "Towards a Theory of Alcoholism," in which he demonstrated the cultural roots of American male alcoholism. Clearly, there are many reasons for drinking to excess. Different cultures and different genders may have patterns all their own. Bateson's research remains brilliantly insightful into certain American cultural patterns that lead to addiction.

Bateson proposes that alcoholism represents an escape from an insane premise. What is that premise? Is it that the "self" or head should unilaterally control the body, as if it were a specific machine? There are few generalizations we can make of all alcoholics, but one of the safest is that their personal relationships are severely attenuated. One way in which this happens is the attempt to control one's spouse, children, subordinates, work colleagues, and so forth, as if one were tinkering with a boiler.

This manipulative lifestyle generates high levels of tension and anxiety, as controllees turn on their would-be controller. The alcoholic's typical reaction is to treat his own body as yet another specific to be managed. When he doses his body with alcohol, a depressant, he orders his body, "Relax!"

Unfortunately, his body is now so desperate to relax, so eager to be rescued from mounting tension, that one drink leads to a craving for more, culminating in total collapse. The body has escaped from the "insane premise" that it is a specific to be controlled by the "self."

Bateson puts "self" in quotes because it has been too narrowly specified and is defined to exclude "the weak flesh!" As with Dimmesdale, the addict is at war with himself, rejecting the idea that body and mind are a unified whole, that his body is trying to tell him something.

Figure 6.3 uses a cusp catastrophe surface to illustrate the two horns of the dilemma. *Catastrophe* (from the Greek, for the "downturn" at the climax of tragic drama) is created by pushing upward tension-generating specificity while at the same time pushing downward the relaxation of diffuse relationships. The effect—raising the upper horizontal edge of this surface while lowering the adjoining vertical edge on the left of the figure—is to produce a cusp or precipice, whereby the alcoholic "falls off the wagon" and "hits bottom" in a sudden, uncontrollable oscillation from overcontrol to loss of control with total collapse.

The Vicious Circle

We can trace the vicious circle by following the drunkard's footsteps. It begins at the top left of Figure 6.3 when he boasts that his willpower, or manipulative self, is stronger than his alcohol-craving body. His willpower will conquer his weakness, or as American postage stamps recently boasted, "Alcoholism: We can lick it." This slogan is not the cure, but a symptom of the malaise itself, which mistakes alcoholism for a noxious thing.

The vicious cycle repeats itself because every failure to remain sober and every collapse only reinforces the alcoholic's "insane premise" that he must control his body. When he wakes up in hospital or jail and relatives weep and reproach him, he simply vows that next time he will fight his own body more successfully. The more his relatives emote, the less he has to, so his emotions atrophy more completely. After all, he must learn to control himself! One wailing spouse is enough. The vicious circle goes on

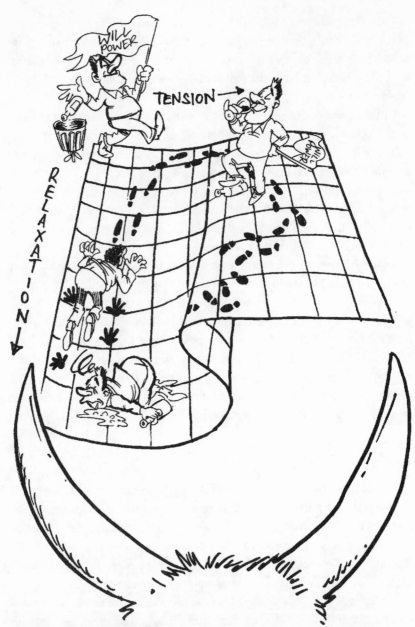

THE DILEMMA OF ALCOHOLISM

Figure 6.3

and on until death intervenes. He never realizes that his mind-body dualism is killing him. He grabs for control only to feel his own body lash back in surrender.

Bateson also explains how Alcoholics Anonymous, a grass-roots self-help organization, has proved more successful than the disease-driven medical model, which specifies alcoholism as an "illness." AA starts by attacking "alcoholic pride," the macho belief in the narrow "willpower" that can "beat the bottle." At AA meetings all members must testify: "My name is [first name]. I am an alcoholic." It is crucial to admit that you are not stronger than your condition and that you cannot drink again, ever. Where this admission is not made, AA will not accept you into diffuse membership. It will typically wait for you to "hit bottom" among the garbage cans and then ask you to try again.

God plays an important part in AA's philosophy, an ecumenical deity more powerful than you, with whom you must co-exist in humility and serenity. Here "God" represents the wider physical, social, and ecological environment that transcends us all. Equally important is the anonymity of the alcoholic. This is not, as some believe, a device to save face or maintain respectability, but a way of countering alcoholic pride. The recovering alcoholic can easily become "intoxicated" by "beating alcoholism," which is where we come in! Only by remaining anonymous and acknowledging help from fellow members can his new balance be preserved.

A crucial part of AA's cure is substituting a diffuse relationship for a specific drug. AA provides a "buddy system," a close friend who will sit with you until the urge to drink passes. This arrangement brings relaxation and balance through an indirect relationship, not a specific dose. It begins the process of repairing social-emotional skills and intimate relationships.

You relax in friendship and conviviality, as illustrated by the two edges of the geometric surface in Figure 6.4 moving back into balance and the cusp or precipice disappearing. This is what AA means by serenity—a gentle, ecological relationship among contrasting values. The Serenity Prayer states: "God grant us the serenity to accept the things we cannot change, the courage to change the things we can, and the wisdom to know the difference."

Among the things we cannot change is our interdependency with others and with our own bodies. If we treat these like specific things, we inflict

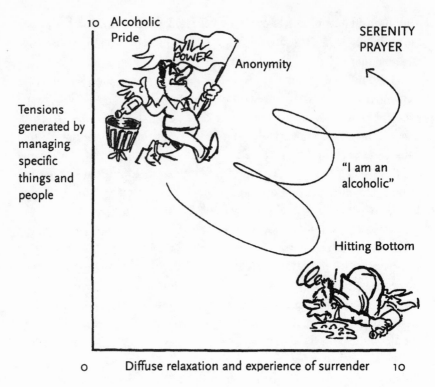

Figure 6.4 Recovering from Alcoholism

misery on ourselves and others. The dilemma and its reconciliation is shown in Figure 6.4.

We may conclude, therefore, that when one value, specificity, dominates, this can lead not only to the oppression of women like Hester Prynne and Fran Kubelik but also to addictive cultural patterns in which we become dependent on specific substances.

America's reliance on carefully specified remedies was never clearer than when the British author was asked to consult upon the "mental health delivery system" envisaged by what was then the National Institute of Mental Health. In evaluating the system, it was proposed to count the number of calls made by psychiatric social workers upon clients. Each call represented the "delivery" of a "unit" of mental health. An average social worker had a caseload of 110 clients, and calls lasted an average of six to seven minutes, during which "mental health" was ostensibly imbibed.

Evaluations showed that while clients expected to be told what to do and to be helped to do it, psychiatric social workers saw themselves as supplying "crucial insights" into the clients' "personal predicaments" that would facilitate them in taking independent action.

Behind this philosophy is the concept of "the helping stranger," the person whose clinical detachment permits the delivery of nuggets of penetrating insight. People who are already lonely and despairing do not need "helping strangers" or pints of psychiatric advice delivered to their doorstep. They need diffuse and personal relationships with their neighbors and family. Where welfare consists of money and other "deliverables," the system stagnates and perpetuates dependency on specifics. The "solution" is part of the problem.

In the business cases that follow, we show in each instance that wealth can be created (as opposed to money made) only by reconciling the specific with the diffuse in a process of sustainable development. We are not speaking of ripping and running, wherein specific gains are usually the aim, but of generating more wealth together than each of us had to begin with. This requires diffuse processes as well as specific elements.

Case 1: The Ungrateful Supervisor

Jeff was a twenty-eight-year-old Israeli, a "local hire" off the streets of Tokyo. He worked for Motorola Nippon, a largely autonomous Japanese subsidiary of Motorola, the American electronics corporation. Jeff was part of a four-person sales force for complex land-mobile products (LMP) sold to companies and municipalities with their own fleets of vehicles or aircraft. LMP allowed all fleet vehicles to communicate with each other and with central control.

Jeff worked under the supervision of Muneo, his Japanese manager. One consequence of being "a local hire" was that Muneo had almost complete authority over him. There were no expatriate arrangements with headquarters. Jeff felt from the beginning that Muneo did not like him. At his first interview he was told his salary was too high. When Jeff met and became engaged to a Japanese woman, Muneo made clear his disapproval, although other Japanese in the office offered their services of mediation and seemed eager to help the young couple in any way.

Muneo also refused Jeff's request for a lower sales quota because of Jeff's difficulty with the Japanese language. However, thanks to his fiancé, soon to be his wife, Jeff's Japanese language skills were improving rapidly.

Like many minorities before him, Jeff believed that he had to prove him-self by working harder. He got up at 6:30 AM and scheduled four sales vis-its a day.

After nine months in the job Jeff was outselling the three other sales ex-ecutives in his unit, all Japanese. After eighteen months he had outsold all three of them put together. This was, he felt, a triumph of hard work and persistence. He was out in the field 95 percent of the time and rarely both-ered his boss.

It was therefore a considerable shock when Jeff received an "average" rating from Muneo at his annual appraisal meeting. This was the lowest mark possible, short of "unacceptable," which would have led to termina-tion. It was also the worst appraisal in the department. Jeff was too angry to argue with Muneo, but appealed his "flagrantly unfair" appraisal to Mo-torola's international human resources function.

After an interval of some months, international HR came down on Jeff's side and his appraisal was revised upward. Muneo not only refused to speak to Jeff, he refused to look at him. Finally Jeff asked for a meeting. Muneo was so angry he could hardly speak.

"You shoot me, I shoot you," he repeated. Jeff's story was told to us in the course of researching a quite different issue. We had not been hired to help him or to consult on this problem. Yet the pain of his situation and the seeming injustice was so palpable that we made the following diagnosis and recommendation.

"Given specific American and Israeli values, you have performed ex-tremely well. Your sales record speaks for itself, as does the long hours you have worked, the number of customers contacted, and the fluency of your Japanese. It is even to your credit that you did this all by yourself and did not bother your boss.

You were also within your rights in appealing his appraisal of you, which does not match the results you achieved. Judged by these specifics, you have a strong case and your treatment was unfair. The facts speak for themselves.

But you are now living and working in Japan, not Israel or the United States, and you must expect to be judged by Japanese values, which are less specific and far more diffuse than the values to which you are accustomed. We have tried to recreate Muneo's objections to your conduct from what we know of Japanese management culture. For your sake, we thought it un-wise to approach him directly and stir up rancor.

Muneo is angry with you because you began by asking for favors rather than concentrating on how you could help him and your team. When your successes began, you did not inform him, solicit his advice, or invite him to share that success. You did not inform other team members about the information and approaches underlying your record sales, so that they could benefit from your knowledge.

"Not bothering him," was seen by Muneo as a snub, not a favor. As your boss he was formally responsible for your successes and wanted to play a genuine part in these. He probably feels you cut him out of participating in your triumphs.

Appealing over his head to the foreign owners of the company is experienced by Muneo as an insult to his authority and as undermining the local autonomy of Japanese management. That you did not warn him of your appeal or discuss it with him first is a rejection of your relationship with him and the ideal of mutual respect between you. To have a local decision reversed by U.S. headquarters is a matter of shame for him. He loses face before other Japanese colleagues by provoking interference in domestic affairs.

We recommend bimonthly meetings with Muneo and the Japanese sales team in which you seek their advice and share the background information on your successes. For Muneo to be pleased, the whole team must succeed and Muneo himself must lead that success. So seek his advice and support for every move you make and from the successes you have enjoyed try to draw conclusions useful to the whole group. Be as modest as you can, and let the value of shared knowledge speak for you."

This case is illustrated in Figure 6.5. Jeff, our "client" in this case, had four choices. He could stand by his specific sales record (top left). He could abandon his own values and embrace not just a Japanese wife but Japanese value preferences (bottom right) by agreeing with Muneo that his performance was "average." He could accept Muneo's invitation to a "shoot-out" (center), or he could reconcile himself to Muneo by helping to build a better-informed team (top right). The last we heard was that Jeff had greatly improved his relationship with his boss and that improved performance had spread to the team.

Case 2: What Type of Airline Service?

The Specific–Diffuse distinction is useful in distinguishing the policies of airlines in different cultures. Do you provide a service that consists of

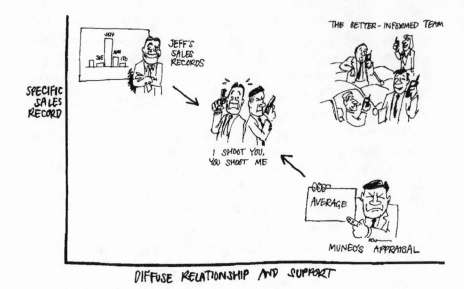

Figure 6.5 The Ungrateful Supervisor

specifics—a seat, a drink, a meal, a video—for which passengers pay on a per-item basis, or do you provide a diffuse and seamless service in which everything is thrown in—champagne, slippers, dinner served by a professional staff?

The problem with diffuse service is that you must pay for it and the frills are expensive. The problem with specific items is that you must fiddle for small change and the airline seems niggardly. They are so worried about giving anything away that in first-class American airline seats at breakfast time, you are lucky to get a pretzel. In contrast, French, British, Dutch, and Belgian airlines will serve you a hot breakfast in the thirty-five minutes of flight time between their capitals, and you pay for it anyway. "Singapore service" is widely regarded as the acme of customer care, but Singapore Airlines is almost exclusively long-haul, with business-class passengers featured prominently, so it is somewhat easier for them to choose between these values.

A fascinating attempt to reconcile these values comes from the writing of Jan Carlzon, one-time head of SAS (Scandinavian Airlines). He introduced the concept of "moments of truth." Passengers do, indeed, want seamless service from their airline but they judge the value of that service from several "moments of truth." Passengers interact with staff somewhere between four and twelve times during a journey, and from these scattered encounters they draw whole impressions of that airline's attitude toward them.

"Moments" are, of course, specific, while "truth" is a diffuse integrity. Passengers catch glimpses of that integrity, or lack of it, from several momentary episodes of service. It follows that several small things can make a big impression. When the Dutch author of this book was seriously late for a presentation to Irish managers, Aer Lingus succeeded in negotiating an early landing at Dublin airport and allowed his limousine onto the edge of the tarmac for a swift getaway.

When airline controllers delayed an SAS flight to Stockholm, the airline offered free champagne in compensation although the fault was not theirs. Passengers know this and interpret the kindness of the airline accordingly. It is a "moment of truth" when passengers with tight connections are allowed to leave the plane first, when unaccompanied children are looked after, when lost possessions are located promptly.

Figure 6.6 depicts the "first-class pretzel" (top left), the ultra-specific so-

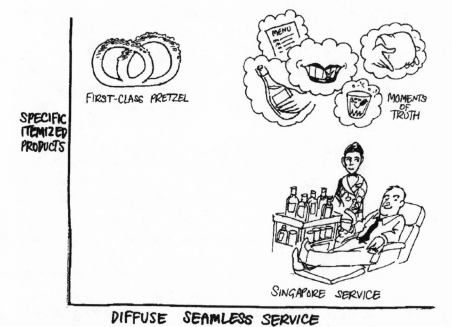

Figure 6.6 Jan Carlzon's "Moments of Truth"

lution, and "Singapore service" (bottom right), a style that fits both Chinese culture and longer flights, both of which tend toward diffuse, continuous caring. Carlzon's concept (top right) is that airline service is judged by "moments of truth," or specific moments by which a diffuse pattern of caring is judged, often by very small indicators.

Case 3: How Ikea Reconciled Diffuse Design with Specific Furniture

We do not necessarily associate Sweden with retailing success. Domestic prices and taxes tend to be high. Ikea is very much an exception, achieving its astonishing international retailing success by an artful combination of diffuse and specific values. It begins with excellence in Swedish furniture design, but to prevent the high costs of these skills from pricing themselves out of the market, it has cross-fertilized these with plentiful supplies of inexpensive domestic wood, largely pine.

As Sweden's slower-growing northern trees have had to compete with faster-growing tropical forests, Ikea has sourced much of its wood abroad, using indigenous carpenters and furniture makers.

This winning combination has been achieved not only by maintaining very high standards of design excellence which diffuse transnationally throughout the Ikea system, but also by combining these with very high-volume, fast-turnover, low-price furniture, locally sourced in countries like Poland, Mexico, and so on.

Consider a glass coffeetable with a wooden stand. Ikea orders 60,000 wooden stands from a local manufacturer and 60,000 oval glass tabletops from local glassmakers. This combination is both high-value in design and low-cost in supply.

The design of Ikea retail stores is also of interest and is depicted in Figure 6.7. Here, Specificity has been switched to the horizontal axis and Diffuseness to the vertical axis, but for good reason. Customers coming to Ikea will typically locate whole "living spaces," diffuse, lighted rooms on the upper floor and specific, boxed pieces of this furniture on the ground floor, which acts as a warehouse.

Arguably, people do not shop for "a chair" or "a bed" but for elegantly furnished spaces in which to live. By showing diffuse arrangements of furniture, Ikea inspires the interior decorator within us, suggests a suite of furniture rather than one chair, and, by means of specific numbers at-

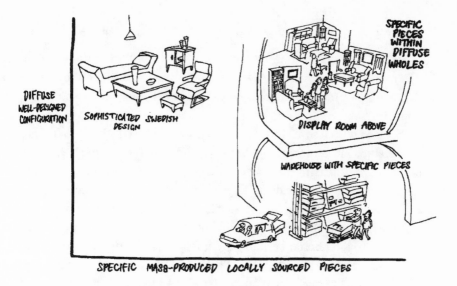

Figure 6.7 Ikea: The Specific–Diffuse Synthesis

tached to the room design, allows us to locate the disassembled pieces in the warehouse below, removing these cheaply in our own cars.

In short, Ikea uses specificity for cheap manufacture, easy storage, and do-it-yourself transport and assembly, while using the diffuse design of whole rooms to achieve aesthetic impact and scenarios for satisfying living. Customers can see the objects they intend to buy as both text and as context, as picture and as frame, as specific figure and as diffuse ground. Those who want new furniture to match existing furniture can visualize what they seek to buy in its most appropriate setting.

Ikea also encourages customers to fix their own boundaries between what the company will do for them and what they will do for themselves. Deliveries can be arranged, as can skilled assembly of furniture in pieces. Customers can save these costs or assume them if their time can be more profitably used in other work.

Ikea illustrates the power of synthesis, that cheap pieces can be used to create high-value, whole configurations of elegance and good taste. It is a reminder of the capacity of the whole to transcend its parts. Good design, like information, is in our heads and is readily communicable and replicable, yet it is capable of transforming the physical universe.

Case 4: Rapport or Report—Women and Minorities in the Workplace

We have already touched in Chapter 5 on Deborah Tannen's observation that men are more oriented toward reports, drawing attention to specific facts, while women are more oriented toward rapport, establishing relationships.

We also saw that some business cultures work from the inside out. They are specific first, get straight to the point, and form relationships with people who are sufficiently interested in their business proposition. Other cultures work from the outside in. They relate diffusely first and finally get to the point only when rapport and trust have been established.

But what interests us is the complementarity of report and rapport, an issue that has import far beyond gender relations. What bedevils communications is that many people do not believe in the truthfulness of negative reports. What is important about the family as a human institution is that it is one of the few contexts in which someone can credibly say to you, "I love you, but I hate what you've just done." Reports delivered in the context of strong rapport are becoming rarer as the family declines.

This observation throws important light on the fate of minority groups, especially minorities in business. These groups seem to suffer least where family structures are strong, as among many East Asian minorities in Western countries. But where family structures are weak, as in many black communities, there arises an almost insoluable dilemma. Certain minorities are predisposed to distrust negative feedback about their conduct.

We all make errors that need correcting. Individuals in the dominant culture tend to trust that criticism is aimed at their mistakes, as opposed to their very existence in an organization. Unfortunately, minorities cannot safely make that assumption. If they fail to develop in the workplace, it may be because they cannot trust their rapport with the superior to whom they report.

A male boss says to a female subordinate that she was "too aggressive" during a recent meeting. Is that statement aimed at helping her and improving her performance or does it state a preference for encountering women in bedrooms, not boardrooms?

In practice, it is extremely difficult for minority members to distinguish attacks on their mistakes from outright rejection of their being. Indeed, they may mistake well-intended criticism for personal prejudice and so fail to amend their conduct.

Many supervisors, in their eagerness not to discriminate, may avoid criticism altogether. But this, too, is a poisoned chalice, because the minority employee never learns why promotion has not come and is denied crucial information.

North American women, who tend to have a stronger orientation toward rapport than do men, may do better when posted to cultures in Southeast Asia and Latin America, where rapport is also a priority. Nancy Adler studied four hundred young women executives posted to these regions and found satisfaction ratings of 80 to 90 percent among the women and among those who sent them—far higher than the satisfaction ratings for men, at around 60 percent. People tend to prosper in compatible cultures.

We have designed programs for corporate clients in which all minorities are asked whether the criticism they receive is

1. Withheld and manifests itself in failure to progress
2. Aimed at their gender or skin, not at improvable conduct
3. Authentically and honestly communicated in an atmosphere of mutual rapport

Only under condition 3 can we reasonably expect the reconciliation of specific reports and close rapport, as illustrated in Figure 6.8. Only strong rapport is able to survive credible reports, which are tough on the recipient. Businesses must face many harsh realities, must accept responsibilities that are painful to bear, must "look on tempests and not be shaken." The health of a corporation can be gauged by asking what if anything is unsayable, too painful to discuss, too tough to contemplate. Men do not strengthen themselves by ignoring the need for close rapport; rather, they weaken their relationship. Equal opportunity does not mean that everyone is allowed to enter a notional "race to the top." There can be no equality of opportunity without a rapport that includes minorities.

We see in Figure 6.8 that report without rapport and rapport without the discipline of having to report are both unsatisfactory. Only very strong rapport can give an unwelcome report credibility. Business communications rely on this synthesis.

Vicious and Virtuous Circles

Are there any signs that the Specific–Diffuse values dilemma is troubling American culture? We have already traced the "addictive" features of

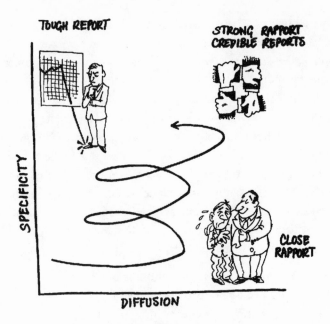

Figure 6.8 Reports Versus Rapport

overreliance on specific remedies and the scourge of alcohol and drugs. But there is a second issue, which may even now be approaching crisis point. This has to do with the conflict of money (specific) versus wealth creation (diffuse). It has been flagged by David C. Korten, author of *When Corporations Rule the World,* and founder of the Positive Futures Network. He is one of the first social critics to emerge from a business education background.

Korten asks why there is suddenly not enough money to provide adequate education for our children. Why expenditures on prisons are overtaking expenditures on education. Why it takes a two-wage family to accomplish living standards once available to one-wage families. Why millions have no health insurance, no savings, no pension, no provision for retirement.

The problem cannot be lack of money. The world's 450 billionaires own as much as the combined annual incomes of half of humanity. Those who remember the sixties will recall that a whole generation questioned whether it was necessary to go on creating, as opposed to more fairly distributing, national wealth. Yet, although we are infinitely richer today than we were then, we are told we cannot afford what once we took for granted. In the middle of the greatest knowledge explosion business has known, state universities have cut back on education. Are we mad?

Korten's thesis is that specific money is eating into and is beginning to destroy the far more diffuse process of creating wealth. The financial system has become predatory, and its demand for ever higher returns is exploiting the "real capital"—human, social, natural, and even physical capital—on which our well-being depends. Money is attacking life. Eighty percent of the world's fund flows are speculative and slosh around the globe like an overfilled bathtub, swamping frail economies.

Korten cites the Malaysian minister for forests, who explained that once all Malaysia's forests were cleared and the monies invested and earning interest Malaysians would be "better off." "The image flashed through my mind of a barren and lifeless world populated only by banks with their computers faithfully and endlessly compounding the interest on the profits from timber." No wonder the more money we have, the less we can afford!

Diffuse wealth creation, explains Korten, consists of "factories, homes, farms, stores, transportation, and communications facilities, the natural productive system of the planet, and people going to work in factories, hospitals, schools, stores, restaurants, publishing houses, and elsewhere to produce the goods and services that sustain us." The money system is supposed to facilitate this process, to be "the dutiful servant of wealth creation." It is intended to complement "an active economy of affection and reciprocity in which people do a great many useful things for one another with no expectation of financial gain."

What has happened is that money has become an end in itself and a way of generating more money, which either ignores or exploits the wealth-creating sector. The financial assets of developed countries in the OECD are growing twice as fast as their underlying economies and are feeding off their hosts.

The biggest profits and salaries are going to those who deal in pure finance. In 1996 the shareholders of the seven largest money center banks reaped an average total return of 44 percent. Mutual funds, specializing in finance, averaged 26.5 percent, significantly higher than technology stocks, which earned only 21 percent. Why make something that is useful for someone else when you can "mainline" on money itself?

Financial bubbles are one more form of cultural "high," as insubstantial as the thrills of addiction, with money to be made by selling on to someone else with identical yearnings. The celebration of "casino capitalism" has re-

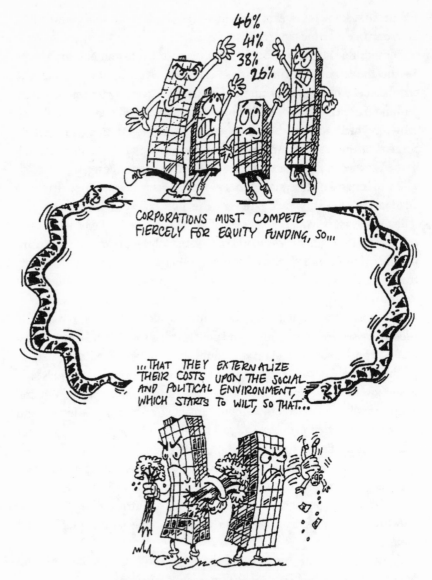

Figure 6.9 The Vicious Corporate Circle

cently claimed even Barings, Britain's venerable merchant bank, laid low by the fraud of a sole trader. Those ostensibly supervising him were gaining from his covert dealing, so that money poisoned wealth.

But it does not take fraud for finance capitalism to help itself to wealth creation and siphon off the gains. Korten cites the takeover by Charles

Hurwitz of the Pacific Lumber Company (PLC). Hurwitz took over not just the company but the generous benefits to employees, the fully funded pension fund, and the substantial holdings of ancient redwood timber in Northern California that PLC had pledged to preserve for the nation. He at once doubled the cutting rate and clear-cut a mile-and-a-half corridor through the virgin forest, which he sneeringly called "our wildlife biologists' study trail." He then siphoned off $55 million from the $93 million pension fund and laid off workers. Wealth that used to belong to the American environment and American workers was turned into money for Hurwitz and his shareholders. Korten poses the question: Has money become a cancer on wealth creation?

Takeover targets include any company that spends heavily on training, skilled employees, environmental protection, pension rights, and health care. You simply buy the company, strip away its diffuse social processes, give these in specific monies to shareholders, then bail out before the company starts to wilt.

Were this simply a moral problem, we might rely on the "good guys" to rally, but Korten sees it as a problem of system design. Figure 6.9 shows clearly the pressures exerted on all industry.

Corporations start to compete for investment funds by progressively raising the returns to shareholders they offer to pay. If you want equity capital, you have to pay more and more for financing, monies that are then wrested from governments, workers, education, and the environment. For example, in 1999 the Ford Motor Company demanded $50 million from the British government to keep its engine works at Bridgend and not move to Spain. Why the British taxpayer should finance Ford for not going away is not explained. It appears to be a question of power: "Pay or we move."

Corporations that compete furiously with each other to make higher returns externalize their costs upon the environments in which they operate. There is a net transfer of funds from wealth creators and taxpayers to finance capital. No wonder we are so rich in gaining, yet so poor in giving, so intent on grinding up our social relationships to feed the moneymakers.

Figure 6.10 depicts our two snakes battling, but in this case the "money snake" appears to be winning and the ideal of a financial system that helps, not bleeds, the processes of wealth creation may be slipping from our grasp.

Are we making more and more money through impoverishing ourselves, through the monetization of what used to be free—the air, the

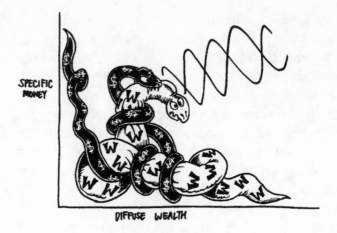

Figure 6.10

forests, the help of neighbors and family? How we define wealth—narrowly or broadly or both—could make all the difference to our futures. That the wealth created by loving parents, inspired teachers, and good neighbors is hard to count is undeniable, but that does not make it any less valuable, nor should it be turned into cash.

7 Achieved–Ascribed Status

THE DILEMMA

How the Dimension Is Defined

Cultures in the developed world have traditionally put a strong emphasis on reputation. You are esteemed for what you have accomplished—your track record, your successes, the position to which you have been promoted, the money you have accumulated, the income you earn.

Essential to the achievement ethic is that contestants have no unfair advantages. There is an "even break" so that winners "make it" by their own determination and ability. If X wins and Y is beaten, it is important to attribute the success of X to his or her "get up and go," as opposed to aunts and uncles pulling strings or the prominence of his or her family.

Given this emphasis, ascribed status is often seen as privilege and special pleading. It is the way contestants "cheat," by invoking the status of their connections. Status is ascribed to people for many reasons, some of which are suspect; other reasons may be entirely justified. Let us deal with the suspect reasons first.

Status is ascribed to those who are "well born," of noble or royal origins, those who speak like gentlemen or ladies, those who are related to or within the social circle of admired persons, those who are physically handsome or beautiful, those from prestigious families, those who are white, male, Protestant, or immigrants of certain European origins.

There is, perhaps, an inevitable spreading of status to connected persons. The wife or husband or child of a celebrated achiever will be treated with a certain degree of deference. One thinks of Dennis Thatcher's relation to Margaret Thatcher, or the dynastic connections among the Kennedy clan.

Yet ascribed status is not simply a question of snobbery, aristocracy, and Old World prejudices. We love our children before they achieve. We value the projects we seek to fulfill before these prove successful. We treat people as valuable prior to any proof of that value and before our judgment is validated. There may, indeed, be persons whose achievements have been unexpected, who have "beat the odds" and surprised us. But there are also many, perhaps more, who have justified our faith and confidence in them, who have fulfilled positive expectations.

Even in an achieving society it is still necessary for individuals to say at some point, "This is worth achieving, but that is not so important." Who is to be the judge, the coach, the impressario? Who is to define a particular form of achievement as important to the nation or the world? Why is running one hundred yards faster than others more important than shooting clay pigeons, or playing darts?

Figure 7.1 depicts the crucial interdependence of achieved status and ascribed status. While "iron men" compete to achieve victory, a woman judge, flanked by the media, defines "men of iron" as those who do the ironing! The joke is not ours but Michael Leunig's, an Australian cartoonist. This redefinition of masculinity as a willingness to do housework re-

Figure 7.1 Achieved Versus Ascribed Status

veals the potential power of ascribing status to one activity rather than another. Indeed, setting up a competition is one important way of celebrating
ascribed values. When women are seen to vie with each other in a Miss
America beauty contest, being beautiful and being American are defined
as very important, consecrated by heroic efforts to win. But note that both
beauty and U.S. nationality are largely ascribed qualities, not achieved
ones.

Similarly, a spelling bee ascribes status to spelling correctly, even where
winning is an achievement. SAT scores ascribe status to test-taking, or occasionally scholarship, even where high scores are achievements. Enough
has been said to show that achieved and ascribed status are not simply polarities but are connected in subtle ways.

How We Measure Achieved–Ascribed Status

We measured this difference by posing a dilemma to respondents and
graphing the results.

"The most important thing in life is to think and act in the manner that
best suits the way you really are, even if you don't get things done."

This proposition describes a sense of self worth that is independent of
what the society around you believes you "ought" to achieve. Those dis-
agreeing with the proposition give priority to achievement or "getting
things done." Those agreeing with the proposition give priority to an au-
thentic sense of being. Achievement is about what you have done. Ascription is about who you are.

The scores are presented in Figure 7.2. We see that Americans opt for
achieved status by six to four, and Australia by fifty-five to forty-five. The
United Kingdom is divided evenly, and much of the rest of the world
prefers ascription. Korea is 76 percent ascriptive, Japan 70 percent, France
65 percent, and Singapore 60 percent. None of this means that achievements are necessarily neglected. It means that across cultures, individuals
first decide what is important before going on to try and achieve it, and
whether or not they succeed is less important than their initial decision
about "who they are."

Achieved status often if not always necessitates a degree of conformity.
To enter a career in plastics, you must agree that plastics constitute an important career challenge worth achieving. To compete as a kick boxer, you
must see this sport as an avenue of success. While at Harvard Business

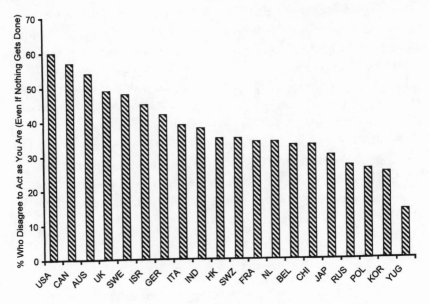

Figure 7.2 Act the Way You Are

School, the British author of this book observed two teams of MBA students competing at a task that consisted of sticking signal dots on a piece of paper in a simple pattern (simple task) and a complex pattern (complex task). He remembers thinking that nothing would induce him to engage in so artificial and trivial an activity and that the experiment and doctoral thesis must surely fail. He was quite wrong! The teams competed fiercely. Sticking dots on paper had been defined as important by HBS, and so it became.

David McClelland, author of *The Achieving Society,* measured achievement motivation via ring-toss games and by rolling colored balls into holes. He found significant correlations with achievement fantasy and subsequent success. Clearly "achieving" is a highly elastic goal. This confirms Michael Maccoby's finding that "the gamesman" is the prime mover in American corporations. He or she seeks to win, whatever "game" is on offer.

Why Is American Culture Achievement-Oriented?

America is among the highest in achievement orientation of any national business culture, for the following historical reasons.

- Justification through works with God as Puritan taskmaster, demanding the building of the Kingdom of Heaven on this earth, requires that these tasks be achieved.
- An immigrant nation, and this includes Australia (also high in achievement), has great difficulty ascribing status to persons of varied national origins. (Who cares that you came from Lithuanian nobility?) What matters is not where you came from, but what you have done recently and what you can contribute now. While ascribed status does not travel well, achieved status can be demonstrated in the New World for all to see.
- America was not merely a set of "new rules" to which immigrants voluntarily subscribed, but a set of new games and level playing fields on which they were invited to compete.
- An important way to ascribe importance to different activities is to let them appeal to the public purse and to vie for the applause of audiences. It follows, then, that football, boxing, and basketball are "important" because their fans make these sports rich. In this way, markets define what is valuable, not just in sport but in business.
- America is a culture given over to empiricism, pragmatism, and "what works." In the business world, achievement is pragmatism applied to commerce.
- International trade has become the substitute for war. To the extent that America wins over world markets, the achievements of its industries and people increase the power of that nation.
- Global markets mean that achievement is now of transnational scope. Wealth flows toward those best able to supply goods and services—the ultimate achievement of national character.
- Achievement is the reality test of potentially valuable ideas. We do not know whether we will like these ideas until someone puts them into action and we can judge their effects. "The marketplace of ideas" presupposes successful applications.

At Its Best . . .

Achieved status inspires the United States to win more Nobel Prizes than any other nation on earth, although Britain and Scandinavia come quite close on a per capita basis. America is especially strong in the sciences, physics, chemistry, and economics and not so strong in poetry, literature, and peace.

Horatio Alger, a Unitarian minister from Massachusetts, wrote scores of successful stories of Ragged Dick and similar characters, who with "luck and pluck" went from rags to riches. His heroes were usually orphans so that their achievement was owed to no one save themselves, not even parental love. They were self-motivated and self-made.

America celebrates its heroes in style. After being fired by President Truman, General Douglas MacArthur, hero of the Pacific Campaign in World War II, returned to a snowstorm of ticker tape as he paraded down Wall Street. Although Truman blamed MacArthur for precipitating Chinese entry into the Korean War, New Yorkers were determined to acknowledge the achievements of MacArthur's lifetime, which included the surrounding and capture of much of the North Korean army.

The Hollywood Oscars are the world's most coveted movie awards and an empirical test of excellence in filmmaking. It is said that "You are as good as your last film," a reminder that achievement must be perpetually renewed. In a world of fantasy, achievements reach their magical heights on screen as millions identify with a small elite of imaginary winners. The lives of stars themselves are rare achievements, picked from thousands of rivals to twinkle in the firmament.

Achievements include the capture of Iwo Jima from the Japanese in World War II, a feat that cost six thousand American lives and was immortalized in the famous photograph by Joe Rosenthal of the American Marine Corps raising the flag. At its finest, achievement includes the keeping of a promise made, the finalizing of commitments undertaken. In the poem "Stopping by Woods on a Snowy Evening," Robert Frost wrote:

> The woods are lovely dark and deep
> But I have promises to keep
> And miles to go before I sleep
> And miles to go before I sleep.

The achiever endures until the promise is redeemed, keeps to the path through the woods.

Americans even have a Hall of Fame for their sporting heroes, a shrine for fans (fanatics) to visit and commemorate bygone feats. What seems to make for "greatness" is a mixture of undoubted skill, but also high visibility and obvious margins of victory or defeat. The feat must be clear enough to be seen by thousands of fans and TV watchers and the contest close enough to engender excitement. The achievement is only partly in the

Figure 7.3

prowess—it is also in the entertainment value of the game, competing with other games for public attention.

Reputations for achievement tend to snowball, feeding on themselves. If an architect like Robert Moses does well by New York City, great powers will be ascribed to him and he will be offered more and more ambitious projects (Figure 7.3). Ascribed status plays a large role in this process since essentially his reputation "goes before him" and people's belief that he can do even better is self-validating. He is propelled by the growing acclamation of others. Yet this whole process originates in achievement, with escalating ascriptions providing the momentum but not the initial spark. Early achievement sets up a generalized expectation that promise will be fulfilled. People want the favorite in any horse race to win. They "follow the money" and "back the sure thing."

But Taken Too Far . . .

Achievement can vulgarize and secularize values thought of as sacred. A TV scriptural expert, for example, was told, "The Holy Bible has sure paid off for you." Not every value is justified by its game-show winnings. Some principles are worth suffering for, even if they "fail."

The "dark side" of winning is that this inevitably multiplies losers. If fifty young women are called to "the meat market" of auditions but only one is chosen, then forty-nine must wait by their telephones in vain, since they have been instructed, "Don't call us, we'll call you." Although an audience of millions identifies with the winner, the losers are actually more numerous. Disappointment is far more common than delight. For the large majority, hope seeps slowly away.

A variation on this theme is the "winner-take-all society," well described by Robert H. Frank and Philip J. Cook in their book by that name. The more "winning" is worshipped, the more creditable performances that did not quite win are eclipsed as a magnifying glass is placed over a small array of successful performances, with the rest marginalized.

It has been a theme throughout this book that people and their performances are diverse. Insisting that varying skills should be rank-ordered on some arbitrary scale of "best-sellers," for example, places serious biography in the same category as *How to Erect a Tepee in Ten Minutes*.

The drive to achieve may also lead to trivial attainments of the kind recorded in *The Guinness Book of Records*. Who can squat at the top of a pole for longest, squeeze the most people into a tiny car, or jump from the greatest height without breaking his silly neck does very little to improve the human condition. When humanity is measured by crude and narrow yardsticks, the latter are elaborated to include feats that are absurd, like counting the follicles on a bearded lady. The desire to be distinct in some way spreads in all directions.

Figure 7.4

Finally, as Figure 7.4 shows, achievement motives can abbreviate childhood, a time for play and experimentation in hundreds of different possible modes of living. But if from the time you can barely lisp you are trained
to perform some "sexy" simulation of adult behavior in children's beauty
contests, then all the artlessness of childhood has gone, channeled into the
ambitions of professional parents. Children dying in the cockpits of aircraft or bumping and grinding in seductive fashion are sacrifices to the
god of success. Their lifestyles have been fatally narrowed by premature
specialization. To perform adult tasks at a ludicrously early age becomes
another way of being "first."

At Its Best . . .

Ascribed status can make its recipients public-spirited. If you have been
born with silver spoons protruding, then you are under some obligation to
return to the society that lavished you with advantages some recompense
for its generosity. This accounts for the enthusiasm of many aristocrats for
military service, for the ethos of the cavalier, musketeer, and volunteer. It
also accounts for the tendency of royalty to espouse worthy causes—in the
case of Charles, Prince of Wales, organic gardening, community building,
and opposition to modernist architecture and genetically modified crops
(Figure 7.5).

Ascribed status is also importantly connected to the foundations of business enterprise in relationships of trust, integrity, and reputation for fair
dealing. If the sole reason for entering a business relationship is personal
gain, then that relationship will, in the final analysis, be exploited for gain.
Only if you have more to lose than money—your good name, your probity,
the admiration of friends and family—is it safe to trust you. Here smaller
countries have an advantage, as do religious sects. If you cheat colleagues
in Holland, Sweden, or Finland, your reputation with that generation of
compatriots is ruined. Declining ethical standards in Lloyds Insurance,
and the City of London generally, have been traced to an increasing number of English-speaking expatriate communities where those of doubtful
character can migrate to be free of reproach.

We have to see that achievement itself presupposes the worthiness of
what is being achieved. In a nation as large as the United States, people
know that you have money but do not necessarily know how you made that
money. If you made it by climbing to the top of a tobacco company, it is le-

Figure 7.5

gitimate to ask whether your life was wasted, despite your "success" and its financial rewards.

That moral conduct is best regarded as independent of commercial and political ambition is envisaged by constitutional monarchy, an institution that helps to guarantee democracy in large parts of the world. The idea is to ascribe status on a hereditary basis to a person "above the fray," who symbolizes enduring values like family life, charitable giving, and civic virtue. Queen Victoria is a notable example, and so are the members of the House of Orange. Such persons, having received royal status as birthright, spend their lives trying to reciprocate this honor.

One problem with giving the highest office in the land to an achiever is that you may hesitate to buy a secondhand car from such a person or trust him with a cigar. Such persons become incapable of rising above the fray, because they are of the fray itself.

But the strongest case for ascribing status is to treat other human beings in a way that elicits their potential, so that their success is a self-fulfilling prophecy. Our children and partners are special to us before they achieve, and believing in them and treating them with respect is what encourages achievement. We have to distinguish prejudicial forms of ascribing status from nonprejudicial forms. If we favor white men of European descent, we thereby disfavor darker women of African or Asian descent. What we give to one group we have snatched from another. But the search for those with potential, nurturing and mentoring them, takes from no one and looks for unique capacity in the diversity of cultural lifestyles.

But Taken Too Far . . .

Ascribed status makes an ass of itself, and it is easy to laugh at its absurdities. The "Ruritanian" trappings at the Nixon White House led to Edward Sorel's famous depiction of Milhous I (Figure 7.6).

The problem with the yearning for grandeur is that it believes its own mythology and the aura eclipses the person. Desperet's famous cartoon of the chariot in the clouds is not a celebration of the victories of Napoleon I but a desperate attempt to dignify Louis Philippe, the Grocer King, possibly the least charismatic monarch in French history! Yet Desperet quoted Ovid to give his monarch the imperial status of Rome: "With these black clouds swirling around him he no longer sees his chariot's giddy career."

It could be argued in favor of achieved status that alternatives can be lethal. One way of imposing upon others status you have ascribed to yourself is through violence, and the history of the twentieth century is replete with examples. At least achieved status is negotiated with a public willing to buy, watch, or vote. It is the very arbitrariness of a Hitler, Stalin, Franco, or Pinochet that requires such status to be violently imposed.

BUT TAKEN TOO FAR...

... IT PUTS ON AIRS

...IT ELEVATES BLUE-BLOODED INCOMPETENTS

...IT DICTATES A VIOLENT IDENTITY

...IT BELIEVES ITS OWN MYTHOLOGY

Figure 7.6

Less threatening but equally absurd is the habit of elevating the "well-bred." Britain at this time of writing *still* hesitates to replace its House of Lords with those who have achieved election. It is an elementary principle of breeding dogs, cats, or racehorses that you "eliminate the duds"—slow horses and ugly dogs. If you stick with the progeny of champions you have a greater chance of reproducing valued, genetic characteristics. But of course, noble and royal lines of descent have never eliminated their incompetents and have rather inflicted them upon the higher offices of the land, a gross mismatch of opportunity with capacity, once memorably satirized on British TV as the "Race of the Upper-Class Twits."

It is a matter of some notoriety that nations given over to achievement are readily seduced by ascribed status. When Edward VII visited Pittsburg in 1909, three thousand Americans were invited to meet him. Six thousand turned up and the floor collapsed. The fuss made of Grace Kelly's wedding to Prince Rainier, the avid following of Princess Diana—all go to show that achievers yearn for a status independent of having always to achieve. Women and men still marry into positions of social advantage. The royal person who chooses a "commoner" as a consort evokes the Cinderella story, and millions of hearts throb at such ascriptions.

Culture Clashes and Derivative Conflicts: In Business and Industry

You can tell whether a business is more oriented to achievement or to ascribing status by some of the derivative dichotomies pictured in Figure 7.7.

Companies favoring achievement will have a policy of up or out. If you are not promoted you should make preparations to leave. In contrast, companies in France or Japan may see it as their duty to nurture home-grown talent for the long term. If a talented employee from a *grand école* is underperforming, the company may blame itself for having underutilized a talent so well certified. A recent applicant to McKinsey from Cambridge University was automatically dropped from consideration because he had not assertively inquired as to why the company had not responded to his interview. It showed "lack of motive to achieve," he was told.

It is currently fashionable in America not to promise recruits to a company either nurturance or long-term careers, but rather enhanced employability. When they are asked to leave they will be more "employable" in the industry generally than when they were recruited. Their capacity to achieve will have been enhanced, but without any commitment to ascribe them status in that company.

There is no clearer distinction between achieved and ascribed status than the contrasting metaphors of high fliers and crown princes. "High Fliers" are people visibly succeeding, usually early in their lives—for example, the youngest account executive in the company. This height and momentum needs to be maintained if their reputations are not to crash. The trick is to achieve more, in less time, than other "fliers."

In contrast, "crown princes" have been picked out by top management as prospects for promotion and eventual elevation to the top. They may be promoted slowly or rotated among key jobs to give them wide perspectives, but they know that they are being groomed for the top and many hints will be dropped to render them more patient. Hence André Laurent reported that French executives believed the strongest influence on their careers and their success was being "identified by top management as having high potential."

Such ascriptions are not as arbitrary as they sound. French, Japanese, and Chinese cultures take scholarship extremely seriously. The Japanese high school and the French lycée are notoriously competitive and achievement-oriented, hence "examination hell." The way cultures that prefer to ascribe status reveal themselves is by bringing competitive achieving to an end relatively early in life. Once you are admitted to a *grand école* or to a prestigious Japanese corporation your ability to achieve competitively has been discovered and certified. From then on you are guaranteed status in return for using your abilities to serve the corporation, its customers, and the nation at large—an academic version of noblesse oblige. "We acknowledge your potential brilliance, now please vindicate our faith in you."

The effect is to help ensure that outstanding talent serves national institutions and humanity, instead of pursuing private aggrandizement. Sometimes the results can be spectacular. For example, the French utility company Suez Lyonnaise des Eaux has long had a formidable reputation domestically for public and municipal integrity. Supplying drinkable water to whole communities and treating waste is a public trust.

This single company now enjoys a 55 percent world market share of foreign-run municipal water and treatment companies. Using its connections to politicians and French diplomacy, it has undertaken to rebuild, reorganize, and update municipal water services, train and reeducate indigenous managers and workers, and, within twenty years, restore to that country effective control over its own vital resources.

The effectiveness of this strategy rests squarely on ascribing to treated water and to the self-determination of foreign countries an elevated status. Respect for the potential of customers to order their own affairs is the cornerstone of all activity. It shows how the French habit of ascribing value to what sustains public health can serve the world.

Achievement-oriented countries use "management by objectives," a strategy devised by Peter Drucker in the fifties. Subordinates are invited to commit to a combination of their own objectives and those of the company, with care to have these overlap as much as possible. They are subsequently evaluated against their own commitments. This method is pure achievement, with subordinates participating in the design of the tasks and the measurements by which they will themselves be assessed.

The corresponding emphasis for cultures who ascribe status is to make that ascription valid by eliciting the subordinate's potential. It is not so much subordinates who achieve as it is their relationships with supervisors and mentors, which call forth their combined abilities. If you admire your supervisors, if your supervisor convinces you that you have the ability to accomplish this task and shows you how, then the eventual achievement is the product of your joint efforts.

These dynamics help to explain the use or nonuse of bonuses, commissions, and incentives. If you and you alone have achieved a task to which you earlier committed yourself, then you are entitled to piecework incentives or bonuses for the completion of that task. So much achievement can earn you so much money, and if the achievement increases so should the money. It can even work the other way around, with enhanced incentives spurring achievement.

But if your superior has coached, inspired, and facilitated your rapid improvement on the job it is by no means clear why the money should all go to you. Is it not reward enough that her faith and education sustained you? Nor are supervisors the only ones involved. The status ascribed to you, the confidence shown in your project, also comes from other team members who support, facilitate, push through, critique, and qualify your contributions.

Teams have an internal culture that makes or breaks personal morale and is capable of lending great significance, excitement, and challenge to what you are trying to do. The group atmosphere may be the chief motivator of joint efforts, and disturbing it in order to distribute individual incentives could wreck everything (Figure 7.7).

Derivative Dichotomies of Achieved–Ascribed Status
in Ethics and Politics

Achieving cultures take pride in creating a meritocracy, a system of upward mobility. This attracts more capable persons to more formidable

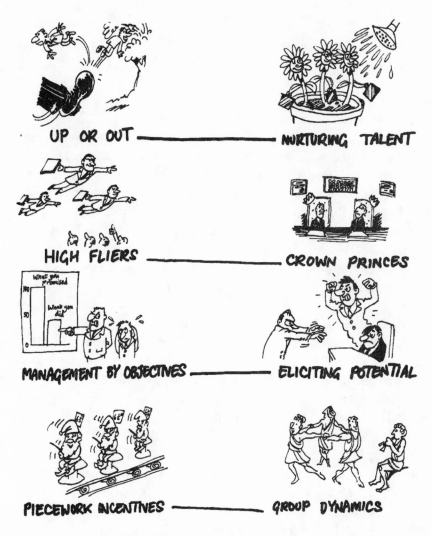

UP OR OUT ————————— NURTURING TALENT

HIGH FLIERS ————————— CROWN PRINCES

MANAGEMENT BY OBJECTIVES ——————— ELICITING POTENTIAL

PIECEWORK INCENTIVES ————— GROUP DYNAMICS

Figure 7.7 Derivative Dichotomies of Achieved–Ascribed Status in Business

challenges and alters patterns of influence toward the more competent. Of course, it can also inflict damage on those who have been outcompeted, resulting in the unseemly scramble pictured at the top of Figure 7.8. Those scrambling to the top may excel in scrambling as opposed to more valuable traits. Achieving in ways that eliminates rather than sustains others may not be of value to the economy as a whole, and could multiply losers, as shown in Figure 7.4.

An alternative is to ascribe preeminent status to your own class, sect, union, ethnic group, or association, which may or may not go on to achieve disproportionately as a consequence. Much will depend on the values of the in-group. Typically, claims to greater moral standing for Protestants in Northern Ireland or the Daughters of the American Revolution in the United States are without much commercial significance and lead to uneconomic forms of discrimination.

Yet certain groups have contributed disproportionately to economic development, such as the English Quakers, French Huguenots, and Chinese immigrants in Southeast Asia. Certain American ethnic groups have extraordinary powers to counter and transform discrimination from the wider world. Morris Rosenberg showed that among American Jewish adolescents, some actually had higher self-esteem in response to "remembered acts of rejection" by non-Jews. Their community had rallied around them, which enhanced their sense of importance. Among the population of American Jewish high school seniors, 85 percent are admitted to college; among Japanese-Americans, 88 percent. Such figures are much higher than those for the white Protestant population.

It is clear from such statistics that communities are at least capable of forming springboards of self-esteem, which may later be used to leap to new heights of achievement. On the other hand, defining yourself as important, independently of achievement, can lead to the kind of genteel decadence portrayed by playwright Tennessee Williams in his characterization of Blanche DuBois in *A Streetcar Named Desire*.

One problem with meritocratic achievement is that it tends to skim off the elites among minority groups. The tendency is to want to be numbered among the stars, so that distance is put between the achiever and his or her ethnic origins. There is also a temptation to attribute success entirely to the achievers themselves, so that their ethnicities are treated as so many obstacles surmounted. For example, some claim, some African Americans have not tried hard enough to achieve. If Clarence Thomas can do it (by agreeing with white conservatives), then they all can.

If we ask how ethnic groups have made it in America, it is not by spreading themselves thinly across occupations and achieving on their own but by networking and mutual assistance. Jews are disproportionately represented in the media, law, finance, garment making, medicine, and the social sciences, among other fields. Irish contractors and city bosses used the sheer numbers of Irish immigrants to vote en bloc in city machines, who then manned police forces and sanitation departments and gave business to Irish contractors, who employed their own. Certainly merit was part of it, but so was the flying wedge.

Finally, there is the ancient quarrel between "new" and "old" money—between the *nouveau riches* and *arrivistes* who have sacrificed their finer sensibilities to the upward scramble, and the "old money" with the *savoir vivre* to spread their bounty fashionably and graciously. It is not surprising that we use French words to describe this polarity. French aristocracy lived on until the end of the eighteenth century and was renewed by Napoleon as the engineer of the Enlightenment. Britain, with its huge country estates created by primogeniture (inheritance by the first born), also associates ascribed status with prime real estate and gracious landscapes.

Yet the United States is not untouched by these dichotomies. Here the split is between those given over to production (achieved status) and those given over to consumption (status ascribed through styles of consuming). In his book on the sixties revolution, *The Cultural Contradictions of Capitalism*, Daniel Bell pointed out that the values of the so-called counterculture were those of consumption. The values of responsiveness, spontaneity, immediacy, permissiveness, instant gratification, and openness were all involved in consumption. The values of initiative, planning, calculation, self-control, delayed gratification, and focused energy were all involved in production. The "contradiction" was that business used mass media advertising to generate its own antithesis.

Ascribed and achieved values are also importantly connected to whether you are a pioneer capitalist country, such as the United States, Canada, the United Kingdom, Australia, the Netherlands, and Belgium, or whether the main strategy is to follow fast and come from behind.

When you are pioneering new technologies, their relative importance is decided only by letting them fight for markets and see who comes out on top. But with the hundreds of recent technologies available in North America, Europe, and Japan, it makes sense in choosing between these to ask what sort of culture you want to become and what you should train your work forces to do so that increased knowledge enriches the culture and so that the value-added per person increases (Figure 7.8).

In short, you must ascribe more value to, say, biotechnology, precision engineering, or electronics than to faster food, new and improved Coke, or mentholated cigarettes. If there is room for only seven industrial clusters

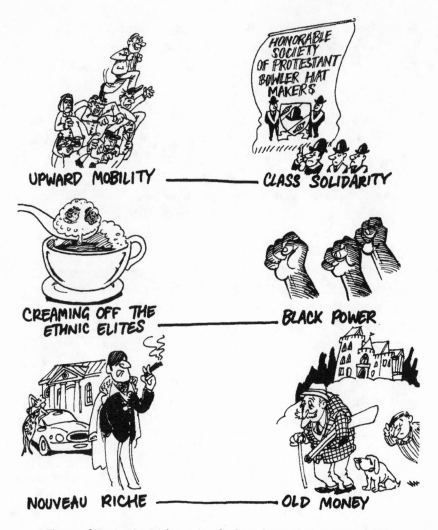

Figure 7.8 Derivative Dichotomies of Achieved–Ascribed Status in Ethics and Politics

in Singapore you must ascribe status to the chosen seven and to others and train your best people to contribute.

Having focused in this chapter on the contradictions and polarities between achieved and ascribed status, we now turn to how these two work together.

8 Reconciling Achieved with Ascribed Status

STORIES AND CASES

As we saw in Chapter 7, achieved status depends crucially upon the worthiness of the goal people set out to achieve. You can make a fortune from drugs, prostitution, pornography, racketeering, and the illegal shipment of desperate immigrants. You can trade in babies, land mines, and plutonium and "achieve" these goals while growing rich.

But competition within such lucrative trades does not redeem the immoral nature of these activities. You can "achieve" and cause considerable harm, unless conscious of the purpose that achievement serves.

In this chapter, we focus on two stories of "doubtful achievements," one adapted from Greek mythology by British and American cultures, the other told by Japanese culture. The stories dramatize the clash of achieved and ascribed values and point to very different paths to reconciliation.

A Story Told by an Achieving Culture

When George Bernard Shaw wrote his play *Pygmalion* between 1912 and 1913, Great Britain was at the zenith of world achievement. The play opened in Vienna, in German, in 1913 and at Her Majesty's Theatre in London in April 1914, three months before the outbreak of World War I. When Alan Jay Lerner and Frederick Loewe adapted the story as a musical in 1956 and as a movie in 1964, entitled *My Fair Lady*, the United States was at the zenith of achievement, commanding 18 percent of all world trade.

Pygmalion is based on the Greek myth about the prince and gifted sculptor of that name who fell in love with Aphrodite, but she rejected the advances of a mere mortal. To assuage his disappointment, Pygmalion carved an ivory statue of his ideal woman, whom he loved only the more for having carved her. The goddess took pity on her rejected suitor and made the statue come to life, so was Galatea made in the image of the goddess of beauty.

Shaw's version of the myth was followed with some fidelity by Lerner and Loewe, with the exception of the story's ending. Professor Henry Higgins is an expert in phonetics, the scientific study of speech. While escaping from a downpour following a performance at the Covent Garden theater, he notices the excruciating Cockney accent of a flower girl, Liza Doolittle. He also meets a longtime admirer, Colonel Pickering, an expert on Indian dialects, and invites him to stay at his house in Wimpole Street.

Higgins mocks Eliza for uttering "depressing and disgusting sounds," a disgrace "to the language of Milton and Shakespeare." Her accent will "keep her in the gutter to the end of her days," he tells Pickering, yet "in three months I could pass that girl off as a duchess at an ambassador's garden party. I could even get her a place as a lady's maid or shop assistant, which requires better English." He could take this "squashed cabbage leaf" and "pass her off as the Queen of Sheba."

But it is the prospect of assisting in a flower shop that draws Liza to Henry's house the next day. She wants to "talk genteel" and will pay a shilling a lesson from her earnings. But what makes the offer tempting is Colonel Pickering's bet that he will pay all expenses and fees if Higgins succeeds in passing her off as a titled lady.

We now need to grasp Henry Higgins' motives. Although socially prominent, he disdains the affectations of his own society and is bored with the social niceties in which he is personally deficient. What better way to revenge himself on this society than to show that its ascriptions of "good breeding" and "gentility" are shams. He can teach a street urchin in six months flat to behave like a lady. His professional achievements can conquer the world of ascribed status, can breach the bastions of polite society.

He will show that the social pretentions of a moribund class system consist of nothing but snobbery about styles of speaking. "I will make a Duchess of this draggletail guttersnipe!" he exclaims. Frederick Loewe's lyrics put it well:

An Englishman's way of speaking
Absolutely classifies him

He has only to open his mouth to make
Some other Englishman despise him

So Liza is given a bath. Her father arrives to collect five pounds, in return
for which he delivers her into the professor's hands. She is subjected to an
exhausting round of drilling and training amid a variety of instruments
that unflinchingly record her Cockney accent. Only the kindness of
Colonel Pickering and the housekeeper, Mrs. Pearce, keeps her going. Higgins swears continuously and threatens to have her walloped and dragged
around the room by her hair, although in fact he never touches her. For uttering the right noises she is rewarded with chocolates, her favorite treat.

Liza turns out to have a very quick ear, to be an excellent mimic, and to
love the music at the concerts she is taken to. So Higgins begins to expose
her to social situations. In the musical version, Liza is taken to the Ascot
horse races, becomes excited, and loudly urges her horse, "Move yer
bloomin' arse!" In the play she visits Higgins' mother and the Eynsford-
Hills, who have also called, and answers "Not bloody likely" when asked if
she will walk home. In both versions, Freddie Eynsford-Hill is smitten with
her.

The play makes the crucial point that it is from Higgins, not her Cockney compatriates, that Liza has learned to swear. After this setback, the
colonel withdraws his bet, but Higgins has the bit between his teeth. He
will achieve his aim, and Liza, too, wants to continue.

The story's climax occurs on the night of the embassy ball for the Prince
of Transylvania. Liza triumphs, and a rival Hungarian phonetics teacher
tells everyone, in confidence, that she is a Hungarian princess!

Henry and the colonel return from the ball, chortling over their success.
But as with any achievement, once accomplished, it loses its attraction.
Higgins confesses himself bored, especially by the ball itself. "Now it's
over and done with, I can go to bed without dreading tomorrow." He proceeds to attack the whole silly claque of fashionable people. "Thank God
it's over!" Then he makes the mistake of asking Liza, still arrayed in her
ball gown and jewels, where his slippers are. She throws them at him.

"I've won your bet for you, haven't I? I don't matter. . . . What's to become of me?" Higgins assures her, "All this irritation is purely subjective."
But Liza laments, "What am I fit for? . . . Where am I to go? What's to become of me?"

We have to understand these questions in their historical context of the early twentieth century. While still a flower girl, Liza could work to support herself, but as a "lady" she could not. If your status was ascribed in those days, you did not even try to achieve. Higgins had tossed her onto the horns of a dilemma, between the clashing values of ascribed and achieved status. That Freddie Eynsford-Hill had fallen in love with her was part of the problem, not the solution, since the Eynsford-Hills were impoverished gentility, hanging on by their fingernails to a lifestyle they could not afford. Liza feels she is a slave to her fine clothes, to the learned outward forms.

It is from this crisis that Liza emerges as a bold and independent woman of the kind Shaw so admired. By next morning she has left Wimpole Street and moved to Mrs. Higgins' house, the redoubtable mother who has formed Higgins' bachelorhood. When the professor and the colonel run to Mrs. Higgins for advice about their runaway pupil, Liza confronts her teacher, and it is Shaw speaking.

First she thanks the colonel for his unfailing kindness and courtesy in teaching her how ladies and gentlemen behave. Then she likens Higgins to a professional dance instructor. It is from the colonel that she learned self-respect.

"You see really and truly, apart from the things that anyone can pick up [the dressing and the proper way of speaking] the difference between a lady and a flower girl is not how she behaves, but how she's treated. I shall always be a flower girl to Professor Higgins, because he always treats me as a flower girl, and always will; but I know I can be a lady to you, because you always treat me as a lady and always will." As she explains, "What I did was not for the dresses and the taxis. I did it because we were pleasant together and I came to care for you."

But Higgins will not let go of his achievement. For this, the contrast between what she once was and now is must be kept alive. He needs her to be a "squashed cabbage leaf" so that the feat of turning her into a duchess is forever celebrated. He will not give to her or the colonel any share in this transformation. Shaw thereby rescues from the ethos of the gentleman its kernel of truth, that people develop intellectually and emotionally if they are treated well.

My Fair Lady ends with Liza returning to her mentor, but is the answer to crucial social dilemmas to be found in lovers' arms? Shaw was made of sterner stuff. Angry when producers of Pygmalion hinted at a happy ending, he wrote a bittersweet postscript, celebrating Liza's courage and independence.

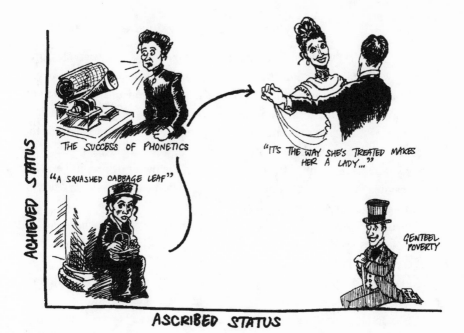

THE SUCCESS OF PHONETICS

"A SQUASHED CABBAGE LEAF"

"IT'S THE WAY SHE'S TREATED MAKES HER A LADY..."

GENTEEL POVERTY

ASCRIBED STATUS

ACHIEVED STATUS

Figure 8.1 My Fair Lady

In the play, Liza marries Freddie for all his faults and poverty, because he loves her passionately in ways Higgins cannot. She cannot live without that validation. She buys and runs her own flower shop and after a few bad months makes it pay. Thanks to the colonel's initial generosity, the young couple survive and prosper and she is always welcome at Wimpole Street, where she uses so well the words and wit that Higgins has taught her that the colonel begs her to be kinder to him.

Figure 8.1 locates achieved status on the vertical axis and ascribed status on the horizontal, while the "squashed cabbage leaf" has neither. Freddie symbolizes genteel poverty, the decadence of a uselessly mannered class (bottom right). He is the Awful Warning of a class-ridden society, too "genteel" to shift for himself. At top right the values of ascription and achievement dance as one. Indeed, "the dance of values" is the theme of all the reconciliations in this story, as in much of this book. The value that the colonel and Freddie ascribe to Liza is enough to enable her to achieve and exercise independence in her life. This was Shaw's dream for all women.

A Story Told by an Ascribing Culture

Tengoku to Jigoku (High and Low) is a film by Akira Kurosawa. It features a hardworking production chief of a Tokyo shoe factory, Gondo. He began work at the factory as a craftsman and was promoted from the shop floor. Gondo is frustrated in his job by the backward-looking policies of his senior colleagues, who resist his pleas for investment in order to upgrade the factory. Gondo cares about quality production. They do not, so he plans secretly to raise the money from the bank and his own resources to buy his colleagues out. It is to be a hostile takeover—quite an "American" way of doing things, rarely seen in Japan.

Visually the movie compares the heights of Yokohama where Gondo lives, to the depths of the town slums where the addicts and criminals lurk. That Gondo is not so far from violence himself is suggested when he chides his son, who is playing "sheriff and outlaw" with his chauffeur's son. "Hide and let him have it. . . . It's kill or be killed."

Gondo lays his plans carefully until on the very day he had planned to seize the company, a kidnapper seizes one of the two boys at play. Father and mother are both aghast when witnesses to the seizure telephone them, but then to their surprise their own son comes running home in a state of agitation. The kidnapper has seized the chauffeur's son by mistake.

The police arrive and the parents wait by the telephone for the ransom demand. When it comes it is massive. It will take all the money Gondo has collected for his takeover bid, and more. There is a poignant moment when the chauffeur throws himself on the ground before his employer, pleading for his son to be ransomed. Gondo steps over the prostrate figure and leaves the room in anger.

After anguished deliberation, Gondo takes the money in a suitcase to the kidnapper, who grabs it after it is thrown from a train. He eludes capture and subsequently releases the boy. The kidnapper has left clues to his identity, and a manhunt is launched.

In the meantime, Gondo has lost his home, which he mortgaged to pay the ransom. He is dismissed from his job when his aborted takeover plan is revealed. Like the kidnapper, he is unemployed. Then the two meet accidentally. Weeks later the kidnapper is caught. He is identified as a drug-running medical intern at the local hospital. He has killed his accomplices in the kidnap and has spent most of the ransom. He is tried, and from his

Figure 8.2 High and Low

condemned cell he asks to see Gondo, who confronts him on the other side of the steel grill.

The kidnapper screams his hate and rage through the screen between them. He had for years looked out from his small, cramped apartment to "the heaven" of Gondo's spacious house. He and Gondo were in the same business, grabbing for what they could get. Why should he have to die and Gondo live? We learn that Gondo is back at work in charge of another shoe factory. He believes this one will do better than the previous one. The kidnapper continues to rail at him, but Gondo and the audience know that the two men are not the same. Figure 8.2 shows the difference.

Both men began by trying to enrich themselves and achieve relative prosperity. But when the child of his employee was in peril, Gondo lived up to his ascribed status as responsible employer and sacrificed all his resources to save the boy. Of course he was right to strive for achievement, to seek the wealth that he managed better than his colleagues, but his duty as an employer, a father, and a leader came first. A man charged with authority must act on behalf of subordinates. That is the nature of the steel grill separating Heaven from Hell, high from low, and Gondo from the kidnapper. He is not afraid of going to hell, the kidnapper shouts, because he has been living in his own private hell for so long.

As he continues to shout, the guards drag him away and a giant steel shutter falls between their two worlds.

Japanese culture, like American, seeks the integration of ascribed and achieved status, but for the Japanese ascription comes first. The kidnapper disgraced his medical status. Gondo lived up to his ascribed status as a responsible employer and put the safety of his employee's son first. That is the division between them (the top right in Figure 8.2, as opposed to the lower left). We socially construct our heaven or our hell. It is a crucially different approach to morality than that expounded by George Bernard Shaw.

Gondo lost everything through no fault of his own, but not his integrity as a craftsman and his responsibility as an employer. We watch him working on the leather of his own briefcase to trap the kidnapper and see that Gondo is a craftsman, a man who can return to his roots to rebuild his position.

The movie is an allegory of Dante and Virgil in hell. The police inspector gives Gondo a guided tour of the lower depths. The difference is that Gondo can ascend again, while a steel grill traps the kidnapper in the hell of his own contrivance.

Kurosawa's film makes an interesting contrast with two Hollywood versions of *Ransom*, in which a successful businessman's son is kidnapped. In both Hollywood versions the industrialists win by using their great achievements against the kidnappers. They refuse to ransom their own sons. Instead they take the ransom demands and put this as a bounty on the heads of the kidnappers. They act not as loving fathers, but as brilliant achievers. Not a penny for their children—rather, all their money goes to fight crime! It is a very different morality.

Case 1: Hawthorne Revisited

This case will be familiar to many readers. Beginning in 1924 and for several years thereafter, a team of researchers from Harvard Business School led by Elton Mayo and Fritz Roethlisberger conducted a series of studies at the Hawthorne works of Western Electric. This is now known as the "Hawthorne Experiment" by those still eager to understand what happened and the "Hawthorne Effect" by those seeking to dismiss its significance.

The researchers set out to discover what antecedent conditions might produce an increase in achieved output among blue-collar workers. In short, this was a classic experiment designed to discover if improved lighting, altered heights of workbenches, longer rest periods, better food, or variations in working hours would "cause" achievement to rise. Each of these "independent variables" was regarded as a possible "cause" of higher achievement.

There were several experiments, but the one most often cited, and typical of the rest, was the relay test room experiment. For this, two Irish immigrant working women were chosen from the plant floor and invited to choose three other female workers. They formed a five-person experimental group isolated in a separate room where they tested and assembled telephone relays, a job they had performed in the larger plant. In this work they were closely observed by the researchers. They were also visited periodically by their supervisor from the plant. When the observers noticed that the supervisor "was upsetting the girls," these visits ceased after a few days at the researchers' request.

The experiment was a total failure in one respect and an extraordinary success in another respect. It failed in regard to the measured effects of the "independent variables," which were supposed to "cause" higher output and achievement. Production rose steadily as the variables were introduced, but they also rose as they were removed. When, at the end of the experiment, conditions reverted to what they had been at the start, productivity remained 39 percent higher! Whatever caused the rise from an average of forty-nine relays per hour to sixty-eight, it was not the experimental variables.

The most common reaction is to dismiss the whole affair as a "bungled experiment." The women came to like the experimenters and so gave them what they obviously wanted, higher output. This is known as the Hawthorne Effect: what happens when unwary researchers show their feelings and fail to sterilize their instruments from emotional "contamination." The problem with this conclusion is that many managers and most industries would eagerly accept a 39 percent gain in production, *however* it was caused! That experimental psychologists are insulted is not very important. Why *shouldn't* workers give their supervisors what they want?

How did this happen? The view taken here is that subtle alterations were made in the status ascribed to the five women, and so their achievement increased as a consequence. How did this occur?

First, they were selected from hundreds on the plant floor. Three women, the ones chosen by the first two, were picked because they were liked, and this regard was probably mutual. In short, this group was self-organizing based on friendship choices. Each person knew she was valued by the others.

Second, the women were treated by the Harvard researchers as co-researchers, not as immigrant blue-collar workers. The researchers treated them as junior academic colleagues. One suspects that the subjects' reaction followed that of Liza Doolittle: "The difference between a researcher and a factory worker is how she is treated. I shall always be a factory girl to the foreman . . . but I know I can be a researcher to Elton Mayo, because he always treats me as a researcher and always will." No wonder the supervisor was "upsetting the girls" and was barred from the room.

Third, the experimenters sought to "observe" and not "interfere" with the climate inside the relay test room. One result of observing closely is that this becomes seen as respect (from *respicere,* "to look at"). One result of not interfering is that the small group develops spontaneously and its own members develop autonomy (literally, "self-rule"). To give them autonomy is to ascribe them status—unprecedented for working women at this level.

Fourth, there was a subtle but crucially important change in the work definitions of these women. On their old plant floor they had been testing and assembling telephone relays, a repetitive and routinized manual task. But now they were inquiring and seeking to discover how telephone relays could better be assembled.

This experiment was both a gift and a wake-up call to industrial relations everywhere. The book that resulted, *Management and the Worker,* by Fritz Roethlisberger and William Dickson, became a best-seller. If the women realized they were co-researching an important discovery, they were not mistaken. But they initially had this status ascribed to them. Only later did they go on to achieve outstanding performance.

Although the independent variables were found to have no significant effect upon performance, taken together they quite clearly had a meaning. If you look at the variables being tested—better nutrition, longer rest periods, better wage incentives, better medical care, better illumination, more comfortable chairs and workbenches—there are no prizes for guessing what Elton Mayo and Fritz Roethlisberger were seeking to accomplish. The theme of the entire experiment was to see if it paid a company back to treat workers with greater consideration. The mistake was to seek a one-to-one specific connection between this or that variable and subsequent productivity. What did work was the general aura of goodwill and the evident social concern for the improvement of work conditions. It was to this the workers responded.

But we have not understood the Hawthorne Experiment until we study the direction and momentum of events. Harvard Business School researchers are not renowned for their modesty and social responsiveness, although Fritz Roethlisberger was a notable exception. There is nothing better calculated to increase one's modesty and responsiveness, however, than the failure of all one's independent variables!

It became clear during the course of the experiment that while the researchers' hypotheses were all wide of the mark, *something* important and exciting must have happened for achievement to have increased so dramatically. So the researchers began to ask the women why they were working better. The researchers sought to rescue from the shattered structure of their experiment ideas of lasting value and interest.

In response, the women began to define their reasons, and the more they defined the more they improved. "We have no bosses!" They told the researchers, "We're treated like human beings." "You pay attention to what we tell you." "We enjoy each other." All are sentiments that Liza Doolittle would have applauded.

As productivity steadily climbed, the researchers gave to the women veto power over any feature of the experiment they did not like. In other words, they were empowered and as a result improved even more.

Frankly, it is hard to see how the absurdly simple job of testing and assembling relays could be improved by so great a margin. The results are testimony to the effectiveness of ascribing new kinds of status to employees who then assume that status. For the fact is that manual work (hands only) loses all status and significance when it is separated from one's mind. What the experiment gave to the workers was the reconnection between mind and work, so that what they did with their hands was to test hypotheses they shared with their researchers. Brain work of this kind signifies not only higher status but also greater meaning. You use your hands to discover something your mind seeks to know.

Finally, we must recognize the soaring group morale and the sheer thrill of having membership in a group that is highly successful and thereby ascribes you high status. At the end of every day the women received their output figures and were able to celebrate the fact that these were climbing.

As the weeks went on and the fame of the experiment spread, a steady stream of visitors came to the assembly room to see for themselves the group whose productivity increase had exceeded first 10 percent, then 20 percent, then 30 percent, and was heading skyward. Never in their lives, before or since, had these young Irish and Polish immigrant women been paid such breathless attention by such august spectators. It was, as we shall see, too good to last. Too much had been happening too quickly for the bewildered academics to comprehend. Their old paradigm had collapsed, but they lacked new ways of thinking.

The Hawthorne Experiment has a sad sequel. The genuine significance of the research was missed. The researchers concluded that positive sentiment among workers was a crucial productive advantage and treating them with kindness paid off. Attempts to institutionalize the findings missed key points.

Management and researchers established a counseling program, whereby workers who were upset for any reason could seek counsel from representatives of management. For this purpose, middle-aged women were hired—at very low expense—and were installed in temporary buildings adjoining the factory. Workers were free to seek their advice after their shifts were over. Counselors were trained to "reflect sympathetically" what workers told them and generally mollify them.

Managers were willing to assent to the idea that "kindness works." But they obviously felt that they should not spend their precious time being tender to undistinguished persons or listening to immigrant workers. The trick was to hire kind, motherly females and plug them into the circuit. Thirty-five years later the counseling program was quietly abandoned, so as not to alert the media. A typical feature of institutions of mass production is the isolation of all social engagement to a cul-de-sac. It was business as usual for Western Electric, with a department of "corporate Momism" hitched incongruously to the rear of the plant where workers could vent their feelings.

A comment the British author of this book wrote in 1970, at the height of cultural revolts and his own rebellion, is still, alas, justified.

The behaviour of Western Electric over the publication of the book *Management and the Worker* is illustrative of the extent to which the Hawthorne findings modified management's attitudes. The book became a best seller, being translated into several languages. Western Electric demanded and re-

Figure 8.3 Lessons from Hawthorne

ceived half the royalties on the grounds that it had hosted the experiment. It then remembered that while Dickson, the junior author, had been working on the book, Western Electric had paid his salary, so it pocketed *his* share as well. (After all, why be generous? There's a special department for that.) Roethlisberger was so upset that he sent half of his quarter-share of the royalties to Dickson. So the company got three quarters and the two authors one eighth of the royalties each. As for the girls, who had told everyone the answers, they got nothing. The moral is that you can lead a horse to water, but you can't stop it drinking your share, and then fouling the water hole.

The Hawthorne research is illustrated in Figure 8.3. At top left is the status quo ante, with the supervisor demanding higher output and "upsetting the girls." At bottom right is the ineffective counseling program, in which kindness and concern has been segregated from tough-minded business as usual and is offered as a safety valve. At top right the (accidentally) transformed nature of the five female workers has led to the most famous experiment in the history of the human relations movement.

Can the Hawthorne gains be replicated or were they a freak occurrence? There is no good reason why industrial work groups cannot recreate key Hawthorne conditions, with workers conducting experiments in how to work better that management is willing to be surprised by and from which they are prepared to learn. Teamwork has become the norm in many companies, and "hot groups" go from strength to strength. Blue-collar workers, thanks to the Japanese challenge, now work smart, using higher math to solve algorithms on the shop floor and assuring quality by mutual oversight. Hawthorne anticipated all this and more.

Case 2: Transforming the Macho Truckers

On some occasions employees have already ascribed to themselves and to each other an extremely tenacious identity that is not necessarily consistent with how management would like them to be.

This was the case for the "Pacific Oil Company's" terminal in California, from which gasoline was distributed throughout northern and central California. The problem was safety, and trying to increase safety consciousness among truckers, organized by the Teamsters union, was a very formidable challenge.

There were two major dilemmas: how to persuade truckers who were tough, macho loners to "please be more careful," and how to persuade terminal workers, which included truckers picking up loads, to report any "unsafe acts" they witnessed so that these acts could be systematically reduced. Being careful did not fit with the self-ascribed status of organized truckers, and snitching on each other to management about "unsafe acts" was contrary to good trade unionism. Let us deal with these dilemmas in turn. We should note that any one company typically has several dilemmas that need to be resolved in a planned sequence of actions. One company–one dilemma is the exception, not the rule.

Dangerous Trucks

Management had been conspicuously unsuccessful in getting the drivers of oil tankers to drive in less hazardous ways. Management demanded that drivers "read" a 250-page safety manual and then sign a form testifying that they had read it. This rule was held in some contempt by drivers and was seen as a device to blame drivers in any legal dispute following an accident. Anyone following the manual to the letter could not possibly deliver his quota of gasoline to thirty stations a day.

There had nearly been a strike the past year when a driver suffered second-degree burns. He woke up in hospital to find the safety manual by his bedside with the key clauses highlighted by his supervisor. He had barely regained consciousness and the blame game had already begun!

Yet management had good reason to be worried. Each truck carried enough gasoline to cause an explosion that could envelop vehicles three hundred yards away in a giant fireball. Were a truck to turn over in a street with adjoining houses, the gasoline could flood the area, leak into cellars, touch off pilot lights, and incinerate a small neighborhood. Punitive damages might run to many millions.

Several complaints had been received from the truck detail of the California Highway Patrol. Truckers were using their CB radios to warn each other about speed traps and patrol cars. There had even been attempts to jam police radio frequencies. A pep talk given by the director of safety to a group of truckers had been ungraciously received. The truckers had many colorful comments about the state of the highways, about inadequate shoulders when their brakes failed, and about how little anyone was concerned for them.

One major issue was that truckers received a bonus for delivering to a given number of gasoline stations per day, but they were fined if spot checks revealed that they were driving too fast or "splash loading" at the terminal, a process in which gasoline spilled on the plastic shell of the tanker while fuel was being loaded. Truckers complained that only dangerous practices allowed them to meet their quotas of delivery. Managers concerned with productivity and managers concerned with safety had conflicting priorities, and drivers were damned either way.

A number of drivers had called in sick, complaining of nausea and "cab nod," a tendency for the cab to nod up and down as they drove. Several trucks had recently been retrofitted, and drivers complained that this had created their problems. Management referred to them as "a bunch of neurotics" and pointed out that 40 percent of the complaints came from drivers whose cabs had never been altered. In management's view, this was a grievance manufactured by the union for its own purposes.

A year earlier, following a serious terminal explosion in New Orleans, the Pacific terminal had launched a safety drive. This consisted of all employees reporting to the safety department any "unsafe act" witnessed. This included bringing cigarettes or matches into the terminal, splash loading, jumping down from the cab to the ground, leaving puddles of fuel anywhere on the ground, and creating "a hazard" for other workers to trip over or run over.

Figure 8.4 The Case of the Macho Drivers

Unfortunately, the unionized terminal workers flatly refused to "snitch" on fellow trades unionists and denounced the safety campaign as a pretext aimed at weakening union solidarity and dividing workers against one another. Very few "unsafe acts" were reported, and those that were came from managers and were typically subject to disputed evidence. When a tanker caught fire it was virtually impossible to obtain any evidence for the inquiry.

The consultants explained that Pacific Oil faced two major dilemmas. The first, illustrated in Figure 8.4, consisted of getting "macho" drivers, eager to achieve their productivity bonus, to drive safely and with social responsibility through the communities located en route to their destinations. The current situation is depicted at top left with "CB cowboys" ganging up to frustrate the Highway Patrol and informing other drivers of their presence. At bottom right is depicted the unsuccessful pleas to "Be more careful." What management feared most is shown in the center and is a consequence of dangerous driving and ignored pleas—also of management's highly legalistic attitude toward accidents, more concerned with blame than with prevention.

The solution suggested by the consultants, and later successfully implemented, was to ascribe to drivers more inclusive identity and a status based on public service to the community, a status consistent with yet broader than the existing image of themselves as lonesome, sleepless cowboys, scorching public highways in a dangerous quest for a living wage.

The "Knights of the Road" were encouraged to use their CB radios to warn of rockslides, broken-down vehicles, ice on the road, and other highway hazards. Volunteers received additional pay to make videos of icy "black spot" locations on the interstate and state highways. Of special concern to truck drivers were entry ramps that were either too steep or too short for a fully loaded tanker to reach fifty miles per hour before it joined the stream of highway traffic. Attempting to join ongoing traffic at slower speeds is extremely hazardous.

Truck drivers were also concerned that shoulders leading to sandtraps, designed to stop a speeding truck with brake failure, were not properly maintained. The sand had hardened and grassed over. Instead of being halted, trucks would be launched into the adjoining fields and explode on impact.

The idea that truck drivers are unconcerned with safety quickly vanished. The videos made were not only shown to all other drivers but were featured in union literature. Once a year the drivers made a presentation to the California Highway Authority on ways in which highways could be made less hazardous. Local TV stations showed some of this footage. A new, illustrated safety manual was created by the drivers themselves. Every year, two or three drivers received Knights of the Road awards for timely warnings, roadside assistance, or well-filmed dangers. These included decals that they affixed to the doors of their cabs.

After one year of operation, road accidents had been halved and fleet insurance rates were negotiated downward.

Case 3: Safety and Unionization

The second dilemma faced by Pacific Oil was the refusal of unionized terminal workers to report members for committing "unsafe acts." The procedure is well established wherever safety is an issue: instead of waiting for an accident to occur, following which all witnesses may be traumatized and/or seeking to avoid blame, you count *near* accidents or unsafe situations and work toward the systematic reduction of such incidents. Where risks are virtually eliminated, real accidents may not occur. Warning of

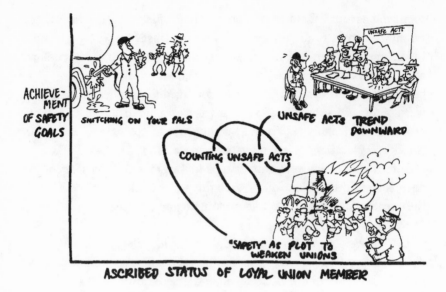

Figure 8.5 Unionized Safety

possible hazards functions like the whiskers of a cat, which closes its eyes reflexively as objects approach its face.

But for such methods to work, unsafe acts must be reported so that they can be registered, counted, and reduced over time as the effectiveness of safety precautions becomes measurable. The refusal of the union to cooperate seriously frustrated safety initiatives.

The dilemma is illustrated in Figure 8.5. In this illustration the system is stuck at bottom right, with union members blocking inquiries into safety infringements for fear that their members will be picked off. What they fear is shown at top left: one union member snitching on another. The outcome of this conflict could be a devastating terminal explosion, as occurred in New Orleans.

The consultants made the following recommendations: Any unionized terminal worker or trucker witnessing an unsafe act could save the worker involved from management sanction by reporting the "unsafe act," even where a manager had also witnessed and reported it. However, that worker must appear before a committee of fellow union members plus the safety manager to explain his negligence. It turned out that workers had strong opinions about safety. During these meetings colorful language was used

about the person endangering all his colleagues, and the negligent individual was left in no doubt about the anger of his peers.

The persistent offender could have the union's support withdrawn, in
which case management sanctions would again apply and he was liable to
be dismissed. But it rarely got that far. One unforgettable appearance before the committee was usually enough to convince the careless individual
of his obligation to others. Pictures of charred bodies from previous terminal fires made the point.

The result was that many more unsafe acts were now reported, and the
numbers trended downward, week by week, as the word went out that errors would not be tolerated. This scenario is depicted at the top right of Figure 8.5.

So it was that Pacific Oil succeeded in both its objectives: persuading
tanker truck drivers to drive more safely and flagging unsafe acts so that
these could be highlighted, counted, and reduced. In both cases, it was
necessary to qualify the status ascribed to truckers and to terminal workers, permitting them to achieve in new ways and along new dimensions.

Case 4: How Fairfield Became the Best Plant
in the Anheuser-Busch System

Those consultants who interview managers or employees as a means of
diagnosing corporate issues often discover a curious, if not altogether surprising, phenomenon. No one seems to have genuinely listened to these
people in years. In interviews, not infrequently they supply the answers
that have eluded those who hired the consultants to help the organization.

The Meridian Group in Berkeley, California, set out to discover if interviewing alone could improve the performance of the Fairfield plant of Anheuser-Busch. If you ascribed status to the lives, the experience, and the aspirations of employees by listening carefully to each person and made no
other intervention, might this have a positive effect on output and measured achievement?

Anheuser-Busch was no stranger to measured achievement. Indeed, the
company suffered at that time from what senior consultant Royal Foote
called "information authoritarianism." For example, because it was two
hours earlier at the St. Louis company headquarters (central time) than it
was in California (Pacific time), managers in Fairfield might be telephoned

during breakfast at home to be told that their "tin wastage" was up 4.0 percent. What did they intend to do about it? Not very much until they got to work in the morning! At the time of the first intervention, the Fairfield plant was a laggard in the Anheuser-Busch network of brewing plants— not quite the worst, but not far off the bottom. Eight years later, with the program entering its ninth year, Fairfield was the best by a significant margin.

The intervention made was extraordinarily simple. Yet, without an understanding of the way ascribed status interacts with achieved status, one would not have expected it to work, especially in a plant employing quite simple technology. Beer was brewed, canned, or bottled, packed into shipping cartons, and delivered to towns in northern and central California.

The intervention was as follows. The consultants interviewed senior management, after which they trained them in interview techniques developed by Professor Nevitt Sanford of the Wright Institute. Top managers then interviewed their direct reports, who interviewed their direct reports, and so on down to the lowest-level supervisors, who interviewed the hourly workers and the truckers. At each level, the techniques of interviewing were explained and taught.

The interviews were focused not on work issues but on any issue that happened to concern the interviewees at that time, including parental, domestic, work, and community concerns. In short, the interviewer asked, "Who are you?" No subject was off limits, and the interviewers were trained to pursue the interviewee's personal concerns. Each employee was treated as "a person worth listening to" in his or her own right, regardless of the job he or she was doing.

This is what anthropologists call "thick description," a very detailed picture of a particular informant's viewpoint.

Over time this led to a "high-context culture," which refers to how much information members of a culture have about one another. The "higher" the context, the richer and more detailed is the mutual knowledge within that culture. The consultants' hypothesis was that high context and the ascription of importance to each person's identity would increase organizational effectiveness, as information was literally "dredged upward" from the lowest levels of the organization to the top.

However, nothing could have prepared the consultants for the total transformation in the fortunes of Fairfield over the decade that followed. As in the case of Pacific Oil, the plant was organized by the Teamsters, a particularly tough and demanding union, whose local chose their own leaders by ballot.

The first major change was the election of the moderate faction of the Teamster's local with previous strike leaders ejected. The new leader argued that although management was still making serious errors, it seemed ready to listen and to learn. Given this apparent goodwill, a policy of dialogue was preferable to confrontation. The work force agreed.

But what really impressed corporate HQ was that Fairfield was posting gains on all major indexes of efficiency and effectiveness. On-time deliveries, sales, profits, and dealer satisfaction were all up. Theft, leakage, tin wastage, absenteeism, turnover, grievances, work stoppages were all down. At the end of five years Fairfield was vying with the best plants in the system. At the end of eight years, it led on twenty-eight of forty indexes of performance.

There is a bittersweet ending to this story. It took eight years for the CEO to acknowledge Fairfield's turnaround, in part because he did not understand the intervention. He understood only that the plant had succeeded. The day came when medals were pinned on the lapels of Fairfield's finest, and the CEO made a congratulatory address. The consultants had retired modestly to the back of the hall, as consultants should. They were somewhat distressed to hear the following peroration by the CEO: "And so we all see that dialogue works better than confrontation, so our duty is clear. Whenever we meet confrontation we must *stamp it out*. Thank you very much. . . ." Eight years of work . . . ah well!

Figure 8.6 illustrates the Fairfield plant's trajectory to success. The dynamic begins at top left, with executives being called at home with critiques of their performance. This practice ceased as a result of interviewing. Now all local executives receive information about their own plant first, so that remedies are in place by the time HQ inquires. The interviewing process moved information from narrowly performance-oriented to broadly person-oriented and was confirmatory of ascribed status. The helix spiraling top right shows the increase in high-context culture and the "thickening" of each person's description. At top right are the many celebrations as Fairfield broke record after record.

The interesting finding is that knowing work colleagues really well pays off in work effectiveness, even where the task is simple. So many are the ways of miscommunicating that knowledge of one another seems to be a successful antidote. We might expect that top research scientists would

INDEXES
OF
ACHIEVED
PLANT
PRODUCTION
AND
EFFICIENCY

INFORMATION AUTHORITARIANISM

HIGH CONTEXT CULTURE

BEST PLANT IN SYSTEM

THICK DESCRIPTION

INTERVIEWING AND RESPECTING WHOLE PERSON

Figure 8.6 How Fairfield Became the Best Plant in the System

need to know one another well, since they deal in subtleties, but that beer is better canned and shipped by people who share intimacies and know each other well is a highly significant finding that tells us much about the human condition. Listening to Fred tell me about his catfish pond and his kid's lost hamster is not wasted time after all.

Case 5: Pygmalion in the Classrooms

Our final case tells us a lot about the power of ascribed status to change the life opportunities of schoolchildren. Two researchers, Robert Rosenthal and Leonore Jacobson, purported to have conducted a detailed study of several classes of high school students. They presented their "findings" to the children's teachers. On the basis of careful studies, they had identified children who, during the following academic year, were expected to "spurt" in their academic achievement.

The children so designated had not been told, and the teachers were asked to say nothing to the children that might bias the researchers' predictions.

A subsequent assessment of the children's grades and their teachers' reports showed that what the researchers had predicted largely came true.

The designated "spurters" had done better. Most of them had performed significantly better than they had a year earlier.

There was only one problem. No study had ever been undertaken. No potential to spurt had ever been discovered. The designated children had been chosen at random, using a random number table. The researchers' real intention had been to discover the effect of teachers' expectations on subsequent performance of children. And indeed it was powerful. The children performed in such a way as to confirm their teachers' prior ascription of status, guaranteed by Harvard. The school had thrown its mantle of prestige on selected children and they had blossomed, even though the selection had been entirely arbitrary. The children had neither achieved nor shown promise of achievement until they were changed by the positive regard of their teachers, who wanted to believe what Harvard had told them.

Liza Doolittle's adage resonates: "It's the way that she's treated that makes her a lady"—or scholar, or achiever.

This dynamic is depicted in Figure 8.7. The top left shows the mythical "level playing field" or "even break," with children or competitors on the same footing. At bottom right, Harvard researches predict that certain children will do better and the mystique descends. At top right we find that the teachers' expectations alone (no one had mentioned Harvard to the children) have elevated the academic status of the children.

Research of this kind leaves a somewhat unpleasant taste. There is the fact that the researchers lied to the teachers and the fact that not every child could be guaranteed by Harvard, so that what was given to one child was necessarily taken from others. However, there is no reason that status cannot be ascribed to all persons on the basis of their unique characteristics and potentials, as it was in the Fairfield case.

There is abundant evidence that certain minority ethnic groups in America and elsewhere succeed despite prejudices against their ethnicity. Such success is almost certainly traceable to strong family structures and to the "undeserved" status of being loved by parents, siblings, and relatives, and to achievement being used as repayment for affection.

We have only to note the number of Asian students at the University of California, and that Chinese immigrants in the United Kingdom are wealthy relative to others in that society, a feat repeated in Malaysia, Indonesia, Thailand, and in most parts of the Chinese diaspora.

No less an authority than Douglas McGregor, a professor at MIT in the

CHILDRENS' RELATIVE ACHIEVE-MENT

LEVEL PLAYING FIELD

SELF-FULFILLING PROPHECY

HARVARD'S AURA

TEACHERS' EXPECTATION THAT CHILDREN WOULD SPURT

Figure 8.7 Pygmalion in the Classroom

sixties and formerly president of Antioch, described the role of ascribed status in business. He argued that the status ascribed to employees was either inconsistent with their heightened achievement or consistent with it. He called the inconsistent ascription Theory X and the consistent ascription Theory Y. He held that both attitudes were self-fulfilling, so that the manager would "discover" what she had initially assumed and then spend much of her career being validated.

Theory X assumes:

• The average individual has an inherent dislike of work and will avoid it if possible.

Therefore:

• Most people must be coerced, controlled, directed, and threatened with punishment to get them to put forth adequate effort.

This is because:

• They prefer to be directed, wish to avoid responsibility, have relatively little ambition, and want security above all.

Theory Y assumes:

- The expenditure of physical and mental effort in work is as natural as play or rest.
- External controls are not the sole means [of motivation] since individuals will exercise self-direction and self-control in the service of objectives to which they are committed.
- Commitment to objectives is a function of the rewards associated with their achievement (which can take the form of actualizing both the self and organizational objectives).
- The average individual learns under proper conditions not only to accept but to seek responsibility.
- The capacity to exercise a relatively high degree of imagination, ingenuity, and creativity in the solution of organizational problems is widely, not narrowly, distributed throughout the population.

Clearly, by anticipating future achievement, Theory Y makes that much more likely to occur. In contrast, Theory X by ascribing an anti-achievement, low-strategy role to employees, makes them hostile toward the manager, the organization, and the achievement ethic.

9 Inner Direction versus Outer Direction

THE DILEMMA

A major issue confronting all cultures is where to locate the origins of virtue. Depending on where virtue is, you steer your conduct and develop your sense of moral direction from two contrasting sources.

How the Dilemma Is Defined

Inner direction	Outer direction
conceives of virtue	conceives of virtue
as *inside* each of us—	as *outside* each of us
in our souls, wills,	in natural rhythms,
convictions, principles,	in the beauties
and core beliefs—in	and power of nature,
the triumph of conscious	in aesthetic environments
purpose	and relationships

While inner-directed cultures believe that "deep down" we know what is right, that we have a soul or inner core of purity and integrity, outer-directed cultures bid their members to emulate Nature—its beauty, majesty, force, seasonality, and ecology. To respond with grace to social and natural forces is the essence of virtue. For example, is mercy within us—"in our bowels," to use a somewhat archaic expression—or does it drop "like gentle dew from heaven?" Any one culture may use both metaphors, but inner- not outer-directed images typically predominate in Judeo-Christian cultures.

If virtue is innate, then expressing it fearlessly and defiantly is among the great moral acts. "No man can do ought against conscience," said Martin Luther. "Here stand I. I cannot do otherwise." Another strand in the Western theme of inner directedness is the ancient battle of Man versus Nature. For most of our time of existence on this earth we have been challenged by natural elements—earthquakes, wind, fire, cold, pestilence, hunger, thirst, and predatory animals. When Francis Bacon wrote that "Knowledge is Power," he meant power over Nature. Nature is "a woman," and we must "torture her secrets from her" while she is "kept in restraint." Hans Jonas comments on Bacon's sado-masochistic imagery of nature as a shrew to be tamed: "Not only is man's relation to nature one of power, but nature herself is conceived in terms of power. Thus, it is a question of either ruling or being ruled; and to be ruled by a nature not noble, kindred or wise means slavery and hence misery. The exercise of man's inherent right is therefore also the response to a basic and continuous emergency: the emergency of a contest decreed by man's condition."

Not surprisingly, perhaps, the nations who led the first wave of industrial revolutions were those that most wanted to see nature tamed and subservient. The inventions of huge machines, the clearing of the wilderness, the slaughter of perhaps ten million buffalo, the colonization of India and Africa, the sending out of missionaries to convert the heathens—all were the works of inner-directed persons.

Two people from two different cultures meet. There is an awkward pause, and the more inner-directed of the two starts to shout commands and/or wave weapons to control his anxiety.

In contrast, the outer-directed person is more likely to adjust himself to external force, to temporize, to bend but not necessarily break, and to study this new force for whatever potential opportunities it presents. Can he harness this force and use its momentum for his own purposes?

The contrast between inner-directed and outer-directed can best be illustrated by comparing two famous generals: Alexander the Great, whose conquests reached from Greece to India, and Sun Tzu, the famous Chinese warrior-strategist and author of *The Art of War*. Alexander the Great died in 323 BC, two years after his successful campaign against Indian forces, in the Indus Valley. Sun Tzu's writings were collected and chronicled at about the same time, but some historians trace the original general to the fifth century BC. It is the writings, not the victories, that survive.

Alexander conquered "the known world"—China and Southeast Asia were not known to him—by dint of brilliant strategic plans that remained largely unchanged, although battle tactics varied. The strategic ingredient was the phalanx of 64 battalions, a closely interlocked unit of 256 men.

The battalions bristled with spears like a porcupine. The front five rows pointed their spears forward. The sixth to ninth rows held their spears at acute angles of ever greater elevation. Rows ten to sixteen deep held their spears in the air tilted slightly forward. The front row presented a row of interlocked shields. The flanks were shielded also. Falling projectiles from above typically struck the spears, which deflected their momentum. If necessary, shields could be placed over heads and shoulders to armor the whole formation.

The formation was strategically unbeatable by any foreign formation. The Indian elephants, pricked by scores of spears, stampeded and killed their own soldiers. The Persian chariots were stopped by several hundred javelin throwers that preceded the battalions. Those that did get through were confounded when the formation parted to let them through and then closed behind them. The formation could face both ways, and the charioteers were trapped between it and the Macedonian rearguard.

It would be an exaggeration to credit this single formation with all Alexander's victories. His siege engines were brilliantly innovative and his cavalry was ferocious. But Alexander had a "winning strategy" in his Macedonian phalanx that no other army could resist, urged on as they were by the men who directed each "porcupine" formation.

Alexander's conquests are clearly a monument to inner-directed strategy. Modern Western business has borrowed this military metaphor to dignify and glamorize its own strategies. The search is for "the winning idea" that no one else can match, the secret formula that when revealed will gain victory for your objectives and spell defeat for your opponents. At its simplest, inner direction means getting your own way by superior means.

Sun Tzu's *Art of War* takes a completely different tack. It is wise where Alexander was merely clever. The Chinese word for the strategy used by Sun Tzu is *ji*, for which no Western word exists. It can be translated as "Think through the whole situation."

Sun Tzu is famous for maxims that at first glance are virtually a negation of force itself, much as outer direction may appear to be a negation of inner direction: "Subdue the enemy without fighting." For Tzu, you fight only when mental agility and cunning fail to win the day. "Wars must be brief," he states. "There has never been a protracted war from which a country has benefited." Wars are won swiftly and with least loss when you know both yourself and your enemy.

Crucial to leadership is the harmony between leader and led, fighting "with one heart" and "animated by the same spirit throughout all its ranks." It is this spirit that makes for successful delegation, with generals responding as their sovereign would have done.

The attack should be less on the enemy than on his strategem, which once confounded will render him perplexed and weak. If you cannot beat his strategy, attack his alliances, cutting him off from assistance. Only then—and only if you must—attack his cities.

The key is to create a situation that traps your opponent, to use natural terrain and natural elements against him "as if one rolls logs or stones down from a mountain." You should "lie in wait" for your enemy—let him exhaust himself finding you, ambushing him when you are rested, provisioned, and poised.

"Generally he who occupies the field of battle first and awaits his enemy is at ease; he who comes later to the scene and rushes to the fight is weary." At first you should be "shy as a maiden," then "swift as a hare." It is crucial to disguise your strength. "When capable, feign incapacity, when active, inactivity, when near make it appear that you are far away, when far away that you are near." Objectives should be approached by indirection.

One wins by closely following the terrain, by adapting to the changing situation more rapidly. "An army may be likened to water, for just as following water avoids the heights and hastens to the lowlands, so an army avoids strength and strikes weakness. And as water shapes its flow in accordance with the ground, so an army manages its victory in accordance with the situation of the enemy. And as water has no constant form, there are in war no constant conditions. Thus, one able to gain the victory by modifying his tactics in accordance with the enemy situation may be said to be divine."

Strictly speaking, Sun Tzu was trying to win, much as Alexander the Great was trying to win. Both shared a concern with successful strategy. Where they differed is that Alexander aimed straight for victory by using overwhelming force, while Sun Tzu won by indirection, by baiting the trap and letting his enemy blunder into it, by reconfiguring the battlefield so that the advantage was his. Alexander was inner directed, conceiving war as a conflict of wills in direct confrontation. Sun Tzu was outer directed, conceiving war as a set of external conditions to which your response must be quicker and by which you aim to bewilder and confuse your opponent.

How We Measure Inner versus Outer Direction

We administered to our multinational samples of managers questions designed to measure the inner direction or personal control of success. We measure inner versus outer direction by a set of questions that stress the advantages of self-determination and inner control versus the advantages of contingency, luck, fate, and circumstance.

In Figure 9.1A executives in different nations reject the proposition that "Without the right breaks one cannot be an effective leader." The United States and Canada reject this most strongly. China and Indonesia reject this the least, with 61 percent of the Chinese agreeing that "the right breaks" are necessary. Similarly, 88 percent of Canadians, 80 percent of Americans, and 83 percent of Germans agree that "Trusting to fate never turned out well" (Figure 9.1B), but only 32 percent of Singaporeans and 49 percent of Japanese agreed with this statement. Canadians and Americans, 42 percent and 38 percent, respectively, claim "There is no such

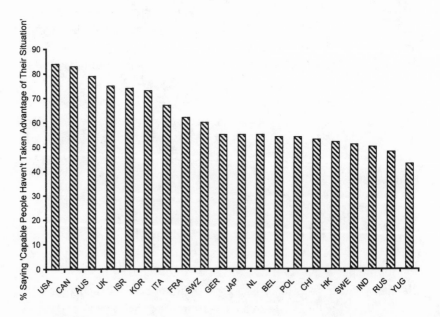

Figure 9.1A Without the Right Break, One Cannot Be an Effective Leader

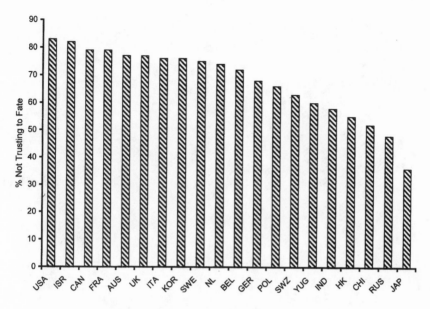

Figure 9.1B Trusting to Fate Never Turned Out Well

thing as luck" (Figure 9.1C). Only 13 percent of Japanese and 14 percent of Chinese endorse this extraordinary statement. Finally, the statement "Getting a good job depends on being in the right place at the right time" (Figure 9.1D) is rejected by 69 percent of Americans and 72 percent of Canadians but by only 44 percent and 40 percent of those in Singapore and Thailand.

Stressing as they do fate, luck, and chance, these statements inadequately explore some of the more subtle qualities of outer directedness. The outer-directed perspective also encourages individuals to use fate, chance, and contingency with more skill than their opponents and by expecting fortune to play a part, make use of its capriciousness.

Why American Culture Is More Inner- than Outer-Directed

- The Protestant Reformation championed the outraged conscience of the dissenting individual.
- Immigration to the New World required a singleness of purpose and putting aside the objections of the social environment the individual was leaving.

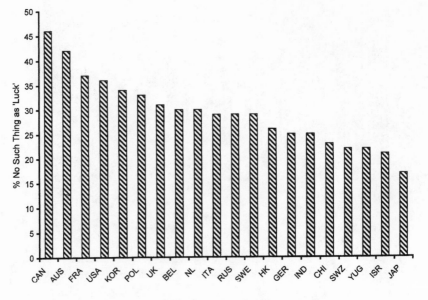

Figure 9.1C There Is No Such Thing as Luck

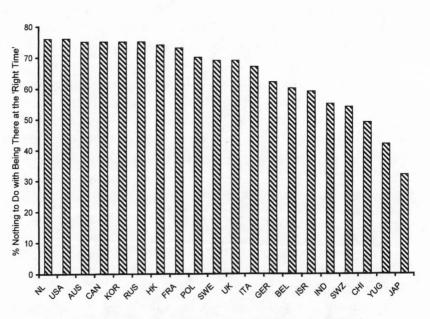

Figure 9.1D Getting a Good Job Depends on Being in the Right Place
at the Right Time

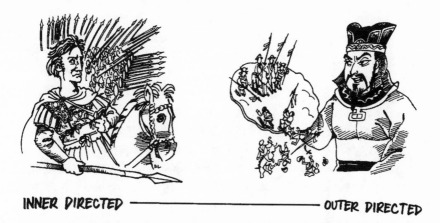

INNER DIRECTED ────────────────────── OUTER DIRECTED

Figure 9.2 Outer Direction Versus Inner Direction

- The dangers and discomforts of so long a journey were overcome only by the dreams and imaginings of what would be possible once the New World had been reached.
- "Justification by works," the Puritan doctrine, meant that the state of an individual's soul or inner purity was proven by external feats of achievement. The individual thereby expressed what was inside.
- Western Newtonian science decreed the prediction, control, and manipulation of objects demonstrably subjugated to our will.
- America's power in the world has been very considerable, until it is today the world's only remaining Superpower. Superior power manifests itself by having its conscious purpose implemented and pressed on to victory over opponents.
- America is a nation born from the ideas of the Enlightenment, conceived by the country's founders and then put into action—a New Jerusalem or Heavenly City. It represents to many the triumph of ideals translated into reality.
- Many Americans have an "innocence" and lack of guile that comes from the literal translation of good intentions and pure thoughts into reality.
- The twentieth century has been, as Harold Evans put it, *The American Century,* in which the United States has put the stamp of its authority upon the world.
- We saw in Chapter 1 that the United States is strongly universalist, or rule-making, in its orientation. This requires that the rules be exported

and imposed internationally. What the United States conceives internally to be true is also deemed true for others, in politics as in science.

- Especially in business, American scholarship and research has led the way and is widely copied. The "mastery" of business administration speaks for itself.

- America's huge size and relatively low population density has much delayed the deleterious effects of human domination over the natural environment and the shrinking biodiversity that accompanies such domination. The United States still obeys the biblical injunction "Multiply and subdue the earth." U.S. corporations lobby fiercely against environmental controls of any kind and externalize their costs on foreign environments. The recent Rio Summit witnessed much U.S. foot-dragging.

- The American legal system is highly adversarial, with many lawyers admitting they play "the devil's advocate" and that "attack is the best defense." Rape survivors say that the resulting legal action is "like being raped again." The search is often not for justice but to uphold the rights of each to fight the other. The "sacred" attorney-client bond is between fellow combatants.

- American culture has of late greatly increased its adversarialism with "shock jocks," and trading epithets about "big fat idiots" and children burned alive in the seige at Waco, Texas. Where each adversary is entirely inner-directed, no hope of reconciliation can survive, no joint search for truth is possible. They preach past each other. Civility and dialogue are casualties.

At Its Best . . .

Inner-directed culture puts private conscience at the helm of social and political affairs. Martin Luther's dissent was echoed by Martin Luther King, by the civil rights campaign, by opponents of the Vietnam War, by the release of the Pentagon Papers. Historically, American dissent has been chronicled by, among others, John F. Kennedy in *Profiles in Courage*. Lawrence Kohlberg, the late Harvard professor and researcher into sequential stages of moral development, placed principle and conscience orientation at the summit of moral development. Individuals rebel for a principle of conscience capable of resolving the moral dilemma they have encountered.

Many American movements, ultimately victorious, have originated from the inner-directed dissent of lone individuals who contrasted the principles within themselves to the horror and chaos surrounding them. In *The Rebel*, Albert Camus wrote, "I rebel, therefore we exist." Shared values have their origins in the fierce assertions of inner-directed individuals. Martin Luther King took *The Rebel* with him to his Birmingham jail. His *Letter from a Birmingham Jail* reveals its influence.

That American and British inner direction had its origin in the Puritan revolt is illustrated by John Milton's words wherein he esteems his own convictions very highly and regards objections to his views as a discordant howling of vile beasts:

> I did but prompt the age to quit their cloggs
> By the known rules of ancient libertie,
> When strait a barbarous noise environs me
> Of Owles and Cuckoes, Asses, Apes and Dogss.

Milton had a low opinion of his social environment.

William Ernest Henley immortalized the inner-directed person in Britain's more confident *Poems of the Empire*, a nineteenth-century tribute to the intrepid imperialist who "thanked whatever gods there be for my Unconquerable Soul." His head was "bloody but unbowed." Colonial expansion clearly necessitates the willpower celebrated in these words:

> It matters not how strait the gate,
> How charged with punishments the scroll,
> I am the master of my fate;
> I am the captain of my soul.

While most of us have been raised to admire such sentiments, they are not without problems.

In the Western idiom we have Frank Sinatra, who proclaimed "I did it my way," and Gene Kelly in the film *An American in Paris*, who climbs a "stairway to paradise," warning the audience not to impede his progress. Indeed, American business is very much impelled by The Big Idea, conceived by the likes of Thomas Edison and Bill Gates and consummated through the compliance of lesser individuals (Figure 9.3).

But Taken Too Far...

Inner directedness can lead to a sense of being driven from within, a compulsion to "succeed"—whatever that means. Inner-directed persons

Figure 9.3

are not necessarily original or creative but may feel compelled to win whatever contest or game is on offer. Michael Maccoby conceived *The Gamesman*, a business executive impelled to win all or any "games" defined by the corporation as worth playing. While ostensibly motivated from within to win at any cost, he ended up serving the purposes of the organization, climbing to "the top" because someone else had so defined it. The determination not to be "a quitter" simply makes the gamesman easier to control by those who have set him in motion.

While all six dimensions explored in this book are really complementarities, this reality is perhaps more obvious in the case of inner and outer directedness. It is obvious, surely, that for A to be inner directed in supervising and managing B, B must be directed from outside himself by A. An inner-directed culture is therefore highly adversarial and argumentative, because each party is attempting to direct the other in accordance with his or her own values. This leads to what Deborah Tannen calls "the argument culture," an issue we expand in this chapter. Here people become rich through publicity and by polarizing debate and slinging mud—a process that essentially kills the reconciliation we have been describing in chapter after chapter—and breaks arguments down into lethal shards. The National Rifle Association likes to quote the Second Amendment to the Constitution ". . . the right . . . to keep and bear Arms, shall not be infringed." But the ellipses at the beginning of this half-sentence give the game away. The full text reads "A well regulated Militia, being necessary to the security of a free state, the right of the people. . . ." State militias were abolished more than a century ago.

Research has found that a gun kept in the home is forty-one times more likely to injure a person in that home than is an intruder attempting to enter illegally. But none of this deters inner-directed individuals, who see themselves as the shooter, not the shot, as achieving their conscious purpose, not as making fatal errors and then blaming others.

Even a series of school massacres, most notably the one in Littleton, Colorado, only moves gun buffs to advocate more father-son bonding around firearms and to urge even small children to be trained in "responsible" gun handling at the earliest possible stage.

America's comicbook superheroes are all exemplars of inner direction. Almost all are stronger than nature, "faster than a speeding bullet," and able to reverse time by flying backward round the earth's rotation and saving those in distress. Because a superman would make an awkward companion, for whom one could do nothing, most superheroes metamorphose from Clark Kent, or his equivalent, to all-powerful embodiments. This allows them to be lovable, simple, and folksy on the outside and enjoy "normal" relationships while being dynamic and all-powerful internally and in their pursuit of "truth, justice, and the American way."

Their inner direction also makes superheroes easier to identify with. "Just like me—shy, friendly, then POW!" This is clearly the stuff of compensatory fantasies toward individuals who frustrate you in achieving your goals.

No clearer example of how business celebrates the inner-directed individual can be found than in *Fortune* magazine's periodic celebration of America's Ten Toughest Bosses—no awards for tenderness! These include such colorful characters as Old Blood and Guts, Loose Cannon, Detail Monger, Megabrain, Commando, Cost Buster, and In-Your-Face (Figure 9.4). One of America's most admired CEOs is Jack Welch of General Electric, called "Neutron Jack" after the projected neutron bomb, which would kill only people but preserve property. Whether Welch deserves this appellation we do not know.

The "dark side" of toughness does, of course, require many subordinates to be humbled and fearful. One boss, according to *Fortune*, was "so tough he tells you when to go to the bathroom." But would that not require a dozen or so subordinates to wait for permission? How much stronger is American management as a whole? If inner direction is for leaders, is not outer direction the fate of all subordinates, of the average person?

It is not the fittest who survive, but the fittingest, those who co-evolve with their natural environment.

American culture has had a long, bitter quarrel with the theory of evolution because it is fundamentally a theory of external fit. The environment allows certain organisms to survive because these find a niche, and it dooms others. So, far from being inner directed by God or by humanity, evolution is externally directed by the environment in a purposeless way. This controversy came to a head in the Scopes Monkey Trial held in Dayton, Tennessee, in 1925, where defense attorney Clarence Darrow clashed with prosecutor William Jennings Bryan.

The modern expression of anti-evolutionism is "creationism," a movement that demands that the biblical account of the creation be taught in public schools alongside the "unproven" theory of evolution. Recently in Kansas, creationists came close to striking evolution from the curriculum

BUT TAKEN TOO FAR ...

... LEADS TO
DRIVENNESS

The Right
to Bear
Arms

... WORSHIPS WEAPONS

... CREATES COMPENSATORY
FANTASIES

IS IT
A BIRD?

IS IT A
PLANE?

...MULTIPLIES AND
SUBDUES THE EARTH

... CELEBRATES FORTUNE'S
TEN TOUGHEST BOSSES

LOOSE
CANNON

COST
BUSTER

DETAIL
MONGER

MEGA
BRAIN

COMMANDO

Figure 9.4

altogether. It is an interesting example of the predisposition of culture to believe and disbelieve key patterns of explanation. A recent poll has found that among Americans, 44 percent believe that "God created man pretty much in his present form some time in the last 10,000 years."

Some of the less agreeable episodes in American history, for example, the Watergate scandal, seem to have had more than their fair share of inner-directed antagonists. The Watergate conspirators generated between them a large number of statements, indicating a fierce, driven inner directedness. John Mitchell, the only U.S. attorney general to be convicted and sent to prison, reminded John Dean of the mantra of inner directedness: "When the going gets tough the tough get going." In other words, you simply intensify your original conviction when encountering opposition. Nixon regarded Mitchell as "a great stone face" who would resist inquiries. In fact, Mitchell had talked to prosecutors much earlier.

Chuck Colson described himself as "willing to run over his grandmother to serve the president." He kept a green beret on his wall and displayed the motto, "If you've got them by the balls, their hearts and minds will follow." In prison he was promptly "born again."

Bob Haldeman announced "Every president needs a son-of-a-bitch and I'm Nixon's. I'm his buffer and his bastard." He so admired Nixon's Checkers speech that he left advertising to join him. He said of Watergate, "There is no excuse. . . . It is inexcusable in every phase and aspect." (still certain!)

John Ehrlichman, who with Haldeman was called "the Prussian Guard," was an Eagle Scout and (with Haldeman) a Christian Scientist (mind-over-body). When L. Patrick Gray's FBI nomination was stalled in Senate committee, he remarked, "Let him hang there, let him twist, slowly, slowly in the wind." "The president *is* the government," he said of his role in Watergate.

G. Gordon Liddy proposed to the Committee to Re-elect the President (CREEP) in front of Mitchell a $1 million program, Gemstone. It proposed kidnapping and drugging hostile demonstrators at the Republican Convention and dumping them over the Mexican border, sabotaging the air conditioning system at the Democratic convention, and bugging Democratic offices—for which they were later caught. Liddy is notorious for holding his left hand above a candle flame and burning his own flesh without flinching. It was always his left, never his right, so he could reach for his gun. He has since become a shock jock on radio and has advised listeners to aim for the heads of federal agents since they wear bulletproof vests.

Inner directedness remains mired in ambiguity. Sometimes Americans seem to revel in outer-directed messages. Such an occasion was the publication of B. F. Skinner's book *Beyond Freedom and Dignity,* which became a best-seller. On the surface its message was bleak. Individuals are entirely the product of conditioning by their environment. "Beyond freedom and dignity" is the design of reinforcement schedules that can be guaranteed to shape all human behavior.

The book had an obvious appeal to specificity (see Chapter 5), with its discrete contingencies, responses, and behaviors—but surely it broke every taboo of inner directedness? Surely its message was an uncompromising view of the person as externally reinforced and at the mercy of the environment?

Not quite—every book has a text and a subtext. The message that human beings can be externally shaped and their freedom and dignity is an illusion is actually rather good news to those investigators intent on doing the shaping. Where there is no freedom in the psychology lab, there could be perfect freedom for behaviorists themselves, who design environments that shape others. Skinner's work was the secret delight of those aiming to control everyone else, the behaviorist elite. It was inner directed, after all.

At Its Best . . .

Outer-directed culture is in touch with the living environment and, like the lyre of Orpheus, resonates with all nature. An obvious feature of East Asian cultures is that their martial arts, like Sun Tzu's *Art of War,* represent conflict by indirection. In ju-jitsu, aikido, bushido, and other activities the ideal is to learn "the way of" (*do*) swords, gentleness, and so on. In judo, you use the momentum of your opponent to flip him or her in the desired direction. You start with his or her inner direction and end by getting your own way. But even here, you are directed by the art of judo itself. "The way of" judo, archery, calligraphy, flower arranging, and so on is more important than are its practitioners. You become a master by surrendering your body and muscular reflexes to "the way" itself. At the height of achievement you are entirely directed by ancient art forms and disciplines. Your body responds automatically to an idea, like the hand of an artist to a vision.

In East Asian cultures, the ritual of bowing has the same pattern of responsiveness, as do small noises made in the back of the throat to denote that you are hearing and paying attention. To bow is to respond, to resonate to take direction from another. The depth of the bow is indicative of the depth of respect. You bow more deeply to a superior than the superior bows to you. The language of relative status is conveyed by physical movements.

Outer-directed cultures are very quick to catch on to technologies originating in the West and ride on the back of these to fame and fortune. While inner-directed cultures may invent on a larger scale, outer-directed cultures may elaborate, improve, refine, and customize more effectively. "Tiger" economies have developed faster than any economies in the history of economics—even in the light of recent banking crises. The outer-directed mind-set notes what is moving fastest—for example, microelectronics, precision engineering, capital goods—and jumps on the back of the "tiger."

These outer-directed government-orchestrated interventions are quite sophisticated, and like Sun Tzu they "tip the battlefield." "Horizontal technologies"—for example, machine tools, microchips, liquid crystal displays—are technologies running across many industries and making major differences to their productivity. The trick is to find a small unit that makes a large difference. Is the technology knowledge-intensive, so that it educates and renders more intelligent all those who design it, make it, distribute it, and use it? Will it increase "the value-added per person" of your economy and so help eliminate low wages and low skills? Do you have trained people in the educational pipeline so that rare skills are not bid up to generate inflation? Will this technology help to form a cluster of interacting competencies that cross-fertilize to create new knowledge and technologies?

Outer-directed governments like Singapore typically advise their industries but do not instruct them. They may create "mechatronic institutes," claiming that machines have more and more electronic components, sensors, regulators, and feedback loops. It is therefore obvious that mechanical engineering needs to be directed by electrical engineering and vice versa. Similar operations may cross-fertilize biology and chip-making, new materials and design, and so on. East Asian "planning" is often a combination of disciplines rather than a precise program driven by a schedule. The guess is that the combination will generate novelties.

Shinto religion is not unconnected to Japan's industrial disciplines. Worshippers craft products carried on the shoulders of celebrants, which are so beautifully and elegantly made that the gods will wish to inhabit them. Shinto gods, who are pantheistic deities of nature, inhabit the wind, rain, storm, river, mountains, and harvests. Worshippers are outer di-rected, emulating their beauty, strength, force, speed, and majesty. The Zen garden and moss garden are cultivated in imitation of natural land-scapes, miniaturized and finely groomed.

The gods hate dirt or pollution of any kind and therefore objects made for their habitation are beautifully finished and immaculate. That you can eat your breakfast off the floor of a modern Honda factory says much for the way religious habits of cleanliness have been brought into the work-place.

Much skill at survival goes into assuaging the gods. Bamboo is grown not simply for its lightness and many uses but for its hollowness and occu-pancy by divine spirits. The bamboo grove is also the safest place to be in an earthquake. Nothing heavy can fall on you, and the long roots create a web beneath fault lines.

Outer-directed cultures are adept at designing environments, since by definition these greatly influence their occupants.

Karaoke is a typical amusement of an outer-directed culture and has spread from Japan throughout East Asia. You are controlled by the accom-panying music, which is typically accompanied by images on a screen, and are expected to sing along cheerfully to a scene contrived for you.

The advantages of outer directedness, then, are preferred by cultures liv-ing in a crowded, turbulent, and potentially threatening terrain. By taking the circuitous route of positively altering the environment, one can in turn improve oneself. Outer directedness teaches survival disciplines that be-come reactive habits and disciplines, minimizing and deflecting violence. Outer-directed cultures often ride upon raging market forces with con-summate skill, fast following at breathtaking speed (Figure 9.5).

But Taken Too Far . . .

Outer directedness can become pathological. East Asian attitudes to-ward death, as part of the process of living, may reveal subtlety and sophis-tication. Death is not an insult and an absurdity, as it is for inner-directed individuals who "rage, rage against the dying of the light." Even so, Japan's

AT ITS BEST, OUTER DIRECTEDNESS...

...GETS ON THE SAME WAVELENGTH

...USES THE MOMENTUM OF ONE'S OPPONENT

...JUMPS ON THE BACK OF A TIGER ECONOMY

...EMULATES THE BEAUTIES OF NATURE

...CRAFTS PRODUCTS WHICH GODS WOULD LIKE TO INHABIT

...SINGS ALONG

Figure 9.5

suicide cults do more than help death on its way. They represent an ethos of self-sacrifice to external authorities. There is nobility in disembowelment and ritual sacrifice—witness the suicide of Yukio Mishima in November 1970.

The kamikaze pilots of World War II were imitating the "divine wind," which twice before had scattered troops gathering to invade Japan. The ideal was to emulate the destructiveness of typhoons that had tracked northward up the Japanese islands for the past two thousand years. To be as angry as a volcano, as destructive as a typhoon, as cold as a mountaintop can lead to violent and cruel behaviors. Nature is not always benign.

More recent, and more practical in its consequences, is that both optimism and pessimism about Japan's economy seem to be self-fulfilling and self-perpetuating, since people reflect the mood outside and around them. Japan's recent recession, largely confined to domestic despondency and not reflected in the overseas operations of Japanese companies, appears to be contagious. Zero interest rates and massive government spending are insufficient to raise the gloom.

The outer-directed perspective is also captured in the "humor" of Japanese TV game shows, where the discomfort and ridicule of contestants is grist for the mill of the audience. Contestants must sit on blocks of ice with their trousers down while their rear ends freeze and they are expected to be "good sports" about it all (Figure 9.6). Especially young contestants are expected to "win their spurs" by diving into pools for eels or immerse themselves in slime. The audience seems to enjoy it when the environment is dominant. There are very real problems in giving the social environment the advantage over human self-direction.

The less than spontaneous demonstrations by the supporters of Chairman Mao, and Great Leaps Forward, which turned out to be a great slide backward, are the fruits of outer directedness.

Finally, outer directedness can produce an artificiality, an overcontrolled "naturalness" that is untrue to nature. Ruth Benedict drew attention to the manicured gardens, miniaturized trees, and oddly clipped and distorted plants, also the overly contrived images of beauty, so that the geisha resembles a painted doll with nearly all humanity expunged. Takeo Doi refers to Japanese children delightful when small, but a few years later docile and with most expressiveness gone, carefully copying the "no-face" and the attitudinal blankness of their elders.

BUT TAKEN TOO FAR ...

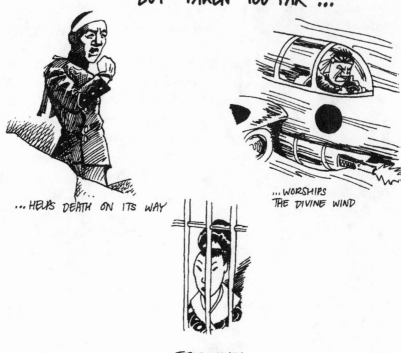

... HE/IS DEATH ON ITS WAY

...WORSHIPS
THE DIVINE WIND

...TURNS WOMEN
INTO DOLLS

... THE ENVIRONMENT ASSAILS YOU
FOR LAUGHS

... CANNOT LIFT ITSELF
OUT OF COLLECTIVE GLOOM

Figure 9.6

Culture Clashes and Derivative Conflicts: In Business and Industry

Many are the derivatives of inner versus outer directedness in the conflicts and issues faced by business.

There is the contrast between the "dauntless decision maker" and the "chief listener," both located at the apex of the organization. In American and European traditions the leader is the originator of strategies and missions. In the English language, "authority" stems from the word *author* or *originator*. Leaders are the most inner directed of all in authoring the corporation's decisions.

Even the word *decision*, from the Latin *de-cido*, means "to cut off." Dauntless decision makers choose an alternative and cut off other alternatives, along with continuing discussions. The die is cast. The decision made. The risk taken. It was Alexander the Great who used his sword to cut through the Gordian knot while lesser men picked and pulled at it.

To be truly inner directed, you must override the opinions of those around you. To the extent that they influence you, you are outer directed. So the height of inner direction is achieved by those who invent the company, the entrepreneurs and, where the company already exists, by those who impose their decisions on subordinates.

Accordingly there is a soft spot in the American psyche for the turnaround specialist, the grand acquisitor, and the downsizer.

In outer-directed cultures those rising to senior ranks tend to talk less and less, such is their wisdom and the significance of their very presence. The Japanese emperor is perhaps the clearest example. But since the outer directedness of one person does by definition elicit the inner directedness of another, the East Asian authority figures become chief listeners to the petitions, requests, and initiatives of their subordinates. To be inner directed is to be young, precocious, aspiring. To be outer directed is to be mature, responsive, and nurturing.

Here the Confucian metaphor of the family looms large. The father takes pleasure and delight in the growing capabilities of his children, who show off for him. This helps to explain the anomalous findings concerning East Asian corporations. They are simultaneously more hierarchical and more adept at getting vital information from the bottom of the corporation to the top and from the field to the center.

Worker suggestions, for example, are ten times more likely to be implemented at Motorola's Penang plant in Malaysia than at its U.S. plants in

Illinois, Texas, and Florida. The difference is that those at the top in East Asia are chief listeners, while those at the top in the United States are inner-directed issuers of deathless decisions, against which the ideas of subordinates cannot prevail. In most Western cultures, steep hierarchy makes this situation worse, so that hierarchy is typically deplored. But in East Asian cultures, the duty to listen and to respond dates back to feudalism. No parent should ignore his or her children. Hierarchy is based on the obligation to be influenced from below and from outside.

The hero of an inner-directed society is the "great inventor," the person who began with an idea inside his or her head, persisted in creating it, and finally established it as a major feature of the external environment. Great American inventors include Alexander Graham Bell, Vannevar Bush, Samuel Colt, George Eastman, Thomas Edison, Henry Ford, Benjamin Franklin, Charles Goodyear, Edwin Land, Samuel F. B. Morse, George Pullman, Frederick W. Taylor, Eli Whitney, and the Wright Brothers— among many others.

The heroes of the outer-directed cultures are those providing the external stimuli—the great trading companies, or *zaibatsu,* the customers who demand numerous refinements, and top managers, who set riddles for subordinates to answer. Instead of great inventions, Japan has largely produced some remarkable *kaizen,* or refinements. This is by no means a simple or riskless process.

For example, Ampex, a U.S. company, invented the video cassette recorder, but it was an expensive machine for television studios, priced at $1,500 and up until Victor and Sony refined the VCR for the consumer market. The investment needed was considerable—over $2 billion—but almost the entire market for VCRs was won for the Japanese, worldwide. It is not enough to start a race. You must finish it. The prize in consumer electronics is the mass market. The closer you get to consumers, the more outer directedness pays off, because consumers have myriad needs, constantly changing, which require rapid adjustment from suppliers. During the eighties, America lost several markets it had originated through its inner directedness to outer-directed Japanese refinements. Robert Reich commented, "Several product histories make the point. Americans invented the solid-state transistor in 1947. Then in 1953, Western electric licenced the technology to Sony for $125,000—the result is history. A few years later RCA licenced several Japanese companies to make colour televisions—that was the beginning of the end of colour television production in the United States."

The inner-directed culture celebrates the giving of direct orders, but because these can be highly problematic, when the order is wrong, they also celebrate defiance of such orders. Hence Chuck House of Hewlett-Packard was ordered by David Packard to get his prototype for a lunar landing monitor "out of the lab," by which Packard meant "Abandon it." House got it out of the lab, all right, and into production. It was used in the Apollo mission, and House was presented with a commemorative plaque "For Defiance." Another example of defiance within a hierarchy is *Mutiny on the Bounty,* a much recounted historical episode featuring both direct orders and mutinous defiance.

The Japanese approach is to act as "riddler"—to give indirect, incomplete, ambiguous, or even paradoxical orders—so that the outer-directed recipient is obliged to interpret what is being asked for and, in so doing, create. In their seminal book *The Knowledge-Creating Company,* Ikujiro Nonaka and Hirotaka Takeuchi give several examples of metaphors or indirect statements given by top Japanese managers to subordinates that could be answered only by a creative response to their environment. For example, the metaphor "Tall Boy" for a vehicle almost spherical in shape, the concept of "Automobile Evolution," and the principle "Man maximum–machine minimum" are all phrases designed to elicit solutions from outer-directed people. It is impossible to conform exactly or to comply because it is unclear what the speaker wants. Like the ancient oracle at Delphi who advised the Greek armies to "Hide within your wooden walls," what the authority prescribes is unclear. That they took their ships and won the Battle of Salamis was a tribute to their powers of creative thinking. The oracle was a stimulus.

"The role of top management," says Ryuzaburo Kaku, chairman of Canon, "is to give employees a sense of crisis as well as a lofty ideal." It deliberately creates an external environment of "creative chaos," "strategic equivocality," and "challenging Detroit."

An important breakthrough in Canon's mini-copier for use in the home occurred when task force leader Hiroshi Tanaka held up an empty aluminum beer can. "How much does it cost to manufacture this?" he asked. The group immediately responded to this stimulus. Ninety percent of faults in the copier involved the drum. Why not make a cheap, detach-

able aluminum drum that could be exchanged at the corner shop for a new
one?

You are also encouraged to learn from your own body or corporeal environment, which may have latent knowledge of the answer. A lowly factory
worker may have extraordinary manual skills, making dies accurate within
a thousandth of an inch. East Asian companies will point cameras at these
hands to discover their secrets. This was done with master bakers at the
Osaka International Hotel to better design a dough-mixing machine for
home baking. The bakers twisted the dough before they squeezed it, in order to trap air. The kneading machines imitated the process. Outer-directed emulation has many advantages (Figure 9.7).

A major difference between inner- and outer-directed selling methods is
the hard versus soft sell. Americans have a curiously charitable view of the
hard-sell huckster, the inner-directed individual. "Professor" Harold Hill
in the musical *The Music Man* could neither read music nor play it. Yet he
had a "vision," a boys' marching band for which he would supply the uni-
forms and instruments. He first frightened the citizens of River City into
subscribing lest their children be attracted to the local pool hall, then
started to machinate. His redemption by true love was incidental.

In *The Wizard of Oz* a traveling charlatan and fortune-teller tries to get
Dorothy home to Auntie Em before a twister strikes. In her dream he meta-
morphoses into the wizard and is up to his old tricks—all of which are considered lovable. A star salesperson purportedly can even sell refrigerators
to Eskimos. Note that getting people to do what they do not want and to buy
what they do not need defines stellar performance for the inner-directed
person, whose will overrides. Gary Larson, the popular "Far Side" cartoonist, has made much sport of insurance salesmen. Figure 9.8 elaborates on
the theme he has made famous.

In contrast, Japanese or East Asian salespeople may be so soft it is in-
comprehensible. Westerners who watch Japanese TV commercials might
well ask the Japanese what is being advertised. The message has an association to an association of which we are not aware. Department stores show
"mood videos" of waves and burbling steams with no clear connection to
any product. The more ready the consumer is to respond to external stimuli, the less hard you have to try and the softer the signals can be. A famous
example of soft sell was the goodlooking young men from Nomura who
called on Japanese housewives in the years following World War II.

So, far from individuals or products showing off, they may reveal them-

DAUNTLESS DECISION MAKER — THE CHIEF LISTENER

THE GREAT INVENTOR — THE REFINER

DIRECT ORDERS/DEFIANCE — THE RIDDLER

Figure 9.7

selves modestly. "I'm sure you have many more deserving candidates than I," began a letter to the British author of this book from a Chinese woman seeking to do her doctorate under his supervision at Cambridge University. On the contrary, her record was outstanding!

In outer-directed cultures where members study their environment carefully and react readily, boasting about yourself or your product can insult consumers. Do you imagine they have not noticed? You need not speak so loudly nor repeat yourself.

A major difference between inner-directed and outer-directed market research is the use of questionnaires by the former and the preference for conversation or for action by the latter. In inner-directed cultures we insist that our knowledge of markets be logically ordered by us. Consumers get to answer questions in our frameworks according to our formulation. Very often they can answer only "yes," "no," "not applicable." Or they may be asked to rate a statement from 0 to 5 for importance. They cannot tell us that the question is foolish, that we have missed the point, that their reasons are quite different. We have essentially confined them to our own frame of reference. We refuse to hear any answer that we have not anticipated!

Japanese and East Asian marketing is much more likely to use conversation to learn about customers and consumers. In a conversation I can tell you that your question is irrelevant to my custom, and I can also tell you what is relevant. I am rejecting a safety seat in my car for a small child not because I disbelieve in its effectiveness but because the child cannot see out and cries because she feels trapped. She has also learned to extricate herself and crawl into the front seat! Inner-directed questionnaires can miss such realizations because they are not open to rival logics.

Outer-directed cultures may also prefer to act rather than ask! When Post-it notes were being launched by 3M, the question "Would you buy repositional notes with weak stickum?" failed to elicit a positive answer. So the notes were distributed to secretarial staff, who within hours wanted more. To actually supply the product on a trial basis is a typical outer-directed tactic.

Magorah Maruyama, a Japan based Japanese-American professor, has contrasted deviation-reducing feedback loops to deviation-enhancing loops. The first are typical of inner-directed cultures. You have, for example, a market objective against which you periodically measure your approximation. Any falling short of this plan is a "deviation" to be "reduced," so that you can come closer and closer to your original objective. But note the unstated assumption, that the original objective was correct.

More unusual in Japan and Southeast Asia is the search for what consumers prefer via a deviation-enhancing loop. The company may deliberately produce 120 variations on, for example, the Honda motor scooter and use these to find out which ones customers prefer. This variety can later be cut back after the company has learned from consumer responses. The premise is the opposite of what it was in our inner-directed example. The

HARD SELL ——————— SOFT SELL

QUESTIONNAIRE ——————— CONVERSATION

VOLVO ——————— MITSUBISHI

Figure 9.8

original premise is but a guess, a general direction. Variations on this guess allow the company to be outer directed by its customers as to what they prefer.

An interesting example of the inner-directed versus outer-directed philosophies in the design of cars is illustrated by the experience of the Dutch author of this book, who was driving a Mitsubishi that collided with a Volvo. The Swedish concept of safety is to make the car as strong as possible to protect the passenger. If possible, the Volvo should come out of any collision with another make of vehicle with far less damage. The Japanese concept of safety is to protect the driver by having the car, not the driver, yield before the impact. When he scrambled indignantly out of his car to confront the other driver, the Mitsubishi had a badly crumpled rear fender, while the Volvo had hardly a scratch. Yet the Dutch author had survived the impact unscathed. The driver of the Volvo had bumped his head.

We are not claiming that the Japanese outer-directed design is necessarily superior—possibly the Volvo driver had not fastened his seat belt. We are only pointing out an alternative approach to safety, which is to let the car absorb the impact of a collision so that the driver is less jarred. Such differences can be instructive.

Culture Clashes and Derivative Conflicts: In Religion, Ethics, and Politics

Inner-directed culture leads inevitably to adversarialism. Each adversary is noble to the extent that he or she, directed from inside, finds him- or herself at odds with the experience of the other. The most important issue in an inner-directed culture is that both contending views get expressed. "Fairness" is defined as letting each side fire an equal number of verbal blasts at each other. We call this "the sound-bite culture." While this might be "fair" or "balanced" between parties to the conflict, it is not balanced between conflict expressions and conflict resolution. People blasting away at people is "entertainment" and "choice." Voters are expected to favor one side or the other. Conflict resolution, on the other hand, is not regarded as entertainment at all. Nor is it usually newsworthy—rather, it is typically regarded as a profound anti-climax.

The sound-bite culture uses values as missiles or bombs. Sometimes these bombs are real, not rhetorical. Whenever President Johnson announced that he was "praying," a wise Vietnamese, North or South, should have ducked. Indeed, an upsurge in moral sentiments typically precedes an upsurge in violence. No wonder that much of the scientific community has given up on value judgments altogether.

A major movement in American high schools uses a method called "values clarification." Values are, of course, more "clear" when they are polarized and decontaminated of their opposites. The process used is to discuss or debate values until they become "clarified" and then leave these to the "free choice" of students. Unfortunately, the "clearer" values become, the less reconcilable they are. Idealism purged of all traces of realism is a disaster waiting to happen, as is realism cleansed of all idealism. Realistic ideals are our only hope, and this applies to all polarities in this book.

Values clarification also implies, even if it avoids stating, that all values are relative. Indeed, once you have reduced them to lethal polarities, they are all equally bad! American conservatives complain with some justice that values clarification produces a wasteland. Alas, imposing the preferred polarities of the Christian Right on everyone else is no solution either.

In contrast to the adversarial sound-bite culture is the principle of *wā*, or harmony (see Figure 9.9). Cultures like Singapore, Malaysia, Japan, and Korea celebrate the harmonious interaction of yin and yang in the Tai-Chi, the Taoist symbol of the supreme ultimate. For the Japanese, *Ameratsu*, the sun god, shines his light on living nature and makes all things grow ecologically, especially his own worshippers.

Is the principle of *wā*, with every living creature responding to a benign environment, necessarily superior to the adversary culture? Not necessarily. The cultural expectation that its members will be "harmonious" is all too easy to abuse. Was it in the long-term interests of America that so many Japanese-Americans went with such docility to internment camps during World War II? Was some protest not in order? Habits of harmony can be used to oppress, as state Shintoism was used in World War II by Japan's military government.

Should we admire Singapore because of its enviable record of social harmony concerning the agenda of the development of an "intelligent island," or should we criticize Singapore for using libel laws to bankrupt opposition politicians? Singapore's position is at least comprehensible. You can "oppose" but not question or disrupt the social ideal of national harmony, and some styles of opposition do this. It remains to be seen whether outer-directed ideals of harmony reduce values diversity and thereby undermine economic and democratic development. In this book, we have seen in chapter after chapter how important value reconciliation can be, but only where the conflict is first expressed and the dilemma accepted as genuine.

A final cultural contrast between inner and outer directedness is dramatized by two mythical characters: Prometheus and the Monkey King. The story of Prometheus represents Western civilization, drawing its inspiration from Greek mythology. The Monkey King derives from Chinese civilization, drawing its inspiration from a famous Buddist story, *Journey to the West* (from China to India, where the origins of Buddhism lie).

The myth of Prometheus is well known in the West and so is sketched very briefly here. Prometheus, a Titan (a mortal superman), is the brother of Atlas. Prometheus—the name means "forethought," hence inner directedness—had a dispute with Zeus about a sacrificial bull. Instead of reserving the best parts for the gods, Prometheus reserved these for fellow mortals. Zeus took back the gift of fire and told Prometheus to eat his meat raw. But Prometheus crept up Mount Olympus and, carrying some burning charcoal in a fennel stalk, "stole fire from the gods."

As punishment, Zeus had Prometheus chained to a pillar in the Caucasus Mountains, where a griffin-vulture ate his liver by day, which grew back overnight. But Prometheus resisted this torture for thirty years, hurling back defiance at the gods. Moved by his courage and at the behest of Heracles, Zeus unbound him. This myth has been celebrated by Aeschylus in his play *Prometheus Bound* and by the poet Shelley in *Prometheus Unbound*. Shelley anticipated the modern mood, scorned Aeschylus' reconciliation of god and man, and made Zeus (or Jupiter) into a vindictive tyrant and Prometheus into the spirit of human freedom and perfectability.

Journey to the West, sometimes called *Monkey* or *The Monkey King,* dates from China's Tang dynasty (fifth century AD). It recounts the journey of a Buddhist priest, Hsuan Tang, to India, the birthplace of Buddhism. In its written form, the story dates from 1580 and is by Wu Chengen of the Ming era. It is perhaps East Asia's most popular children's story owing to the similarity between the Monkey King's naughtiness and the need for children to grow up and accept discipline.

The Monkey King bursts fully formed from rock eggs atop Huaguo Shan (Flower Fruit Mountain) on Penglai island when a bolt of lightning strikes the rock. He immediately declares himself king of the startled monkey inhabitants, who submit to his leadership.

Showing off as usual, a few days later he dives into a waterfall and discovers beyond it a waterfall cave full of fruit and flowers, in which his followers luxuriate. When one aged monkey dies, the king is aghast. Why are not monkeys immortal? He leaves straightaway to discover how he can become a god.

He consults a Taoist ancient who confers upon him the name Sun Wukong, "Little One of Enlightened Emptiness," suggesting he has great potential to learn. He discovers seventy-two powers. His two favorites are "flying somersault over the clouds," by which he can make his escape, and "little monkeys from a pulled hair."

It is this second trick by which the Monkey King recaptures the waterfall cave, taken over by a water monster. From a single hair of his body come scores of fighting monkeys who slay the monster.

But success is going to the Monkey King's head. He steals from the Dragon King of the Sea and causes chaos at a banquet given by the Great Jade Emperor, who gives him a minor post as officer of his stables. Stung by the insignificance of his office, he kills the horses.

The Jade Emperor sends his forces against the Monkey King, but the battle is interrupted by the Buddha Rulai, who takes the Monkey King in his hand and then challenges him to jump out. The Monkey King does his famous flying somersault and lands near four pillars, which mark, as he believes, the ends of the universe. He scrawls graffiti on the "pillars," which turn out to be the four fingers of Buddha's hand, for Buddha is everywhere. The embodiment of inner directedness, he had been within those hands all the time.

Buddha places a huge stone upon the Monkey King, who lies there imprisoned until rescued by Tang Sansgang, a Buddhist monk, who recites a sutra and the rock explodes. Although he has promised to accompany Tang on "the journey to the west," he quickly tires of his commitment and is in the act of departing when a gold band flies down from heaven and encircles his head. It quickly tightens as he departs from his promised path, and only another sutra uttered by Tang stops the pain. Thereafter, the band tightens whenever the Monkey King needlessly hurts others or strays from his journey.

On this journey he picks up traveling companions. The Pig of Eight Prohibitions has been expelled from heaven for gluttony and lechery. They also recruit a water demon.

Their final obstacle is in the shape of a monstrous dilemma. The Bull Devil King sits atop a blazing mountain whose flames are fed by his consort, the Fan Princess, who uses a huge iron fan. The Monkey King, given temporary immortality by the Lord of the Earth, another Taoist deity, seizes the iron fan and beats out the flames, thus using the same instrument for a different purpose. Then he thrusts his sword, matador-like, into the heart of the bull. The successful travelers are blessed by Rulai Buddha and carry seventy-two Sutras back to China.

There are many variations of this story. In Thailand, Monkey is a Lothario. In Japan it is a long-running soap opera, featuring a martial arts expert traveling through time. In Stan Lai's Taipei national opera, "Chinese civilization" is on a gigantic operating table being poked at by global surgeons. Will Chinese culture survive?

What runs through all these versions is the need to tame and to socialize

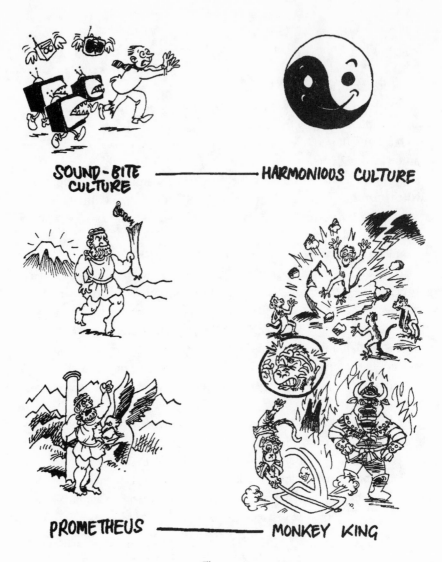

SOUND-BITE ——————— HARMONIOUS CULTURE
CULTURE

PROMETHEUS ——————— MONKEY KING

Figure 9.9

child-like fantasy and exuberance in a way that preserves a culture of ingenuity and a spirit of youthfulness, yet teaches it to serve a larger purpose.
The tightening gold band and the ubiquity of Buddha's hands are the symbols of East Asian outer directedness controlling child-like impulses—the
counterpoint to the story of Prometheus. See Figure 9.9.

To the artful reconciliation between inner and outer directedness in order to create value and generate wealth, we now turn.

10 Reconciling Inner and Outer Direction

STORIES AND CASES

As we saw repeatedly in Chapter 9, those whose moral position and direction is fiercely determined from within may require other persons and other groups to comply with this direction—in short, to be directed from outside. Neither inner nor outer direction is without its problems. The latter can reduce its followers to a predatory gang. The former can lead to stiff-necked, insufferable righteousness, along with moral dictatorship.

Below we compare two films about the history of a culture. Both are encounters with death. Both seek to explore how inner- and outer-directed individuals, respectively, deal with their own mortality to find meaning in their lives. In both cases the search is arduous and heroic. In both there is every reason to despair of the human condition, to conclude that God is dead. The two totally opposed postures of defiance and acceptance tell us much about the cultures concerned.

A Story Told by an Inner-Directed Culture

In 1957 Ingmar Bergman unveiled what many regard as one of the world's finest films, *The Seventh Seal*, winner of the Cannes Film Festival. This is very much an art-house production. The subject is too grim to appeal to the box office. Yet its fame in the West is sufficient to qualify it as a milestone of cultural expression.

It opens on a desolate seashore of stones and rocks, under a threatening sky with a circling bird of prey. Two figures—the knight, Antonius Block, and his squire, Jons, are just waking up. They are on their journey home to Sweden after a crusade to the Holy Land. It is the fourteenth century and

Sweden and much of Europe are being ravaged by the Black Death, a plague that took the lives of an estimated one-third of Europe's population. It seems a scant reward for those in search of the Holy Grail.

The knight is barely awake when a figure in a black cloak announces that he is Death. He has come to take the knight and squire. But the knight is not ready. It is less that he fears death than that he has not solved the riddle of life. On impulse, he challenges Death to a game of chess, on the condition that he continues to live until he loses. Throughout the film, Death reappears at intervals as the dual between them continues.

Block first goes to confession and tells his hooded confessor, "I cry to Him in the dark but there seems to be no one there. My whole life has been a meaningless search. I need to find one significant act." But as he peers beneath the confessor's hood, he sees it is Death. He next encounters a 14-year-old "witch" with carnal knowledge of the Devil. He stares into her eyes. If he can see the Devil then perhaps he can find God, his adversary. But in the child's eyes he sees only fear and pain. He accosts the monk, who accompanies the doomed girl. Again, it is Death.

He meets an artist painting a church frescoe called the Dance of Death. Death with his scythe leads a procession of revelry toward a dark land.

The knight and squire cross the path of a caravan of traveling players from regions to which the plague has not yet spread: Jof, a juggler, Mia, and their baby son Mikael. Jof and Mia, along with Skat and other members of the troupe, are enacting a bawdy comedy. The performance is interrupted by a grim procession of flagellants, scourging themselves and crying doom.

In a tavern after the performance, Jof is almost killed by local inebriates, who see actors as spreading sin and sickness. When Skat seduces the blacksmith's wife, all artists are fair game. The squire rescues Jof, and in gratitude the knight and squire are invited to eat with the family.

It is at this moment that sunshine breaks through the clouds and illumination comes to Antonius Block. As the radiant young couple serve them milk with wild strawberries and Mikael chases butterflies, the knight eats his "last supper of existentialism" on the grass beside them. To think that he had butchered his way to Jerusalem and all the time the meaning he sought was right here and now, in this small circle of conviviality, in the beauty of human faces.

He has found his "one significant act." He will protect this frail human caravan, conserve this oasis of affection. But Death appears to him once more. The game must go on. On a rock, some distance from the caravan, the knight and Death match wits once more. But Death is taking an interest in this family. Suddenly Block deliberately upsets the board and the chess pieces tumble. As Death replaces the pieces, saying "I never forget," Jof and Mia have climbed into their caravan and crept away.

In the meantime, Death has cheated in replacing the chess pieces, and a few moves later the knight is in checkmate. "When we meet again, I will come for you and your companions." The knight finally reaches home, where his lady awaits him. It is a somber reunion. Both have changed. He recalls their amorous frolics of earlier years, all sacrificed to abstract ideals. They read from the book of *Revelation* about breaking the Seventh Seal, and as the passage ends there comes a thunderous knocking. Death has come for them.

But not all of them. Because of the inner-directed defiance of the knight who challenged Death, a small caravan of three people escapes across the horizon. Jof, Mia, and Mikael will survive.

Figure 10.1 illustrates this triumph of the inner-directed, existential individual. The knight was able to find meaning in the face of pestilence by thrusting the idealism and hope he finds within him into the very face of absurdity. At top left is the chess game, with the knight and Death locked in inner-directed confrontation. At bottom right is the Dance of Death. Is "civilization" more than a frenzied revel leading toward darkness? The reconciliation, approached via the knight's defiance and inner direction, is that we engage in significant action before time runs out. That death is upon us only increases the urgency to act. The last supper and the escaping caravan are the consequences of Block's commitment.

In a very real sense this film is about the agony of Europe's postwar intelligensia—either occupied like France, Holland, and Norway, or neutral like Sweden—but all helpless to halt "the black death" of Nazi expansion and able to save only small islands of sanity.

The film is also about Bergman's private struggle with the strict Lutheranism of his pastor-father. He left home at 18 after his father struck both him and his mother and he had returned the blow. In *Fanny and Alexander,* a semi-autobiographical film of Bergman's childhood, he depicts his father being burned alive after his religious robes catch fire. Hence his depiction of religion as Death in various disguises, which occur throughout *The Seventh Seal,* is no passing fancy but the conflict at the center of his life.

A final point is that Bergman made a troupe of actors into his Holy Fam-

Figure 10.1 *The Seventh Seal*

ily. Jof and Mia translate into Joseph and Mary. Bergman believed that the artist is culture's conduit for transmission. So long as we can play and simulate, we can learn how better to live. He described himself as a stonemason in a large cathedral.

A Story Told by an Outer-Directed Culture

Few Western filmgoers will have heard of the Japanese classic *The Ballad of Narayama,* written and directed by Shohei Imamura and starring Ken Ogata and Sumiko Sakamoto. The film won the Grand Prix at the Cannes Film Festival in 1983. It does not appeal to popular audiences in the West because its moral narrative is largely alien to us.

Based on a novel by Shichiro Fakazawa, *Ubasutteyama,* the film is set in the nineteenth century in a desperately poor, subsistence farming community in the north of Japan, at the foot of Mount Narayama. This is popular Japanese entertainment and has audiences in tears.

The story's chief protagonists are a 69-year-old widow called Orin and her recently widowed son Tatsuhei, whose wife fell accidentally from a cliff. The fate of Orin's husband is more mysterious. He deserted her thirty years ago after physically abusing her and being unfaithful. Orin is the matriarch of the family. She has two grandchildren, now young men, Kesa and Risuke. Kesa is very much a ladies' man and sports in the woods with Matsu, of the neighboring Ameya family, who becomes pregnant.

The story opens in the last days of winter. Orin has already decided that she must "go to Narayama" by the onset of next winter. The mountain, an object of Shinto-type worship, is where its surrounding people come from and where they must return, helped by their sons, who carry them to the snow line and leave them to die. It is a cultural and religious adaptation to shortages of food.

The film concerns itself with Orin's final months of life as she prepares herself stoically for her final journey. Her son must find a new wife, and they obtain a homely, hefty woman from the nearby village through the agency of the salt-seller. Her name is Tama, and Orin teaches her all she knows, especially the secret of catching fish from a secret pool in the forest.

The community's desperation over scarce food supplies is revealed when Aleya, the father of Matsu, is caught stealing. The villagers raid his house and find stocks of stolen food, even potatoes pulled from the ground while still small. Aleya's own father was also a thief. The furious villagers divide the store between them, leaving the family with nothing.

Matsu, who is five months pregnant, has moved into Orin's house to live with Kesa. But she steals from her in-laws to provide food for her disgraced family. Tatsuhei catches her and dangles her above a pit where thieves are thrown and buried, before relenting. But tragedy driven by hunger is building. Orin gives Matsu some rice cakes to take to her family and make a meal for them. As they are eating, the villagers rush the house carrying nets. They ensnare the entire family, including children, and bury them in the pit, even as Kesa screams that Matsu is carrying his child.

All of this only increases Orin's determination "to go to Narayama." An alternative to killing the young is for the old to yield gracefully, leaving the available food for the new generation. In a tense confrontation with Tatsuhei about her impending death, he reveals the truth about her missing husband. Tatsuhei, age 15, had killed his own father, when he had contemptuously refused to carry his mother (Tatsuhei's grandmother) up the mountain. Must he now kill his mother, too?

He must, Orin tells him. Rites are performed, and in the quiet of the early morning, without farewells, Tatsuhei begins his long climb up Mount Narayama. He carries Orin on his back. On and on he struggles, his mother quietly yet insistently egging him on. A bridge is down, a rockslide bars the way, but still they struggle upward. This last climb symbolizes the torturous hardship of their lives. As they climb above the treeline, the landscape becomes harsh and ugly. There is the first shock of a skeleton among the rocks, then more and more skeletons grotesquely strewn among the stones, while black carrion-eating birds squawk and flutter at the prospect of new arrivals.

Two hundred yards away, a neighbor from the village is leaving his father, but the latter panics at the prospect of being abandoned and clings to his son's trousers. In the struggle the old man falls and rolls down the mountain as a bloodied corpse.

With extraordinary dignity, Orin sits upright on a small rock and motions her son to leave her. She has three balls of white rice, symbolizing purity. It is her last supper. Her expression is peaceful and resigned. Tatsuhei is ten or more minutes into his descent when the first snow of winter starts to fall. It is the fulfillment of the old ballad that snow falls to bless the living sacrifice and bring a swift and merciful death. He runs back up the mountainside to where he has left Orin. "The snow has come, Mother, the snow!" And indeed it has transformed the whole landscape with a blanket of whiteness and purity—the Japanese color of death.

Orin sits upright as ever. The snow is beginning to cover her head and shoulders, yet with a gesture, sad yet imperious, she orders Tatsuhei to leave. In a physical existence indescribably harsh and cruel, human love and dignity and the integrity of the family have triumphed. One old woman has returned to the mountain.

The moral of this story is the obverse, the mirror image, of *The Seventh Seal*, just as white death is the obverse of black death. Virtue triumphs by outer direction, by accepting the harsh realities of life and adjusting to them, by going along with the process of aging and death (Orin even knocks out her own front teeth to look old). Yet by this very act she makes it possible for others to be nourished in her place, for life to continue for her family.

Figure 10.2 follows the outer-directed path up the mountain in preference to the inner direction of thievery and killing by people fighting over food. As Westerners, we confess to admiring this story, not enjoying it. Matsu's fate, in which Orin was probably complicit, makes the horror more real to us than the beauty. Not all communal directions should be followed.

But we must stress the reconciliatory side of death acceptance. If you are

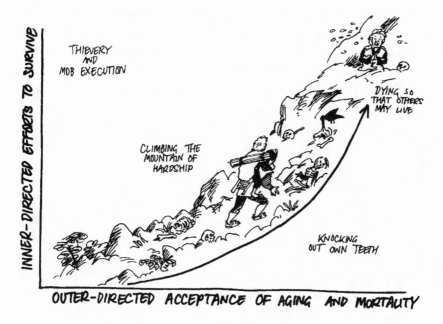

Figure 10.2 The Ballad of Narayama

prepared to die, you will live for all those people and things that you cannot take with you. You will realize that what ultimately matters is giving, not grabbing. In both stories, the significant action is aimed at sustaining the lives of others.

Have these two grim stories the remotest connection with how we conduct business? They have, as it happens. The Ford Motor Company in the United States reported to us that a spiritual crisis afflicts a large proportion of its most senior managers promoted to the "E-roll," the top two hundred persons in the company. In a few years they will be retired. What has it all meant? They have clawed their way to "the top" and have at last "arrived." There is a sense of profound anti-climax. Is this all? As Antonius Block put it, "My whole life has been a meaningless search." Does the heap look any better from the top?

Motorola has asked its senior officers, "What will be your legacy?" Can they change the company, its products and its processes, in some significant way so that they leave their mark? Can they mentor and develop subordinates so that these talents flourish after they have gone?

The reconciliation of inner and outer directedness has to do with transcendence, a form of continuous change. Can some part of us leave our minds and bodies to become forever part of an ongoing, flowing world? This happens in part through our children, but can it also happen through our work and innovation? Companies who have grasped this dynamic can do very well for themselves, as we shall see.

Do inner-directed and outer-directed cultures misunderstand each other? They do! One of the authors of this book was flying on Singapore Airlines when a drunken member of an American business delegation contrived to push a stewardess, so that she overbalanced and sat down on his lap. He then pretended that she had done this purposely and that she was more than welcome.

He was immediately confronted by the chief purser, who told him that if he apologized to the stewardess the matter could end there. Unfortunately he was sitting next to an American lawyer who urged him to "admit nothing" on the grounds that this would weaken his defense. The lawyer clearly assumed an inner-directed adversary system. On arrival in Singapore the businessman was arrested in the cabin and taken to jail.

What the Singaporeans wanted was an acknowledgment of their customs of good order and a sign that this visitor was prepared to be directed (from the outside) by these customs. The actual offense was minor. The failure to willingly adjust to Singaporean customs was a major source of challenge to that culture, for which he then suffered.

Let us now consider several cases in which inner and outer direction first clashed dysfunctionally but later came together.

Case 1: The Perils of Acquisition

One of the commonest clashes occurs when companies acquire other companies. An acquisition policy is inner directed by definition. "Grand acquisitors" like BTR, Hanson Trust, and the late Jimmy Goldsmith make large profits. What they have significantly failed to do is grow companies in their portfolios, and they have suffered serious stock market declines as a consequence so that the conglomerate is largely discredited as an effective corporate structure. What happened is that acquisitors' inner directedness often rides roughshod over the directions of acquired companies, which soon begin to wilt.

A company is a living system with its own sense of direction and integrity. The process of acquisition all too often destroys this direction and integrity by substituting its own culture for that of the acquired company.

We have studied several disastrous takeovers by Delphi, the former General Motors parts and systems supplier, and by Rockwell Automation. In most cases, the company, having been expensively acquired by making a higher bid than anyone else, actually loses values within days or weeks of being acquired.

If the acquisition is small or medium-sized and a big company bureaucracy is imposed upon it, the result is rather like a "bear hug" in which the life is squeezed out of the smaller and weaker system. As a result of acquisition the founders may retire, but even if they stay on the zest has likely gone out of their activities. The company is no longer theirs. They have to take orders. The acquirer does not understand them. The new procedures, however effective in the parent company, are inappropriate in another country, for another technology, or in another industry.

In many cases both companies, the acquisitor and the acquisition, have grown strong through inner direction, but now the acquired company receives a big, compulsory dose of outer direction and starts to expire. Especially vulnerable is the creativity of smaller companies. When they were small it was easy to get permission to take risks. They were close to their customers, fleet of foot, fast to respond. But once they have been incorporated into a giant company, permission alone can take months. Huge energies are absorbed by incorporation, or by trying to resist its worst effects. The dilemma is illustrated in Figure 10.3.

Note that the acquired company can also prove unruly and impetuous. This typically happens when a clearing bank like Barclays takes over an investment bank like BZW. The acquired company is more dynamic, smarter, and closer to the leading edge than its parent. Thus when West Deutsche Landesbank, a regional, government-owned German wholesale bank, took over Pamuir Gordon, a small city brokerage in London, the latter proved restive. Personnel often demand salaries, bonuses, or equity shares larger than their owners pay themselves. Such an acquisition tends to be a runaway company (shown at bottom right of Figure 10.3).

There may be a lesson to be learned from the more outer-directed Japanese on this issue. While Americans typically go for a majority shareholding, which will give them control ("You work for *me*, Buster!"), Japanese companies tend to buy minority shares in other companies and learn from these without at first trying to shape their policies. If you join a company and observe its accustomed manner of successful operation, you can later take control if you want to, once you have internalized its way of working.

This strategy of acclimatization avoids serious errors. For example, Rockwell Automation brought I-Com, a software producer. It was a smart move, given that software is increasingly the cutting edge in the sales of automation hardware. Unfortunately, I-Com's logo was expunged and its products rebranded "Allen Bradley," a distinguished hardware automation supplier but with little reputation in the software industry. Customers complained that I-Com had actually done more for Rockwell before it was acquired than afterward. The hardware and software cultures were simply incompatible.

In our consulting practice, we follow a policy of minimalism concerning the involvement of an acquired company in the culture of its acquisition. We follow the American maxim that "Least government is best government"—at any rate, until you have studied and learned how and why your acquisition became successful enough to attract you.

As consultants, we produce a narrative history of the acquired company, discuss the various crises that have shaped it, and interview in depth to discover what visions and aspirations those running the acquired company entertain. Since the acquirer brings new capital, these visions are sometimes ambitious and exciting. We then study how the acquired company's reporting system can, with the fewest possible changes, be adapted to the information the parent wants to receive.

During the extended process of "taking over" this new acquisition, we measure its value in the marketplace. It is our concern that its value should increase, not decrease. Any increase in value is a measure of the success of the takeover. What is typically required is a new strategy that uses the acquired company to give its parent company new height, so the latter is riding high (Figure 10.3).

Case 2: Is Designed Strategy a Cultural Illusion?

According to Henry Mintzberg, professor at McGill University, nothing excites the American corporate imagination like a brilliantly conceived and designed strategy. Reminiscent of the world conquests of Alexander the Great, an all-powerful strategy is the archetype of the inner-directed individual (see Chapter 9). Brilliant top managers conceive an unbeatable series of moves, faithfully implemented by subordinates, by which opponents are swept from the field. Sheer ingenuity and imagination have triumphed.

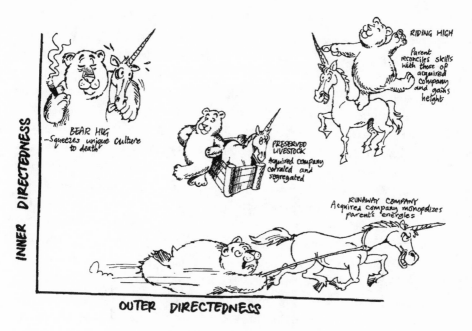

Figure 10.3 Perils of Acquisition

Except that this is not how it actually happens. Mintzberg studied what business executives actually did—and planning, organizing, commanding, and controlling, those idealized concepts of top management, were noticeable by their rarity. Executives spent most of their time adjusting, improvising, reacting to outside inputs, fighting fires, anticipating problems, and seeking information.

Mintzberg likened the pretentions of those managers, filled with academic nostrums, to those of battlefield commanders. He was reminded of the disastrous advance of Allied soldiers at the Battle of Passchendaele, in which 20,000 died because senior commanders remained largely ignorant of the waterlogged terrain. What we need, claims Mintzberg, is not the "heroic" view of strategy as some inner-directed act of genius but a way of operating that emerges from the actual experiences of those on the front lines. He wrote in his first published article: "Man's beginnings were described in the Bible in terms of conscious planning and grand strategy. The opposing theory of Charles Darwin suggested no such grand design existed but that environmental forces gradually shaped man's evolution."

Mintzberg was destined to become the "Darwin" who haunted the "Established Church" at Harvard Business School, whom he views as Creationists, although he now increasingly examines the business interaction between plans and environmental contingencies, between inner and outer directedness.

His reconciliation of the two has been that strategy is crafted. Upon watching his former wife, a potter, working with clay at her wheel, touching and shaping it here and there, he wrote: "Craft evokes traditional skill, dedication, perfection, through the mastery of detail. What springs to mind is not so much thinking and reason as involvement, a feeling of intimacy and harmony with the materials at hand, developed through long experience and commitment. Formulation and implementation merge into a process of learning."

There are many instances of effective change without strategy. The Canadian Film Board switched from making movies for cinemas to making them for TV, without any instruction from the top at all. Independent producers saw the opportunities shift and moved with these. Honda's designed strategy to introduce its 350-cc motorbike to the U.S. market collapsed when the bike could not handle America's high-mileage requirements. When troubled executives saw a crowd of Los Angeles citizens staring longingly at the Super Cub 50 cc, a product they used themselves but had no plans to import, they suddenly changed their minds. It was the Super Cub, sold through "sports stores," which spearheaded Honda's brilliantly successful invasion of the U.S. market. The product that happened to be parked one day on the sidewalk changed everything. A strategy had emerged to be crafted.

Mintzberg's reconciliation of inner-directed, designed strategy and outer-directed, emergent strategy are depicted in Figure 10.4. The disaster at Passchendaele is in the center and is the consequence of designed strategy ignorant of the terrain, markets, or culture intended to implement that design.

What really happens is that scores of "strategies" emerge phoenix-like from creative, ad hoc attempts to satisfy customers. The better of these are asked for repeatedly and are soon copied by other companies. Top management's job is to craft these emerging initiatives into useful generalizations—to identify, applaud, and disseminate those initiatives that work best and mold them into pragmatic, workable strategies by combining their best features. Strategy evolves by hundreds of small acceptances and rejections in the market environment. Managers craft with what works

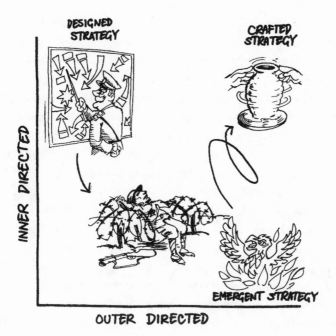

Figure 10.4 Strategic Styles

and reject what fails until there emerges something with most of its details road-tested for effectiveness. Figure 10.4 charts the developing spiral between inner-directed conception and outer-directed fit with the environment.

Case 3: Strategic Direction and Intent and the Quest for Core Competence

Two other prominent gurus who have softened the implacable edges of inner-directed strategy are the academics-cum-consultants Gary Hamel and C. K. Prahalad. They speak of strategic intention, of proceeding in an agreed direction, and of accumulating core competencies as this path is trodden, so that learning and knowledge are cumulative.

Unlike Mintzberg, these two scholars lean toward inner, not outer direction, but they are keenly aware of the limitations of tunnel vision and aiming straight for your original goal, without being "distracted" by changes in the environment. The direction they want to set is an intention only, but it remains vital that employees share this intention if only to know what model is being tested and whether the time has come to change their direction.

Strategic intent is an "animating dream" that provides the emotional and intellectual energy to take a journey guided by the "strategic architecture" of the brain. It is intent that stretches you, that creates a misfit between resources and opportunities and hence drives the accumulation of more resources. Strategic intent is about the future—not just about where you are heading but about where *it* is heading, so that a rendezvous between inner and outer direction can occur in that future.

It includes a sense of discovery so that the future is "out there," not "in here." Without a direction, employees are subject to a babel of slogans: "lower costs," "faster cycle times," "improved profitability." But all these beg the question, "Why?" unless they know where they are going and what the cost cutting is for. How much "delegation" and "empowerment" is enough? There are answers to these questions only if there is a purpose to empowerment, if it's getting you or not getting you somewhere.

But in order to plot your approximate direction, chosen perhaps because opportunities strew the path, it is necessary to take stock of your core competencies. What is unique about the configuration of your skills and resources, and in what direction can you move as a result of these competencies? What additional competencies will you need to get there?

Whether or not a corporation thinks in the way Hamel and Prahalad prescribe, the fact is that products tend to build cumulatively upon the logics a corporation has assembled. Where they stray outside their core competence, there is no reason why they should do better than a score of other competitors. Rare skills develop through focused study and long accretion. Hence companies are likely to fail when they stray from their expertise and succeed when they "stick to their knitting." Research by Richard Rumelt has found that diversifications are much more likely to succeed when they are related to the existing business of the company than when they were unrelated.

Hamel and Prahalad's thinking has been applied by Jaap Leemhuis, president of the Global Business Network in Europe, to the development of Motorola.

Consider the product history of Motorola. Its first product was a capacitator, a battery eliminator for automobiles. Its second product, which gave it its name, was a car radio with which the car engine did not interfere.

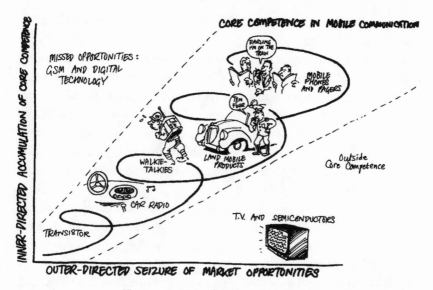

Figure 10.5 Motorola's Core Competence

With World War II coming, Motorola sold the walkie-talkie—jokingly known as the "breakie backie"—to Allied troops in the field. The next big jump was to land mobile products, including two-way radios fitted to police cars, ambulances, and aircraft. The cellular, or mobile, phone was next, together with the pager. The iridium satellite system, to which Motorola was a major contributor, has now proved a disaster as it has literally crashed to earth.

What do such products suggest about core competence? Leemhuis suggests that what Motorola has historically succeeded in is the combination of communication with mobility. When it has strayed from this path, as with stand-alone radios, TV sets, and semiconductors, it has been forced to discontinue these or spin them off.

Motorola's path is depicted in Figure 10.5. The strategic direction is the broad swathe moving from bottom left to top right, as Motorola's core competence recognized and seized new outer-directed opportunities and used them for self-renewal. We cannot take these opportunities for granted. Motorola nearly missed the move into cellular phones. It was made only because one employee fought stubbornly for the chance. Likewise, the move into battlefield communications, the walkie-talkie, came only because Paul Galvin visited Europe as war was approaching.

If outer direction is vital for success, it is not sufficient by itself. At Motorola, manufacturing and selling television sets had to be abandoned because imports were cheaper. Semiconductors are also in the process of being divested (see bottom right). Among the opportunities Motorola has missed because of its "America first" policy is the European GSM (global standard for mobile phones) system, seized upon by its rivals Ericsson and Nokia. In this instance the company suffered an excess of inner directedness, pushing the American CDMA (collision detection multiple access) standard and dismissing GSM. Opportunities in digital technology have been missed too.

Although this illustrates the powerful impact of core competence, it is not true that Motorola was consciously steered by the logic of mobile communications. Rather, the company kept rediscovering its own strengths. Henry Mintzberg was right. Even the effect of a core competence emerges from day-to-day experiences over time. With the benefit of hindsight and by this reading of its own history, a new strategic intent could be crafted as Motorola continues to discover its strengths in what succeeds and its weaknesses in what does not.

Case 4: Riding the Tiger—Why Southeast Asia and China Have Developed so Rapidly

We saw in Chapter 9 that most nations in Southeast Asia with rapid economic development are outer directed. This includes China, Japan, Singapore, Malaysia, Hong Kong, and Thailand (but not South Korea). These nations, before the recent banking crisis, were growing at over 7.0 percent per annum and are now returning to this growth rate.

To put these feats in proportion we have to realize that Britain grew at little more than 1.0 percent or less during its own industrial "revolution," and the United States seldom more than 3.0 percent. Why is each subsequent wave of industrialization faster than the one before? Why, if Southeast Asia is so enterprising now, was it not more enterprising earlier?

Our answer is that Western inner directedness and pioneer capitalism, when combined with East Asian outer directedness and catch-up capitalism, are much more effective than either inner or outer direction on its own. Inner direction causes slow growth because of excessive adversarialism. Outer direction caused no growth for centuries because the members of its cultures were "directed" by feudal and rural traditions. But when economic development became a national and global imperative, East Asians became very skilled at harnessing their own growth to the best international corporations and the best technologies the West and Japan have to offer.

Consider the rapid economic development of Singapore. Forty years ago, Singaporeans still served as "coolies" to the British, not permitted to work as staff in the best restaurants and nightspots. One venerable British resident would promenade in the park with his "culture cane," striking at any native who came near him.

Today, Singapore's gross domestic product per person is once again higher than that of its former colonial master and could match that of Switzerland by 2005. How was this accomplished? By reconciling foreign, mostly Western inner-directed technology with a Singaporean outer-directed and well-educated work force who learned swiftly about that technology.

Being a small, densely populated island, as well as a hospitable and strategic venue for foreign corporations, Singapore can afford to select who is let into its island to conduct business and who is not. Hence Singapore will select transnational corporations whose technologies have already succeeded, provided these technologies are intelligent, teaching Singaporeans cutting-edge skills and increasing the value-added per person on the island.

If you have a low-tech product, say, a bottling plant, Singapore will gladly host your headquarters, where highly skilled work is done, but will suggest that the actual product be mixed with water elsewhere—somewhere outside the country. Singapore has a high-wage, high-skill policy, and lesser work is pushed across its borders.

The knowledge intensity and skill inherent in foreign technology is not enough. Singapore will want to locate you in one of several clusters—for example, precision engineering, microelectronics, financial services, oil and chemicals, multimedia, aviation—so that you will cross-fertilize with companies in the same industry and indigenous suppliers can best serve you.

The Economic Development Board (EDB) is famous for its intelligence and responsiveness to foreign companies. Its members have been educated abroad and typically will have detailed knowledge of the inquiring organization, which may be persuaded to contribute to shared research and training facilities.

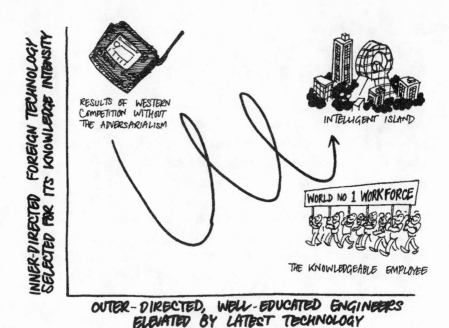

INNER-DIRECTED FOREIGN TECHNOLOGY SELECTED FOR ITS KNOWLEDGE INTENSITY

RESULTS OF WESTERN COMPETITION WITHOUT THE ADVERSARIALISM

INTELLIGENT ISLAND

WORLD NO 1 WORKFORCE

THE KNOWLEDGEABLE EMPLOYEE

OUTER-DIRECTED, WELL-EDUCATED ENGINEERS ELEVATED BY LATEST TECHNOLOGY

Figure 10.6 Outer-Directed Accelerated Development

The growth dynamic Singapore has constructed with its Mandarin love of learning is illustrated in Figure 10.6. Note that Singapore benefits from the fruits or results of foreign competition without the adversarialism it so dislikes. It can choose the smartest, cleanest technologies in the world, and usually does. It then readies a highly educated, predominantly technical work force to be directed by the potentials and opportunities of this new technology, in order to build an increasingly "intelligent island." The more knowledge and intelligence crammed into a product, the scarcer that product will be and the higher will be the price it can command and the wages that can be paid to employees. Singapore actually outlaws low wages by forcing those who pay less than the government's standard to contribute to a worker reeducation fund.

What is so noteworthy about this reconciliation is that all the nations concerned excel at what they do best—the United States and the West at innovation and Singapore at using the resulting technology to create a wealthy, harmonious society of people guided from the outside. It is an example of how the nations of the world can combine their respective values.

Case 5: Picking up a Tailwind—The Record Flight
of Thomas Weisel Partners

We should not assume that inner- and outer-directed reconciliations require Western–Asian partnerships. Increasingly, many kinds of selling depend on the growing success of one's customer. If you select a customer according to an accurate judgment that the customer is likely to succeed, then you will be repaid handsomely for appreciating a logic of development—a logic that is not your own but is outside you.

A service industry that gains immeasurably by selecting and financing successful customers is the investment banking industry, especially those companies that specialize in startups, initial public offerings (IPOs), and rapid-growth entrepreneurial enterprises. It is in these areas that the external logics of hundreds of different companies with diverse ideas, in new fields, must surely baffle the inner-directed logic of investment rationality.

Thomas Weisel Partners, which grew out of a highly successful merchant bank called Montgomery, is arguably the most successful and fastest-growing investment house in the world, earning $2.4 billion in profits for its sixty-six partners in 1998 and upping its growth forecast by 50 percent in the same year.

What is involved in the process known as leverage is the joining of the calculations of scores of the most original and enterprising entrepreneurs to the partnership's own inner-directed logic of investment success. What is rare is not the desire to make money, which is the commonest feature of the investment community. What is rare is the capacity to comprehend and to assess ideas so innovative that in most cases customers have still to record their verdicts. How do you pick winning ideas from the buzzing, blooming confusion on the innovative edges of many marketplaces? Recall that failure is still more common than success. The excitable entrepreneur who talks up a storm is no guarantor of growth.

Thomas Weisel Partners specializes, if only because an investor cannot know everything about every area of innovation. The areas of specialization are shown in Figure 10.7, together with the estimated growth prospects for these areas between 1998 and 2002. It is clear that these seven sectors, which grew from $2.7 trillion in 1990 to $6.1 trillion in 1998, are expected to grow to $9 trillion by 2002. The partnership does not confine itself to these seven categories; some 22 percent of business is done on personal judgment alone, from which new categories of special-ization may arise.

But Thomas Weisel's radar does not stop there. It also classifies invest-ments according to themes discovered within the fastest-growing compa-nies. These themes include membership on the Internet, with "accumu-lating returns" made possible by increasing net customers. A second theme is increasing bandwidth, a process by which huge amounts of in-formation can be downloaded so rapidly that, for example, this book could be sent in one minute to destinations anywhere in the world. ISDN (Inte-grated Services Data Network) is its best-known manifestation.

Third and fourth themes are outsourcing and consolidation. Outsourc-ing involves the creation of virtual organizations, where specialists per-

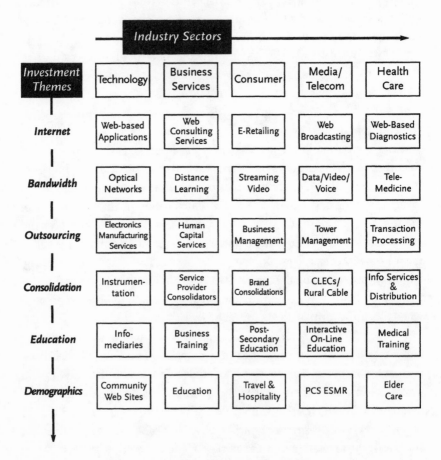

Figure 10.7 "Tailwind" Organizational Structure

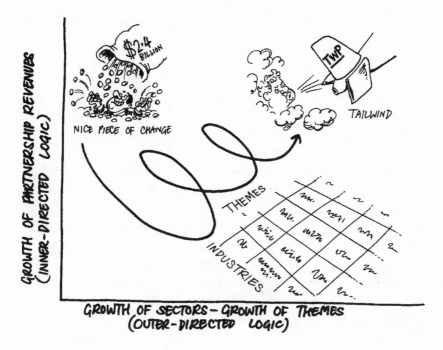

Figure 10.8 Thomas Weisel's "Tailwind"

form functions previously performed in-house but now assessed electron-
ically. Because this process tends to fragment the organization, there has
been a corresponding move toward consolidation, to have outsourced
functions performed by a sole supplier. And, of course, there is consolidation in general—previous joint venture partners or customers and suppliers combining.

Education speaks for itself. The number of skills that have to be learned
ever faster rises exponentially. Demographics have to do with population
moves and a large increase in the elderly population.

When the company combines investment areas with investment
themes, this creates the "tailwind" organizational matrix structure detailed
in Figure 10.7. Note that this matrix is not just a strategic tool but the way
the partnership structures its organization, so that strategy follows structure, which follows strategy.

One result of cross-fertilizing fast-growing sectors with fast-growing
themes is that the areas of most profitable investment jump out at you—
for example, Web-based applications, optical networks, tele-medicine, E-

retailing—so that the partnership can focus its research in these areas with pinpoint accuracy. The partnership also uses an Enterpreneurs Founders Circle to advise it on what is likely to succeed and what is not. How the logics of inner direction and outer direction are combined is illustrated in Figure 10.8.

Virtuous and Vicious Circles

Now that we have examined several virtuous circles, the time has come to look at the perils of excess—of how fatally easy it is to set off a vicious circle that will, in the end, suck down even the person who set it in motion. While mass society can be relied upon to punish excessive inner direction so that its proponents visibly fail, the same cannot be said for the mass media, who deal in cultural clichés and celebrate the same. Hence even those whose policies are catastrophic live on in the public imagination and on our screens, insisting to talk show hosts that their motives were too pure for this wicked world.

Here we shall briefly trace the rise and fall of Al Dunlap (between 1995 and 1998), the ex-paratrooper who could "never see the top without going over it." For USA Today he posed voluntarily in ammunition belts, bandeau, and two automatic pistols, worn over conventional business trousers, shirt, and tie, calling himself "the Rambo of the boardroom." Similar nicknames for Dunlap were "Rambo in pinstripes," "Chainsaw Al," and "the Darth Vader of Downsizing" (Figure 10.9). He saw himself as "an enemy of socialism." "People want a leader they can look up to. The outside world thinks 'this guy is tough' and I am tough, damned tough." He called his book Mean Business.

"Tough" and "mean" translated into forcing people out of work in massive lay-offs. It meant firing friends, ending relationships. "If you want a friend, get a dog," Dunlap wrote. "I'm taking no chances. I've got two dogs." What distinguished Dunlap from the fifty-nine "corporate killers" Newsweek wanted to interview was that only he would talk about corporate cruelty and do so with pride and relish.

Dunlap maneuvered himself into situations where corporations were in such disastrous condition that radical surgery was essential. Hence, Kerry Packer, the Australian tycoon, hired him to turn around ANI, a $300 million acquisition that was losing $200 million a year. In such circumstances, any agent of change would have reached for an ax, but Dunlap was

SHAREHOLDERS' INTERESTS

CORPORATE MANAGEMENT'S INTERESTS

Figure 10.9 Divide and Conquer

searching for such opportunities and loved chopping. The way he tells it, everyone he meets deserves this treatment.

Of course, among the 55,000 workers Dunlap has boasted of laying off were thousands guilty only of being badly managed. Kerry Packer and Jimmy Goldsmith, who also retained Dunlap, never claimed to be any good as managers—they were self-described raiders and dealers. Dunlap was essentially sent in after raiders failed to grow their companies, in order to strip the remaining assets. According to his philosophy, a failing organization is often more valuable without its people. You get rid of what cannot be easily manipulated by one individual.

If we look carefully at Al Dunlap's record, he failed consistently. Yet he certainly boosted the shareholders' take in the short run and was most adept at self-promotion. Millions of Americans want to believe that Rambo is more than an excess of testosterone and celluloid make-believe. Kerry Packer sold ANI for a £180 million profit after costs were cut, but while the financials had improved the spirit had gone. Within a year of his leaving, ANI was hemorrhaging again. The trick is to cash in your stock while the markets are still high on Rambo, and then get out quick before the hangover.

Dunlap did not grow or develop companies, he chopped them up, moving across each organization to cut up cozy management's soft furnishings. It is a straight grab in which employee interests are externalized (Figure 10.9).

Money is simply taken away from employees and redistributed to shareholders.

The reasons carve-ups fail are not difficult to identify. Anyone who is any good gets out before Dunlap arrives, especially as his reputation precedes ever further before him. To ax one person in ten destroys nine relationships in which information is stored. Knowledge leaks out of the organization as through a sieve. Corporate claims to be a "learning organization" are derided. Employees also start to pass on to the customer the way they are themselves being treated. But such human problems take time to work through the system. In the short run, that which financial analysts can see looks better. Revenues are off only slightly, costs have been slashed, hence profits are up.

In the case of Sunbeam, the share price climbed from $12 to $18 within weeks of Dunlap's arrival. It hit an astounding $52 after an apparent "surge" in sales.

Share prices climb not necessarily because businesses are about to succeed but because investors think that markets think they will succeed. The bubble is formed by psychology and culture, by the desperate need to believe in Rambo and the inner-directed individual who wages war on the unproductive. What eventually happens to the stock is not the speculator's concern.

In early 1998 Sunbeam announced a $44.6 million loss. The surge in sales earlier had been contrived by dealer discounts for early purchase, and then the hangover hit. Dunlap immediately announced more job cuts. Like a medieval doctor carrying leeches, he prescribed this cure for everything. About his own job he told Patricia Sellars of *Fortune,* "Am I afraid of losing my job? Get goddamn serious!" But with its share price down to $14, almost where he started, Sunbeam fired him.

What markets like is a volatile stock with plenty of hype, so money can be made on both the up side and the down side. Rambo certainly provided that.

Dunlap now lives off media appearances, talk shows, and public debates. This seems somehow fitting, since from the beginning he was essentially a showman, celebrating cultural excess, pushing what most people believe that much further, so as to be culturally safe yet prominent.

The Argument Culture

Does any of this matter? Is Dunlap more than a business buffoon? Is he, however unpleasant, necessary, like a funeral director, albeit one who relishes morbidity? We think it does matter, because Chainsaw Al is one more symbol of Deborah Tannen's "argument culture," a male-dominated contest. She refers to "a ritual war-like stance, a programmed contentiousness—a prepatterned, unthinking use of fighting to accomplish goals."

Since the presidency of JFK and the "Camelot" era, the press has gone "from lapdog to attack dog," their appetite having been whetted by Watergate. It ignores what is constructive and worthwhile—like President Clinton's Americorps, a program in which college students earn tuition in return for participating in public work projects. Instead, at the ceremony to launch the program, the press focused on a single hostile question from one of its members: "How can you talk about service when you did not go to Vietnam?"

As a result the press is increasingly hated. Witness the $223 million awarded against the *Wall Street Journal* for its criticism of a small brokerage firm; 90 percent of the award was punitive damages. Typically, journalists express more hostility than they feel. While 53 percent of journalists in a *Times Mirror* study "thought that public officials as a class were more honourable and honest than the general public was," this was not the impression they left with the general public, 80 percent of whom believe "that politicians' morals were worse than those of the average citizen." An equal percentage thought "political authorities could never be trusted to do the right thing," up from only 30 percent during the Kennedy era.

The consequences are everywhere. Having given up on being liked by the general public, politicians increasingly focus on expensive televised "attack ads" upon opponents, in the awareness that negativity can mean credibility, and that integrity is suspect. Fewer and fewer Americans bother to vote, despite the millions of dollars spent on boosting the gladiatorial spectacle and breathless blow-by-blow commentaries on TV and radio. The public is increasingly saddened by the negativity—for example, by the "moral" crusaders who released Monica Lewinsky's detailed testimony as publicly subsidized pornography. The desire "to beat" the president overrode any residual principles about the protection of the public from moral corruption.

The argument culture has long afflicted the practice of law. Philip Morris answered a "discovery" motion by the ABC television network by printing its documents on red paper so they could not be scanned by computer for content or photocopied. Female plaintiffs in the case of the Dalkon shield, a contraceptive device, were questioned by lawyers on their sexual histories, with the transparent intention of causing so much embarrassment that they would withdraw from the lawsuit.

American law is keener to uphold the rights of combatants than to discover the truth.

The media, in a desperate bid for viewership and readership, bills almost every encounter as a "war" or "shoot-out." The television show *Crossfire* features two combatants with equal time to hurl invective at one another. Anyone with the temerity to agree is labeled "boring," anyone who offers praise is sycophantic and teased by other combatants. No wonder Colin Powell refused to enter the 1996 presidential race, and Bobby Ray Inman withdrew as a nominee for secretary of defense. The price of public office is to be publicly pilloried.

All issues are held to have "two sides," so that the Holocaust for example has to be asserted and denied! It is hard to think of any event in world history for which the evidence is more plentiful or appalling. But the argument culture taken to its culmination disputes everything—evolution, genocide, the assassination of JFK—all are "really" the opposite of what is claimed, a truth lurking behind a cover-up.

In chapter after chapter of this book we have seen that polarizations, however dramatic and entertaining, lead only to frustration, to oscillation between opposing values, and, most serious, to vicious circles, downward vortices that can tear institutions and societies apart.

There is no objection by Deborah Tannen or by the authors of this book to the need for vigorous discussion of controversial issues, for the discovery that we disagree and that values themselves are differences upon a continuum, with the middle often excluded. The problem lies in leaving the problem there, in extracting excitement from a debate and focusing only on the drama and accusations. The problem lies in believing that only two sides exist, that one side must "beat" the other, that any position between

Figure 10.10 The Argument Culture

these polarities is vague, boring, morally compromised, and unprincipled. By Tannen's own accounts, she is being totally misrepresented. Her public appearances are billed as "confrontations," and when she demurs she is represented as pleading "that everyone be nicer to each other," a travesty of her position.

In Chapters 2, 4, 6, 8, and 10 we have shown that the alternative to polarized conflict is not just compromise, but that wealth and value are created by reconciliation, that the new creative synthesis is to be found in the cultural space between disputants, that a virtuous circle can encompass both conflicting values.

The argument culture is trapped in the vicious circle depicted in Figure 10.10, wherein argument without end escalates into violence. Ironically it is in business, the private sector despised by the Old Left, where most win-win solutions are now evident, and it is from business that culture, politics, the media, and the legal system must learn.

11 Sequential and Synchronous Time

THE DILEMMA

Time is an enigma, as Elliott Jaques has written. You cannot see, touch, hear, or smell time. It is not a thing at all. Yet all cultures are conscious of time, and all cultures organize themselves around their conceptions of time. It is because time is both so pervasive yet so elusive that it teaches us more about cultures than about itself. It is through and over time that cultures reveal themselves.

How the Dilemma Is Defined

Sequential time	Synchronous time
(seriatim or clock time,	(recurrent or cyclical time,
time as an arrow)	good timing)

While one distinction we can make is between varying cultural emphases on past, present, and future, our chief concern here is to describe sequential time, where increments go hurrying along in an irreversible sequence of seconds, minutes, hours, days, months, and years. Here time is seriatim. It "waits for no man." Once it is gone, you lose it forever. "Procrastination is the thief of time." "Never put off till tomorrow." And so on. The contrast is with synchronous time, which is circular or cyclical. In synchronous time it is events and opportunities that repeat themselves. We take timely advantage of such recurrences by "seizing the time," by noting that "there is a tide in the affairs of men that taken in the flood leads on to fortune."

The cultures of both ancient China and ancient Greece distinguished

CHRONOS ——————————— KAIROS
GOD OF CLOCK TIME   GOD OF TIME AND OPPORTUNITY

Figure 11.1 Concepts of Time

between these views of time. The Chinese thought of time as a thread (*ji*) joining the past to the present and stretching out into an interminable future. It was especially important to trace the line of your descent. But time was also a winding or circular track (*li*) where cycles of growth and decay, birth and death, springtime and autumn promised a harmony with nature and perpetual regeneration. The two concepts of *ji* and *li* operated in concert, like yin and yang.

Despite the ideal of harmony, the two concepts could collide, and great care had to be taken to avoid this. Official orders made on a linear basis were not to interfere with the cycle of being, which included propitious and unpropitious days.

It is from Greek mythology that we shall take our two personifications of time. Chronos was the god of clock time, bearing the hourglass and scythe. From his name come the words "chronology," "chronometer," and so forth. Kairos was the god of time and opportunity, or of "good timing." Chronos is our familiar "Father Time," announcing the end of the year, the century, the millennium, or our own life spans. Kairos is less well known, in part because the Romans did not re-create him. Indeed, there is no surviving image of Kairos. We know from written accounts that he was winged and youthful and carried a pair of scales on a razor's edge (Figure 11.1). Since time has to be synchronized with opportunity, we take Kairos to be the god of synchronous time.

How We Measure Sequential versus Synchronous Time

We measure contrasting images of time by two methods. One is Tom Cottle's Circles Test, where respondents draw circles that represent to them past, present, and future. This test is especially useful in contrasting the United States with Japan. In our early research, respondents from the United States clearly expressed the sequential view of time. Their circles were barely touching each other, like footprints in the sands of time. This perspective on time held sway until the mid-nineties. But as our work spread to workers in American electronics companies and investment bankers, the circles started to converge. American synchrony is growing apace, and this may be connected to innovation and the networked economy where fleeting opportunities must be seized (Figure 11.2). Japan's view of time has always been highly synchronous.

A second way we measure the discreteness versus overlap of concepts of time is to ask managers when their past, present, and future began and ended. We ask the following question.

Consider the relative significance of the past, present, and future. You will be asked to indicate your relative time horizons for the past, present, and future by giving a number.

7 = years
6 = months
5 = weeks
4 = days

USA
(Sequential)

Japan
(Synchronous)

Figure 11.2 Measuring Time

3 = hours
2 = minutes
1 = seconds

My past started ———— ago, and ended ———— ago.
My present started ———— ago, and ended ———— from now.
My future started ———— from now, and ended ———— from now.

From this data we can measure the overlap (synchrony) of past and present to get the results shown in Figure 11.3.

Hong Kong, Israel, and South Korea are the most overlapped or synchronous, while Turkey, India, and the United States are relatively sequential.

We can also calculate the overlap or synchronous nature of present and future. This is shown in Figure 11.4.

The surprise here is Singapore, which sees its past and present joined but its future as discontinuous—perhaps a quantum leap forward. The United States is once again more sequential, and Hong Kong, China, and South Korea are more overlapped or synchronous.

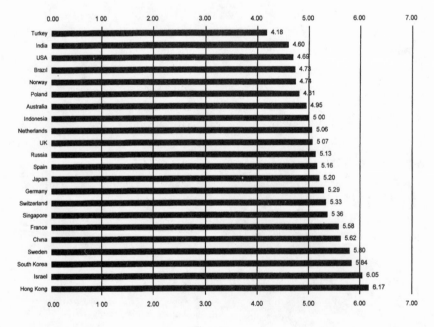

Figure 11.3

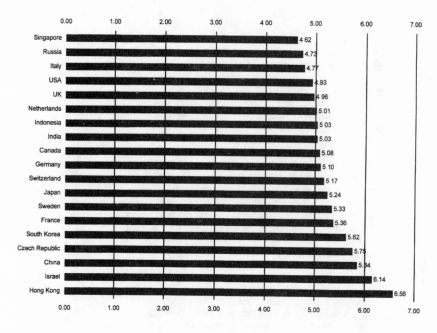

Figure 11.4

In Figure 11.5, we can also look at the sheer length of the past and the sheer extension of the future to gauge short-term versus long-term. Here we see that the United States is relatively short-term, a fact much complained of and noted, while Hong Kong, South Korea, China, and much of Scandinavia are longer-term. The Philippines, a client state of the United States, is extremely short-term, as is Brazil. Short-termism is at least in part a consequence of the feeling that time is racing by and that as much money as possible must be made in the least possible time. But if time is recurrent and generative, then the seeds planted now will bear fruit continuously in future years. That said, the correspondence between short-termism and sequential time and long-termism and synchronous time is more complex than indicated.

Why Is American Culture Sequential?

The preponderance of sequential thinking in American culture can be traced to a number of historical events.

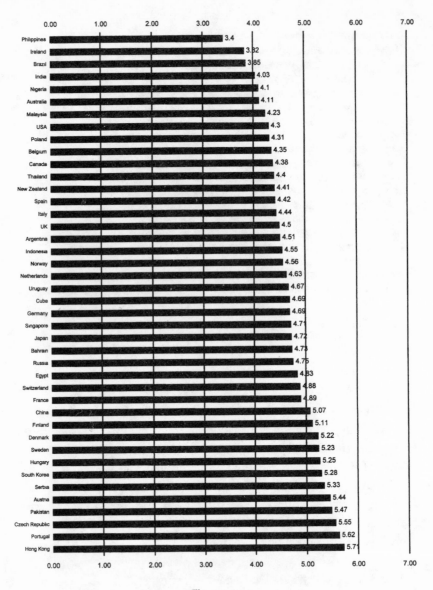

Figure 11.5

- Protestants were covenanted to build the Kingdom of Heaven on this earth and, given the perilously short life spans of the seventeenth and eighteenth centuries, had very little time in which to do this.
- Immigration gives people a second or third chance to make something

of their lives, but since earlier chances have come and gone, the individual experiences a "pursuit of happiness" as a quarry to be chased.

- Puritan science was squarely founded on the vision of a cosmic clock, wound up by God and ticking on. Uncovering its secrets was holy work.
- For a vast continent like the United States, which encompasses many time zones, standardizing time within a single nation was a major historical accomplishment.
- Owing to the vast distances that had to be traversed and the sheer distance between the thickly populated East and West coasts, speed became crucial—from the Pony Express to the railroads to the national highway system to modern air transport.
- A major feature of the Machine Age was the sheer speed of production, much as the computer revolution is driven by lightning speeds of calculation.
- Fordism and Taylorism, two major movements by which America revolutionized industrial production, were squarely based on sequential time and producing more and more in shorter and shorter time intervals.
- Popular almanacs like Ripley's *Believe It or Not* and *The Guinness Book of Records* are linear to the core, recording sequential units of speed, height, length, volume, and so on.
- Rewards and incentive payments have for years been calculated based on ratios of time and output.
- To compete against the clock is to dedicate yourself to continuous improvement regardless of the progress of adversaries. You are never good enough.
- Clock time is the person's inner disciplinarian, the individual's universal yardstick, a specific measure of heightened achievement. It thereby incorporates the five other values in this book on which Americans score high.
- In a Space Age where rockets point toward heaven and countdowns to blastoff are celebrated, we are witness to the symbols of a sequential world.

At Its Best . . .

Sequential culture conceived the whole cosmos to be a giant celestial clock. Figure 11.6 shows the orrery made for Harvard College in 1767 by

AT ITS BEST, SEQUENTIAL TIME...

... is the origin of time
and motion studies

... conceived of the cosmos as
a giant clock

...Had we but world enough and time,
This coyness, lady, were no crime...

... celebrates youth

... sees that
time is money

... celebrates the
quick buck

Figure 11.6

Benjamin Martin of London, a famous instrument maker. The orrery was a mechanical recorder of the orbital time of planets circling the sun, operated by gravitational force. It was the paragon of nature's order, a Newtonian model of a Newtonian universe.

Although this paradigm is now dated, we should be under no illusion about its power and influence or the important role it played in the history of science. Above all, it convinced our forebears that humanity could find order in the terrifying vagaries of nature. The Puritan temper has always been in a hurry, less puritanical about sex than about the time taken in courtship and preliminaries. Consider Andrew Marvell's delightful *To His Coy Mistress:*

Had we but world enough, and time,
This coyness, lady, were no crime . . .
But at my back I always hear
Time's winged chariot hurrying near;
And yonder all before us lie
Deserts of vast eternity . . .
The grave's a fine and private place,
But none, I think, do there embrace.

Marvell was a Puritan poet, tutor to the ward of Oliver Cromwell and assistant to John Milton. His poem celebrates youth, when we can make love while there is still time, and dreads "Time's winged chariot." It is this same sense of urgency that we find in American "get-up-and-go" and in the satirical character "Rabbi Zeal-of-the-Land-Busy" in Ben Jonson's plays. It helps us understand such slogans as "Trust no one over thirty," once uttered by Hippies now in their fifties and sixties.

For Americans, youth is golden. Indeed, success is typically measured by what you have achieved by age 16, 24, 30, and so on. Late developers are at a distinct disadvantage unless they move on. It was no less a sage than Benjamin Franklin who said, "Time is money." Legal contracts typically have time clauses. Dr. Faustus enjoyed himself until the Devil came for his soul. In vain he prayed: "Stand still ye ever moving spheres of heaven / That time may cease and midnight never come."

Sequential time brings judgment and death inexorably closer, hence Franklin's "Nothing can be said to be certain, except death and taxes."

Perhaps it is for this reason that Americans celebrate "the quick buck." The more money you can make before the tax man or the undertaker calls, the better off you are. "If you value life, value time, for time is the stuff that life is made of," observed Franklin.

Time and motion studies are among America's major legacies to industrial civilization. Essentially, more motion is crammed into the smallest increment of time, with hundreds of successive increments and motions joined into a single sequence.

You cannot visit Disneyland or the Epcot Center without marveling at the American genius for forming lines, coiled up against one another like snakes. Even when you enter an exhibit you are conveyed by "people movers" through the hall and out the back—no lingering, no stopping, only continuous machination; which is why the lines diminish as rapidly as your money. The "experience industry" is just that—great white (plastic) sharks assailing boatloads of tourists at seven-minute intervals at Universal Studios.

But Taken Too Far . . .

You find yourself in an interminable race with the clock, which, as a machine that measures abstractions, is the final victor and will run you to exhaustion. As the workers sang in *Pajama Game*, the Broadway musical satire of the fifties,

> When you're racing with the clock
> When you're racing with the clock
> The second hand doesn't understand
> That your back's all ache
> And your fingers break
> And your constitution isn't made of rock.

The stage is illumined by a giant clock, and the dance ensemble conveys its impact by short, jerky movements of their limbs.

Studies of the mental health of workers have revealed that machine-timed, semiskilled workers report five times as many symptoms of mental disorder (e.g., sweating, palpitations, sleeplessness, breathlessness) compared with autonomous, skilled workers who control their own machines. Gareth Morgan, in his classic *Images of Organization*, cites biographical details of F. W. Taylor, suggesting that he was more than a bit mad. He would regiment the children he played with. "Before playing a game of baseball he would often insist an accurate measurement be made of the field, so that everything would be perfect, even though most of the sunny morning was spent ... measuring. ... On cross-country walks he would experiment with his legs to discover how to cover the greatest distance with a minimum of energy. ... As an adolescent before going to a dance, he would make lists of attractive and unattractive girls likely to be present, so that he could spend equal time with each. ... Taylor suffered from fearful nightmares and insomnia. Noticing that the worst dreams occurred while he was on his back, he constructed a harness of straps and wooden points which would wake him whenever he was in danger of getting into this position."

The nightmares of the machine-timed workers were not too dissimilar. In fact, sequential time has a haunting, death-like quality, made light of by damsels tied to railway tracks as in *The Perils of Pauline*. At the end of the sequence is our own demise, as scores of medieval paintings remind us. Victorian poet Francis Thompson wrote of being relentlessly pursued by the Hound of Heaven.

I fled Him, down the nights and down the days;
I fled Him, down the arches of the years;
I fled Him down the labyrinthine ways
Of my own mind; and in the midst of tears
I hid from Him, and under running laughter.

But with unhurrying chase,
And unperturbed pace,
Deliberate speed, majestic instancy,
They beat—and a Voice beat
More instant than the Feet—
'All things betray thee, who betrayest Me.'

All too clearly, the "sequential individual" does not simply "pursue happiness," she is pursued by fantasized beasts.

Perhaps the most telling commentary on sequential time comes from William Blake in his *Europe: A Prophecy*. A bearded man of titanic proportion called Urizen ("your reason") is trying to banish darkness and chaos with a compass, using mathematics and scientific deduction, which is sequential—if ... then. This is *not* a benign or god-like act, as Blake's text makes clear, but an attempt to subdivide and fragment the imagination and destroy all understanding of the infinite.

Blake inveighs not only against the "natural religion" (Newtonian sci-

Figure 11.7

ence) of the Puritans but against Plato, who banished artists and drama-
tists from his logical *Republic*.

When we reason, we use a sequential process in which conclusions follow from premises. Traditional science searches for sequences of cause
and effect. Hierarchies employ "chains of command" with authority flowing down from the top to the bottom. All this banishes creative syntheses,
lateral thinking, fused processes, spontaneous interaction, systems thinking, negative feedback, and other synchronous phenomena from an equal
place in the citadels of science. Chaos had been confronted, but at a price.
Measurement is a defense against anxiety.

The final problem with sequential thinking is that it frequently cuts us
off from the "here and now." In Thornton Wilder's *Our Town*, Emily, who
dies during childbirth, is allowed to revisit her life on one day of her choosing. She selects her sixteenth birthday. Of course, her parents are blind to
the joy and uniqueness of the moment. While she stands there rejoicing in
the preciousness of each second they pester her with the minutiae of sequential living. The one-day visit, which was to be a celebration of youth, is
instead an indictment of sequential time and how it blinkers our apprecia-
tion of the here and now.

At Its Best . . .

Synchronous culture studies the recurrent features of time and its
events, so as to make crucial interventions. The hero arrives in the nick of
time to untie the heroine from the railroad tracks. We wish each other
"many happy returns of the day" as important anniversaries and significant days in the calendar come around again.

While sequential people like to do one thing at a time and are distressed
to be thrown off schedule by sudden happenings, synchronous people do
many things at a time. The Dutch author of this book remembers being
served by an Italian woman in a ticket office in Rome. She was writing his
ticket, talking on the telephone, admiring the baby of a colleague, and
handing over tickets to another customer—all at the same time!

Our research shows that women tend to be more synchronous than
men, possibly the result of family members making pressing and simultaneous demands upon them.

Synchronous time is much concerned with timing and keeping time.
The universe is rhythmic in its repetitions—hence, "the music of time."

Many cultures define health, vitality, and vibrancy as being in tune with the music of the spheres, as the adjustment of our body clocks to ecological time. For the truth is that the cycle of the moon pulls the tides in and out, coordinating the feeding cycles of thousands of sea creatures and entraining even our own bodies in rhythms of sleeping and waking. One cause of jet lag is that our bodies are out of phase with the gravitational pull of lunar cycles, and we tend to respond by slowing down or speeding up to get back in sync.

The cultures of East Asia are, as we have seen, among the more synchronous. The Chinese Emperor's legitimacy, his "mandate from heaven" to rule, depended crucially upon actions taken on auspicious days—timing was everything. Rival rulers and warlords in China would impose their own calendars and specify the days and hours on which things should be done. Divisions of time symbolized imperial legitimacy. The Buddhist religion, with its cycles of birth, death, and rebirth, relied on imperial astronomy. The doctrine of reincarnation is synchronous time taken to its fulfillment. Taoism preaches a cycle of eternal return. Twelve animals represent cycles of twelve years—for example, 1998 to 2000 were the years of the tiger, the hare, and the dragon. The signs of the zodiac also symbolize circular or synchronous time. The American sixties counterculture made much of the Age of Aquarius.

In early imperial Chinese funeral rites, the ideal to be attained was one of perfect harmony, with the sequential trajectory of a single life joining synchronously with the eternal rhythm of the universe and spinning around with the cosmos itself, rejoining the heavens from which the emperor's mandate came.

Another East Asian culture based in synchronous time is Japan. New Year is the most important festival, crucial to the notion of starting afresh and being reborn. *Toki* ("time") denotes not an ongoing increment but a momentous occasion or auspicious moment. As if anticipating Einstein, the *kanji* (Chinese character) for "time" includes "space," so that time is folded like Einstein's universe. Another *kanji* pairs "time" with "change" to mean renewal. Indeed, *kanji* are word composites, synchronous in themselves. "Pessimism" can be combined with "optimistic possibilities" to mean "pessimism aware of optimistic possibilities." "Crisis" can be paired with "opportunity" to mean "crisis in which an opportunity can be found."

The combining of past and present is revealed in the way the Japanese mark their calendars with the names of bygone emperors. As one dies, the next is born. Japanese Buddhism differs crucially from other variants of Buddhism in that your ancestors never leave you and reincarnation is not entrapment. In *genso-eku*, preached by Shinran, the dead keep returning to save and sustain the living. On memorial days especially, the spirits of the departed dwell with their ancestors and may slip into the womb of a great great granddaughter to be born anew.

Various birth signs are held to ensure the happiness of marriage when these are co-joined. Others may be fatal, as when a woman is associated with fire and with the year of the horse. Such dangerous conjunctions are often used to escape an unwanted bride or groom. Business deals may be unaccountably delayed because they fall on a bad day in the Buddhist calendar, for example *butsumetsu* ("day of great danger") and *shakko* ("day of red mouth").

In a renewal ritual, the Japanese rebuild wooden shrines and temples, sometimes yards from where they originally stood and even in the same place. The point is not for these structures to stand forever but to be reborn in cycles of renewed worship.

Not surprisingly, Japan's concern with synchronization has left an industrial legacy: the just-in-time delivery of supplies and split-second coordination of activities within the factory. Americans, with their emphasis on sequential speed, tend to run their machines at the highest possible speeds. If a machine runs out of widgets to work on, high inventories are in place so that the machine will not have to stop. The Japanese, with their emphasis on synchronization, tend to keep inventories at a minimum, regarding large inventories in general as a sign of poor coordination, as when widgets pile up between a faster and slower workstation.

While speed is a cost reducer, so are lowered inventories, since they include sizable carrying costs. Japanese and Americans saved costs of manufacture in diametrically opposed ways. The Japanese learned speed from Ford and Taylor. The Americans learned "just in time" efficiency from Taichi Ohno, the celebrated chief of Toyota's flexible manufacturing (Figure 11.8). In this case, the conflict between cultures has been creative.

But Taken Too Far . . .

Synchronous concepts of time are no guarantee of an effective culture. Slavish adherence to astrology, for example, will blank out whole sections of your calendar and force delays upon you. The difficulty is that you have

AT ITS BEST, SYNCHRONOUS TIME...

... brings many happy returns of the day

... arrives in the nick of time

... can do many things simultaneously

... conceives of life as a dance

... delivers "just in time"

Figure 11.8

to respond to another culture's rhythm, which may not be your own. For example, Southern Europeans may take a siesta in the heat of early afternoon, then eat dinner at 9 or 10 PM.

Edward Hall noticed that Japanese negotiators would make their demands just as sequential Americans were due to fly home and were looking at their watches. He trained U.S. executives to respond to inquiries about their schedules with the reply, "As long as it takes."

The Vietnamese correctly estimated that Americans would run out of patience in the Asian quagmire, while Vietnam had fought, on and off, for a thousand years. Vain hopes about "the light at the end of the tunnel" testified to American sequentialism and desperation for the war to conclude.

To those not used to it, synchronous cultures are chronically distracting. Everyone seems to demand your attention at the same moment. No one seems willing to wait. Noise levels during religious services strike many Westerners as extraordinary. Noise at night makes it almost impossible to sleep. If you are engaged in a task and see a friend, you may seriously injure his feelings unless you lay aside the task to greet him. A South Korean former student returning to visit his American professor was insulted when the teacher continued to speak in turn with a line of students at his desk and did not break off to greet an old friend who had just entered the classroom. Although he had studied in the United States, he still found himself surprised at this behavior.

Synchronous cultures are less likely to form lines. Rather, a mob forms in the place the bus is likely to stop, and people press all around to squeeze their way in. The Western convention of space around your body is violated by an unaccustomed form of physical propinquity (Figure 11.9).

The most irritating aspect of many synchronous cultures for Americans and Northwest Europeans is the misuse of one's own time to elevate the status of superior persons in that culture. You are expected "to give people time" if you meet them accidentally on your way to a scheduled meeting. It is rude to wave and rush past, especially if they are your seniors or distinguished in some way. You must respond to their physical presence even if those you agreed to meet are waiting.

Indeed, prominent people expect to be waited upon. Seniority means that subordinates wait upon their superiors' whim and convenience. At a meeting in South Korea, the British author of this book entered punctually and sat down. He was bidden by a flustered official to wait outside, as the

Figure 11.9

visiting speaker, and to enter immediately before the president, who was twenty minutes late—sufficient time for all lesser mortals to assemble. Four young women by the door bowed to everyone entering, their bows becoming deeper with passing time as more exalted personages entered the room, until the president had them at an angle of ninety degrees or more.

Readers who believe there is no trace of this in American custom are invited to read a passage in *Odyssey* (1987), by John Sculley, then CEO of Apple, reminiscing about his job at Pepsi, where Neilsen presented its relative market shares. Here, too, persons entered the room in reverse order of status, so the lesser waited upon the greater and the data were ceremoniously unveiled, leading the CEO to smile or glower upon those assembled.

All this can leave at least one party aggrieved. The British author of this book happened to meet the president of a Brazilian university at a reception. The president asked to see him early in the following week and offered to send his car to the author's hotel.

On the appointed day the car finally arrived fifty minutes late, proceeding to drive quite slowly to the university. The author was shown into the anteroom of the president's office, where at least twenty-five people were gathered drinking strong Brazilian coffee.

The president finally appeared twenty minutes later and walked through the gathering, pumping hands and pressing shoulders. He exchanged only two or three sentences with the author before moving on, but four or five of his entourage questioned the author in turn about the role of corporate universities.

After about forty minutes the president left and the room quickly emptied. The author did not feel he had made good use of his time. The president, on the other hand, looked content.

Culture Clashes and Derivative Conflicts: In Business and Industry

The clash between sequential and synchronous modes takes several forms. The Dutch author of this book recalls a visit to his local butcher shop, where at least twenty customers waited patiently in line, on a first-come, first-served basis. He would wait with dwindling patience for his turn to come and had plenty of time to reflect on how service might be speeded up. Much time was expended in unwrapping the meat, carving it, and then wrapping it again. If four different cuts were demanded by a customer, this was done four times. At least half the time was spent wrapping and unwrapping.

A few weeks later, he happened to be vacationing in Italy and visited a butcher shop. There was no line, but the shop was crowded. The butcher, having unwrapped some pork, decided to serve everyone who wanted pork. The packets were passed over the heads of the crowd to those signaling. He then turned to the beef. The author left the Italian shop rather faster than he had left the Dutch shop, and decided that less time had been spent in wrapping and unwrapping.

An interesting mix of these methods was encountered by the British author of this book at the airport in Singapore. The check-out person at the airport bookshop took his book and credit card and then served the next person. When he complained that he had been abandoned, she informed him that his credit details were being checked. Sure enough, the confirmation came through, she returned to the first person in line, and completed the transaction. In fact, she had saved herself and those waiting about 50 percent of the time spent in line. The credit check took about twenty seconds, and by that time she had begun processing the next customer's card.

Another important distinction that shows up regularly in business is that distinction between cause and effect, sequential thinking, and triggering a response from living systems, which is virtually instantaneous and synchronous. It really does make a difference whether you kick a soccer ball made of long-dead cattle hide, or whether you kick a live pit-bull (Figure 11.10). Live creatures react to your behavior, often with ferocity. You do not "cause" them to behave, for the simple reason that they have their own energy and vitality stored within them, together with their own interests and motives. All you can really do is elicit reactions or trigger actions.

There is much posturing among some American executives. "I run this shop," snarls the plant manager. The worker promptly closes his machine and replies, "OK, then, you run it!" Of course, the manager has no idea how the machine should be operated. An executive can "tell" her secretary what to do, but since in many cases she cannot perform those tasks herself, what she really has is her secretary's tacit agreement. The secretary places his skill and discretion at the executive's disposal.

In Western cultures, the temptation to treat living systems like dead objects is founded not only on Newtonian science but also on the sequential structure of most Indo-European languages, in which a subject uses a transitive verb to do something to an object. "I really sold that customer!" The customer's account will differ substantially, and he probably does not see himself as a sales target. We tend to lock ourselves within sequential conceits, while the real world of subtle interaction remains unreflected in our language. The words are not the reality. The map is not the territory. It is of note that Japanese and Chinese languages are nonsequential in their structure.

America has made straight-line production famous. Americans speak of "the line organization," of line and staff, of the assembly line, of the bottom line, and of the place where the buck stops.

Increasing the speed and efficiency of the line is, of course, only one way of getting the product out more quickly. Another way is to create four lines, not one, all running in parallel, known as parallel processing. Instead of "winning the race" on a fixed racecourse, you cut the length of the course by three quarters and work simultaneously on the four quarter-lengths. Of course, because the four shortened lengths must be synchronized, parallel processing appeals more to synchronous cultures, especially Taiwan, Singapore, Hong Kong, China, and Japan.

A similar important distinction is between push strategies, where managers are "progress chasers" hurrying along any project that looks like it might be late, and pull strategies, where operations converge with the customers' needs at some future time. The advantage of the pull strategy is that the customer may also be late (or early), and you can reschedule to pull the resources toward her on cue. If you are early for your rendezvous, you decrease worker hours. If you are late for your rendezvous, you increase worker hours. Either way, the customer wants it when she wants it, and being early will cost both of you, whether or not the original schedule has been met.

Business cultures vary greatly in whether they regard time as rigid and exact or as soft and flexible (Figure 11.10). Is the future "out there," many miles away, even if it is rushing toward you, or is the future with you now, in the boardroom, contained within "the seeds of time," some of which will flower in season? Is the past left behind and forgotten or is it with you still in the form of traumatic memories and forebodings?

At a business lunch, German managers might grind their teeth as French managers pass around the menu during the early part of the meeting. For Germans, time is exact and precise, a promise adhered to. For the

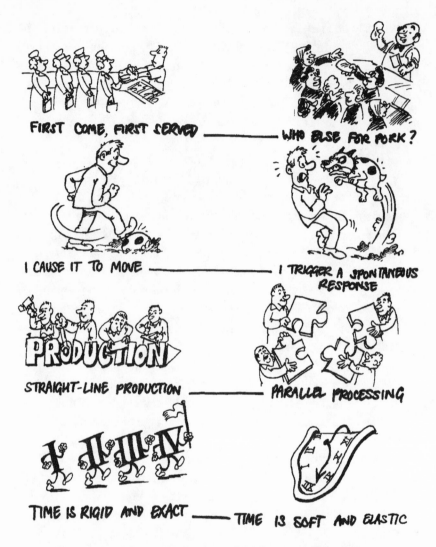

Figure 11.10 Dichotomies of Sequence/Synchrony of Time in Business

French, it is soft and flexible, something to be folded and molded. Is time a discipline both cultures can agree to accept, or is it a variable to be shaped and formed?

Culture Clashes and Derivative Conflicts: In Ethics and Philosophy

It was Isaiah Berlin who contrasted the fox, who "knows just one thing," with the hedgehog, "who knows many things." Western sequential and specific thinkers have historically pursued, fox-like, single propositions that, when verified, pile up in a somewhat untidy heap of truths. In contrast, synchronous and diffuse thinkers have tried to mold many propositions into one grand theory or synthesis in which all points converge, in an effort to make them aesthetic and harmonious in their combination.

Berlin insists that "hedgehog" cultures make bigger and more disastrous errors through their insistence on some grand synthesis. In contrast, "foxy" findings that accumulate as a weight of evidence are more modest in their ambitions and less dangerous in their frustrations. This is an interesting Cold War debate that we hope to reconcile, not referee, in Chapter 12.

One consequence of sequential thinking is that older people tend to be pitied and undervalued. Elderly individuals have very little sequential time left. If you conceive of time rushing onward, the old get left behind, can no longer run with the others, and should be "put out to pasture" like old horses. Sequentialists treat time as objective. Time is "out there" in public space, a train of continuously passing events, so that when you retire you lose touch and become steadily more confused.

Synchronous time, in contrast, bestows respect and advantage on the elderly. They have seen it all before, noting the patterns and themes of recurring events. With age comes not cleverness but wisdom, the capacity to integrate and synthesize a lifetime of experiences. If you have had a "career," you come to the end of that sequence. But if you have taken a circuitous path of many job rotations, as is the Japanese pattern, you have learned to see things in the round and from every conceivable angle. You are a trusted adviser and intermediary.

As you age, as memories outnumber activities, the capacity for synchronous thinking is crucial. Can you make your life meaningful, whole, coherent? No wonder the Chinese worship longevity and give respect to the aged. Shou-xing (or, in another manifestation, Shou-lai) is the Chinese star of longevity, with a bulging forehead that symbolizes wisdom. His mantle is covered in star constellations to reveal his oneness with the universe. He is supposed to know and to have written the time of every person's death—but, as befits a synchronous thinker, he will juggle with the numbers in the interests of supplicants! He makes a strong contrast with Ronald Reagan, a victim of Alzheimer's disease who may have been "over the hill" while still in office.

Apollo rode the sun chariot across the heavens at such imposing speed that demigods and underlings petitioned Zeus to let them drive, with catastrophic results. Even here sequentialism was suspect, since Apollo appeared on the opposite horizon the following morning. In contrast, the world of everlasting cycles is beautifully captured in Jean Dampt's sculpture "The Grandmother's Kiss." Dampt's work of art communicates the

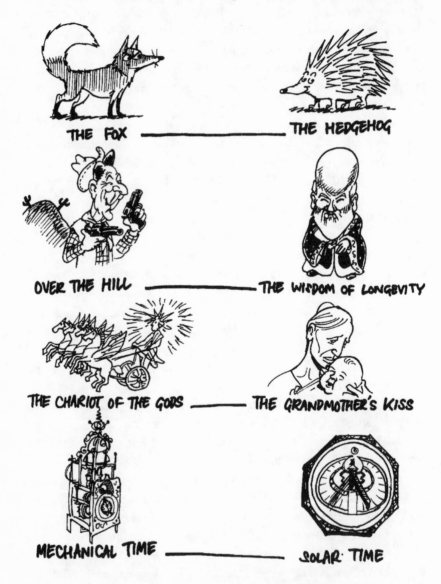

THE FOX ————————— THE HEDGEHOG

OVER THE HILL ————————— THE WISDOM OF LONGEVITY

THE CHARIOT OF THE GODS ———— THE GRANDMOTHER'S KISS

MECHANICAL TIME ————————— SOLAR TIME

Figure 11.11 Dichotomies of Sequence/Synchrony in Ethics and Philosophy

idea that love and instruction pass from life cycle to life cycle, that these conjunctions are vital in improving the human condition. Each one of us is potentially immortalized in the generational cycles that follow our own—they have known our love, read our books, or learned by our example.

Sequential time is in reality mechanical time, itself abstracted from the world we experience. In fact, most clocks are partly digitalized and sequential and partly circular and recurrent. In digital clocks and watches, the circularity disappears and "time marches on."

The sundial on which early clocks were based, much as the horseless carriage was based on the horse carriage, is almost entirely circular and synchronous in its function, directing a shadow upon a circular dial. In this sense, synchronous time is "older" than sequential time. As we shall see in Chapter 12, however, we need both to live and work effectively.

Yet, differences in conceptions of time can lead to conflict. A Motorola manager told me the following story, which illustrates this point.

> We had won a contract to install two-way radios in a fleet of Japanese air ambulances. We were discussing with the president of the ambulance company when our installation team could start.
>
> "I will make sure you get access in time," said the president.
>
> "What does *that* mean?" I said. "What we need to know is *when*."
>
> "You will have sufficient time to complete the project, I promise that," said the president.
>
> "Can't you give us a date and time?" I asked.
>
> He rose to his feet and left the room. He never spoke to me again!

What the president promised was an agreed and synchronized time, which would provide sufficient time for the work to be completed. What the Americans wanted was a specific, sequential time interval.

The president probably lacked the detailed knowledge of operations that would allow him to give a date. He felt his personal promise and guarantee were being brushed aside. The Americans did not trust his judgment about "sufficient time." He was offended.

12 Reconciling Sequential with Synchronous Time

STORIES AND CASES

We have seen that most cultures entertain at least two contrasting concepts of time; time as a sequential series of increments and time as a propitious conjunction or synchrony of events, so that "what goes around comes around." While it can be useful to make this distinction, the dichotomy, like most others in this book, is in itself sterile. Discovery, innovation, insight and the creation of value all lie between these concepts, in the subtle interaction of one with the other.

Since this is the last chapter, we shall also take the opportunity of explaining how the models we have used throughout this book borrow from the two concepts of time and portray their reconciliation. The management of time could be a new frontier for management studies. No less an authority than Peter Drucker admonished managers to "Know Thy Time." We do not simply have to manage our daily schedules, but understand the sequences and circles all around us, with their "windows of opportunity" opening and shutting before our eyes.

A Story Told by Sequential Culture

The Hollywood film *Groundhog Day* is a vivid story of sequential time. The main character is Phil, an egotistical television weatherman who has been sent, for the fourth time, to cover the Groundhog Festival in the small Pennsylvania town of Punxsutawney, in the company of his producer, Rita, and cameraman, Larry.

According to legend, the groundhog surfaces on February 2 and if he sees his own shadow, this is a prediction that winter will last another six weeks. At the climax of the festival, the groundhog, "Punxsutawney Phil" is produced to prognosticate in "groundhog-ese" that winter will last a bit longer, amid cheers and laughter.

Phil is contemptuous of small-town hicks, irritated by rival weather forecasters, and bored by the repetition of his assignment. His abrasive conduct irritates his colleagues. He is even more annoyed when his forecast for that evening proves wrong. A blizzard is moving in. The state highway is closed. He is trapped for a second night in the town he so detests.

Early next morning, as 6 AM clicks into place on Phil's digital clock radio, we hear the same music and voices as the day before. "It's cold out there" exclaims the announcer. "Nice going, boys, you're playing yesterday's tape," Phil complains, but in fact Groundhog Day is beginning all over again. Some vengeful spirit has trapped him in a midwinter time warp where he is condemned to repeat the day he despises in the town he disdains.

Culturally and psychologically, the film has much to tell its audience. Those who use sequential time to manipulate other people *do* find their lives repeating endlessly. They are trapped in their own linear stratagems and the hostile responses to them. That Phil alone is caught up in this recurrence of a single day while others respond afresh is also a clever portrait of narcissism, where everyone else is the naive pawn on the narcissist's chessboard. That Phil is a weatherman whose job is prediction simply reinforces his manipulative personality.

His first instinct when Groundhog Day begins to repeat is to seek help from his companions, but they do not know what he is talking about. His second instinct is to be totally irresponsible. Nothing he does counts. No one seems to remember the crimes and misdemeanors he has committed. Jailed at night, he wakes up next morning in the room of his bed and breakfast. He even steals the groundhog and drives over a precipice. Although the truck is incinerated, he wakes up next morning unscathed as Groundhog Day begins again.

Finally, Phil decides to take advantage of the insight he has gleaned through constantly repeating the same day. He plies his producer, Rita, with questions about her tastes and childhood and then uses these disclosures to seduce her. Unfortunately he has only one day to make his conquest, so every evening ends with him pushing his luck and piling on so many "sensitive" insights that Rita's suspicions mount and she accuses him of having researched her tastes.

Figure 12.1 Groundhog Day

Although sequential time has been abridged for Phil, he is still using one-day forecasts to get one-night stands, safe in the knowledge that Rita will not remember his attempts. If anything, his short-termism and sequential manipulations have intensified.

Figure 12.1 shows the vicious circle of endless iterations in which Phil is trapped, getting his face slapped at the end of each day, perpetually frustrated.

Gradually, Phil begins to learn something else from his manipulations. He has discovered how kind Rita is, how delighted and responsive she is to his advances (until the coincidences multiply and she becomes suspicious), how genuinely she likes the locals and the festivities. If he is to win her, he must learn to love what she loves.

Phil decides to use his accumulated social intelligence for quite another purpose. Knowing what will happen next in the course of the day (sequential knowledge) gives him the opportunity to intervene to help people (synchronous knowledge). He catches the boy who falls from the tree at the same moment each day. He changes the flat tire on a car transporting three old ladies. He saves a middle-aged man who is choking, soothes the pre-wedding nerves of two lovers, and learns to play the piano.

All these good deeds are done on what turns out to be the last day of Phil's entrapment. He has convinced Rita of his deja vu experiences, and she offers to stay with him overnight to witness the phenomenon. At one point during the evening, he utters the words that will free him from the perpetual winter of his own devices: "No matter what happens tomorrow and for the rest of my life, I'm happy now and I love you." He is at last present in the lived moment. Exhausted after a busy day, he falls asleep on his bed beside Rita, without attempting to seduce her. Next morning, the radio alarm clicks to 6 AM. It is a new day, white and fresh from the passing blizzard. Time has moved on, and with it two lives are now synchronously entwined.

The story is clearly a fable about the dominance of "forecast behavior" and its timely qualification by the cycles of love and renewal. The comedy sends up the excesses of sequentialism and macho machination.

A Story Told by a Synchronous Culture

Shall We Dance? is one of the more recent examples of Japanese films that have been heavily influenced, some would say swamped, by Anglo-American culture. We hope to show, however, that despite these extensive borrowings, the film remains true to Japanese culture and is one of the best examples of the Japanese cultural dynamic. The title is taken from the theme song of *The King and I*, in which an English governess dances with the King of Siam.

This film is about Shohei Sugiyama, a Japanese middle manager and accountant who records numerical sequences at work and commutes daily along straight railway lines.

It is from the window of his commuter train that he first spies Mai Kishikawa, who runs a Western-style ballroom dancing studio and whose inspiration is the Winter Garden in Blackpool, England, where international competitions are hosted. What Shohei sees each day is a melancholy young woman, Mai, standing at the bay window of her studio, with shadows whirling behind her.

Having seen her repeatedly on his journeys to and from his office, Shohei finally ventures timidly to join her dancing school. He cannot afford individual lessons, so he joins two other students, a pint-sized, chirpy man and a somewhat large, shy, overweight executive. Taking private, "foreign" dancing lessons is regarded as mildly scandalous. Indeed, all three have very private reasons for wanting to dance, as has a fourth man, disguised in an elaborate wig. This is Mr. Aoki, a work colleague of Mr. Sugiyama, who becomes bold and wild when dancing, in complete contrast to his office behavior.

Mr. Sugiyama is disappointed to learn that Mai is not his teacher; only occasionally does she fill in for her colleagues. He is disappointed again when she refuses to see him after work. If he has joined the group in order to meet her, she warns him, he has made a mistake. She takes dancing seriously. And so does Shohei—in an attempt to prove her wrong, and to like what she likes.

Shohei's dancing rapidly improves and transforms his whole morale. He discovers a lightness of step, a *joie de vivre*, a new source of energy. His wife is at first delighted, then worries. His shirts smell of perfume. She reluctantly hires a detective, who reports that there is no affair going on. He is simply dancing.

As Shohei's skill improves, he enters a local dance competition with one of his instructresses, Toyoko, a quick-tempered woman whose invective has already reduced the two others in the class to rage and tears. Mai refuses to dance in the competition. She is nursing a secret sorrow.

One evening, Mai confides in Shohei. As a child visiting Blackpool, she was enchanted by dancing. A couple who looked like winners caught her eye, but then they fell heavily to the floor. The man had protected his partner as they fell, and young Mai was filled with admiration. Dancing was a metaphor for life itself—for skill, devotion, and harmony.

Years later, Mai had reached the finals with her partner, once more in Blackpool. As she and her partner were nearing victory, however, another couple crashed into them. When Mai fell, her partner did not protect her. Worse, he blamed her for the accident. She ended their partnership and quit competitive dancing. To make a living, she began to teach.

Until she met Shohei, Mai had not wanted to dance again. But watching him practice his dance steps on the train station platform below her window each day, watching him become more graceful and buoyant, she had begun to believe again in the magic of dance.

Cheered by Mai's confidence, Shohei and Toyoko dance in the competition. They reach the finals amid great excitement. At this moment, Shohei's wife and daughter enter the dance hall. His daughter shouts out in excitement at her father's prowess. He is startled and collides with another couple. His private synchronous world has collided with his public

Figure 12.2 Shall We Dance?

sequential world. He tries to prevent his partner from falling but steps on her dress, which rips, leaving her half naked. The catastrophe is total (Figure 12.2).

Chastened by his ordeal, Shohei promises his wife never to dance again, but she is ambivalent. He was so happy, so alive when he was dancing, she says wistfully. Their daughter makes him teach her mother to dance, but the effort seems halfhearted. They cry in each other's arms. A delegation from the dance studio visits him, begging him to return. He was so nearly successful. Mai is going away to Thailand—won't he at least come to her farewell party? He equivocates.

On the night of the party he cannot bring himself to go, until he sees in the window of the studio "Shall We Dance, Mr. Sugiyama?" He arrives at the party just as Mai is choosing her partner for the final dance. The spotlight circles the floor twice until it illuminates him, still holding his briefcase. They make their first and last triumphant circuits of the floor, dancing to the music of time, carried along by the theme song.

Shall we dance?
On a bright cloud of music
Shall we fly?
And perchance . . .

Most of the elements here are American and British. Right? Not quite. The dream of life as *wā*, as one harmonious whole, the idea of dance etiquette as a guide for human relationships, the celebration of artful timing as the key to love and sociability, these are quintessentially Japanese themes, as is the protest against a world of straight lines and accumulating numbers.

So long as executives' feet move surreptitiously beneath their desks or pirouette in the washroom, as they do in this film, the rhythms of life will never be completely suppressed. Indeed, they can even help in running a business, as we shall see. Five business cases follow.

F. W. Taylor and Taichi Ohno: The Revolution in Automobile Manufacturing

Whatever Japan's financial problems and the weakness of its banks, it has already revolutionized world automobile manufacturing and the rest of us are still struggling to catch up. We know what Japanese workers do, and if we could imitate them we would. But culture is a form of mental and physical programming, a "software of the mind." It is very hard to copy if you have not been raised to think that way.

In the early twenties, automobile mass manufacturing began with Frederick Winslow Taylor, the engineer-inventor of carbon steel tools. A second major exemplar was Henry Ford. "Taylorism" and "Fordism" are often used interchangeably. The key invention was the sequential, ever-moving assembly line with which workers had to keep pace. There were very American reasons for taking this process so far. First was the huge automobile market—cars could be sold much more cheaply if their volume was increased. When Henry Ford suddenly doubled the wages of his work force—much to the outrage of his shareholders—he put the Model T within range of his own workers. The more he produced, the more were bought and prices headed downward.

The second giant impetus to Taylorism were the sheer numbers of foreign immigrants pouring into America, many of them with scant English vocabularies. Taylorism subdivided work so minutely and made it so simple that a low-wage immigrant laborer could be taught in two hours, hired, and fired, as others stepped off the boat.

In Japan and Europe, markets were much smaller and craft traditions had survived. The Japanese were mightily impressed by Taylor and Ford and studied their methods minutely, but they had identified a serious source of waste that Americans had missed. Machines worked very fast, so fast that they were often considered by Americans as superior to workers. Indeed, for many years the American dream had been total automation.

In order to keep the machines running at top speed, American factories, into the late eighties, would buffer these with huge piles of inventory. If any one machine ran out of components to work on, it, and perhaps the whole line, would have to stop. To forestall this dreaded eventuality, American factories were awash in inventory—both components delivered by suppliers and in-process inventory—the piles accumulating between workstations.

It was Taichi Ohno, the fabled plant manager of the Toyota flagship factory, who first regarded inventory as waste. It is waste because you have to pay for it and then carry it until the supplies have been assembled and sold to customers.

But there is another defect that high inventories signify: poor synchronization and coordination. If one worker is working rapidly and another more slowly, inventory will accumulate between the workstations of the first and the second. Far better, argued Ohno, to give the fast worker more to do so that each person's work cycle synchronizes perfectly with the other.

In addition, Ohno observed, suppliers should be trained to deliver inventory "just in time," a matter of minutes before it is needed at a workstation. In this way, the company does not have to pay for the cost and duration of warehousing. Ohno would express his hatred of large inventories by launching a ferocious kick at supplies whenever he found them on the factory floor (Figure 12.3).

While faster sequences and better synchrony are very different principles, championed by American and Japanese culture, respectively, their combination saves even more cost than either principle taken singly. In combination, they form what is known as *flexible manufacturing*. In this process the assembly line still moves as rapidly as it ever did for Ford, but because the arrival of special components has been carefully synchronized, what comes out at the end of line are not three hundred identical black cars but twenty to forty varieties of vehicle, each of which was created by key combinations of components reaching the assembly line "just in time."

Flexible manufacturing gives you speed with variety. It gives you mass

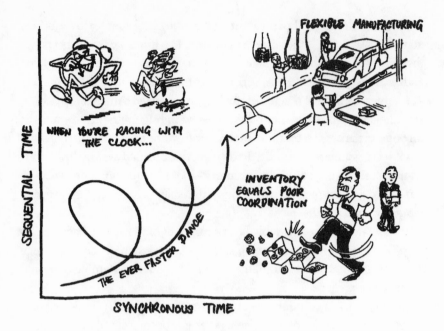

Figure 12.3 Sequential and Synchronous Time

customization with mass-produced components synchronized in customized packages. While sequentialism is a race and synchronization resembles a dance, the helix that improves both axes is the ever faster dance.

Elliott Jaques and the Time Span of Discretion

It was from the work of Elliott Jaques that we have taken the distinction between Chronos and Kairos, discussed in Chapter 11. Jaques is a Canadian psychiatrist who joined the Tavistock Institute in its golden years, heading the Glacier Metal Studies. He typically poses questions so vast in their ramifications that lesser individuals tend to avoid them. He asked two interlocked questions: What is the justification for paying one employee more than another? Is there a way of paying differential wages that is intuitively recognized as fair by most members of a company?

There is a tacit avoidance of hierarchy in American management literature. It is as if the subject is somehow obscene and no one wants to speak either of his own subordination or of the subordination of others. Because the topic is evaded, hierarchies persist almost by default and are considered to be the barely legitimate habitations of the power-mad.

Jaques has a brilliant definition of the "responsibility hierarchy," as he calls it. We are paid for the time span of our discretion, that is, for how long the sequence is, before our work is supervised (or synchronized) with that of higher authority. A CEO enjoys a long time span—two or three years before the shareholders check up on her. Her contract will typically specify this interval. Her staff will have, say, six months to a year, their employees three to six months, all the way down to the hourly worker, who is not just paid by the hour but supervised every quarter or half hour to make sure he has not erred in his conduct.

The crucial fact to grasp about time spans of discretion is that you cannot cheat over them—at least, not without serious repercussions. If you supervise someone too closely, this wastes money because supervision is expensive. If you supervise someone inadequately, that is expensive too, because any mistake will have compounded itself over time. The rhythm or synchronicity of supervision is thus an act of judgment on timing. The time span must match the fitness of the individual to go unsupervised.

This relationship is depicted in Figure 12.4. Note that "freedom" is measurable by the time elapsing between one point of supervision and the next. You feel less free immediately after and before being supervised, and most free equidistant between. The level of responsibility also rises on the

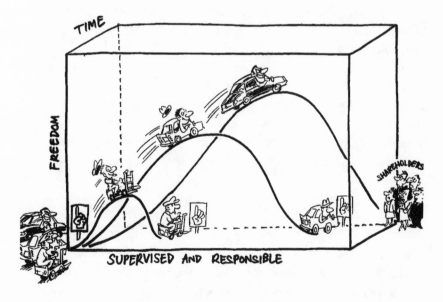

Figure 12.4 The Time Span of Discretion

vertical axis because you have a longer time span during which you are held responsible. What you are paid for is your autonomy, literally "self-rule," for which you must account.

Note also that our dual-axis diagram has become a cube. How? The third dimension is time and the fourth dimension is the curving trajectory of time and space. It is over time that freedom is gained and through periodic reporting that responsibility is established. In fact, all the reconciliation diagrams used in this book are really cubes. The helixes are three-dimensional, and their progress through time is the fourth dimension. Dilemmas get synchronized over sequences of time. The time interval has to be just right, like the interval between periods of supervision. Responsibility means that you respond to those who delegated power to you. It is axiomatic that our freedom increases with our responsibility. You cannot have one without the other.

Jaques has shown that highly capable leaders look at the long term. Senior generals in the Pentagon, where he conducted extensive research, felt responsible for the state of American defense ten to twenty years ahead. That they would be dead or retired was not the point; the foundations of long-term policy must be laid now. That other persons wish, for their own purposes, to retire you or supervise you does not necessarily limit the long-term responsibility a leader feels for present policies that will bear fruit over the years. Jaques has demonstrated that fitness and desire to lead is measurable by the time span to which leaders aspire, not necessarily the time span they are given.

Jaques recommends that leaders be chosen according to the time spans in which they think and aspire to be responsible. His research shows that selection on these grounds is successful. His research has also revealed that the time span of discretion correlates most highly with the measure concerning fair and just payment for work. It is a logic of differential rewards that work forces are most likely to accept.

The Sponsorship of Teams to Solve Problems—at Motorola and Advanced Micro Devices

One of the major developments in corporate effectiveness over the past decade has been the use of teams. As problems grow in complexity, their solutions have the quality of whole, new systems. Increasingly, teams have become necessary to improve or create these systems.

A team task force working in Analog Devices, for example, was charged with solving the problem of late deliveries. It carefully researched the problem, came up with six of the commonest reasons for late deliveries, and then eliminated these causes one by one. Such teams do "real work"; that is, they do not delegate responsibility to others but take direct action and are co-responsible for the results arising from this action. Teams often have their own "dashboards," or indicators of ongoing progress and success. This can help turn them into "hot groups," in which excitement runs high and esprit de corps is much evident.

The great advantage of short-term, ad hoc teams is that their membership can be matched precisely with the issue to be tackled. It is usually possible to estimate what skills and knowledge will be needed to solve a particular problem, and volunteers with the requisite motivation and competencies can form themselves around that problem. Small groups typically "develop" over time as the group's shared culture gathers knowledge about the social styles and personal capacities of the various members. The growing intimacy and sensitivity among members, combined with the novelty of a fresh combination of skills, makes the group maximally effective after a number of meetings. The trick is to match this peak effectiveness with the problem at hand.

Another advantage of problem-solving or innovating teams is that they can be drawn from several departments, cultures, or even nations and then returned from whence they came. The solutions they come up with are not foreign to the cultures involved, having been wrought by their own members and representatives. Teams are, therefore, an excellent means of solving problems within a microcosm of the wider problem, and then helping the various cultures to communicate more effectively with the team's understanding as a guide.

Consultants face the problem that their solutions may not "take." They are often rejected not for being wrong, but for representing "foreign tissue." In contrast, the team is of the same tissue as its host.

There remains a serious problem of authority, hierarchy, and delegation. How is the team to fit into the responsibility hierarchy of the corporation? What is its role?

Some years ago, Motorola began to teach "team sponsorship." It is the responsibility of senior managers, not to know all the answers but to define the problems, the dilemmas, the challenges, and issues, and then to sponsor a team to shape the answers.

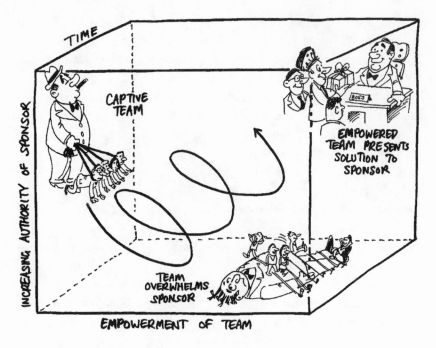

Figure 12.5 Teams and Authority

The leaders delegate powers to the teams they have sponsored, much as they might to subordinates, giving these teams resources, empowerment, and rights of inquiry. The teams then report back to their sponsors after an interval of time sufficient to give them a sense of responsibility for their common task. A team enjoys autonomy and empowerment to the extent that its sponsor does not check up on it or issue frequent commands but allows it to form, to think, to solve, and to decide. The dynamic is illustrated in Figure 12.5.

The real challenge to any sponsor is: Can he give his power away? Delegating to a team is much more dangerous than delegating to a single subordinate. Team members know and usually like each other more than their sponsor. If they take the bit between their teeth, it may be impossible to rein them in. What if they depart from their task and suggest something that is impossible, essentially wasting many hours of work and the resources put at their disposal? The sponsor could look very foolish, and she might face rebellious subordinates angry that their contributions have been suppressed.

This is why many sponsors hold their teams on such a short leash that they are rendered useless (Figure 12.5, top left). In such cases the team members are the sponsor's creatures, placed there to do his bidding and reporting back either publicly or secretly on a daily basis. The team never solves any problems because it can only second-guess what the sponsor seeks.

What the sponsor dreads, and the reason he uses his leash, is that the team may overwhelm him, tying him down by its dominant deliberations (Figure 12.5, bottom right). The real art of sponsoring a team is to know how long to leave it alone before asking members to report back to you. The longer this interval, or the further apart the turns of the helix, the more the team is empowered and respected. Of course, it helps to have an exciting task, to ask a really crucial question to which an answer is discoverable, to form the team out of people who seriously wish to meet this challenge.

Once again, the relationship between sequential time (how long the team is left alone) and synchronous time (when the team reports back) is a crucial act of judgment. No wonder that Dennis Romig, consultant to Advanced Micro Devices (AMD) and others, found that semi-autonomous teams are more effective than totally autonomous teams. You cannot let teams simply go their own way. They will lose touch with what the organization needs, with what their boss needs to do for shareholders. The responsibility hierarchy cannot be evaded.

Of course there are ways of fine-tuning sequence and synchrony. You can ask the team to contact you as sponsor, if it has any doubts about whether a new approach falls within the parameters of the task. These consultations are voluntary. You can shorten the intervals at the team's request. You can discuss the results you seek, not the means you propose. As the team develops a track record, intervals will typically lengthen as mutual confidence between sponsor and team increases.

The important point depicted at the top right corner of Figure 12.5, "empowered team presents solution to sponsor," is that the sponsor's authority has actually been increased, as has the empowerment of the team. The sponsor has discovered an answer to a major issue or challenge facing the organization and, as a result, may be promoted. The team is responsible for having found that solution with a sense of zest and accomplishment. Each member has learned to trust the other with a heightened degree of freedom. Interrogatory management poses questions and dilemmas to teams and seeks their answers so that all can learn.

Note that once again the dual axis has become a box, with time synchronized in cultural space as the fourth and crucial dimension. This chart was actually used to monitor team sponsorship by Martin Gillo at AMD's fabrication plant for microprocessors in Dresden. Among most East Germans and some West Germans, the idea of sponsoring the freedom and empowerment of teams was unfamiliar, although not necessarily unwelcome. That the "Dresden Fab" is now the flagship of AMD's plants worldwide is not unconnected with training in the sponsored autonomy of teams.

Flow Experiences and the Curious Distortion of Time: The Research of Mihaly Csikszentmihalyi

Chicago psychologist Mihaly Csikszentmihalyi has spent a lifetime studying *flow experiences*, an important source of happiness and peak experience. Flow is occasioned by the same kind of "fine-tuning" among "opposed" elements that we have been discussing in this book.

When you are engaged in an absorbing task, there is a sudden experience of dissolved boundaries. The skier has become the mountain and intuits its changing contours. The singer resonates to her audience. The actor is the character he plays, with all his grief and anguish. The dancer is caught up in the rhythm and whirl of the dance. Flow is *autotelic*, meaning that means and ends fuse as the process itself becomes a reason for being.

> I must down to the sea again
> To the lonely sea and the sky
> And all I ask is a tall ship
> And a star to steer her by.

John Masefield's verse, aptly called "Sea Fever," tells of sailing as an end in itself, as a sensing of "the wheel's kick, the wind's song, and the white sail's shaking."

Flow experience, according to Csikszentmihalyi, depends on quick and accurate feedback, which allows you to make minute yet crucial adjustments so that the fit is perfect and the adjustment fine. Flow involves a sudden transformation in the quality of experience, so that the singer no longer fears her audience, or the skier the mountain, or the sailor the sea. Rather the singer is wafted on waves of applause, the skier leans into the curvature of the mountain, and the sailor carves through the crests of the wave as persons and environments are reconciled.

Industry reveals many examples of flow–if we can recognize them: the worker on the punch press who can make dies accurately within one-thousandth of an inch, the salesclerk whose counter and department displays raise sales by $50 per square foot per day, the negotiator who has finally crafted the win-win solution.

Csikszentmihalyi discusses the conditions that typically give rise to flow. Consider an issue with a high degree of challenge confronting a newly sponsored team. Let us suppose that the team does not have the skill sufficient to meet that challenge, for whatever reason. Perhaps its members were safe nominees, not aspiring volunteers. Perhaps the challenge was simply too great for the levels of knowledge and training available. In any case, the result is anxiety (Figure 12.6).

Now consider the opposite situation, where the challenge is small yet the skills are more than enough to meet it. This would probably result in boredom, resulting from the insufficient challenge. When a "flow experience" occurs, however, a very precise fit has been achieved between the

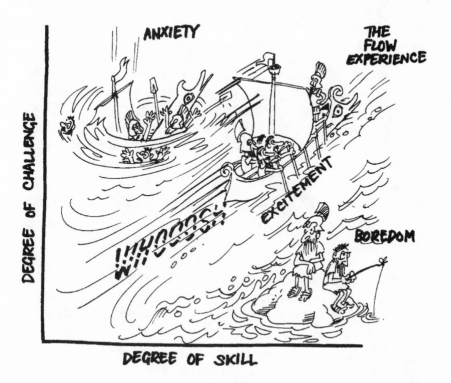

Figure 12.6 Optimal Experience

challenge facing the team and the combination of skills its members bring to the project (Figure 12.6, center to top right). In this case, the team has something important to discover about itself—some goals only inches away to stretch for, new records to break, new points to prove, and a problem that dissolves all of a sudden when the right interventions are made. No wonder, then, that the experience is heady and triumphant, that each member feels he or she has made vital contributions to the overall goal and shares the victory.

What is important in the light of this chapter is that Csikszentmihalyi reports from his research subjects a transformation in the sense of time. Hours seem to go by in the course of minutes—so intense is the absorption—as "momentous" or synchronous time bends and folds the sense of sequential time. Sometimes, time slows and the seconds are savored. Sometimes there is a sense of suspension in time. Sometimes familiarity combines with discovery or, in the words of T. S. Eliot:

> We shall not cease from exploration
> And the end of all our exploring
> Will be to arrive where we started
> And know the place for the first time.

One more turn of the helix and a new awareness breaks. In every act of creation there is a "shock of recognition." The axes and ingredients are somehow familiar, yet the combination is new—never before has it been reconciled quite like this. We need to see that challenge and skill, sequential and synchronous time, familiarity and discovery, usually vie with one another in relentless conflict. But there comes a transformative moment when this conflict gives way to synergy, when we rejoice in the mountain we have climbed and are thrilled by the new resources discovered in ourselves to meet the challenge.

The new combinations shaped by reconciling these contrasts are irreversible. Something new has been formed and created. Between the rock and the whirlpool is a current that sweeps us through to new levels of awareness. Time no longer ticks quietly on. There is a rush of enthusiasm, a great surge of movement. Kairos and Chronos have engaged each other at an opportune moment.

The happiness that flow experiences bring may depart as quickly and mysteriously as they came, leaving us wistful.

Business and the Balanced Scorecard

In 1992, Robert S. Kaplan and David Norton published two articles in the *Harvard Business Review*. Ever since, these two academics and consultants and their "balanced scorecard" have been very much in vogue. Their body of research and consulting picks up on another aspect of time in addition to sequence and synchrony: the relative importance given to past, present, and future. Many executives, according to the authors, have given up on financial measures like return on equity and earnings per share. This is not because these are not important or that shareholders are indifferent—quite the opposite—but because these are verdicts on the past not the present or future.

In some industries this past may be long passed. In the oil industry, for example, earnings flow from twenty- to thirty-year-old investments. However good these are, they cannot tell you what to do tomorrow. Profits may be all important. They may even be "what it is all about," although we doubt this. The fact remains that they are reported too late to steer by.

Another favorite source of indicators is operational measures. How does our company do against key benchmarks? How does it compare to its industry? The problem here is that a company is measuring itself by yardsticks it personally chose. Not only may these measures be out of date—the market is demanding other qualities—but the company does not know what others think about its performance and service, especially customers.

It is possible to beat all extant benchmarks in producing something in which your customers have lost interest. Benchmarks themselves tend to lag some months or years behind new customer needs and innovations to meet these. You cannot start to measure an operation until it is routinized, and routines have an ever briefer life span.

You may actually make things worse by enthusiastically measuring and celebrating past performances and internal calibrations, which is one reason companies deemed "excellent" may already be heading downward and have notoriously short moments in the sun. The problem with these scorecards is that they are unbalanced. They neglect the future, and they fail to consult customers as the company falls prey to self-congratulations.

Kaplan and Norton use two axes, contrasting four sets of indicators, as shown in Figure 12.7. The top and bottom boxes represent past and future, while the left and right boxes use the dichotomy discussed in Chapters 9

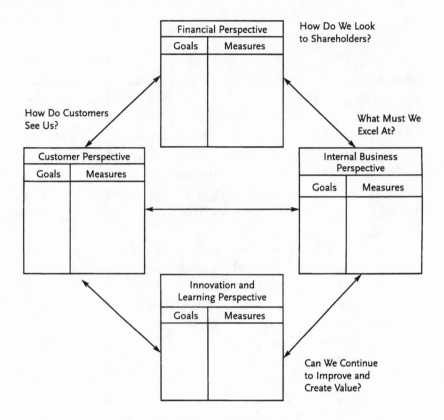

Figure 12.7 The Balanced Scorecard Links Performance Measures

and 10 of this book: outer-directed (customer) orientation versus inner-directed (strategy) orientation. The measures within the boxes are all sequential, but the connections between the boxes are synchronous.

This approach reminds us of an important lesson. Dilemmas are almost always plural and not singular. Your problems include not only speed versus timing and past versus future, but also rules versus exceptions (Chapters 1 and 2), individuals versus communities (Chapters 3 and 4), and inner-directed companies versus outside customer verdicts (Chapters 9 and 10).

Indeed, one criticism we have of the balanced scorecard is that it deals with only two dilemmas, while for us all six dilemmas featured in this book should be mapped and scored systematically. Too often companies fall into the trap of measuring what is easiest to measure. The past is nearly always more definitively measurable than the future. Our own pet yardsticks are

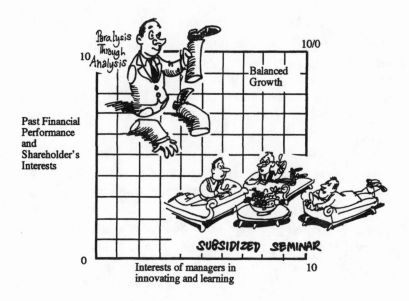

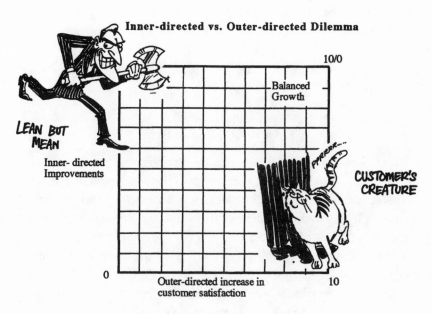

Figure 12.8 Past Versus Future Dilemma

nearly always clearer than our customers' yardsticks. Management by exception measures the infringement of rules and the violation of expectations but generally takes a hostile view of the unexpected and tries to bring everyone back into line. Exceptions should be eagerly studied, whether these are errors or opportunities or both.

Figure 12.8 shows our scorecards for the past–future dilemma and the inner-directed–outer-directed dilemma.

We are all accustomed to excesses of financial analysis about matters no longer relevant to us, hence paralysis through analysis (top left of upper grid). However, the interests of managers in innovating and learning can also be carried too far and resemble a "subsidized seminar" (bottom right).

Inner-directed improvements may take an ax to everyone, cutting out not just the fat but the muscle and bone (lower grid). Of course, customers will suffer when disgruntled, and fearful employees pass on this treatment. But you can also go too far cozying up to customers and becoming the "customers' creature," an ingratiating fat cat who has lost all integrity and inner purpose. In both cases the answer is balanced growth. But Kaplan and Norton have little to say about the dynamics at the point of balance or the transformations possible. Their advice, however, is important. Measure yourself on contrasting axes and with balance—growth will occur. On this they are almost certainly right.

From Helix to Double Helix

Throughout this book we have used the helix to reconcile, as depicted in Figure 12.9. It should be clear by now that the helix is a synthesis between circular and sequential time. It winds its way between axes, synchronizing them, but it also makes sequential progress toward the top right corner and upon both axes of the dilemma.

But why just one helix? Usually there are at least two parties involved, each championing its favorite value, each with a different sequence of reconciliation that puts its favorite value first. This presupposes a double helix, with Alpha moving toward the values of Omega, while Omega moves toward the values of Alpha, as illustrated in Figure 12.10.

The more Alpha can see the values complementary to her own, which Omega espouses, the more she can move in that direction. The more Omega can see that Alpha's values give contrast and meaning to his own, the more willing he is to join those values. The two "waltz" around each

Figure 12.9 Helix as Synthesis Between Line and Circle

other, which helps explain why dance has been such a powerful metaphor in this chapter—the climax in both our stories.

The double helix is, of course, the template of life. We do not seek to steal the biologist's mantle of science, only to borrow a metaphor from what is alive rather than dead, from what grows rather than "is." The social

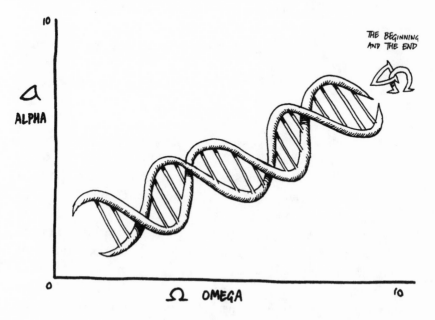

Figure 12.10 . . . Arrive Where We Started . . .

Figure 12.11 The Third God of Time

sciences have always borrowed. Freud's limited energy model of the mind was a Victorian steam engine in human guise. Brain researchers now tell us that the mind is a computer, or a hologram. We regard the double helix not as a law or theory of multiculturalism but as a model to serve until its usefulness ends.

In Search of the Third God

We began this chapter with Chronos and Kairos, personifying the two contrasting embodiments of time. But there was a third god of time known as Phanes, or Aion. Phanes sprang from an egg fashioned by Chronos, from which he burst suddenly in the fullness of time. He was the god of renewal or creative time, one of the Orphic mysteries.

The god (depicted in Figure 12.11) is from the second to third century AD and stands in the Galleria e Medagleira in Modena, Italy. Its meaning still puzzles historians. A young man bursts from an egg in a blaze of fire. The whole length of his body is encased in the helical coils of a large serpent. The youth is winged, and animal heads representing past, present, and future sprout from his chest. He has a linear staff in one hand and a sheaf of lightning bolts in the other. What can it all mean?

We take a rather perverse pleasure in speculating that the ancients had worked it all out twenty centuries ago or more, which brings us back to T. S. Eliot's poetry, cited earlier, in which we

> . . . arrive where we started
> And know the place for the first time.

Appendix 1   Dilemma Theory and Its Origins

Intellectual Origins

Dilemma theory has taken some thirty years to work out. It derives from many sources. We have borrowed widely yet selectively and do not accept in their entireties the theories from which we have borrowed.

1. *From classic Greek tragedy* we borrow the idea that values get personified and endowed with god-like powers. The more these are vaunted, the more likely they are to turn into their opposites and clash destructively. The antidotes to such excess are comedy and, if you fail to share the fun, tragedy. The ideal is *harmonia,* or *symphronasis,* in which conflicts are reconciled.

2. *From Sigmund Freud and neo-Freudians* Jung, Adler, Reich, Rank, and Fromm, all of whom were much influenced by classic mythology, we have borrowed both the drama of forces in psyche struggling against each other and the idea that some of these forces are denied conscious awareness. We see the "unconscious" not as a repository, but as the consequence of Aristotelian logic, which has made it difficult for Westerners to entertain two opposing propositions. Hence one "horn" of each dilemma tends to be repressed from conscious awareness in favor of the other.

3. *From cognitive consistency theorists*—especially George Kelly, Prescott Lecky, and Leon Festinger—we have derived the notion that persons struggle for consistency among their personal constructs and that how such consistency is achieved has fateful consequences.

4. *From structural anthropologists*—especially Frances Densmore, Clyde Kluckhohn, Ruth Benedict, Gregory Bateson, Claude Lévi-Strauss, and Edmund Leach—we got the idea of values as binary and as differences on a continuum. Hence values are contrasting pairs of attributes, and cultures repre-

sent the mind writ large. Values are *corybantic* (i.e., they dance to and fro on these continua).

5. *From humanistic psychologists*—especially Abraham Maslow (who credited Ruth Benedict)—we get the concept of synergy. Similar ideas are found in the work of Rollo May and Carl Rogers. People develop through the reconciliation of opposite endowments, as do groups, organizations, and cultures. The downside is well captured in the catastrophe theory of René Thom and Christopher Zeeman. (From the "down turn," *catastrophe*, in Greek tragic drama.)

6. *From brain researchers*— especially those studying the split brain, such as Roger Sperry, Michael Gazzaniga and John E. Bogen–we get the notion of lateral functions coordinated between brain hemispheres. The work of Karl Pribram and the Papez-MaClean theory propose similar specializations and integrations.

7. *From systems theorists*—particularly Ludwig von Bertalanffy, Geoffrey Vickers, West Churchman, Magorah Maruyama, Francisco Varela, and Humberto Maturana—we derive the idea of self-organizing systems which spontaneously seek higher levels of development and complexity. These are governed by positive and negative feedback, which may seek to reduce deviance or elaborate it.

8. *From the field of organizational behavior,* we have built on problems identified by Fritz Roethlisberger (formal versus informal systems), Douglas McGregor (Theory X or Y), Robert Blake and Jane Mouton (concern with task or people), Paul Lawrence and Jay Lorsch (differentiation versus integration of subsystems), Eric Trist and Fred Emery (socio-technical systems), Chris Argyris and Donald Schön (Model I versus Model II behaviors), Michael Porter (low costs versus premium strategy), Henry Mintzberg (designed versus emerging strategy), and many others.

9. *From political science, sociology and cultural studies,* we have borrowed many insights into American society. We are especially indebted to Talcott Parsons, Seymour Martin Lipset, Daniel Bell, Christopher Jencks, Richard Hofstadter, Robert Bellah, David Halberstam, Robert B. Reich, Richard Sennett, George C. Lodge, and Lester Thurow.

10. *From East Asian studies* we are indebted to Ezra Vogel, James Abegglen and George Stalk, Ikujiro Nonaka and Hirotaka Takeuchi, Akio Morita, Takie Sugiyama Lebra, Rosalie L. Tung, Shotaro Ishinomori, and Kisho Kurokawa. Most have shown that East Asian value preferences are the mirror image of our own.

11. *From epistemology and the philosophy of science* we are indebted to Floyd Mat-

son's critique of Newtonian science, T. S. Kuhn's insight into scientific revolutions, and the seminal epistemologies of Henri Bergson, Kisho Kurokawa, Alfred Schutz, Russ Ackoff, and Hannah Arendt, along with the marvelous elucidations of inquiry by Abraham Kaplan.

12. *From studies in creativity* we are grateful for the work of Arthur Koestler on janus phenomena, holons, and bisociation. We have learned much from Frank Barron on creative resilience and from Liam Hudson, Jacob Getzel, and Philip Jackson on the dynamics of divergence-convergence.

13. *From moral development studies* we have learned the necessity of creating a mini-crisis or dilemma in the respondent's mind, a practice followed by Jean Piaget and Lawrence Kohlberg. More serious crises were simulated by Richard Crutchfield and Stanley Milgram with studies on conformity and obedience.

14. *From architecture and design,* we owe a debt to Buckminster Fuller and his demonstrations of synergy—also to Kisho Kurokawa and his metabolism movement.

15. *From chaos theory and the patterns of fractals* our debt is to James Gleick and John Briggs for their different expositions and to Benoit Mandelbrot, Paul Rapp, Ilya Prigogine, Mitchell Feigenbaum, and many others.

Experiential Origins

The British author of this book quit Harvard in 1972 and moved into a halfway house for ex-convicts in San Francisco, called the Delancey Street Foundation, about which he sought to write a book, *Sane Asylum* (New York, William Morrow, 1974). This proved quite a culture shock for his privileged and academic background, yet the rehabilitation process was undoubtedly successful and he was obliged to account for this.

The ethos of this organization was a curious hybrid of left- and right-wing doctrines. In its public face, Delancey Street was quite liberal in exposing the excesses of the penal system and pleading for a second chance. In its private face, it was highly familial and conservative, stressing hard work, self-reliance, and tough love. It taught both that society generates criminality and that change can come only from cutting the strings of that causality and taking personal responsibility.

It stressed that right- versus left-wing debates are a pathological discourse with poor Americans as footballs in a contrived game. In three-day, sleepless sessions of psychodrama, elaborate comedy and satire of criminal pretentiousness was climaxed by tragic reenactments of wasted lives. The author encountered not simply persons from a different world but emotions of excruciating intensity, with rehabilitation achieved against all odds.

Dilemma theory is an attempt to pick up the pieces of those extraordinary and moving experiences of a genuine community.

Dilemma Theory: A Summary

We thus describe dilemma theory as follows:

1. Values deemed virtuous, god-like, and personified by heroes inevitably conflict and must achieve harmony if protagonists are not to clash tragically.
2. Among conflicting values, one is often consciously and culturally preferred to the other which is buried and repressed.
3. The personality constantly struggles for consistency and may successfully integrate opposing values or repress and deny one side.
4. These values, properly conceived, are differences on an often tacit continuum and thereby structure the patterns of a culture and the minds of its members.
5. These combinations of values may grow synergistically and humanistically, or regress with catastrophic consequences.
6. Much of this inherent opposition and unity has been found in contrasting brain functions.
7. Values form open systems which spontaneously self-organize and steer by getting feedback from their environment.
8. Many of the tensions within living systems have been found in organization behavior. Industries and workplaces confront dilemmas which they must resolve to generate wealth.
9. Similar dilemmas pattern the politics and sociology of American and other societies and must be resolved if those societies are to continue developing.
10. The ways Americans resolve dilemmas are often the mirror image of the ways East Asians resolve theirs, leading to considerable misunderstandings and culture shock.
11. Searching into and resolving dilemmas is a form of human and organizational learning.
12. It requires creativity and innovation.
13. May involve moral development.
14. Is reflected in architecture and design.
15. And enables us to bring order to chaotic events and manage the fractal patterns which arise.

Appendix 2 Exercises in Reconciliation

Every country, organization, and individual faces certain universal problems or dilemmas. A culture is expressed in the way people approach these dilemmas. Intercultural competence can be achieved by recognizing cultural differences, respecting them, and ultimately reconciling them. When working across cultures, it is important to keep the following in mind:

- Values working together make the organization more powerful.
- Unresolved conflicts tend to diminish individual and group energies.
- Reconciling values leads to better products and services.
- The need to reconcile value differences is never ending.
- By increasing cultural competence in reconciling dilemmas, conflicting values can be transformed into complementary values.

Table A2.1 delineates the steps to take when you come across a (business) problem related to (seemingly) opposing values.

The Logic of the Double Helix

In order to grasp the reasoning behind our five approaches, it is best to view these as successive approximations to the double helix illustrated at the end of Chapter 12.

- The strands of each helix are developmental processes.
- If you look at the double helix from the side, you will see the strands closest to you, framed by the strands farthest away. If you go around to the other side, "picture" and "frame," text and context, will change places.

Table A2.1   Strategies for Achieving Cross-Cultural Competence

Action	Why	How
Step 1: Eliciting dilemmas Find issues and check for dilemmas • Identify the main differences in perspective involved in the issue. • Identify the opposing values. • Identify the dimension(s) involved	Because: • Greater value is created by reconciling value differences within vision, mission, strategy, structure, products, and services. • If in the issue you can identify the value tension of one of the dimensions, you can be sure that the issue represents a real dilemma.	Tools: • Interviews • Questionnaires • (Participant) observation • Document/ process analysis • Cartoons • Discussion
Step 2: Charting Chart the dilemma • Draw a dual-axis diagram. • Label the axes according to the most relevant dimension(s). • Add labels that reflect the (seemingly) opposing values of the dilemma. Be specific. • Chart the positions of the actors. • Make a list of positives of the extreme value orientation.	Because: • By doing so you will visualize the key issues and challenges confronting you and/or your company. • You will locate yourself and the other actors in a "field of meaning." • This will help you to respect the different positions and (later on) find a proper reconciliation.	Tools: Look at the BBG for labeling axes.

Table A2.1   Continued

Action	Why	How
Step 3: "Stretch" the dilemma (list positives and negatives and find epithets) Qualify extreme and non-desirable solutions: • Make a list of positives of the extreme use of each value orientation (1, 10) and (10, 1) • Make a list of negatives of the extreme use of each orientation • Find negative epithets (stigmatizing labels to emphasize these negative extremes) • Also find a negative epithet for the compromise position (5, 5)	Because: This will help you to respect the different positions and (later on) find a proper reconciliation • It is forcing you to break out of your own frame of reference • You will see the negative consequences of taking a value to its extreme • You will see what positions are to be avoided	Tools: • Combine the negative words that describe each value extreme and choose the most poisonous, negative, expressive, cynical, and creative label • The positives may help as well: make the epithets sweet and sour
Step 4: Possible (nondesirable) solutions: • What are the extreme solutions for regarding your value and their value? • What is the compromise solution? Use negative slogans (epithets) to emphasize the extremes.	Because: • You are forced to break out of your own frame of reference. • You will see the negative consequences by taking a value to its extreme. • You will see what positions to avoid.	• Make a list of negatives and positives of the extreme use of an orientation. • Combine the words that described the extreme value (positive and negative). • Choose the most cynical ones.

Table A2.1   Continued

Action	Why	How
Step 5: Reconcile the dilemma (5 phases)	Because:	
• **Processing**: Change nouns into present participles, e.g., universalizing.	• Use of the present participle suggests a process rather than a thing. Reconciliation is done in a process.	• **Processing**: Change nouns into present participles; e.g., instead of universal truths see univers-*alizing* truth.
• **Framing**: Consider the context.	• A frame or context contains and constrains the picture or text.	• **Framing**: Consider value A and put it into the context of value B, and vice versa (use graphics).
• **Sequencing**: Realize one value first, then realize the second; e.g., strengthen your particular relation-ship, then generalize from this.	• Sequencing allows us to express one value now and through that expression promote the complementary value.	• **Sequencing**: We develop orientation A first so that orien-tation B will grow in the future.
• **Waving/circling**: Realize one value through the other.	• By joining the ends of the sequence, we can create a circle, a feedback loop, and a value system.	• **Waving/circling**: Realize value A through the value of B.
• **Synergizing**: Any circle which improves and develops values is a helix.	• Values are synergistic when expressed through one another as a virtuous circle. The strength of both values can develop indefinitely, provided these continuously feed into each other.	• **Synergizing**: Through value A we improve value B, which in turn improves value A, etc.

- The helical strands are sequences, moving between the ends of each rung of the ladder in alternation.
- Such sequences are waveforms or circles which spiral up and around.
- These helixes are synergistic in their creation of vitality and growth, generated by their interaction.

Appendix 3 Measuring Transcultural Competence: Old and New Questionnaires

All the results recorded in this book come from our old questionnaire, which presents respondents with a straight choice between universal rules versus particular exceptions, individual advantages versus community responsibilities, specific versus diffuse criteria of judgment, and so on.

When we pose a dilemma, we also impose an either/or choice upon respondents. In essence, we assail their value systems. We force them to make a stand upon one or the other end of a continuum. They must commit to what they see as the most fundamental of two virtues. Under normal circumstances, for example, the individualist would venture forth to serve one or more communities, while the communitarian would consider the effect of community influence on individual nurture. But under siege conditions, both hunker down to defend individualism or communitarianism respectively.

Inevitably we finish up by measuring not just the responses of managers, but the conditions of siege we have ourselves created.

Might people respond differently when not besieged or assailed by alternative choices? This is the purpose of our new questionnaire. Here we give not two choices, but five. Respondents can choose either exclusive alternative, as in the old questionnaire, they can select one or another reconciliation which uses alternative sequences, or they can choose to compromise. What respondents realize when scanning all five alternatives is that they do not have to choose between these values, unless they wish to. They can choose both, in three varieties of combination, or they can choose either one while rejecting the other.

This tells us far more about how respondents function in "normal conditions," when researchers are not seeking to slice their value systems in two or assail their integrity. In both questionnaires we can use very similar narratives, but in the new questionnaire we widen the range and the complexity of choices.

Take, for example, the traffic accident dilemma presented in Chapter 1, which posed the conflict between telling the truth in a court of law (universalism) or remaining loyal to a special friend (particularism). You are riding in a car driven by a close friend. He hits a pedestrian. You know he was going at least thirty-five miles per hour in an area of the city where the maximum allowed speed is twenty miles per hour. There are no witnesses. His lawyer says that if you testify under oath that he was driving only twenty miles per hour it may save him from serious consequences.

What right has your friend to expect you to protect him?

Here the responding manager must either side with his friend or bear truthful witness in a court of law. There is no possibility of integrating opposites, no opportunity to display transcultural competence by reconciling this dilemma.

This typifies all dilemmas in the old questionnaire. There is a stark choice. In the new questionnaire we offer five responses.

a. There is a general obligation to tell the truth as a witness. I will not perjure myself before the court. Nor should any real friend expect this from me.
b. There is a general obligation to tell the truth in court, and I will do so, but I owe my friend an explanation and all the social and financial support I can organize.
c. My friend in trouble always comes first. I am not going to desert him before a court of strangers based on some abstract principle.
d. My friend in trouble gets my support, whatever his testimony, yet I would urge him to find in our friendship the strength that allows us both to tell the truth.
e. I will testify that my friend was going a little faster than the allowed speed and say that it was difficult to read the speedometer.

Figure A3.1 is a dual-axis map that graphs the range of responses.

a. (10/1) is a polarized response in which the law is affirmed but the friend is rejected (universalism excludes particularism).
b. (10/10) is an integrated response in which the rule is first affirmed and then everything possible is done for the friend (universalism joins with particularism).
c. (1/10) is a polarized response in which the friend is affirmed as an exception to the rule, which is then rejected (particularism excludes universalism).
d. (10/10) is an integrated response in which exceptional friendship is affirmed and then joined to the rule of law (particularism joins with universalism).
e. (5/5) is a stand-off or fudge, in which both the rule of law and loyalty to friends is blunted (universalism compromises with particularism).

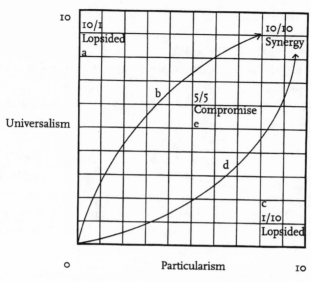

Figure A3.1

Our calculation is as follows:

- Integrated responses b and d show more transcultural competence than do polarized responses a and c, and compromised response e.
- While American managers will typically put universalism first, and East Asian/southern European managers will typically put particularism first, each can integrate his or her priority with its opposite.
- From which it follows that there are at least two paths to integrity, not "one best way."

Or consider the conflict between individualism and communitarianism presented in Chapter 3. Two people were discussing ways in which individuals could improve the quality of life.

A. One said: "It is obvious that if individuals have as much freedom as possible and the maximum opportunity to develop themselves, the quality of their life will improve as a result."

B. The other said: "If individuals are continuously taking care of their fellow human beings the quality of life will improve for everyone, even if it obstructs individual freedom and individual development."

The old questionnaire makes it a straight choice between A and B, but the new questionnaire offers five alternatives.

a. I work for increased freedom and independence, for never having to depend on someone else's favors, and to free myself as far as possible from social control.

b. I work principally to benefit my family, my friends at work, and my company. When I succeed in this, they gladly grant me all the freedom and independence I could ask for.

c. I work for increased freedom and independence, so that I can make myself valuable to others on my own terms and contribute to society in my own ways.

d. I work principally to benefit my family, my friends at work, and my company. I prefer this to selfishness and much prefer it to being the victim of others' selfishness.

e. I work both for myself and the communities (friends, family, company) that surround me. Sometimes it means self-sacrifice, while at other times the larger community needs to adapt.

We can now locate these answers on the dual-axis map shown in Figure A3.2. The choices are scored as follows:

a. Champions individualism, rejects communitarianism.
b. Integrates communitarianism with individualism.
c. Integrates individualism with communitarianism.

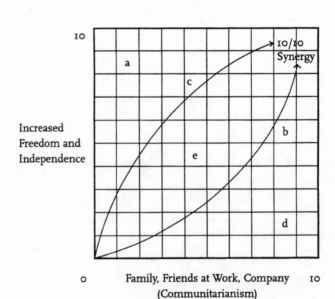

Figure A3.2

d. Champions communitarianism, rejects individualism.

e. Compromises both principles.

Those choosing b and c have chosen alternative paths to reconciliation, corresponding to Rick's choice in *Casablanca* (c) and Watanabe's choice in *Ikiru* (b), both of which integrate the two values.

What We Found

The questionnaire based on these logics has been administered to the following groups: U.S. executives with both extensive and limited experience of international management at Applied Materials; Chinese "high fliers" working for a U.S. multinational corporation; trainees attending the Intercultural Communications Institute summer school near Portland; 1,000 employees of Bombardier, the French-Canadian engineering company; and several European samples. The following trends are already evident.

- There is a capacity to deal with and reconcile values in general. Respondents who reconcile dilemmas are likely to employ similar logics across the board, as do "compromisers" and "polarizers."
- Cross-cultural competence as measured by our questionnaire correlates strongly, consistently, and significantly with

a. Extent of experience with international assignments.

b. Rating by superiors on "suitability for" and "success in" overseas postings and partnerships.

c. High positive evaluations via "360-degree feedback." Arguably, this reconciles equality versus hierarchy, since the verdicts of peers, superiors, and subordinates are compared.

d. Success in a strategy simulation exercise.

e. Being promoted over the last three years at Bombardier as opposed to being laterally transferred or remaining in the same position.

f. Having a reputation as an "outstanding leader" who was interviewed for our forthcoming publication *21 Leaders for the 21st Century.*

Interestingly, there is a negative correlation with assessed technical competence, which warns us that manipulative logics may impede us from relating to living systems.

But—and here is the surprise—with the exception of Chinese "high fliers" who have been recently influenced by American training, the transculturally competent do not necessarily put their own cultural stereotype ahead of foreign values in a logical sequence. For example, American transcultural competents

(TCs) are as likely to argue that good communities and teams generate outstanding individuals as the reverse proposition. TCs can begin with the foreigner's sociotype and join this to their own.

This probably reveals skill at negotiating and entering dialogue, where you share understanding of the other's position in the hope of reciprocity. It may also reveal a case-by-case adoption of foreign methods where these are considered appropriate, along with curiosity about "the road less traveled" by one's own culture.

Finally, we would like to suggest that transcultural competence may be only the tip of the iceberg, representing the most visible manifestation of human diversity in general. The role of leaders and managers is increasingly to manage diversity per se, whatever its origins in culture, industry, discipline, socioeconomic group, or gender. If there is indeed a way of thinking which integrates values as opposed to "adding value," the implications are far-reaching.

An Uncertainty Principle for the Social Sciences

Werner Heisenberg's "uncertainty principle" is well known. It states that because the investigator looms so large when measuring subatomic realities, we can be sure of a particle's position or of its momentum, but not both. If we concentrate on fixing its position, we lose sight of its momentum. If we concentrate on measuring its momentum, its position becomes uncertain.

We believe that this is the difference between our old and new questionnaires. The old questionnaire fixes the respondents' positions at either end of a continuum. By assailing them with dilemmas, we push them into fixed, defensive positions. The new questionnaire lifts this siege and invites respondents to move to and fro upon values continua. In other words, it measures momentum.

Why should there be similarities between subatomic phenomena and cultural phenomena? Because both respond to the investigator. Subatomic entities respond because they are comparatively so small. Cultural elements respond because they are alive and the researcher participates in relationships with them. In both cases you can fix their positions or give them room to move. Our old questionnaire fixes the respondent's position. Our new questionnaire looks for a momentum which is corybantic, that dances between value opposites, so that the dance itself can become the potential reconciler of contrasts. It is no coincidence that Chapters 8, 10, and 12 feature dancing metaphors among their reconciliations.

Appendix 4 The Space Between Dimensions

In this book we concentrate on two ranges of phenomena: the diversity produced by the values and the ends of our six dimensions, and the consequences of reconciling these values "virtuously" or polarizing them "viciously."

We have not had the time and space to consider the interactions between these six dimensions, although some are fruitful and illuminating. We can examine these interactions by crossing our axes and labeling the four quadrants.

Different Principles of Social Order

Consider, for example, crossing dimensions 1 and 2, Universalism–Particularism and Individualism–Communitarianism. Doing this allows us to understand what principles of social order various countries employ to maintain their civic cultures.

Individualism and Particularism by themselves are likely to promote disorder, because if everyone feels unconstrained by their group, and if everyone feels they are an exception to that culture's laws, there is little left to restrain anti-social behavior.

Similarly Universalism and Communitarianism will tend to promote order, because keeping to laws and regarding the community, family, or state as more important than yourself is likely to put effective curbs on anti-social behavior.

In practice, successful economies use universalism or communitarianism to maintain a "freedom within the law," as depicted in Figure A4.1. The most successful models are those at top left, the "harness for self-interest," exemplified by the United States, United Kingdom, and much of Western Europe. Another successful model is at bottom right, the "harmonious society," exemplified by

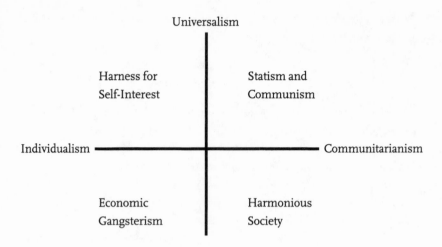

Figure A4.1

Singapore, Japan, Hong Kong, Malaysia, and South Korea. These feature a higher degree of particularism, originating from Confucian family values and higher degrees of communitarianism. What stops the communitarianism from becoming totalitarian is the particularity of each family and each person.

A failed attempt at universalist communitarianism was the Soviet and former Warsaw Pact countries and Mao's China. Such regimes suffer from an excess of imposed order which acts to stifle economic freedoms. Being both communitarian and universalist made these cultures coercive and dictatorial. Their people were unable to develop.

Finally, we come to the quadrant at the bottom left of Figure A4.1, which is both individualist and particularist and so lacks any viable principle of social order. A glance at our research results in Chapters 1 and 3 shows that Russia now falls into this quadrant. Its communitarianism died with the collapse of the Soviet Union, and the mix of its traditional particularism and new-found individualism may have produced "economic gangsterism," with self-interested gangs preying on one another. In such circumstances order can come only from power imposed from above, and such societies oscillate between anarchy and draconian order.

Moving with deliberation and continuity from the top right of the figure to the bottom right has rewarded China with annual economic growth rates of between 7 and 14 percent for fifteen years or more. Abrupt Westernization does not appear to have served Russia or the former Warsaw Pact countries well. Cultural continuity may be more important than trying to imitate the United States.

Varied Corporate Cultures

A second set of insights created by crossing dimensions has to do with the spaces between dimensions 1 and 4, or Universalism–Particularism and Achieved–Ascribed Status, as depicted in Figure A4.2. Here we have a typology of corporate cultures instead of national economic systems.

At the bottom left we have the family culture, represented by *le patron*, the father figure who takes the weight of the world on his shoulders. His status is ascribed by reason of being born into his position, and much revolves around his particular personality. A majority of the world's corporations are family-owned.

The Eiffel tower also depends on the positions and roles ascribed to key bureaucrats and operatives. They may have achieved in the past, for example, at some *grande ecole* but their current authority depends largely on their formal position, on their ascribed expertise rather than on recent successes.

The major characteristic of this culture is its strong rule orientation and system of subordination. It is governed by those who apply the rules and regulate conduct. It is slow to ask, "Do these rules work? Are they effective?"

The "guided missile" culture is oriented around teamwork and project groups. Teams solve problems and achieve set tasks while measuring their successes on group "dashboards." They are rule-oriented insofar as they are trying

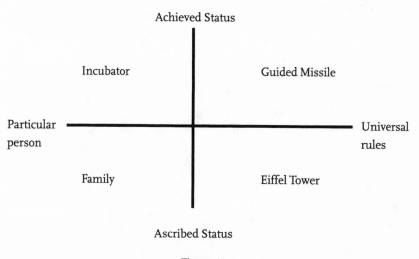

Figure A4.2

to generate new products, systems, and regulations and are searching for the regularities of core competencies and industrial disciplines. NASA pioneered the use of project groups when varieties of different engineering disciplines solved complex aeronautical challenges.

Finally, the "incubator culture" is achievement-motivated but oriented to the particular genius of the entrepreneur or innovator. Employees join the company because of its unique qualities and idiosyncratic quest. Typically these are small start-up companies in Silicon Valley, Taipei, Bangalore, Cambridge, and so on. Everyone knows everyone's first name and special capabilities. All share an enthusiasm for incubating new processes.

We find that cultures favoring ascription and particularism, such as China, Singapore, Hong Kong, and Thailand, produce most of the family-owned companies, while cultures favoring universalism, such as America, the United Kingdom, and northwest Europe produce most of the guided missile and incubator cultures, although Taipei and Bangalore have been successful at the intersection of family and incubator cultures.

Bureaucracies, or Eiffel towers, are found in many countries, but the tower in Paris is of German origins and Max Weber was the first to celebrate the rational forms of bureaucracy. Both France and Germany put great stress on formal schooling and education but thereafter rely on an "expert culture" which tends to be ascriptive and rule-bound. You achieve *because* of your expert status. It is expected and taken for granted. When Americans shower experts with congratulations, it is seen as redundant and as hype. A soft *"pas mal"* ("not bad") is all that is necessary to confirm a professional's status.

How Managers Conceive of Success and Progress

If we cross-correlate dimension 5 with dimension 2, Inner–Outer directedness with Individualism–Communitarianism, we discover differences of some subtlety which might otherwise elude us (Figure A4.3).

Superficially, individualism and inner directedness may seem to be the same but they are not. Individualism puts the person before the group. Inner directedness finds the source of moral direction within the individual's conscience or psyche. In nations like France, revolutions have taken a communitarian form with spontaneous outbursts of anger and passion. But the origin of that anger was inside the souls and consciences of the protagonists.

Hence for France, we have the "barricade," in which whole communities are inflamed by righteous indignation. For the United States, the United Kingdom, and the Netherlands the career ladder, or "Stairway to the Stars," celebrates the individual climbing to success, through inner determination.

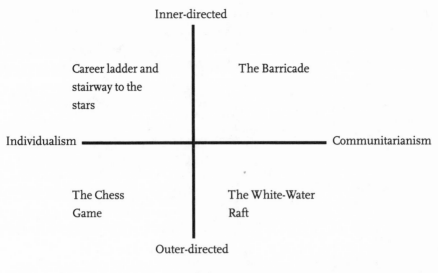

Figure A4.3

For nations not powerful enough to get their way in the world, like Sweden, a melancholic determination toward individual responsibility, despite overpowering opposition, leads to the "chess game," as in Ingmar Bergman's *The Seventh Seal*, in which the knight challenges Death, despite insuperable odds. Finally, the Japanese celebrate their "white-water men," managers paddling their raft down the rapids, going with the surging flow of economic events but managing to remain afloat—a combination of outer direction and communitarianism.

The Logic of Industrial Development

Finally we have Figure A4.4, which shows the logics employed by various countries in hastening their development. This cross-connects Individualism–Communitarianism with Achieved–Ascribed status and has to do with the legitimacy of government interference with the economy. For pioneer capitalist countries such as the United Kingdom, the United States, Belgium, and Holland, the government is more of a referee, guaranteeing the fairness of the game and not taking sides as individuals vie with one another to achieve.

Those who believe in free markets typically opt for the top left quadrant. The government has a judicial role in ensuring a level playing field.

But for economies trying to catch up—such as Japan, Korea, Taiwan, Singapore, and China—it may pay to ascribe to governments the status of a coach, encouraging and facilitating national enterprise. The coach represents Japan or

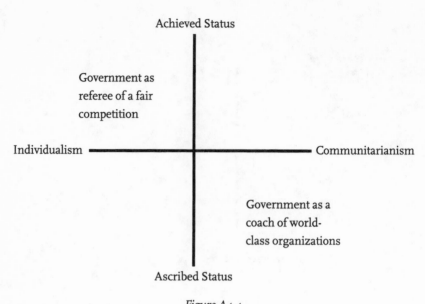

Figure A4.4

Singapore or South Korea as a whole and tries to resolve sectional quarrels between businesses in order to benefit the whole economy.

The government may also take charge of the supply of educated and skilled labor and try as public policy to increase the knowledge intensity of the economy on the grounds that superior knowledge generates scarcity and hence profitability.

Bibliography

Abegglen, James C. and George Stalk, Jr, *Kaisha: The Japanese Corporation*, New York: Basic Books, 1985.

Adler, Nancy J., *Competitive Frontiers*, Oxford: Blackwell Business, 1994.

Allinson, R. E., et al., *Understanding the Chinese Mind*, Hong Kong: Oxford University Press, 1989.

Amon Carter Museum, *The Image of America in Caricature and Cartoon*, Fort Worth: The Museum, 1975.

Argyris, Chris, *Inner Contradictions of Rigorous Research*, New York: Academic Press, 1980.

———. "Skilled Incompetence," *Harvard Business Review*, Sept./Oct. 1986.

———. *Strategy, Change and Defensive Routines*, Boston: Pitman, 1985.

Argyris, Chris, with R. Putnam and D. M. Smith, *Action Science*, San Francisco: Jossey-Bass, 1985.

Argyris, Chris and David Schön, *Organizational Learning*, Reading, MA: Addison-Wesley, 1978.

Barber, Benjamin R., *Jihad vs. McWorld*, New York: Times Books, 1995.

Bartlett, Christopher A. and Sumantra Ghoshal, *Managing Across Borders*. Boston, MA: Harvard Business School Press, 1991.

Bateson, Gregory, *Steps to an Ecology of Mind*, New York: Jason Aronson, 1978.

Bateson, Mary Catherine, *Our Own Metaphor*, Washington, DC: Smithsonian Institution Press, 1991.

Bell, Daniel, *The Coming of Post-Industrial Society*, New York: Basic Books, 1976.

———. *The Cultural Contradictions of Capitalism*, New York: Basic Books, 1976.

Bellah, Robert N., *Tokugawa Religion—The Cultural Roots of Modern Japan*, New York: Free Press, 1985.

Bellah, Robert N. *et al.*, *Habits of the Heart*, Berkeley, CA: University of California Press, 1985.

Bennis, Warren, *On Becoming a Leader*, Reading, MA: Addison-Wesley, 1989.

Bennis, Warren and Bert Nanus, *Leaders: The Strategies for Taking Charge*, New York: Harper and Row, 1985.

Bennis, Warren and Robert Townsend. *Reinventing Leadership*, New York: William Morrow, 1995.

Berlin, Isaiah. *Two Concepts of Liberty*, Oxford: Clarendon, 1958.

———. *The Hedgehog and the Fox*, New York: Simon & Schuster, 1953.

Blake, Robert R. and Jane S. Mouton. *The Managerial Grid*, Houston: Gulf Publishing, 1964.

Bohm, David. *On Dialogue*, New York: Routledge, 1996.

Boisot, Max. *Information and Organization*, London: Fontana, 1987.

———. *Information Space*, London: Routledge, 1996.

———. *Knowledge Assets: Securing Competitive Advantage in the Information Economy*, Oxford: Oxford University Press, 1998.

Boisot, Max and John Child, "The Iron Law of Fiefs and the Problem of Governance in Chinese Economic Reforms," *Administrative Science Quarterly*, 33, December 1988.

Bogen, Joseph E. "Educational Aspects of Hemispherical Specialisation," *UCLA Educator*, Spring 1975.

de Bono, Edward. *Lateral Thinking*, London: Penguin, 1982.

———. *Water Logic*, London: Penguin, 1994.

Brand, Stewart. *The Clock of the Long Now*, New York: Basic Books, 1999.

Brandenburger, Adam M. and Barry J. Nalebuff. *Co-opetition*, New York: Doubleday, 1996.

Briggs, John. *Fractals: The Patterns of Chaos*, London: Thames and Hudson, 1994.

Briggs, John and F. D. Peat. *The Turbulent Mirror*, New York: Harper & Row, 1989.

Burns, James MacGregor. *Leadership*, New York: Harper and Row, 1978.

Burns, Tom and G. M. Stalker, *The Management of Innovation*, London: Tavistock, 1961.

Capra, Fritjof. *The Tao of Physics*, Berkeley, CA: Shambhala, 1975.

Carlzon, Jan. *Moments of Truth*, New York: Harper and Row, 1986.

Carrol, Raymonde. *Cultural Misunderstandings*, Chicago: University of Chicago Press, 1988.

Christopher, Robert C. *The Japanese Mind*, London: Pan, 1984.

Chua, Beng-Huat. *Communitarian Ideology and Democracy in Singapore*, London: Routledge, 1995.

Collins, James C. and Jerry I. Porras. *Built to Last*, London: Century, 1994.

Corning, Peter A. and Susan Corning. *Winning with Synergy*, New York: Harper and Row, 1986.

Cottle, Tom J. "The Location of Experience: A Manifest Time Orientation," *Acta Psychologica*, 28, 1968, 129–149.

Crutchfield, Richard S. "Conformity and Character," *American Psychologist*, 10, 1955.

Csikszentmihalyi, Mihaly. *Flow: The Psychology of Optimal Experience*, New York: Harper, 1990.

Davis, Stan and Christopher Meyer. *Blur: The Speed of Change in the Connected Economy*, Reading, MA: Addison-Wesley, 1998.

de Geus, Arie P. *The Living Company*, London: Nicholas Brealey, 1997.

——. "Planning as Learning," *Harvard Business Review*, March/April 1988.

De Mente, Boye Lafeyette. *Japanese Etiquette and Ethics in Business*, Lincolnwood, IL: NTC Business Books, 1989.

Deming, W. Edwards. *Out of the Crisis*, Cambridge, MA: Technology Center for Advanced Engineering Study, 1986.

Dertouzos, Michael L., Richard K. Lester and Robert M. Solow. *Made in America: Regaining the Productive Edge*, Cambridge, MA: MIT Press, 1989.

Doi, Takeo. *The Anatomy of Dependence*, New York: Kodansha/Harper, 1973.

Dore, Ronald, *Taking Japan Seriously*, Stanford: Stanford University Press, 1987.

Dunbar, Nicholas. *Inventing Money*, New York: John Wiley, 1999.

Dunlap, Albert J. *Mean Business*, New York: Random House, 1996.

Durkheim, Emile. *The Division of Labour in Society*, New York: Harper and Row, 1964.

Eliot, T. S. *Four Quartets*, New York: Harcourt, Brace and World, 1943.

Emerson, Ralph Waldo. "Freedom," *Poems*, William Heinemann, 1927.

Emery, Fred, and Eric Trist. *Towards a Social Ecology*, New York: Plenum, 1975.

Evans, Harold. *The American Century*, London: Jonathan Cape, 1998.

Fayol, Henri. *General Industrial Management*, London: Pitman, 1949.

Festinger, Leon. *A Theory of Cognitive Dissonance*, Evanston, IL: Row Peterson, 1957.

Follette, Mary Parker. *Freedom and Coordination: Lectures in Business Organization*, New York: Garland, 1987.

Frank, Robert H. and Philip J. Cook. *The Winner-Take-All-Society*, New York: Free Press, 1995.

Franken, Al. *Rush Limbaugh Is a Big Fat Idiot*, New York: Dell, 1996.

Friedman, Milton and Rose Friedman. *Free to Choose*, New York: Avon, 1981.

Fromm, Erich. *Man for Himself*, New York: Rinehart, 1947.

Fukuyama, Francis. *Trust: Social Virtues and the Creation of Prosperity,* New York: Free Press, 1995.

Garratt, Bob. *Learning to Lead,* London: Fontana, 1990.

———. *The Learning Organization,* London: Fontana, 1987.

Gazzaniga, Michael S. "The Split Brain in Man," *Scientific American,* January 1964.

Giddens, Anthony. *The Third Way. The Renewal of Social Democracy,* Malden, MA: Blackwell, 1988.

Gleik, James. *Chaos: Making a New Science,* New York: Viking Penguin, 1993.

Gray, John. *Men Are from Mars, Women are from Venus,* New York: HarperCollins, 1992.

Gusfield, Joseph R. *Symbolic Crusade,* Urbana: University of Illinois Press, 1963.

Halberstam, David. *The Reckoning,* New York: Avon, 1988.

Hall, Edward T. *The Cultures of France and Germany,* New York: Intercultural Press, 1989.

———. *Dance of Life: The Other Dimension of Time,* New York: Anchor, Doubleday, 1983.

———, and Mildred Reed Hall. *Hidden Differences: Doing Business with the Japanese,* New York: Doubleday, 1987.

———. *The Silent Language,* New York: Doubleday, 1959.

Hamel, Gary and C. K. Prahalad. *Something for the Future,* Boston: Harvard Business School Press, 1994.

———. "Strategic Intent," *Harvard Business Review,* May–June 1989.

Hampden-Turner, Charles M. "Approaching Dilemmas," *Shell Guides to Planning,* No. 3, 1985.

———. *Charting the Corporate Mind: From Dilemma to Strategy,* Oxford: Basil Blackwell, 1994.

———. *Creating Corporate Culture,* Reading, MA: Addison-Wesley, 1992.

———. *Gentlemen and Tradesmen,* London: Routledge and Kegan Paul, 1984.

———. *Maps of the Mind,* New York: Macmillan, 1981.

———. *Radical Man: Towards a Theory of Psycho-social Development,* London: Duckworth, 1973.

———. *Sane Asylum: Inside the Delancey Street Foundation,* New York: William Morrow, 1974.

Handy, Charles. *The Age of Paradox,* Boston, MA: Harvard Business School Press, 1994 (published in the UK as *The Empty Raincoat*).

———. *The Age of Unreason,* London: Business Books, 1989.

———. *The Gods of Management,* London: Souvenir Press, 1978.

Hawthorne, Nathaniel. *The Scarlet Letter,* New York: Mentor, 1968.

Herrmann, Ned. *The Creative Brain*, Lake Lure, NC: Brain Books, 1988.

Hofstede, Geert. *Cultures' Consequences*. Beverly Hills: Sage, 1980.

———. *Cultures and Organizations: Software of the Mind*, New York: McGraw-Hill, 1991.

Huizinga, John. *Homo Ludens: A Study of the Play Element in Culture*, New York: Harper, 1970.

Hurst, David K. "Of Boxes, Bubbles and Effective Management," *Harvard Business Review*, May/June 1984.

———. *Crisis and Renewal*, Boston: Harvard Business School Press, 1995.

Inzerilli, George and André Laurent. "Managerial Views of Organization Structure in France and the USA," *International Studies of Management and Organization*, XIII(1-2), 1983.

Ishihara, Shintaro. *The Japan that Can Say "No,"* New York: Simon & Schuster, 1991.

Ishinomori, Shotaro. *Japan Inc.*, Berkeley: University of California Press, 1988.

James, William. *Essays in Pragmatism*, New York: Hafner Publishing, 1949.

Jantsch, Erich. *The Self-Organizing Universe*, New York: Pergamon Press, 1980.

Jaques, Elliott. *The Form of Time*, New York: Crane Russak, 1982.

———. *Free Enterprise, Fair Employment*, New York: Crane Russak, 1982.

———. *A General Theory of Bureaucracy*, London: Heinemann, 1976.

Johnson, Barry. *Polarity Management: Identifying and Managing Unsolvable Problems*, Amherst: HRD Press, 1992.

Johnson, Chalmers. *MITI and the Japanese Miracle*, Stanford: Stanford University Press, 1982.

Jonas, Hans, "The Practical Uses of Theory," *Social Research* 26(2), 1959.

Kao, John. *Entrepreneurship, Creativity and Organization*, Englewood Cliffs, NJ: Prentice Hall, 1989.

Kaplan, Abraham. *The Conduct of Inquiry*, San Francisco: Chandler, 1964.

Kaplan, Robert S. and David P. Norton, "The Balanced Scorecard: Measures that Drive Performance," *Harvard Business Review*, January 1992.

Kelly, George. *The Psychology of Personal Constructs*, McGraw-Hill, 1963.

Kennedy, John F. *Profiles in Courage*, New York: Harper, 1956.

Ketudat, Sippanondha and Robert B. Textor. *The Middle Path for the Future of Thailand*, Hawaii: East-West Center, 1990.

Keynes, John Maynard. "Economic Possibilities for Our Grandchildren" in *Essays in Persuasion*, Cambridge: Cambridge University Press, 1930.

Kidder, Rushworth M. *How Good People Make Tough Choices*, New York: William Morrow, 1995.

King, Martin Luther, "Letter from Birmingham City Jail," in *Why We Cannot Wait*, New York: Harper & Row, 1963.

Kluckhohn, F. and F. L. Strodtbeck, et al. *Variations in Value Orientations*, Evanston, IL: Row, Peterson, 1961.

Koestler, Arthur. *The Act of Creation*, New York: Macmillan, 1964.

Koestler, Arthur, J. R. Smythies, eds. *Beyond Reductionism: New Perspectives in the Life Sciences*, Boston: Beacon, 1969.

Kohlberg, Lawrence. *The Philosophy of Moral Development*, New York: Harper and Row, 1981.

Korten, David C. *When Corporations Rule the World*, San Francisco: Barrett-Koehler, 1995.

Kuhn, Thomas. *The Structure of Scientific Revolutions*, Chicago: University of Chicago Press, 1970.

Kurokawa, Kisho. *Each One a Hero*, Tokyo: Kodansha International, 1996.

———. *The Philosophy of Symbiosis*, London: Academic Press, 1994.

Laing, Ronald. *The Divided Self*, New York: Penguin, 1965.

Laurent, André. "The Cross Cultural Puzzle of International Human Resource Management," *Human Resource Management*, 25(1), 1986.

———. "Cross Cultural Management for Pan European Companies," in Spyros Makridiakis (ed.), *Europe 1992 and Beyond*, San Francisco, CA: Jossey-Bass, 1991.

———. "The Cultural Diversity of Western Conceptions of Management," *International Studies of Management and Organization*, XIII (1–2), 1983.

Lawler, Edward E. *High Involvement Management*, San Francisco, CA: Jossey-Bass, 1986.

Lawrence, Paul R. and Jay W. Lorsch. *Organization and Environment*, Boston: Harvard Division of Research, 1967.

Lebra, Takie Sugiyama. *Japanese Patterns of Behavior*, Honolulu: University Press of Hawaii, 1976.

Lecky, Prescott. *Self-Consistency—A Theory of Personality*, New York: Island Press, 1945.

Lewin, Kurt. *Field Theory in Social Science*, New York: Harper, 1951.

Lippincott, Kristin. *The Story of Time*, London: Merrell Holberton (with the Maritime Museum) 1999.

Lipset, Seymour M. *Political Man*, New York: Anchor Books, 1960.

Lodge, George C. *The American Disease*, New York: Knopf, 1984.

Lodge, George C. and Erza F. Vogel (eds.), *Ideology and National Competitiveness*, Boston: Harvard Business School Press, 1987.

Lorenz, Edward. *The Essence of Chaos*, London: UCL Press, 1995.

Lux, Kenneth. *Adam Smith's Mistake,* Boston: Shambhala, 1990.

Maccoby, Michael. *The Gamesman,* New York: Simon and Schuster, 1976.

McGregor, Douglas. *The Human Side of Enterprise,* New York: McGraw-Hill, 1960.

Magaziner, Ira and Mark Pantinkin. *The Silent War,* New York: Random House, 1989.

Mahizhnan, Arun and Lee Tsao Yuan, eds. *Singapore Re-engineering Success,* Singapore: Oxford University Press, 1998.

Mandelbrot, Benoit B. *The Fractal Geometry of Nature,* San Francisco: Freeman, 1982.

Mant, Alistair. *The Rise and Fall of the British Manager,* London: Macmillan, 1977.

March, Robert M. *The Japanese Negotiator,* Tokyo/New York: Kodansha Int., 1988.

Marquand, David. *The Unprincipled Society: New Demands and Old Politics,* London: Cape, 1988.

Martin, Joanne, Martha S. Feldman and Mary Jo Hatch. "The Uniqueness Paradox in Organizational Performance," *Administrative Science Quarterly,* 28(3), 1983.

Martin, Joanne and C. Shiel."Organizational Culture and Counter Culture: An Uneasy Symbiosis," *Organizational Dynamics,* 12, 1983.

Maruyama, Magorah. "Epistemological Sources of New Business Problems in the International Environment," *Human Systems Management,* 1989.

———. "New Mindscapes for Future Business Policy and Management," *Technological Forecasting and Social Change,* 21, 1982.

———. "The Second Cybernetics," *American Scientist,* 51, 1963.

Maslow, Abraham. *Motivation and Personality,* New York: Harper and Row, 1954.

Matson, Floyd. *The Broken Image,* New York: Braziller, 1964.

May, Rollo. *Freedom and Destiny,* New York: Norton, 1981.

Michael, Donald N. *On Learning to Plan and Planning to Learn,* San Francisco: Jossey-Bass, 1973.

Mill, John S. *Autobiography,* New York: Columbia University Press, 1924.

———. *On Liberty,* London: Watts, 1946.

Mintzberg, Henry. "Crafting Strategy," *Harvard Business Review,* March/April 1987, pp. 66–75.

———. "The Manager's Job: Folklore or Fact?" *Harvard Business Review,* July/August 1976.

———. "Opening Up the Definition of Strategy," in J. B. Quinn, H. Mintzberg, and R. M. James (eds.), *The Strategy Process,* Englewood Cliffs: Prentice-Hall, 1988.

————. "Planning on the Left Side, Managing on the Right," *Harvard Business Review,* July/August 1976.

Monks, Robert A. G. *The Emperor's Nightingale,* Oxford: Capstone, 1998.

Morgan, Gareth. *Images of Organization,* Beverly Hills: Sage, 1986.

Morita, Akio. *Made in Japan,* New York: Dutton, 1986.

Natanson, M. (ed.). *Philosophy of the Social Sciences,* New York: Random House, 1963.

Nock, Samuel L. and P. H. Rossi. "Achievement vs. Ascription in the Attribution of Family Social Status," *American Journal of Sociology,* 84(3), 1978.

Nonaka, Ikujiro and Hirotaka Takeuchi. *The Knowledge-Creating Company,* New York: Oxford University Press, 1995.

Ogilvy, James A. *Many Dimensional Man,* New York: Oxford University Press, 1977.

————. *Social Issues and Trends: The Maturation of America,* Menlo Park, CA: Values and Lifestyles Program, SRI International, 1984.

Ohno, Taichi. *Toyota Production Systems,* Cambridge, Mass: Productivity Press, 1988.

Olson, Mancur. *The Rise and Decline of Nations,* New Haven: Yale University Press, 1982.

Ornstein, Robert. *The Psychology of Consciousness.* San Francisco: W. H. Freeman, 1972.

Ouchi, William. *The M-form Society,* Reading, MA: Addison-Wesley, 1984.

————. *Theory Z: How American Business Can Meet the Japanese Challenge,* Reading, MA: Addison-Wesley, 1981.

Ozbekhan, H. "Planning and Human Action," P. A. Weiss, ed., *Systems in Theory and Practice,* New York: Hafner, 1971.

Parsons, Talcott and Edward A. Shils. *Towards a General Theory of Action,* Cambridge, MA: Harvard University Press, 1951.

Pascale, Richard T. "Perspectives in Strategy: The Real Story behind Honda's Success," *California Management Review,* 26(3), 1984.

Pascale, R. T. and A. G. Athos. *The Art of Japanese Management,* New York: Simon & Schuster, 1981.

Peebles, Gavin and Peter Wilson. *The Singapore Economy,* Cheltenham: Edward Elgar, 1996.

Penang Skills Development Center. *The Pangkor Review,* Penang, 1996.

————. *Update: Bayan Lepas,* Penang, 1996.

Peters, T. and R. H. Waterman. *In Search of Excellence,* New York: Harper & Row, 1982.

Pfeffer, Jeffrey. *Competitive Advantage Through People,* Boston: Harvard Business School Press, 1994.

Pine, B. Joseph. *Mass Customization*, Boston: Harvard Business School Press, 1993.

Porras, Jerry I. *Stream Analysis*, Reading, MA: Addison-Wesley, 1987.

Porter, Michael E. *The Competitive Advantage of Nations*, New York: Free Press, 1990.

———. *Competitive Strategy: Techniques for Analyzing Industries and Competitors*, New York: Free Press, 1980.

Prestowitz, Clyde V. *Trading Places*, New York: Basic Books, 1989.

Pribram, Karl. *Languages of the Brain*, Englewood Cliffs, NJ: Prentice-Hall, 1971.

Prigogine, Ilya and Isabelle Stengers. *Order out of Chaos*, New York: Bantam, 1984.

Pugh, Derek S, ed. *Organization Theory*, London: Penguin Books, 1983.

Quinn, James B., Henry Mintzberg and Robert M. James. *The Strategy Process*, Englewood Cliffs, NJ: Prentice-Hall, 1988.

Quinn, Robert E. *Beyond Rational Management*, San Francisco: Jossey-Bass, 1988.

Raine, Kathleen. *William Blake*, London: Thames and Hudson, 1996.

Redding, S. Gordon. *The Spirit of Chinese Capitalism*, New York: Walter de Gruyter, 1990.

Reich, Robert B. *Tales of a New America*, New York: Times Books, 1987.

———. *The Work of Nations*, New York: Knopf, 1991.

Reich, Robert B. and Eric D. Mankin, "Joint Ventures with Japan Give Away America's Future," *Harvard Business Review*, March/April 1986.

Rhinesmith, Stephen H., *A Manager's Guide to Globalization: Six Keys to Success in a Changing World*, Homewood, IL: Irwin, 1993.

Richie, Donald. *The Films of Akiro Kurosawa*, Berkeley: University of California Press, 1984.

Robbins, Harvey and Michael Finley. *Transcompetition*, New York: McGraw-Hill, 1998.

Robbins, Lionel. *An Essay on the Nature and Significance of Economic Science*, London: Macmillan, 1932.

Roethlisberger, Fritz and William Dickson. *Management and the Worker*, Cambridge, MA: Harvard University Press, 1939.

Rohwer, Jim. *Asia Rising*, London: Nicholas Brealey, 1996.

Romig, Dennis A. *Breakthrough Teamwork*, Chicago: Irwin Professional, 1996.

Rosenberg, Morris. *Society and the Adolescent Self Image*, Princeton: Princeton University Press, 1965.

Rosenthal, Robert and Lenore Jacobson. *Pygmalion in the Classroom*, New York: Holt, Rinehart & Winston, 1969.

Rotter, J. B. "Generalized Experiences of Internal vs. External Control of Reinforcement," *Psychological Monographs*, 609, 1996.

Savage, Charles M. *5th Generation Management,* Boston: Butterworth-Heinemann, 1996.

Saxenian, AnnaLee. *Silicon Valley's New Immigrant Entrepreneurs,* Public Policy Institute of California, San Francisco, 1999.

Schein, Edgar H. *Organization, Culture and Leadership,* San Francisco, CA: Jossey-Bass, 1985.

———. *Strategic Pragmatism,* Cambridge, MA: MIT Press, 1996.

Schön, Donald A., *Beyond the Stable State,* New York: Random House, 1971.

———. "Creative Metaphor: A Perspective on Problem Setting in Social Policy," in A. Ortony (ed.), *Metaphor and Thought,* Cambridge: Cambridge University Press, 1979.

———. *The Reflective Practitioner,* New York: Basic Books, 1983.

Schwartz, Peter. *The Art of the Long View,* New York: Currency Books, Doubleday, 1991.

Schwartz, Peter, Peter Leyden and Joel Hyatt. *The Long Boom,* Reading, MA: Perseus, 1999.

Scott, Bruce R. and George C. Lodge (eds.) *US Competitiveness in the World Economy,* Boston, MA: Harvard Business School Press, 1985.

Shaw, George Bernard. *Pygmalion,* London: Penguin, 1985.

Simon, Sidney B. et al. *Values Clarification,* New York: Hart Publishing, 1972.

Slater, Phil. *Earthwalk,* New York: Doubleday, 1974.

Smircich, Linda. "Concepts of Culture and Organizational Analysis," *Administrative Science Quarterly,* 28(3), 1983.

Smith, Kerwyn K. and Valerie M. Simmons. "The Rumplestiltskin Organization: Metaphors on Metaphors in Field Research," *Administrative Science Quarterly,* 2(3), 1983.

Sperry, Roger W. "The Great Cerebral Commissure," *Scientific American,* January 1964.

———. *Science and Moral Priority,* New York: Columbia University Press, 1983.

Stouffer, S. A. and J. Toby. "Role Conflict and Personality," *American Journal of Sociology,* I, VI-5, 1951.

Tannen, Deborah. *The Argument Culture,* New York: Random House, 1998.

———. *You Just Don't Understand,* New York: Ballantine Books, 1990.

Tatsuno, Sheridan M. *Created in Japan,* New York: Morrow, 1990.

Taylor, Frederick Winslow. *The Principles of Scientific Management,* New York: Norton, 1947.

Thomson, George. *Aeschylus and Athens,* New York: Haskell, 1967.

Thoreau, Henry David. *Walden,* New York: NAL, 1956.

Thurow, Lester C. *Head to Head: The Coming Economic Battle Among Japan, Europe and America,* New York: William Morrow, 1992.

————. *The Zero Sum Society,* New York: McGraw-Hill, 1980.

Toffler, Alvin. *Future Shock,* New York: Bantam, 1970.

————. Introduction to *Order Out of Chaos* by Ilya Prigogine. New York: Bantam, 1984.

————. *The Third Wave,* New York: Morrow, 1976.

Trompenaars, Fons. "The Organization of Meaning and the Meaning of Organization," unpublished doctoral dissertation, Wharton School, University of Pennsylvania, 1981.

Trompenaars, Fons and Charles Hampden-Turner. *Riding the Waves of Culture,* New York: McGraw-Hill, 1998.

————. *21 Leaders for the 21st Century,* New York: McGraw-Hill, 2000.

Tung, Rosalie L. "Managing in Asia: Cross-Cultural Dimensions," in Pat Joynt and Malcolm Warner (eds.), *Managing Across Cultures,* Singapore: International Thompson, 1997.

————. *The New Expatriates,* Cambridge, MA: Ballinger, 1988.

Van der Haag, Ernest, "Of Happiness and Despair We Have No Measure," in B. Rosenberg and D. White (eds.), *Mass Culture,* Glencoe, IL: Free Press, 1957.

Vogel, Ezra. *Comeback, Case by Case: Building the Resurgence of American Business,* New York: Simon and Schuster, 1985.

————. *The Four Little Dragons,* Cambridge, MA: Harvard University Press, 1991.

————. *Japan as Number One,* Cambridge, MA: Harvard University Press, 1979.

Waldrop, Mitchell M. *Complexity: The Emerging Science at the Edge of Order and Chaos,* New York: Simon and Schuster, 1992.

Warner, Malcolm. *Comparative Management: A Reader,* London: Routledge (4 vols.), 1996.

Watzlawick, Paul. *How Real Is Real?* New York: Vintage, 1977.

Watzlawick, Paul, J. H. Beavin and D. D. Jackson, *Pragmatics of Human Communication,* New York: Norton, 1967.

Wenzhong, Hu and Cornelius Grove. *Encountering the Chinese,* Yarmouth, ME: Intercultural Press, 1991.

Wilder, Thornton. *Our Town and Other Plays,* New York: Penguin, 1962.

Williamson, Oliver E. "Transaction-Cost Economics: Governing Economic Exchanges," *Journal of Law and Economics,* 22, 1979.

Womack, James P., Daniel T. Jones and Daniel Roos. *The Machine that Changed the World,* New York: Harper, 1991.

Yoshikawa, Muneo. *Communicating with the Japanese,* Portland, OR: Summer Institute for Cross Cultural Communication, 1992.

Zohar, Danah. *The Quantum Self,* London: Bloomsbury, 1993.

————. *The Quantum Society,* London: Bloomsbury, 1995.

Filmography

The Apartment (1960, US, 125 min., black and white).   director/producer: Billy
   Wilder; screenplay: Billy Wilder, I. A. L. Diamond; photography: Joseph La
   Shelle; editing: Daniel Mandell; ad: Alexandre Trauner; music: Adolph
   Deutsch

The Ballad of Narayama (*Narayama Bushi-ko*) (1983, Japan, 130 min.).   director:
   Shohei Imamura; producers: Jiro Tomoda, Goro Kusakabe; screenplay:
   Shohei Imamura; photography: Masao Tochizawa; editing: Hajime Okayasu;
   ad: Toshio Inagaki; music: Shinichiro Ikebe

Casablanca (1942, US, 102 min., black and white).   director: Michael Curtiz;
   producer: Hal B. Wallis; screenplay: Julius J. Epstein, Philip G. Epstein,
   Howard Koch; photography: Arthur Edeson; editing: Owen Marks; ad: Carl
   Jules Weyl; music: Max Steiner

Groundhog Day (1993, US, 101 min.).   director: Harold Ramis; producers:
   Trevor Albert, Harold Ramis; screenplay: Danny Rubin, Harold Ramis; photography: John Bailey; editing: Pembroke J. Herring; ad: David Nichols; music: George Fenton

High and Low (*Tengoku to Jigoku*) (1963, Japan, 143 min., black and white).   director: Akira Kurosawa; producers: Tomoyuki Tanaka, Ryuzo Kikushima;
   screenplay: Hideo Oguni, Ryuzo Kikushima, Eijiro Hisaito, Akira Kurosawa;
   photography: Asakazu Nakai, Takao Saito; ad: Yoshiro Muraki; music: Masaru
   Sato

High Noon (1952, US, 85 min., black and white).   director: Fred Zinnemann;
   producer: Stanley Kramer; screenplay: Carl Foreman; photography: Floyd
   Crosby; editing: Elmo Williams; ad: Rudolph Sternad; music: Dimitri
   Tiomkin

Ikiru (*Living/To Live*) (1952, Japan, 143 min., black and white).   director: Akira

Kurosawa; producer: Shojiro Motoki; screenplay: Shinobu Hashimoto, Hideo Oguni, Akira Kurosawa; photography: Asaichi Nakai; editing: Akira Kurosawa; ad: So Matsuyama; music: Fumio Hayasaka

Les Miserables. 10th Anniversary Concert, 1995. based on novel by Victor Hugo; lyrics and music: Alain Boublil, Claude-Michel Schonberg; original direction: John Caird, Trevor Nunn; producer: Cameron Mackintosh; directed for TV: Gavin Taylor; HD-Thames Primetime TV; co-production with BBC

My Fair Lady (1964, US, 175 min.).   director: George Cukor; producer: Jack L. Warner; screenplay: Alan Jay Lerner; photography: Harry Stradling; editing: William Ziegler; ad: Gene Allen, Cecil Beaton; music: Frederick Loewe; lyrics: Alan Jay Lerner

The Seventh Seal (Det Sjunde Inseglet) (1956, Sweden, 95 min., black and white). director: Ingmar Bergman; producer: Allan Ekelund; screenplay: Ingmar Bergman; photography: Gunnar Fischer; editing: Lennart Wallén; ad: P. A. Lundgren; music: Erik Nordgren

Shall We Dance? (1995, Japan, 136 min.).   director: Masayuki Suo; producer: Yasuyoshi Tokuma; screenplay: Masayuki Suo; photography: Naoki Kayano; editing: Junichi Kikuchi; ad: Kyoko Heya; music: Yoshikazu Suo

Index